HORACE GREELEY

AND THE REPUBLICAN PARTY

HORACE GREELEY

AND THE

REPUBLICAN PARTY

1853-1861

A STUDY OF
THE NEW YORK TRIBUNE

By Jeter Allen Isely

1965
OCTAGON BOOKS, INC.
New York

Reprinted 1965
by special arrangement with Princeton University Press

OCTAGON BOOKS, INC.
175 FIFTH AVENUE
NEW YORK, N. Y. 10010

LIBRARY OF CONGRESS CATALOG CARD NUMBER: 65-25891

Printed in U.S.A. by
NOBLE OFFSET PRINTERS, INC.
NEW YORK 3, N. Y.

To M. P. I.

PREFACE AND ACKNOWLEDGMENTS

FEW men in American history rival the number of written words Horace Greeley has left to posterity. As an editor, journalist, literary critic, lecturer, and politician, he discussed and wrote upon every major topic of his day and thousands of minor ones. Nor is the task of his biographer simplified by the confused status of the Greeley material. His private utterances offer a substantial basis for evaluating his public pronouncements, but there is no large repository of Greeley letters. Most useful in this respect are the Greeley-Colfax Correspondence in the New York Public Library and the Greeley Manuscripts in the Library of Congress, but the bulk of Greeley's letters must be sought among the papers of other notable men with whom he corresponded. This job is made more difficult by a fire which destroyed the Greeley home at Chappaqua, New York shortly after the editor's death, and which is said to have demolished quantities of letters written to him.

For the purpose of this book, an effort has been made to study everything Greeley wrote during the period covered. The files of his newspaper, the New York *Tribune* from 1853 through 1861, have been examined with care and deliberation. It is among his editorials that the student must devote the greater portion of research time and energy. The work is complicated by the fact that, in the pre-Civil War era, there were three *Tribune* editions, *Daily*, *Semi-Weekly*, and *Weekly*. With rare exception, the editorials in the *Weekly* had previously been carried in the *Semi-Weekly*, and had first appeared in the *Daily*. Most important was the *Weekly*, with a circulation spreading throughout the free states, and on the eve of the Civil War totaling well over 200,000 copies, thereby exceeding the readers of the *Daily* more than fourfold. The *Semi-Weekly* had relatively few subscribers, except during presidential campaigns, when it was converted to an election sheet at reduced rates. For the sake of continuity in research and narrative, it was found advisable to follow the *Daily* closely, especially scrutinizing those editorials which were reprinted in the *Weekly*, and, during presidential contests, in the *Semi-Weekly*. The reader will find the great bulk of the citations to the *Daily*, but the selections were made with an eye to their appearance in the more widely read issues.

I am deeply indebted to those institutions and friends assisting in the preparation of this study. Financial aid has been tendered by the Julius Rosenwald Fund and the Princeton Department of History. Librarians throughout the east and middle west, either with correspondence or personal attention, have generously given their time and the benefit of their knowledge. Months were spent in the Library of Congress, and without exception I found those members of the staff with whom I came in contact to be cordial, qualified, and anxious to help. The cartoons used are from originals and are reproduced through the courtesy of the Library of Congress. Most considerate among librarians were John R. Russell of the Rush Rhees Library, University of Rochester, and Julian Boyd and Malcolm O. Young of the Princeton University Library.

More appreciation is due those scholars who gave me constant encouragement and advice, despite a four-year publication delay caused by the recent war. Outstanding is the late Professor Clifton R. Hall of Princeton University, to whose concise and patient criticism in every phase of research and writing most of the merit of this book may be attributed. Professor Raymond J. Sontag of the University of California, Professor Joseph R. Strayer of Princeton University, Thomas Riggs of Washington, D. C., and Dr. Roger Shugg of New York City, have carefully read the work in manuscript and stimulated me with valuable suggestions. The American Historical Association committee on the John H. Dunning Prize for the year 1944, kindly extended this monograph, while still in manuscript form, honorable mention for excellence in the field of national political history. Finally, the contribution of Lisette Isely in polishing the study for the press gains my sincere thanks.

My chief concern has been and remains the background and causes of the Civil War. In Greeley's career during the eight years between the passage of the Kansas-Nebraska bill and the first battle of Bull Run is found a lesson for those who would prevent war in the future. A characteristic common to the years before modern armed conflicts begin is the misunderstanding each of the contestants nurtures for its prospective opponent. This misunderstanding is spread and aggravated by propaganda, which is falsified either by virtue of ignorance or of willful misrepresentation.

Greeley was an honest man, but his responsibility for the Civil War is none the less great. Before the outbreak of that encounter he decided that the south would never fight because the non-slaveholders were deeply unionist by conviction and for economic and social reasons detested their more wealthy and powerful plantation neighbors. He felt assured that the secessionists were threatening to leave the Union only in order to cause the free states to compromise and retreat from the position taken by the Republican party in the presidential contest of 1860. Southern leaders were gambling, Greeley reasoned, and once their bluff was called, they would be cast into political oblivion.

Possessing a poorly disciplined and stubborn mind, Greeley was not one to alter his convictions at anything short of a catastrophe. His mistaken views of the slave states penetrated the northern consciousness. Too late for rectification he saw his errors.

JETER A. ISELY

Princeton, 1947.

CONTENTS

ILLUSTRATIONS

HORACE GREELEY

AND THE REPUBLICAN PARTY

I . . . recall enough of the time to feel the influence of this political bible, as it was termed, and I can emphatically say that if you want to penetrate into the thoughts, feelings, and ground of decision of the 1,866,000 men who voted for Lincoln in 1860, you should study with care the New York weekly *Tribune*.— JAMES FORD RHODES, *Atlantic Monthly,* May, 1909.

1. Brady Portrait of Horace Greeley, about 1858

2. Typical first page of *Daily Tribune,* Pre-Civil War Period

First page of *Weekly Tribune* and *Semi-Weekly Tribune* consisted of news and articles

CHAPTER 1

GREELEY AND HIS TRIBUNE

Saw Greel[e]y for the first time—Recognized him at first sight. Remarkable
looking man—Orville H. Browning,
Diary, December 1, 1855.

THE cohesive force of the antislavery movement created the
Republican party and held it together during the vociferous
years preceding the Civil War. Its members were otherwise
at odds, a conglomeration of former Whigs and Free Soil
Democrats, prohibitionists and men who liked their whiskey
straight, adherents of nativism and foreign born. Even upon
the slavery question they failed to concur fully, since they
drew their convictions from dissimilar sources and espoused
them with varying degrees of intensity. Pugnacious Theodore Parker thought human bondage a sin and a curse which
should be cast from the body politic; well-tailored Charles
Sumner felt it an insult to his cultural conceptions; gruff
Ben Wade harangued the Ohio voter and collected antislavery dividends at the ballot box. The rank and file—the
muscular Michigan farmers, the Plymouth spinsters of unblemished reputation, the respectable ministers who rode the
circuit in Indiana—were scarcely better agreed. But by and
large, it is safe to hazard that they read the New York *Tribune*. After the passage of the Kansas-Nebraska bill in 1854,
and the advent of enforced negro labor in those territories,
increasing thousands of workers and intellectuals, merchants
and manufacturers, studied and believed the *Tribune*. It was
more than a metropolitan journal, it was a sectional oracle.

3

Its founder and editor was Horace Greeley, a spectacular and impetuous Yankee. He was responsible for the columns of propaganda which kept the slavery problem poised before the northern mind, a feat which popularized far and wide the growing Republican party. His influence rocketed as he participated in this controversy, but other factors contributed to his prominence.[1] His dynamic character, the clarity of his style, and the brilliance of his staff raised the standard of his profession. Mechanical developments in printing and transportation furnished him the means of attaining a vast reading family; while provincial journalists, unable to duplicate the New Yorker's services, were compelled to issue papers of local interest only. An editor in Iowa, for example, would receive his cosmopolitan news in the same mail which brought many of his fellow townsmen their copies of the *Weekly Tribune*, turned out by the tens of thousands on Hoe's steam driven press and sped westward by a steam locomotive.

Greeley enjoyed this advantage because New York City was the emporium of journalism as well as of trade. Intelligence from abroad flowed almost exclusively through its shipping channels, for the cable was a dream of the future. Even the telegraph was in a primitive state, costly and not fully reliable; and the Associated Press, later such a stimulus to the smaller papers, was hardly more than an experiment recently inaugurated by the larger metropolitan concerns.[2]

Of course other Manhattan scribes shared Greeley's avenues of information and his highroads of dissemination. Indeed, within the city the vulgar and erratic James Gordon Bennett of the *Herald* and the calculating Henry J. Raymond of the *Times* spoke to larger audiences, but neither approached Greeley's popularity among the rural inhabitants of the north. *Tribune* circulation was spread with consider-

---

[1] It is estimated that the *Tribune's* aggregate circulation jumped from some 72,000 to over 140,000 during the years 1852-1853. These figures seem excessive, but are indicative of the paper's strength independent of the Republican crusade against slavery. Willard G. Bleyer, *Main Currents in the History of American Journalism* (Boston, 1927), 228.

[2] Frank L. Mott, *American Journalism* (New York, 1941), 3-326.

able uniformity among almost all the free states. Much of New England and some regions of the middle west had as high a per capita ratio of *Tribune* subscribers to voting population as did New York state itself. To his northern readers, Greeley was more than a distant journalist. Hundreds had shaken his hand, and thousands had been spellbound by his shrill, earnest voice as he discussed topics of interest from Maine to California. The lyceum then functioned as the radio and the cinema, and Greeley was a star attraction at the box office.[3]

It is true that his appeal was sectional, but his refusal to condone the expansion of slavery increased rather than diminished the number and fervor of the *Tribune's* audience. By 1860, well over 200,000 northerners were taking the *Weekly Tribune* alone. Many treasured the paper and were anxious to proselytize their neighbors with its abundance of partisan articles. Greeley urged his friends to circularize their used copies widely. Certainly the *Tribune's* readers far exceeded its subscribers.

Nor was the *Weekly* Greeley's only edition. *Daily* and *Semi-Weekly Tribunes* were published, and his press room remained an uproar even with these jobs completed. Scores of pamphlets were printed to satisfy a demand which mounted during campaign months; and thousands of *Tribune Almanacs*, replete with political advice, hung beside northern bedsteads.[4]

---

[3] James Parton, *The Life of Horace Greeley* (Cambridge, 1896), 294. Joel Benton, "Reminiscences of Horace Greeley," *Greeley on Lincoln, with Mr. Greeley's Letters to Charles A. Dana and a Lady Friend* (hereafter referred to as Greeley, *Letters*), ed. Benton (New York, 1893), 245-271. *Harper's Weekly*, IV (Sept. 15, 1860), 581-582.
For the spread of *Tribune* circulation, see appendix A.

[4] The *Whig Almanac* first appeared in 1838. The title was changed with the volume for 1856. It sold for 12½ cents each, twelve for $1.
Except for occasional "supplementary" issues, which ran to ten pages, each *Tribune* edition, 1853-1861, was eight pages in length, with six columns per page. A single copy of the *Daily* cost 2 cents. The yearly rates were $5 for the *Daily*, $3 for the *Semi-Weekly*, and $2 for the *Weekly*; however, most *Tribune* subscribers belonged to "clubs," whereby a number of copies were sent to a post office, broken open, and called for individually. Under this system, two copies of the *Semi-Weekly* sold for $5

The source of this stream of ink was a four story building on the corner of Nassau and Spruce streets. From the huge press rooms below, it rose through a maze of offices to the compositors' gallery. On the third floor were located the desks of the principal editorial assistants. These were the chosen of their occupation, for as the discerning creator of the *Nation*, Edwin L. Godkin, recalled of the pre-Civil War period, "to get admission to the columns of the *Tribune* almost gave the young writer a patent of literary nobility, and Greeley . . . welcomed talent, male and female, from any quarter and in every field."[5]

While it is true that the *Tribune* employed enterprising correspondents and feature artists regardless of their political leanings, the managing and associate editors never diverged materially from Greeley's policies. All were progressive, most were radical, and their aspirations for the republic were known to accord with Greeley's before they were hired.[6] They looked with favor upon the reform movement which for a number of years had been liberalizing social institutions as it gained momentum throughout the free states. After 1853, their hearts as well as their minds were engaged in making their paper the foremost antislavery organ in the country.

Charles A. Dana as the managing editor was the most valuable of Greeley's assistants. He was a man of broad, general intelligence, a hard worker, a good administrator, and an informed and charming conversationalist. Educated at Harvard, he soon thereafter joined other New England transcendentalists in operating the communal experiment at Brook Farm, and this introduced him to Greeley who both applauded the undertaking and advised young Dana how it

yearly and five for $11.25. The annual cost of the *Weekly* was little under the club arrangement, eight copies for $10 and twenty for $20. A graph of *Tribune* circulation, 1853-1861, may be found in appendix B.

[5] Edwin Lawrence Godkin, *Life and Letters of . . .* , ed. Rollo Ogden (New York, 1907), I, 167. This and all subsequent omissions made within quotations are mine.

[6] Charles T. Congdon, *Reminiscences of a Journalist* (Boston, 1880), 230-231. For a different and apologetic view see John R. Young, *Men and Memories,* ed. May D. R. Young (New York, 1901), I, 112-119.

should be conducted.[7] Immediately upon joining the *Tribune*, Dana went abroad to cover the 1848 revolutions in Europe, where he came under the influence of the socialist Pierre Joseph Proudhon, and where he met Karl Marx, whom he subsequently engaged as a London correspondent for the *Tribune*. Dana returned to New York City in 1849, and until the Civil War was regarded as the " 'rising hope of the stern and unbending' Radicals."[8] His style was concise and firm. He was well versed in several languages, and enjoyed expounding foreign economic, political, and military complexities. Greeley was frequently absent from New York City, leaving Dana lord of all he surveyed. He was a real power on the *Tribune*, for he was first in Greeley's confidence and at all times supervised the other members of the staff.[9]

The number and personnel of the associate editors altered only slightly in the seven years before the Civil War. Most notable among them were James Sheppard Pike, William H. Fry, Charles T. Congdon, and Richard Hildreth. These men shared with Greeley and Dana the burden of editorial writing.

Pike's background was that of a successful business man from Calais, Maine. Having accumulated a modest fortune, he retired early in life in order to devote his attention to free lance journalism. He took intermittent vacations, but worked feverishly when inspired. He journeyed to the nation's cap-

[7] Greeley to Dana, Oct. 10, Dec. 13, 1842. Greeley MSS., Library of Congress (hereafter referred to as LC).

[8] Godkin, *Letters*, I, 168. The most convenient source for the influence Proudhon exercised over Dana is *Proudhon's Solution of the Social Problem*, ed. Henry Cohen (New York, 1927). Marx's *Tribune* correspondence began late in 1851, and by the spring of 1855 totaled over one hundred and thirty contributions. Indications are that he stopped of his own volition, disgusted with a paper which paid Bayard Taylor more than it offered Karl Marx. Marx to Frederick Engels, Apr. 22, 1854; June 15 (1855), *Karl Marx, Friedrich Engels; Historisch-kritische Gesamtausgabe, Werke, Schriften, Briefe*, pt. 3, II (Berlin, 1930), 21-23, 89-90. See also Marx and Engels, *The Civil War in the United States*, ed. Richard Enmale (New York, 1937), x-xi; and Marx, *The Eastern Question*, ed. Eleanor M. and Edward Aveling (London, 1897).

[9] Greeley to John R. Young, May 13, 1856, Young MSS., I, LC. There is no satisfactory account of Dana's early career. The bulk of the work done on him treats his editorship of the New York *Sun*, and the full length biography takes the approach that Dana had not matured until after he left the *Tribune*, James H. Wilson, *The Life of* . . . (New York, 1907).

ital late in the 1840's to try his hand as a political commentator. His ability caught the eye of Greeley, who absorbed him into the *Tribune* in 1850. Pike won instant acclaim with his articles written from Washington which appeared over his initials. However, as Democratic officials at the capital despised him, Greeley, throughout the 1850's, kept James E. Harvey in Washington to cover the administrative side of the news. Harvey, a native of South Carolina and later editor of the Philadelphia *North American,* signed his letters "Index." Pike was more of a columnist than a reporter, preferring to interpret rather than to record the news. Some of the best products of his fearless pen were carried unsigned on the editorial page. At times he disagreed with Greeley on economic matters. He was if anything more antislavery than his superior, and on one occasion at least he embarrassed the *Tribune* by suggesting that the north secede from the slave states.[10]

Fry, Congdon, and Hildreth were impressive stylists highly adept at satire. Fry, a native of Philadelphia, achieved early recognition as the composer of an opera, *Leonora,* and he served as the *Tribune's* music critic; but he was a versatile writer, and the bulk of his contributions covered current political and social themes.[11] Both Congdon and Hildreth, in common with the majority of the staff, were New Englanders. Congdon came to the *Tribune* in 1857 by way of the Boston *Atlas.* A fluent author of prose and poetry, he singled out slave owners and their apologists for special treatment, and his reasoning is punctuated with an irony which has been

[10] Many of Pike's contributions to the *Tribune,* as well as letters from prominent men received by him, may be studied in his *First Blows of the Civil War* (New York, 1879). For Greeley's embarrassment over his colleague's disunionist tendencies, see the *Daily Tribune* (hereafter referred to as *DTri.,* and all *Tribune* citations, unless otherwise indicated in the text or notes, may be found on the editorial page), Jan. 3, 21, 1857. Dana to Pike, Apr. 21, 1856, Pike MSS., Calais (Me.) Public Library (notes on this collection were kindly loaned the author by Miss Elizabeth Ring of Portland).

See also note 2, chapter VIII.

[11] *Dictionary of American Biography,* ed. Allen Johnson and Dumas Malone, VII (New York, 1931), 49-50.

accurately termed "small-sword practice."[12] Hildreth is best known today for his famous *History of the United States,* which marks him as the first outstanding economic interpreter among American historians. He had by 1854 completed his treatise, and his health was already failing; but his mental vigor was unabated, and he toiled with an uncompromising seriousness. He detested slavery and fought it by exposing the historical fallacies embedded in the pronouncements of its supporters.[13]

In addition to its editorial writers and the various correspondents at home and overseas, the *Tribune's* departmental heads deserve credit for its ascendancy. The most important were George Ripley, literary editor; Solon Robinson, agricultural editor; and Bayard Taylor, poet and globe trotter.

Ripley, older than the others, imparted a paternal air to the *Tribune* office. He too was a New Englander and a Harvard man. Impelled by the spirit of transcendentalism, he left the Unitarian ministry and inaugurated Brook Farm, but his career was to be made with his pen. By 1860, he was the most renowned critic in America. His standards were none too high, for he deemed it his first duty to foster the quantity of literary output within the young republic, and he knew this could best be done by encouragement. His condemnation was reserved for authors who attempted to uphold slavery or to slander New England customs.[14]

Much of the *Tribune's* appeal to the farmers was due to Solon Robinson. Formerly a frontiersman in Indiana, he was the proud possessor of two descriptive nicknames—"Chief Big Knife," friend of the Potawatomi Indians, and "King of

12 Fitz-Henry Warren to Pike, Mar. 10, 1858, Pike, *First Blows,* 393-394. See also Congdon, *Reminiscences;* and *Tribune Essays . . . 1857 to 1863* (New York, 1869).
13 Hildreth's *History* was completed with vol. VI in 1852. The best indication of his editorial style and purpose, however, may be obtained from his *Despotism in America . . .* (Boston, 1854); *Theory of Politics . . .* (New York, 1854); and *Archy Moore, the White Slave . . .* (New York, 1857).
14 Octavius B. Frothingham, *George Ripley* (Boston, 1883). Lisette Riggs, *George and Sophia Ripley,* unpublished doctoral thesis, University of Maryland Library, College Park.

the Squatters," protector of the local settlers against land speculators. Much of his frontier preoccupation was absorbed by other interests when he became a *Tribune* editor in 1853; but he remained a benefactor of the weak, as is attested by a melodramatic and sensational book entitled *Hot Corn*, in which he exposed New York City slums. His crop reports and market estimates compiled for the *Tribune* were invaluable to rural readers, and national repute came to him as an expert on the science of agriculture.[15]

Bayard Taylor, who was "not so good a journalist as a voyager," was the most colorful among a group of feature writers whom Greeley employed. Taylor's ambition was to became a great poet, but his worthiest effort in that field is a translation of Goethe's *Faust*. The fame of his travel accounts gained him a permanent place on the *Tribune* roster. His expeditions to California during the gold rush, to Japan with Commodore Matthew C. Perry, and to other areas all over the globe were pursued with vicarious pleasure by thousands of subscribers.[16]

The driving leadership which gave the *Tribune* its power emanated from the third floor office of the editor-in-chief. Partitioned from the noise of the inner editorial room, it was airy and well lighted. Its windows opened across Washington Square, and from them at around noon each day one could look below to see Greeley rushing along the dirty streets toward the *Tribune* building.

His appearance was so unusual that strangers recognized him easily from his description alone. He was of average height and weight, but his shoulders drooped, his large head jutted forward, and his nearsighted eyes peered from behind

[15] Introduction to *Solon Robinson, Pioneer and Agriculturist; Selected Writings*, ed. Herbert A. Kellar, I, (Indianapolis, 1936), is excellent. A storehouse of Robinson's agrarian advice and rough wit is his *Facts for Farmers* . . . (New York, 1864).
[16] Quotation attributed to Dana by Young, *Memories*, I, 18. Bayard Taylor, *The Life and Letters of* . . . , ed. Marie Hansen-Taylor and Horace Scudder (Cambridge, 1884), 2 vols. Most of Taylor's prolific travel accounts have been published in book form, such as *At Home and Abroad* (New York, 1860).

thick lenses. A white duster or a baggy overcoat, its pockets stuffed with documents ready for the typesetter and the morning edition, draped sack-like over his upper body. His suits were poorly fitted, with one or both trouser legs caught carelessly along the top of muddy boots, but his linen was scrupulously clean. A flaxen throat beard, reinforced by wisps of pale yellow hair from beneath a white hat, partially hid his collar. His complexion was clear, and his round face normally wore a pleasant, absent-minded expression. Although a gentle looking man everything about him was conspicuous, and there is no evidence that he wished it otherwise. As a contemporary periodical commented: ". . . he can to-morrow morning, if he chooses, come into Broadway dressed as men occupying his station in society dress, and he can pass unknown and unnoticed through the crowd, if his vanity would permit him to do it."[17]

He hurried up the dusty stairs and entered an office as ill-kept as his clothes were ill-cut. Piles of pamphlets, papers, books, and manuscripts lay in confusion about his desk. Seated with his nose close to a screeching quill, he scribbled at a furious speed. Greeley had a mission in life. To fulfill it, he had been busy since that day he was born, February 3, 1811, on a farm near Amherst, New Hampshire.

His youth, in the best Alger style, was a difficult one. He toiled long hours helping his poverty-stricken parents extract a wretched living from rocky, stump-ridden hillsides. There was little opportunity for schooling, but he made the best of what was offered. He read diligently the few books he could locate and startled his elders with his aptitude in spelling bees. A local minister guaranteed the promising boy an education at Phillips Exeter Academy, but his father and mother summoned up their Scotch-Irish pride and refused the charitable offer. What effect this training would have had upon Greeley's mind will forever remain a mystery; the fact is that

[17] *Frank Leslie's Illustrated Newspaper,* IV (Aug. 8, 1857), 150.

he gained his knowledge in the more arduous, and unfortunately less systematic, college of hard knocks.

He was a morose lad, serious and studious, who refused to play with other children and frowned upon the environment which surrounded him. From the first, he was a reformer who reacted unfavorably to the tobacco-smoking, rum-drinking, carousing, and hell-fire-and-damnation revivalism of his family and their neighbors. He never smoked, very early pledged himself never to drink, and, he tells us, was a Universalist from the moment he could meditate upon matters religious. The towheaded youth appeared so delicate and spiritual to village wags that they dubbed him "the Ghost."

A love for books instilled in his mind the ambition of becoming a printer, and when he was fifteen his father apprenticed him to a small weekly paper in East Poultney, Vermont. This firm soon collapsed from want of funds, and indefatigable Greeley went to New York City in quest of employment. He was at the time a greenhorn aged twenty, with ten dollars in his pocket and a small assortment of clothing wrapped in a kerchief. It was an auspicious entrance for a man who would later delight in being compared with Benjamin Franklin.

With neither money nor friends, Greeley's swift climb in the expanding field of printing testifies to his talents and industry. He began as a poorly paid compositor, but soon set up a business for himself which, thanks to the demand for lottery advertisements, managed to pay from the start.

He was interested in the finer letters, and his first successful venture in journalism was a literary weekly, the *New Yorker*. But political opinions sometimes found their way into his columns, and he was glad to supplement his meager income with contributions to partisan papers. His striking editorials soon drew the attention of upstate politicians. In 1838 he was approached by Thurlow Weed, the lanky, generous, good-natured editor of the Albany *Evening Journal* and mentor to the Whig gubernatorial candidate of that year, a redheaded young lawyer from Auburn named William Henry

Seward. Sponsored by Weed and backed by Whig party funds, Greeley entered political journalism under favorable circumstances. He went to work on a campaign sheet, the *Jeffersonian*, which served its purpose in helping to undermine President Martin Van Buren's home state Democratic strength and elect Seward governor. The next year, Greeley was chosen to edit the Whig presidential campaign weekly, called the *Log Cabin*. Never since in American history has a national contest equaled the tumultuous warmth of the 1840 race between Van Buren and William Henry Harrison. The *Log Cabin* throve, growing to the almost unbelievable circulation of 80,000.

This success trumpeted Greeley's capabilities before the public, and he seized his opportunity to fortify himself in political journalism. There was no cheap Whig paper in New York City. Soon after Harrison's triumph the *Log Cabin* carried a prospectus for the forthcoming *Daily Tribune*, which hit the newsstands on the morning of April 10, 1841, and appeared thereafter six days a week until the Civil War made Sunday issues advisable. In September, 1841, the *New Yorker* was converted into the *Weekly Tribune*. The *Semi-Weekly Tribune*, which although highly political in tone tended to resemble the *New Yorker* by stressing literary materials more than any other edition, was begun in 1842. Almost without exception the same editorials appeared in all three *Tribunes*, with an increasing amount of selectivity, because of space, in the *Semi-Weeklies* and *Weeklies*. Greeley's rise after the launching of the *Tribunes* was steady, and by 1854 he was at the summit of his prestige. The exasperating financial worries of his early days were behind him. He had almost completely divorced himself from the business end of his paper, and Dana handled the details of the editorial office. Greeley had at last arrived at that point in his career when he could devote his time to interpreting the events of the day. He read the newspaper and periodical exchanges, the letters from regular and occasional correspondents, and the scanty telegraphic dispatches, and digested the whole into an opinionated essay. He alone shaped *Tribune* policy.

The words Greeley scrawled upon the foolscap before him formed a compact prose, clearly conveying his intent and sparkling with wit and anecdote. For over a quarter of a century he had cultivated a simple, unmistakable style which gave force to his ideas.

In another respect he had failed to develop. His brain had been touched with genius, but never disciplined. He was prone to quick decisions and deemed his judgment infallible, for as a self-made man he had little else upon which to rely. He lacked the ability to see all facets of a problem, a characteristic the more dangerous as the issues leading to the Civil War became increasingly complex. This shortcoming was particularly noticeable because he had become a politician and prided himself as a practitioner of the art of expediency. Almost any means was justified to his mind in consideration of the end sought. Never did he knowingly deviate from his aim of a social democracy, but in withholding blows here and in giving ground there, he began to confuse the techniques employed with the final objective. When he had taken up the cudgels for a cause, be it basic or merely opportune, he would pound his way relentlessly but dexterously toward its accomplishment. Success in some instances ran at cross-purpose to his overall plan, and his lack of intellectual breadth may be said to have hastened an outcome altogether different from that which he sought.[18]

[18] The account of Greeley's early career, comprising much of this chapter, is based primarily upon his *Recollections of a Busy Life* (New York, 1868); a long autobiographical letter to Moses A. Cortland, Apr. 14, 1845, Ford Ltrs. (hereafter referred to as Greeley MSS.), New York Public Library (hereafter referred to as NYPL); and Parton's life of Greeley, 1896 edition, which is perhaps the best existing full length study. A superb analysis of Greeley's character, purportedly a review of Parton's first edition (New York, 1855), may be read in *Putnam's Magazine*, VI (July, 1855), 76-85; this article, attributed by Frothingham, *Ripley*, 213, to George Ripley, is listed in Ripley's handwriting as his in an unsigned autobiographical sketch in the Massachusetts Historical Society Library (hereafter referred to as MHSL).

Other biographers of Greeley have, in the main, followed his *Recollections* and Parton. In the order of their value, their works are: Logan U.

In contrast to Greeley's ever present idealism, and account-
ing for a large degree of his expedience, was a hunger for
personal glory which seemed insatiable. One of his most intimate associates, Thurlow Weed, confessed: "I shall never
comprehend Greeley, for I can never discern the personal considerations which sway and govern him." Greeley believed
that his paper's influence gave him a weight in the councils
of government above that bestowed upon the people's representatives, and he sought to implement his policies as if they
stemmed directly from the electorate. He was conceited
enough to feel that he could serve the public better than any
other man, and he boiled with anxiety for elective office. It
was contrary to his ethics to advance himself in the *Tribune's*
columns as a contender, and in his personal correspondence—
after he had failed of nomination—he would disavow such a
desire; but any and all efforts to place his name on the ballot
received the wholehearted encouragement of himself and his
closest supporters. Not without reason did Godkin castigate
him for being "as time-serving and ambitious and scheming
an old fellow as any of them."[19]

Greeley had what some considered another shortcoming.
His was a sensitive soul! To attack his policies was to impeach his personal integrity, and he answered his calumniators with an abusive tongue. He seldom hesitated to call an
antagonist a liar or a villain or both, as the situation seemed
to require. James Gordon Bennett was once damned as a

Reavis, *A Representative Life of* . . . (New York, 1872); Don C. Seitz,
Horace Greeley (Indianapolis, 1926); Lurton D. Ingersoll, *The Life of* . . .
(Chicago, 1873); Charles Sotheran, . . . *and Other Pioneers of American
Socialism* (New York, 1915); Whitelaw Reid, *Horace Greeley* (New York,
1879); William A. Linn, *Horace Greeley* (New York, 1903); William M.
Cornell, *The Life and Public Career of* . . . (Boston, 1882); and Francis N.
Zabriskie, *Horace Greeley* . . . (New York, 1890). Another highly
sympathetic account appeared while this work was in press, Henry L.
Stoddard, *Horace Greeley* . . . (New York, 1946).

Carl Sandburg has an inimitable word portrait of Greeley in *Abraham
Lincoln; the War Years* (New York, 1939), I, 403-408.

[19] Godkin, *Letters*, I, 292. Weed to Seward, May 11 (1856), Seward
Collection, Rush Rhees Library (hereafter referred to as RRL), University
of Rochester (this quotation was kindly furnished by Prof. Glyndon G.
Van Deusen).

"low-mouthed, blatant, witless, brutal scoundrel."[20] Greeley sought to justify such vituperation with a typical anecdote. He was reminded of the Irish soldier who was reproved for having bayoneted a dog as the animal charged with open mouth and savage purpose.

"You should have struck him with the butt of your gun, Patrick," admonished an officer.

"And so I wud, yer honor, if the baste had run at me with his tail." [21]

There is truth in this explanation. In Greeley's day journalists customarily indulged in derogatory verbal combat; but to this Greeley added a passion seldom rivaled, and not all who received his blasts deserved them. He had gained fame the hard way, and was, for example, resentful of men who had been favored with a college education and who took pride in their social positions. This contempt was frequently reciprocated. Some of his more highly cultured contemporaries considered him vulgar. Richard Henry Dana, Jr., a blue-blooded Bostonian, wasted no words: "Think him coarse and cunning."[22] But to the great majority of *Tribune* readers, Greeley's aggressive language was a sign of his sincerity and sagacity. To them he was a likeable philosopher who attacked the traducers of honesty, industry, and frugality.

Nor was his popularity restricted to the more rustic among his fellow citizens. Of the famous men and women of his age, hundreds responded to the depth of his convictions. They knew of his desire to assist young authors who showed literary promise, of his abiding concern for the underprivileged, and of his generosity to the destitute. Those closely connected with his everyday activities watched him give away to political campaign chests, to beggars, and to charitable organizations, and spend on his small, experimental farm up the Hudson river at Chappaqua, not only much of his salary and the

20 *DTri.*, Dec. 15, 1853.
21 *DTri.*, Aug. 27, 1857.
22 Charles F. Adams, *Richard Henry Dana* (Boston, 1890), I, 177.

return from his books but also much of his stock in the *Tribune*.

Greeley's friends were inclined to forgive him his oddities and conspicuous displays because they sympathized with him as a man without a congenial home life. In 1836 he had wed Connecticut school mistress Mary Y. Cheney, who was slender of figure and had long, curly, brunette hair. The marriage was hardly successful, but much can be said for Mary Greeley. She had, in the beginning, a quick mind and a deep interest in the welfare of her sex. It was she who acquainted her husband with the brilliant Margaret Fuller, and induced him to bring that gifted woman into their metropolitan residence and to set her up in the literary department of the *Tribune*. But at some point along the line, Mrs. Greeley's mind cracked. She became high-strung and irritable. Omnipresent fears depressed her. An ardent spiritualist, she threw herself into the intangible realm of the supernatural where she sought the causes of worldly and imagined events.

There was ample explanation for much of this emotional instability. She bore seven children at intervals of slightly more than two years from the day of her nuptials. Five of them died at a very early age—two sons tragically. Such fate was enough to break any woman. As early as 1841, Greeley had noted that she was "in her usual bad health." She got worse, never better. Six years later she was a crank, and her constant complaints and nervous quirks made a madhouse of their home. It was difficult to find a servant whom she could endure, and who could put up with her. Greeley once regretted turning down a prospective household employee, but hoped she could find another place, "a home not so desolate and barren as ours habitually is—one where they habitually have breakfast, at least."[23] Such outbursts of self-pity doubtless failed to soothe Mrs. Greeley's nerves, but handicapped in his efforts to work and irritated at the insults to his guests,

[23] Greeley to Emma Whiting, July 28, 1847; to B. F. Ransom, Nov. 13, 1841, Greeley Transcripts, LC.

her husband spent many of his free hours in a furnished room where he could write in peace.

Whoever or whatever was to blame for Mary Greeley's condition, her spouse clung to her with a tender affection, and this endeared him to all who were aware of the inner story of his domestic grief. They were awed by his capacity for punishment. The sorrow of his family life seemed to make him strive the harder for the elevation of his fellow man. He refused to rest. He labored over his desk until boils compelled him to ease up; yet even when traveling on lecture tours or on vacations in Europe, he rose with the sun and continued to pour editorials and letters into the columns of the *Tribune*. He was suspicious of medical advice. He would not relax: "I believe in good, solid work, nothing else."[24]

Greeley's titanic struggle against all the evils in the universe was a large part of his personality, but intermixed was picturesqueness which intrigued his associates. His memory was phenomenal, and in conversation he would rattle off historical dates and election statistics with as great a facility as he could spell the most improbable of words. His knowledge may have been an abundance of half truths—as Godkin asserts[25]—but his interpretation was always fresh and reassuring. Everything about Greeley breathed democracy. The grandeur in his hope for America was contagious. Whether he talked of steam plows and subsoil drainage, of Central Park and the new municipal horse cars, of the 1851 exposition in London and Manhattan's own Crystal Palace, or of art and literature, foremost in his conscience was the betterment of society. He looked upon "Shakespeare as a man of great mind and infinite humor, but he despised the man on account of his ultra-toryism."[26]

[24] Greeley to Ransom, Sept. 2, 1843, Greeley Transcripts, LC.
[25] Godkin, *Letters*, I, 254.
[26] A lecture on "Poets and Poetry," as reported in the Cleveland *Leader*, Jan. 16, 1858, *Annals of Cleveland, 1818-1935*, XLI, pt. 1 (Cleveland, 1937), abs. no. 2007, p. 262.

3. Patent Balancing by an Amateur, by J. Baillie

The Weekly Tribune.

NEW-YORK, THURSDAY, JUNE 1, 1854.

The circulation of THE WEEKLY TRIBUNE is **110,000.** Advertisements inserted for FIFTY CENTS per line each insertion.

SLAVERY AND THE UNION.

Just published at this Office.

THE NORTH AND THE SOUTH.
A PAMPHLET OF FORTY PAGES.

Containing a series of articles reprinted from THE NEW-YORK TRIBUNE.

CONTENTS.

I.—SLAVERY AND THE UNION.
II.—RELATIVE POWER OF THE NORTH AND SOUTH.
III.—THE COMMERCE OF THE NORTH AND SOUTH.
IV.—COST OF THE UNION.
V.—THE GREAT STRUGGLE.
VI.—THE SOUTH AND NORTHERN INTERESTS.
VII.—PROTECTION AND SOUTHERN INTERESTS.
VIII.—NORTH AND SOUTH.
IX.—THE CASE AS IT STANDS.
X.—VIRGINIA.

Price, 10 cents single; $6 per hundred.

BE IT REMEMBERED,

That so much of the Missouri Compromise of 1820 as prohibited forever the legalization of Human Slavery in any part of the territory of the United States north of N. lat. 36° 30′ and east of the Rocky Mountains—that is, all of the Missouri Compromise which was favorable to Freedom—has been *repealed* by the passage of the Nebraska-Kansas bill of Stephen Arnold Douglas—and that the Representatives from the Free States who voted therefor are as follows:

MAINE—Moses McDonald—1. MASSACHUSETTS—None.
NEW-HAMPSHIRE—Harry Hibbard—1.
CONNECTICUT—Colin M. Ingersoll—1.
VERMONT—None. RHODE ISLAND—None.
NEW-YORK—Thomas W. Cumming, Francis B. Cutting, Peter Rowe, John J. Taylor, William M. Tweed, Hiram Walbridge, William A. Walker, Mike Walsh, Theodore R. Westbrook—9.
PENNSYLVANIA—Samuel A. Bridges, John L. Dawson, Thomas B. Florence, J. Glancy Jones, William H. Kurtz, John McNeir, Asa Packer, John Robbins, Jr., Christian M. Straub, William H. Witte, Hendrick B. Wright—11.
NEW-JERSEY—Samuel Lilly, George Vail—2.
OHIO—David T. Disney, Frederick W. Green, Edson B. Olds, Wilson Shannon—4.
INDIANA—John G. Davis, Cyrus L. Dunham, Norman Eddy, Wm. H. English, Thomas A. Hendricks, Jas. H. Lane, Smith Miller—7.
ILLINOIS—James C. Allen, Willis Allen, Wm. A. Richardson—3.
MICHIGAN—Saml. Clark, David Stuart—2.
IOWA—Bernhardt Henn—1. WISCONSIN—None.
CALIFORNIA—Milton S. Latham, Jas. A. McDougall—2.
Total—14.

The same bill passed the Senate without amendment on the 25th, 35 to 13—Senators from the Free States voting for it—as follows:

NEW-HAMPSHIRE—Moses Norris, Jr., Jared W. Williams.
CONNECTICUT—Isaac Toucey.
NEW-JERSEY—John R. Thomson, William Wright.
PENNSYLVANIA—Richard Brodhead, Jr.
INDIANA—John Petit.
ILLINOIS—Stephen A. Douglas, James Shields.
MICHIGAN—Lewis Cass, Charles E. Stuart.
CALIFORNIA—William M. Gwin, John B. Weller.
IOWA—George W. Jones. Total 14.

By the votes of these men, representing Free Labor constituencies, One Million square miles of Territory, heretofore shielded FOREVER from Slavery by a bargain, forced by the South upon a reluctant and struggling North—(and whereof all that part enuring to the advantage of Slavery has been fully secured and enjoyed)—has been opened to slaveholding immigration and settlement, and so exposed to be brought into the Union as Slave States. Shall not Free People mark their betrayers?

SLAVE-CATCHING.

An intelligent, capable, powerful, "forehanded" man claims to be the owner of one ignorant, humble, friendless, penniless. The latter is ignorant, because

"every yoke and let the oppressed go free." Look you that it be not on your part disobeyed!

THE FUGITIVE LAW AND TRIAL BY JURY.

The public tranquillity demands the modification of the Fugitive Slave law, at least to the extent of giving to the alleged fugitive the right of *trial by jury* in the place where he is arrested. No smaller concession than this will prevent, in several of the Northern States, the most serious consequences in the future. It can hardly be doubted that systematic, organized, revolutionary resistance to the business of kidnapping men from the soil of the Free States will sooner or later be resorted to, unless this concession is granted; and we call upon Congress to give their earnest attention to the pressing necessity of a modification of the law to the extent we have indicated.

The theory of this Government is that the People shall make their own laws and be their own governors. And the universal respect and obedience to law which characterizes the people of the Free States rests upon their conviction that the majority ought to govern. But the Fugitive Slave law is of an anomalous character and reposes upon no such basis. It is not a law made or concurred in by a majority of the people of those States wherein lies the sole theater of its application. It is thus totally distinct from all other laws which the people of the Free States are called upon to obey. Instead of its being a law enacted by the people's representatives to operate upon those who enacted it, it is a law made by an outside interest, by those who do not feel its burdens and who are not subject to its penalties; and who framed it and rendered it harsh and odious for the sake of imposing obedience and humiliation at the same time upon those who were to be subjected to its operation. In a word, it is a law made by the slaveholders to operate, not upon themselves but upon the people of the Free States. It is just as much a law of extreme hardship, imposed by a foreign ruler upon a distant and unwilling people, as was the Stamp Act of revolutionary memory. Obedience to it receives no sanction from our theory of government, and, in its present form, refusing as it does the trial by jury, it is a law finding no sanction in the Constitution.

It is for these reasons that the law is resisted, and will be resisted, unless its repeal, or some such modification as we have suggested, shall follow. We call upon the members of Congress from the free States to pay heed to the signs of the times, and to take early steps to compose and tranquillize the public mind on this question. If they fail to do it, a fearful responsibility will rest upon their heads. We appeal to them with the more readiness since the majority of both branches have so lately been full of protestations in favor of submitting the question of Slavery to the people of the States where the slave or slaves are. We do not profess to ask a popular verdict in each fugitive slave case, but we do ask that the ordinary course of justice and the uniform proceedings at common law shall not be subverted and defied in the Free States, and that, in all cases where it shall be demanded, a Jury of twelve men shall be allowed to decide the question of a man's right to his freedom. In no other case but in that of an alleged fugitive is the right of trial by jury denied, and it is time that that exception should cease to exist. In the great cycle of events upon which we are now entering, it will assuredly come to this, and the sooner therefore

Among those who were inspired by Greeley's honesty of intention and captivated by his unorthodox manner were the talented biographer James Parton, the fragile sister poets, Alice and Phoebe Cary, the showman P. T. Barnum, the philanthropist Robert Owen, the saintly minister Edwin H. Chapin, and the wily politician Schuyler Colfax. With these and others Greeley mingled on Sunday evenings as he came and went among New York's literary salons. He was welcomed at these gatherings, where he drank cambric tea, munched crullers, gesticulated volubly—and dashed off to pen the Monday morning leader for the *Tribune*.[27]

Greeley's rapid emergence from obscurity had been remarkable. His entry into New York City in 1831 coincided with the beginning of an era in American history which has been well described in the title, *The Rise of the Common Man*.[28] His early career paralleled that surge of freedom, and he was instrumental in the reform movement which brought it about. His zeal drew strength from belief in the equality of opportunity, in a just distribution of the economic

[27] Among Greeley's papers, the Greeley MSS., NYPL, from which many of the Library of Congress Transcripts are taken, and the Greeley-Colfax Correspondence, also in NYPL, are the best for autobiographical data.

The above draws heavily from Greeley's *Recollections* and from other published memoirs and letters, of which there are hundreds of volumes in this period. The most valuable are: Beman Brockway, *Fifty Years in Journalism* . . . (Watertown, N. Y., 1891). Mary C. Ames, *Outlines of Men, Women and Things* (New York, 1873); *A Memorial of Alice and Phoebe Cary* . . . (New York, 1875). Congdon, *Reminiscences*. Young, *Memories*, 2 vols. Godkin, *Letters*, 2 vols. Anne Charlotte Lynch Botta, *Memoirs of* . . . , ed. Vincenzo Botta (New York, 1894). Thurlow Weed, *Life of* . . . , *including his Autobiography and a Memoir*, ed. Harriet A. Weed, and T. W. Barnes, author of the memoir (Boston, 1884), 2 vols. Frederick W. Seward, *Seward at Washington* . . . *a Memoir of his Life, with Selections from his Letters, 1846-1861* (New York, 1891). Ralph Waldo Emerson, *The Letters of* . . . , ed. Ralph L. Rusk (New York, 1939), 6 vols. Rufus W. Griswold, *Passages from the Correspondence and Other Papers of* . . . , ed. W. M. Griswold (Cambridge, 1898). Alexander K. McClure, *Recollections of Half a Century* (Salem, Mass., 1902). John W. Forney, *Anecdotes of Public Men*, 2 vols. (New York, 1873, 1881). Hansen-Taylor, *On Two Continents; Memories of Half a Century* (New York, 1905). Maunsell B. Field, *Memories of Many Men and of Some Women* . . . (New York, 1874). Frothingham, *Recollections and Impressions, 1822-1890* (New York, 1891).

[28] Carl R. Fish, *The Rise of the Common Man* (New York, 1927).

benefits of the industrial revolution, and in the fraternity of man as taught by Christ.

There was reason for Greeley and his fellow citizens to experience a resurgent faith in the democracy which their forefathers had shaped from the frontier. Untouched natural resources promised wealth and glory, and new methods of exploitation stirred imaginations. Electric wires flashed messages with the speed of light, engines made of iron puffed over mountains and through valleys, giant looms wove cotton and wool into sturdy cloth, and monstrous reapers lumbered across the fields doing the job of a score of men with scythe and cradle. To Greeley, the prospect was rosy. Surely such inventions were ushering in a better social order. He greeted each scientific discovery as a "Sign of the Times," and repetitiously summarized his optimism over the "Progress of the Age."[29]

Much of Greeley's confidence was based upon mechanical contrivances, but he relied to a greater extent upon his religion. He was more than a Universalist who believed in salvation for every man; he felt that God was actively engaged in improving the world: " . . . our Father in Heaven will, in his own good time, bring the whole human race into a state of willing and perfect reconciliation to himself and obedience to his laws—consequently one of complete and unending happiness."[30] Greeley's trust was so implicit that it led him to extremes, for he had found merit in spiritualism and had eagerly prepared for the hereafter by purifying his body and soul on a diet of wheat bread and vegetables. Indeed, he had met his wife while both were under the stern influence of Sylvester Graham, for whom a cracker is named. Greeley once told a lecture audience that he was a mere popularizer of the teachings of Ralph Waldo Emerson,[31] but he was more than a

[29] Greeley to Dana, Apr. 7, 9, 1856, Greeley, *Letters,* 142-148. Examples, *DTri.,* Oct. 8, 1853; Jan. 7, 1854; Sept. 22, 1855; Nov. 24, 1856; May 29, 1857; Aug. 6, 1858; Apr. 30, July 10, 1860.
[30] Greeley to J. M. Austin, Feb. 10, 1855, *Weekly Tribune* (hereafter referred to as *WTri.*), Mar. 3, 1855. Quoted in Parton, *Greeley,* 523-524.
[31] Greeley, *Hints Toward Reforms* . . . (New York, 1854), 86.

transcendentalist. He was a militant Christian socialist, and as such was his brother's keeper charged with the responsibility of uplifting society. As he wrote in 1858, "Christianity is . . . a radical, belligerent, innovating religion. It must advance, and assail, and impeach, and condemn, so long as there shall be evil to combat and good to achieve. It is at war with all shapes and shades of wrong-doing—with all that seeks personal gain or ease at the expense of general well-being." It was "Absolute Justice, Absolute Morality, impelled by Universal Love."[32] Greeley abhorred comfortable pews.and the pallid counsel of expensive ministers. He said that such parsons would have considered "Jesus . . . a young man of rare abilities, high courage, and blameless life, who might do vast good if he would only abandon his radical notions and low associates, and conform to the orthodox creeds and conservative instincts of his time." Greeley tried to follow in his Master's footsteps by searching for truth among "the lowly, the despised, and the outcast."[33] His duty was clear. He must see to it that the poor were fed and housed, for otherwise they would never seek refuge in Christ: "Morality, Religion are but words to him who fishes in the gutters for the means of sustaining life and crouches behind barrels in the street for shelter from the cutting blasts of a winter's night."[34]

More than any other factor, these convictions impelled Greeley to place the *Tribune* in the vanguard of the reform movement, and much was accomplished by him and other leaders. Laws were passed improving working conditions; public elementary schools became the rule rather than the exception; imprisonment for debt was abolished; criminal codes were revised in order to eliminate savage punishments, and prisons capable of regenerating the wayward were built. The insane, the deaf mute, and the blind were attended, and efforts made to adjust them to the normal functions of society.

[32] Greeley *et al., The Religious Aspects of the Age* . . . (New York, 1858), 54-62.
[33] Greeley to John Scoville, Apr. 25, 1853, N. Y. *Sun,* Nov. 26, 1893.
[34] Greeley to Pauline W. Davis, Sept. 1, 1852, Greeley Transcripts, LC.

It is true that more was undertaken than was effected and that the movement was halted at the peak of its strength. Greeley himself wished to prohibit by law the commercial distribution of alcohol, to abolish the army and navy and rely upon the militia alone for defense, to grant the female equality with the male, to do away with capital punishment, and to enfranchise the negroes in the north. Where this progressive impulse might have led but for the advent of the antislavery crusade, no one can say.[35]

A mere listing of its gains does an injustice to the reform movement as a whole. Greeley had in mind a completely new social structure to be brought about through far-reaching economic and political changes. He desired above all else a system which would divide equitably the wealth of the industrial revolution. This he pictured as a decentralized society of industries, handicraft and agriculture, so constituted that every man would own at least a part of his tools of production and be able to rear his family close to the soil, far from the crowded cities and the ills generated by slums.

The beginnings of industrialization in America promised no such Utopia. The panic of 1837 and its resultant depression made this fact obvious to Greeley. The miseries and suffering he witnessed in New York City gave him determination to uplift the downtrodden. A ten year period of thought and experimentation on the problem followed, during which he matured his program; but at this early date, far in advance of his time, he became an advocate of the inherent right of an individual to a job and a wage on which he and his family could not only subsist but also contribute to an improved society.[36]

This laudable desire introduced Greeley to a trail-blazing group of New England reformers, the transcendentalists, and he watched their venture at Brook Farm with expectancy.

[35] Alice F. Tyler, *Freedom's Ferment* (Minneapolis, 1944). Reavis, *Greeley*, 548. Greeley to Seward, Nov. 19, 1857, Seward MSS., Auburn. *DTri.*, Oct. 8, 1853; Sept. 22, 1855; July 13, 1857.
[36] Greeley, *Recollections*, 144-147.

They failed, however, to command his enthusiastic attention. He was more susceptible to the social philosophy first introduced to America by Albert Brisbane in 1834.

Brisbane was a well-to-do New Yorker who had traveled widely in Europe and Asiatic Turkey. While in Paris, he had fallen under the influence of Charles Fourier, whom he grew to admire and whose chief American disciple he became. Fourier, a follower of the eighteenth century rationalists and a keen student of psychology, had compiled a set of social laws which were to him as irrefutable as the Newtonian formulas on gravitation.

The Frenchman deduced that social maladjustments stem from two causes, man's inability to pursue the occupation of his choice and the waste apparent in a competitive economic system. His remedy was known as "Association." He would harmonize human endeavors by giving each person the opportunity to select his vocation and by regrouping society on a decentralized, communal basis. Each such unit was termed a "phalanx" and was to consist of 1620 men working 5000 acres of land. It was to be self-sufficient, but world-wide peace and prosperity were expected to emerge from cultural relations and an interchange of goods between phalanxes. The profits from this trade were to be distributed proportionately among labor, management, and capital, thereby encouraging individual industry, initiative, and thrift.

Greeley, it seems, was first attracted to Fourierism by a book which Brisbane produced on the subject in 1840. Shortly thereafter the two men were sponsoring Fourierist periodicals, and for a time Brisbane ran a *Tribune* column on his favorite topic. Greeley became an ardent pupil of Fourier. There is an indication that he was too impatient even for Brisbane.[37] At any rate, Greeley was chief among the

[37] Brisbane refused to enter into politics, and of course Greeley disagreed on this count. He complained that Brisbane was too exclusive, and would not cooperate with other reformers. "My way is different. I think Association is the most natural thing in the world for a properly civilized and Christianized Society—the very point to which all the Progress of the last century has tended by a natural law." Greeley to Dana, Oct. 10, 1842,

zealots who launched, prematurely, two associations. The first was the Sylvania Phalanx on a barren plot of ground in northern Pennsylvania; the second was the more prosperous North American Phalanx near Red Bank, New Jersey. Greeley was also instrumental in converting Brook Farm from a transcendentalist colony into a Fourierist association.[38]

None of these experiments was more than temporarily successful, and this fact dampened Greeley's fervor. Other developments helped put a stop to his direct advocacy of Fourierism. A number of its enthusiasts were not family-worshiping, God-fearing men, and their attachment to free love and free thought embarrassed their friend of the *Tribune*.[39] Greeley not only preached chastity for the unwed and strict fidelity between husband and wife, but his theories of biology and phrenology made him fear that promiscuous sexual relations would prove catastrophic for the next generation. When visiting the Mormons in Utah, he recorded with satisfaction his impression that children born in polygamy seemed to have subnormal heads.[40] The Bible was to him the law of God, and he interpreted it as sanctioning a legal separation only on proof of adultery. Galley after galley of type

Greeley MSS., LC. See also Charles A. Madison, "Albert Brisbane: Social Dreamer," *American Scholar*, xii (Summer, 1943), 284-296.

[38] Sotheran, *Greeley*, 2-145.

Albert Brisbane, *Social Destiny of Man; or, Association and Reorganization of Industry* (Philadelphia, 1840); *Association; or, A Concise Exposition of the Practical Part of Fourier's Social Science* (New York, 1843); and . . . *A Mental Biography with a Character Study* by his wife Redelia Brisbane (Boston, 1893).

[39] Albert Post, *Popular Freethought in America, 1825-1850.* (New York, 1943).

A news report in *DTri.*, Oct. 19, 1855, tells of Brisbane's arrest on a charge of disorderly conduct in connection with his attendance at what purported to be a free love meeting. See also *DTri.*, Sept. 10, Oct. 16, 18, 29, 1855; Nov. 8, 1858.

Greeley stood up well for a time against the charges that his friends were freethinkers. He wrote Colfax on Sept. 23, 1845, Greeley-Colfax Correspondence (hereafter this source will be understood in any exchange of letters between these two men), NYPL, that he did not mind rumors current about his having attended an infidel meeting: "I am not afraid of such stuff, and shall publish some things soon for Robert Owen, who is very thick-headed in his Theology, but a more Christ-like man than any fat parson in New York." In the end, the opprobrium was too much for Greeley.

[40] From Salt Lake City, July 18, *DTri.*, Sept. 3, 1859.

was spent in debating this point with the brilliant essayist
and one-time *Tribune* Paris correspondent, Henry James,
Sr., and with the instigator of Indiana's lax divorce procedure, the unorthodox Robert Dale Owen.[41]

In embracing precepts which were widely attacked as las-
civious and ungodly, the Fourierists alienated their most
vocal collaborator. Nor was Greeley's partner and business
manager of the *Tribune*, money-minded, ex-attorney Thomas
McElrath, pleased with the socialism expounded in his paper,
claiming that its presence there was diminishing advertising
and curtailing circulation.[42] Finally, and most important,
Greeley had by 1848 evolved a philosophy of his own which
was more peculiarly American.

Fourier's influence remained. It furnished Greeley with a
background for belief in individualism—the right of every
man to pick his means of livelihood. Such an outlook was
necessarily in conflict with the doctrine of enforced labor,
and Greeley's opposition to slavery was intensified by humanitarian sympathies. Also, Fourier had clung to capitalism.
Removing communal life from his preceptor's philosophy,
Greeley substituted harmony among economic classes (that
is, simple good feeling) and association between management
and labor (that is, purchase by workers of part ownership),
and emerged with a program that was hardly revolutionary.
Greeley recognized this fact, yet he continued to consider
himself a radical. He saw nothing inconsistent about this. To
his mind, public affairs should be given mobility by the fresh
wind of progressive idealism and stability by the counterpoise of enlightened conservatism.

The search for a proper ballast led Greeley into the least
progressive of the country's political parties, the Whig.
Since youth he had admired the brilliant Kentucky states-

---

[41] These debates appeared in *DTri.* in the springs of 1859 and 1860. The
controversy with Owen, the later of the two, also appeared in a pamphlet,
"Divorce: Being a Correspondence Between . . . " (New York, 1860), but
may be most conveniently found in Greeley, *Recollections,* 571-618.

[42] McElrath to the editor of the *Tribune,* Dec. 24, 1887 (clipping),
Greeley MSS., LC.

man, Henry Clay, and the weighty doctrines of the latter's "American System," with its internal improvements, high tariff, and national bank.[43] One of Greeley's first propaganda tasks within the ranks of the Whig party was to convince a large crew of farmers and urban laborers that they should heave this heavy cargo aboard the ship of state.[44] As Greeley went about this job, his love for the sturdy hull of the American republic grew, and he became more and more an economic nationalist. He was anxious to increase the powers of the central government, for he believed it charged with the duty of bringing prosperity and health to the people by supervising the expansion of capitalism and by improving the public morale. He advocated neither state socialism nor laissez faire. The government at Washington should neither keep hands off nor engage in business, but rather should do "much *positive good*"[45] for the national economy. It should foster individual and corporate outlays of capital by empowering federal banks to issue an elastic currency backed with bullion, by protecting infant industries and creating new ones with levies against imports, and by subsidizing river, harbor, railway, and other transportation developments.

At the same time, Greeley adhered to certain radical views as a means of trimming the sail to the breeze. He wished to elevate the working man and for this reason was active in the support of trade unionism. Its function was not, as he saw it, collective bargaining. The strike was both disharmonizing and a waste of time. In the early nineteenth century, laborers joined together primarily for benevolent purposes, and to this Greeley wished to add the accumulation of capital reserves in order to establish producers' cooperatives. He at-

[43] Greeley, *Recollections*, 106.
[44] Greeley began publishing a protectionist periodical, *American Laborer* . . . , in Apr., 1842. It ran for twelve monthly issues, and was doubtless stopped because of the passage of the 1842 tariff, which was joyously announced in the Sept. number. See also William Atkinson, "Principles of Political Economy, with an Introduction by Horace Greeley" (pamphlet) (New York, 1843).
[45] *DTri.*, June 23, 1852. Greeley's italics.

tempted to put this practice into effect in his own industry. He was the first president of the powerful New York Typographical Union No. 6, and he sponsored the formation of the *Tribune* Association, which took the place of his partnership with McElrath in 1849. This was not a Fourierist experiment, but a joint stock company in which any member of the *Tribune* family—clerk, printer, compositor, or editor— could participate by saving his money and purchasing a share.[46]

Greeley wished above all else to intrench the laborer in the enterprise of which he was part owner, thus making him a capitalist-worker. Internal improvements were to open to exploitation the vast reaches of the interior, where an elastic currency would foster the growth of industries. A high tariff, he felt, would abet this expansion, and would also encourage inventive genius and promote frugality by curtailing the entrance of luxuries such as wines and silks into American ports. Greeley expected his protective policy chiefly to benefit the artisan and small farmer by diversifying employment, decentralizing industry, and placing the urban consumer near the agrarian producer. In this manner society would eliminate all the unnecessary, and to Greeley's mind parasitic, middlemen who were thriving by transporting goods long distances and marketing them at exorbitant profits.

The key to Greeley's plan for social improvement was land reform.[47] He considered the law of supply and demand a

[46] Dana to Pike, Mar. 26, Apr. 8, 25, Oct. 6, 1851, Pike, *First Blows*, 87-90, 97-98.
George A. Stevens, *New York Typographical Union No. 6* (Albany, 1913) is filled with material on Greeley's early union activities.
[47] "The basis of union of the true democracy of the next twenty years is to be *land reform*, not alone as applied to public lands, but to *all* lands. With this goes *labor reform* or the ten-hour legislation. To these articles I hope another will attach itself, viz: *abolition of the army and navy.*" Greeley to Brockway, Nov. 13, 1847, Brockway, *Fifty Years*, 115-116. Greeley's italics.
See also Roy M. Robbins, "Horace Greeley: Land Reform and Unemployment, 1837-1862," *Agricultural History*, vii (Jan., 1933), 18-41; *Our Landed Heritage, the Public Domain, 1776-1936* (Princeton, 1942), 76-216. John R. Commons, "Horace Greeley and the Working Class Origins of the Republican Party," *Political Science Quarterly*, xxiv (Sept., 1909), 468-488.

basic consideration in setting wages. He did not promote collective bargaining. If eastern workers were to be well paid
and thus enabled to participate in factory ownership, it was
necessary that the labor surplus be drained westward to virgin soil. These settlers, in turn, must be guarded from land
speculators so that they could make the frontier flourish and
prepare the way for small industries. Greeley entered actively
into the agrarian movement sponsored by George Henry
Evans and placed first on his political agenda the legislation
necessary for homesteads.[48]

Thus Greeley's social program, carried to its logical conclusions, inevitably ran athwart the aims of those southerners
who wished to extend and perpetuate their system of plantation economy. Fortunately cr unfortunately, his ideas took
definite shape just as the long dormant slavery controversy
was revived by the Mexican War.

The Missouri Compromise in 1820 had given the nation almost three decades of comparative peace between sections.
This law restricted slavery from all the Louisiana territory
lying north of 36° 30', with the exception of Missouri, which
was at that time organized as a slave state. As mid-century
approached, the southerners became increasingly conscious
of the tremendous population gains made through immigration into the north and westward to free soil. This flood tide
of people, they reasoned, could best be prevented from destroying the equilibrium between the free and slave states by
the adoption of economic policies which were the reverse of
those advocated by Greeley. The famous Webster-Hayne debates, for example, arose from a congressional clash over
western land policy.[49] Most southerners opposed homesteads,

[48] This survey of Greeley's economic philosophy is taken primarily from
Hints; "Why I Am a Whig," *Whig Almanac . . . 1852* (New York, 1851),
19-26; *Essays . . . [on] Political Economy . . . as a System of National
Cooperation for the Elevation of Labor* (Philadelphia, 1869); and "Capital
and Labor," *Wood's Household Magazine* (Nov., 1871) (clipping), Greeley
MSS., LC.
[49] Claude M. Fuess, *Daniel Webster* (Boston, 1930) I, 361-385.

internal improvements, the protective tariff, and a national
bank.

Acrimonious controversy between the north and the south
as to the disposition of newly acquired western lands broke
out even before the treaty of peace at Guadalupe Hidalgo in
1848. This settlement ended the war with Mexico and, along
with the Oregon treaty with England in 1846, carried the
boundary of the United States along its present lines westward from the Louisiana territory and Texas to the Pacific.[50]
A reconciliation over slavery was temporarily effected with
the Compromise of 1850. Provisions of this law instituted
popular sovereignty for all annexed Mexican soil save that of
California, which was simultaneously admitted to the Union
with a free constitution. The bitter subject of slavery was to
be removed from congress and hence from the public mind by
allowing the territorial inhabitants of the area to decide for
themselves as they entered the Union whether or not they
wished to be citizens of slave states.

There was no legal connection between the 1850 adjustment, which applied only to the land seized from Mexico, and
the accord reached in 1820, which held only for the unorgan-
ized portion of the region purchased from France. However,
the vast majority of the southerners and some northerners
contended that popular sovereignty had abrogated, morally
at least, the restrictive feature of the Missouri Compromise.
In 1854 when Kansas and Nebraska were cut from the Louisiana territory, the article of the 1820 settlement prohibiting
slavery was repealed and the doctrine of popular sovereignty
substituted.

This blow struck at the heart of Greeley's social program.
It threatened his land policy by opening the western regions
to the slave system, characterized as it was by the plantation,
the production of staple crops, and non-industrialization.
Should the southerners and their northern allies win in this

[50] The Gadsden purchase, in expectation of railway construction, was
obtained from Mexico in 1853.

encounter, he feared that his dream of small farms backed by free and diversified labor would be shattered. He jettisoned other reforms in which he was interested, marched with screaming headlines against the apologists for human bondage, and helped inaugurate the Republican party.

The results of such decisions as Greeley's were formidable. The Republicans, assisted by the force of political and economic circumstance, were able to bind together disjointed groups of voters; while the Democrats, handicapped by the ineptness of most of their leaders, were demoralized and divided by the assaults upon their party. For seven tumultuous years the country argued whether to restrict or to extend slavery. A choice might have been avoided had the doctrine of popular sovereignty been successful, but its application increased sectionalism. Yankees battled southerners across the plains of Kansas, and their tussles were exaggerated in the minds of congress and the people. A logical approach to the problem became difficult as it grew more involved, and the Dred Scott decision with its constitutional technicalities made matters worse. The financial panic of 1857 emphasized the economic divergences between free and slave communities. Crisis begot crisis. Nerves frayed. Understanding of one section by the other lessened day by day and hour by hour. Every issue seemed to spin itself into a thread of strength for the Republican party, and in 1860 the strands were collectively woven into a national campaign victory. To this historical fabric, *Tribune* propaganda supplied the warp.

When joining the antislavery crusade, Greeley accepted the risk of armed conflict because he believed he could avoid such a calamity and because he judged the quarantine of slavery essential to his program. Had he foreseen the outcome clearly, he would have toiled to prevent it. The triumph of the Republicans led to the Civil War.

CHAPTER 2

FREE SOIL, HERITAGE
OF LIBERTY

The passage of the Kansas-Nebraska bill by the traitors in the Senate of the United States is one further step of Southern chivalry toward effecting the brutal degradation of all Mechanical and Laboring men, white and black, in the United States.—*Daily Tribune*, March 25, 1854.

IN the fall of 1853, Greeley looked from his office window beyond the garbage and dust which lay on the cobblestones below. Although this filth was the topic of frequent editorial growls,[1] he was more aware of the harbor and the newly erected buildings which reached toward the sky. The port was growing at a rapid pace, and this was evidence of an industrious people. He took pride in the future of the United States, for he was a nationalist who gloried in the republic which promised to become a shining example of social justice for the world.

Of course the country had its faults. Enforced negro labor ranked high upon the list, but that as well as the dirt beneath his window would be removed when his fellow citizens realized their better interests. He was doing his part by carrying on an educational campaign against all such evils, but he stood in awe of sectional discord over slavery. He knew that freedom would be more easily and more permanently achieved if it came by virtue of economic changes. Internal improvements, homesteads, and a high tariff must first eradicate the sweatshops and other forms of servitude which permeated the alleys and side streets of his and other cities. Factories paying

[1] Examples, *DTri.*, Oct. 28, 1853; Mar. 6, June 1, July 7, Sept. 7, 1854.

31

a more than subsistence wage must be spread over the nation.
"The thinking men of the South," Greeley claimed, "well understand that slavery can only be maintained in an agricultural country . . ."[22] Industrialization must diversify labor
and largely replace staple with truck farming by creating
urban markets. Scientific advancements and improved communications would then weld the sections more closely together, and newspapers such as the *Tribune* could flood the
south with irresistible torrents of democracy, extinguishing
the plantation system.

This attitude won Greeley scant popularity among the
abolitionists, a small but vocal group of northern voters. They
regarded him as disloyal, for they knew him to be in theoret-
ical agreement with their aim and failed to understand his
attacks upon them as misguided devotees of a single and impracticable political idea. It was not that he neglected to ex-
plain his policy to these gentlemen. While visiting London in
1851 he startled an international antislavery convention when
he argued that the best way to effect liberation in the south
was by elevating the white working class in America and especially in Great Britain. He was more emphatic two years
later when writing for the partisan publication of the Rochester Ladies' Anti-Slavery Society. Those who toiled were detested because "too many seek to engross the product of
others' work, yet do little or none themselves. If the secret
were but out, *that no man can really enjoy more than his own
moderate daily labor would produce, and none can truly enjoy this without doing the work*, the death-knell of Slavery in
general—in its subtler as well as its grosser forms—would be
rung. Until that truth shall be thoroughly diffused, the cunning and strong will be able to prey upon the simple and
feeble, whether the latter be called slaves or something else."
The friends of human bondage, he concluded, were those who
caused labor to be looked down upon: snobbish women, men
who degenerated in luxury, and "every rich Abolitionist, who

2 *DTri.*, May 13, 1853.

is ashamed of being caught . . . digging in his garden or plowing in the field."[3]

His solution was more constructive than that of William Lloyd Garrison, northern disunionist and editor of the *Liberator*. Greeley wanted emancipation to transpire along with and because of economic changes in the slave states. Meanwhile precedents in keeping with a virulent democracy should be established for the negroes in the free commonwealths. His paper pleaded that they be educated and receive industrial training. He believed phrenology, history, literature, and those scientific advancements made by fellow whites proved the black man to be, temporarily, inferior. White men in the United States enjoyed civil rights irrespective of ability, and Greeley urged that, in order to develop innate capabilities, the negro be similarly treated: "We hold it unjust and cruel to aggravate his natural disabilities by legal or social degradations; we hold that Man's inalienable right to equality under the laws is not at all invalidated by his intellectual deficiencies, but rather fortified and hallowed by them—that robbing an inferior race of Political Franchise and Social immunities, is as cowardly and detestable as striking a woman . . ."[4]

Nothing in this reasoning endeared Greeley to the slaveholders. Besides, he had adopted an aggressive procedure for maintaining aversion to thralldom in the minds of his followers which was most offensive to southerners and their sympathizers. Several times each month the *Tribune* carried a column frequently headed "FACTS OF SLAVERY," but sometimes given even more alluring titles such as "A SCENE OF CRUELTY AND BLOODSHED," "THE SHAME OF VIRGINIA," or "MECHANICS BOUGHT AND SOLD." The featured material was generally reprinted from

[3] Greeley, "The Dishonor of Labor," *Autographs for Freedom*, ed. Julia Griffiths, 2nd series (Auburn, N.Y., 1854), 194-197. Greeley's italics. From London, May 23, 1851, to the *Tribune*, reprinted in Greeley, *Glances at Europe* . . . (New York, 1851), 83-86.
[4] *DTri.*, May 31, 1853. See also *DTri.*, Sept. 27, Nov. 7, 1853.

stories and advertisements found in southern newspapers, but occasionally a surreptitious reporter on the scene managed to forward his findings to New York. With gusto the data presented savage executions of slaves and exhibited mulattoes running from the dripping jaws of bloodhounds. It was never heavy reading, and was often spiced with sexual atrocities. The moral involved was unobscured by circumlocution. Bondsmen were portrayed as suffering human beings, yearning for escape. Perusers were led to wonder, if nearly white-complexioned mechanics and field hands were sold, tortured, and murdered, what protected northern workers from a similar fate.[5]

The laborer who glanced at the *Tribune* was warned against expecting aid and comfort from the Democrats. According to hundreds of editorials, they not only tolerated the plague but connived to extend it. Slavery in the United States was said to constitute one of the most serious obstacles to democratic progress not only in the western hemisphere but throughout the world.[6] The Democratic party was therefore a diabolical political organization. Its name alone, Greeley was sure, gave it thousands of unsuspecting adherents, and he usually spoke of it as "Sham Democracy." He instructed his staff to employ similar adjectives of abuse when referring to the Democrats; otherwise, as he complained to Pike, "they may have a roast baby for breakfast every morning, with missionary steaks for dinner, and yet rule the country forever."[7]

Greeley was quick to defend himself when this treatment of slavery and the Democratic party was condemned as "agitation." He countered that he was battling the insidious penetration of the spirit of human bondage into the minds of freemen just as he would "Chinese idolatry or South Sea licentiousness . . . by the diffusion of light and truth and the

[5] Examples, *DTri.,* Sept. 7, 12, Dec. 2, 1853; Jan. 17, 18, 21, Feb. 6, 14, 15, 1854.
[6] *DTri.,* Sept. 20, 1853.
[7] Greeley to Pike, Apr. 28, 1850, Pike, *First Blows,* 49.

quiet rebuke of a consistent testimony." Southern editors rejoined that the north, in spite of liberty, had its full quota of rape and homicide. To which Greeley retorted that while northern felonies were punishable by law, southern crimes were abetted by slave codes, and he proved his case by pointing to "the advertisements of quadroon girls, maimed and branded runaways, negro bloodhounds, and rewards for fugitives . . . "[8]

However annoying this brand of journalism may have been to some, it cannot be termed political abolitionism. Indeed, Greeley confessed that as a resident of New York he had no constitutional right to interfere with the domestic affairs of other states.[9] In national politics there was but one legal method by which he could oppose slavery, by insisting that the federal government halt its advance westward.

Because of the Missouri Compromise he had no grievance as long as the United States held only the Louisiana territory. But the task of restricting slavery became acute with the annexation of Texas, the Mexican conquest, and the Oregon treaty with England. That Greeley restrained himself from rushing pell-mell into this controversial problem is illustrative of his caution. He armed himself with the single propaganda weapon of antislavery only when, some years later, the issue had been clearly drawn by the Kansas-Nebraska bill.

In his private correspondence, he revealed fears that the war with Mexico was waged in order to intrench slavery in the southwest, and he wished to secure state and national Whig resolutions against such a misfortune. He was anxious that his party's presidential candidates be men who concurred with him, and in 1848 held out to the bitter end against the selection of Louisiana slaveholder Zachary Taylor. He favored Henry Clay not only because the Kentuckian was a statesman rather than a militarist but chiefly because he was "for none

[8] *DTri.*, Dec. 27, Nov. 26, 1853.
[9] Speech delivered at Osawatomie, K. T., May 18, *DTri.*, May 31, 1859.

other but free territory, though he don't want any."[10] Defeat
would be preferable to triumph with Taylor, for Greeley supposed that the campaign would drive antislavery Whigs from
the party: "The off-set to Abolition will ruin us. I wash my
hands of the business."[11]

No such disaster met Taylor as the Whig nominee, possibly because the convention which named him sidestepped
trouble by refusing to draw up any platform. This timidity
elicited groans from the *Tribune* that Whig principles had
been slaughtered, but the paper gave Taylor reluctant support. The principles of the Free Soilers, who were running
ex-President Martin Van Buren, had Greeley's sympathies,
but to his mind there was no excuse for a third party because
the Whigs should have advocated both slavery restriction and
homesteads. Nevertheless, he contended that he was doing all
he could for "the banditti" responsible for Taylor's choice,
although that despicable group deserved defeat and the
people probably merited a visitation of "that fat-bellied,
mutton-headed, cucumber-souled" Lewis Cass, the Democratic nominee from Michigan.[12]

Taylor won in 1848, and Greeley was simultaneously
elected to fill out an unexpired term of three months in the
house of representatives. As far as the slavery question was
concerned, he conducted himself with moderation. At this
time he was willing to forget about the Wilmot proviso, an
amendment, shelved by the senate, to an appropriation bill,
which would have flatly prohibited enforced negro labor on
former Mexican soil. A part of Greeley's basic strategy was
to maneuver the north into a favorable relative position for
a compromise which was seen to be forthcoming.[13] His parlia-

[10] Greeley to Weed, Jan. 31, 1848, New York Historical Society Library
(hereafter referred to as NYHSL). See also Greeley to Weed, Aug. 25,
1848, NYHSL. Seward to his home, Jan. 29, Apr. 11, 1848, F. Seward,
Seward, 62, 67. Seitz, *Greeley,* 136-145.
[11] Greeley to Colfax, Apr. 3, 1848, NYPL.
[12] Greeley to Colfax, Oct. 2, 1848, NYPL. George W. Julian, *The Life of
Joshua R. Giddings* (Chicago, 1892), 252.
[13] Greeley to Colfax, Jan. 2, 29, Feb. 16, 1849, NYPL.

mentary interests were retrenchments in operating expenditures, a project for renaming the country "Columbia," and
his cherished economic measures. He reported to his constituents as he left congress that he had "shunned and deplored
any needless agitation respecting slavery," and he "especially
condemned the interminable speech-making on this theme to
which a full half the session was absurdly and perniciously
devoted."[14]

Such was Greeley's frame of mind as the critical Compromise of 1850, covering the disposition of slavery in the recently conquered western lands, was being evolved in Washington. He wanted to avoid sectional antagonism, and his
objections to the spirit of compromise were overridden by his
desire to soothe ruffled southern feelings. An important aspect of the problem as he saw it was the threatened annexation
of New Mexico by Texas, for this would introduce bondsmen
into that area and might later result in the creation of another
slave state. Henry Clay's proposals in congress lessened this
danger by making New Mexico a distinct new territory, and
Greeley approved such a solution. In fact, Clay's allurement
was in part responsible for Greeley's willingness to accept
the Compromise of 1850,[15] and his view of that legislation
may best be taken from his biography of the Kentuckian.

Greeley proclaimed the 1850 settlement a clear-cut victory
for the north. Expressing at this early date an idea which
later became fundamental in Republican party doctrine, he
maintained that bondage could exist only where sanctioned
by statute. He observed that the accord reached failed to uphold it in the southwest, and that Mexican law forbade it.
The adjustment was therefore "calculated and intended to
exclude Slavery from all the territory acquired from Mexico
by treaty." The north made other gains: the admission of

14 Reavis, *Greeley*, 315-323, quoted from the *Tribune*, Mar. 9, 1849.
Congressional Globe, 30th Congress, 2nd sess. (Washington, 1849), 57, 65,
71, 85, 108, 111, 147, 203, 229-230, 269-283, 534, 605-610, 694.
15 Greeley to Colfax, Jan. 2, 1849; June 26, 1850; Jan. 18, 1853, NYPL.
To Weed, May 27, 1850, NYHSL.

California as a free state, and the abolition of the slave trade in the District of Columbia. The settlement included a more rigorous law for the return of fugitives to their owners, but Greeley looked upon this as temporary. As for popular sovereignty, which was really the basis of the reconciliation, he believed this to be mere verbiage, necessary in order to mollify the south.[16]

To Greeley's mind the north was doing well enough without resorting to agitation. More than anything else he had dreaded a continuation of the Missouri Compromise line of 36° 30′ to the Pacific, for this would certainly have opened the southwest to enforced negro labor.[17] Too much controversy in 1850 would probably have had just such a result. Ten years later, on the eve of the Civil War, it was all he and his fellow Republicans could do to block a similar agreement; but in 1850 he coasted along the easier road of expediency when accepting popular sovereignty, and he was destined to receive a terrific jolt in 1854 when he learned that a majority of congress held a view of the Compromise of 1850 differing radically from his own.

This shock came because most southerners, and some northerners, thought the legislation permitted the spread of slavery. They concurred with men of Greeley's persuasion on but one point: the dubious phrasing of popular sovereignty was needed, but only in order to calm antislavery sentiment. When the day of reckoning dawned, discord multiplied as each faction charged the other with bad faith.

For the time being, both sides were pleased. The early 1850's promised prosperity unclouded by disputes between the north and south. Increased immigration furnished the cheap labor needed for speculations in canals, railways, and industries. The young republic felt impelled by Manifest Destiny to assume her rightful place as guardian and ex-

---

[16] Epes Sargent, *The Life and Public Services of Henry Clay, Down to 1848.* Edited and completed at Mr. Clay's death by Horace Greeley (Philadelphia, 1852), 347-367.
[17] Greeley to Colfax, Jan. 2, 1849; Aug. 10, 1850, NYPL.

ploiter of the western hemisphere. Sectional peace seemed the one essential to an era of milk and honey, and both major parties hastened to claim "finality" for the Compromise of 1850. Greeley would have none of this nonsense. The word finality had no place in his democratic vocabulary. He looked upon the adjustment as a mile post, from which the country would walk into the bright land of freedom. How could any settlement be conclusive which included an obnoxious law for the rendition of fugitives and implied the perpetuity of slavery in the south? His America was not one of external expansion, but of internal development and moral and social elevation. He fought against a declaration by the Whig party and its candidates upholding the permanency of the 1850 adjustment; and failing in that battle, he assumed full political independence for the *Tribune*.

Nor was Greeley alone. Despite a bullish financial market and widespread optimism, there was a growing disaffection among antislavery Whigs and Democrats occasioned by the enforcements of the fugitive slave law. Greeley hoped that these dissenters would wield the balance of power in the 1852 national elections. The leading contender for the Whig honors was another soldier of Mexican War renown, Winfield Scott. The general's nativist leanings repelled Greeley, and he had described Scott as a "good soldier but immeasurably conceited, aristocratic, arbitrary ass";[18] but he accepted the choice as inevitable and without much hesitation. This time, Greeley feared the forthcoming platform. What he wanted to do was to turn the tables on the southern Whigs. Scott was known to be under the sway of the progressive bloc of the party, and Greeley wished to see him nominated without a platform, just as General Taylor had been named four years earlier.

On Greeley's return from a European vacation in 1851, it was apparent that a plank praising the 1850 settlement as

[18] Greeley to Colfax, Mar. 17, 1850, NYPL. See also Greeley to Colfax, Feb. 12, 1851, NYPL.

final in sectional disputes could not be avoided, but Greeley was not downcast. He showed himself to be a practical politician, and concocted a plan which would have divorced Scott from the party's platform. He advised the progressive delegates to ballot against the despised plank and to try to swing a homestead resolution as a counterpoise, but not to create a disturbance. After Scott had been selected, they were to reveal their domination over their favorite by having him say absolutely nothing about the 1850 agreement. Other antislavery leaders differed, and extracted a promise from the general that upon being notified of his nomination, he would condemn the fugitive slave law. Greeley regretted this decision, as he would have preferred Scott to lie low and keep quiet until safely in the White House. Nevertheless he submitted a tentative letter of acceptance for Scott, which neither ignored the problem nor denounced the law, but ostensibly threw the question into the lap of congress by a promise to withhold the veto power if a modification were passed.

"Old Fuss and Feathers" Scott upset his friends. As an army man, he was unsuited for the stormy sea of politics. He publicly pledged his support of the platform just after his nomination, thus tying his candidacy into a knot about the ponderous anchor of finality. To Greeley's mind, matters were worse than in 1848. The Whig hopeful had openly supported the southern position on the slavery issue.[19]

The *Tribune* backed Scott in the race which followed, but Greeley would have nothing to do with the Whig resolutions. He published his own platform, protesting the fugitive law, declaring against slavery and demanding free territories, and calling for his pet economic schemes. But there was a limit

[19] Charles W. Elliott, *Winfield Scott* (New York, 1937), esp. 622. Greeley to Colfax, Apr. 22, June 9, 13, 1852, NYPL. To Pike, May 29, June 13, 1852, and Greeley's proposed acceptance letter, dated at Washington, June 20, 1852; Dana to Pike, May (?), June 21, 1852, Pike, *First Blows*, 139, 146-147, 140-142, 148, 149.

to his intransigence. He later toned down his paper and tried to unite the party.[20]

All such efforts were in vain. The Democratic nominee, leather-faced Franklin Pierce, also of Mexican War fame, crushed General Scott beneath an avalanche of electoral votes. Greeley had predicted this outcome. As he saw it, his party had refused any intimation that it stood against the extension of slavery and for a revision of the fugitive law, and now it was dead in fact as well as in principle. It had failed to appeal to the progressives, and the conservatives had stabbed it in the back. Whigs of northern sympathies had been revolted by the platform, while those of southern leanings had been repulsed by the candidate. None of the blame for this sad state of affairs could be pinned on Greeley, and he was rather pleased to see those who had rebuffed his advice now squirming in discomfort. Their lack of political acumen reminded him of the duelist "whose brains *couldn't* have been injured by the bullet through his head—'cause if he had any brains, he wouldn't have been in any such predicament."[21]

Greeley believed that the Whig national organization had been shattered beyond repair. It had been so mishandled that it had served as a hoop to the Democratic barrel staves. He complained to Colfax that in "the wide world, there is just one obstacle to carrying on the Government on Whig principles, and that is the Whig party." With its tattered banner buried underground, perhaps the Democrats could be split and Greeley's economic ideas adopted. This possibility was so pleasant to contemplate that Greeley assumed political independence for the *Tribune*, but he refrained from affiliating with the radical Free Soilers and abolitionists. Rather, he publicly indulged in a rash promise. He had done his share "at shouting, screeching, hurrahing, exhorting, entreating" his readers into voting this or that ticket. Such exuberance

[20] Greeley to Elihu B. Washburne, Sept. 15, 1852, Washburne MSS., II, LC. Reavis, *Greeley*, 290-292.
[21] Greeley to Colfax, Jan. 18, 1853, NYPL. Greeley's italics. See also *DTri.*, May 5, Sept. 12, 1853.

41

may have been very well when he was younger, but he said he had outgrown the feeling which impelled it.[22] In the future, the *Tribune* would be faithful to his economic and social convictions irrespective of his former party allegiance, and it would continue its educational tussle against human bondage: " . . . while it does not propose to make Anti-Slavery the basis of Political action, other than defensive, it will neglect no opportunity, remit no effort, so to diffuse Light and Truth as to render the continuance of Slavery impossible in a land irradiated by the sun of Christianity and boasting itself the great exemplar of Political Justice and law-guarded Freedom."[23]

There is much merit in Greeley's estimate of the Whig collapse and in his hope for a Democratic schism. Defeat prostrated the Whigs in 1852, but the Democrats fared none too well in victory. Sectional agitation was weakening the triumphant party. It managed to stay on its feet until 1860 only because it possessed the greater nation-wide strength and a forceful champion. This dynamic leader was Senator Stephen A. Douglas of Illinois, known as the "Little Giant" because of his booming voice and stocky figure. Pierce, the newly elected president, was inexperienced and incompetent, and his cabinet was weak and divided.[24]

On his return from a European holiday in the fall of 1853, Douglas sought to inject new life into his party. He wished to restore order and harmony, to reduce the tariff, and to dispose of the treasury surplus. By appealing to the national impulse for conquest and expansion, he anticipated another Democratic landslide in 1856, but the rapid growth of the republic thrust upon his shoulders a burden which would have broken the back of a lesser man.

The task which faced Douglas stemmed directly from the country's need for railways, but its ramifications reached

[22] *DTri.*, Nov. 3, 1853. Greeley to Colfax, Jan. 18, 1853, NYPL.
[23] *DTri.* (prospectus), Sept. 1, 1853.
[24] Roy F. Nichols, *The Democratic Machine, 1850-1854* (New York, 1923).

into every crevice of economic and social life. Since entering politics, he had favored building the much discussed transcontinental railroad, and was eager to run it west from Chicago. As the central portion of the federal domain appeared vast and inhospitable, it was generally conceded that one route would suffice for years to come, and a battle for its eastern terminus raged up and down the Mississippi. Secretary of War Jefferson Davis was already far advanced with a project for a line out of Vicksburg, and merchants in both Memphis and St. Louis were clamoring for the coveted prize.

An essential preliminary to any road due west from Chicago or St. Louis was the elevation of the Nebraska region, comprising the present states of Nebraska and Kansas, to territorial status. Otherwise no right of way could be obtained beyond the western borders of Iowa and Missouri, for no legal government existed which could allocate the land. This area was within the zone which had been declared forever free from slavery by the Missouri Compromise. A bill to organize it was introduced into the senate in December, 1853 by Augustus C. Dodge, Iowa Democrat, and was referred to Douglas' powerful committee on territories. Similar legislation had failed in the previous congress because proslavery members had refused to abide by that feature of the 1820 settlement which restricted slavery.

The Little Giant was in a tight spot, but he set about his job with bold determination. To conciliate his southern friends, he reported out of committee a plan which would allow the inhabitants to decide the slavery issue both while in territorial status and when entering upon statehood, and which was vague enough meanwhile to permit slaveholders to migrate westward with their negroes. This proposal contradicted the Missouri Compromise, but Douglas believed that the relevancy of that adjustment had been impaired six years before when northern representatives had blocked an effort to extend the 36° 30' line to the Pacific, and that it had been superseded by the doctrine of popular sovereignty incorpo-

43

rated in the Compromise of 1850. The phrases which Greeley considered mere verbiage Douglas accepted as his great principle to control all future territorial dispositions.

Douglas' intention was to undermine the 1820 accord and to stir up as little controversy as possible, but his hand was called by northern and southern radicals. He was compelled to clarify his bill by repealing outright that part of the earlier law which excluded slavery, and this change intensified sectional discord. An additional complication altered the measure. Conflicting economic interests as well as the enormous size of the Platte country caused Douglas to divide it into two sections, Kansas and Nebraska. This led to more trouble, for the *Tribune* claimed a plot was brewing whereby the southern territory was to be slave and the northern free.[25] The final draft was ready for the senate floor late in January, 1854.

Greeley was alert to these moves. The range and depth of his political knowledge were as great as the *Tribune's* circulation, and as profound as twenty-five years of study and experience could make them. He realized the possibility of such legislation while Douglas was sojourning in Europe. As a consistent advocate of federal aid to transportation developments, he was, if anything, more anxious to span the continent with steel than Douglas, but to barter free soil for that end was unthinkable.

To the contrary, one of Greeley's chief reasons for favoring a transcontinental railway was his belief that its construction would stimulate industralization, extend free soil, and unify the nation. He was willing to sacrifice one of his

[25] *DTri.*, Jan. 24, 1854.
Frank H. Hodder, "The Railroad Background of the Kansas-Nebraska Act," and Robert R. Russel, "The Pacific Railway Issue in Politics Prior to the Civil War," *Mississippi Valley Historical Review*, xii (June, Sept., 1925), 3-22, 187-201. Hodder, "The Genesis of the Kansas-Nebraska Act," *Proceedings* of the State Historical Society of Wisconsin, *1912* (Madison, 1913), 69-86. See also Allen Johnson, *Stephen A. Douglas* . . . (New York, 1908), 217-259. George F. Milton, *The Eve of Conflict; Stephen A. Douglas and the Needless War* (Boston, 1934), 98-128. James F. Rhodes, *History of the United States* . . . , i (New York, 1893), 441-495.

long favored economic principles to this end: "We do not care even to revive the Tariff controversy," he told his readers in the spring of 1853, "if our antagonists therein will unite with us in urging forward the great Pacific Railroad, since we believe many branches of our Manufacture already so solidly established as to need no other Protection than such as the merest Revenue duty will afford, and look to that Railroad to do more for American Manufacturers than any Tariff has done or could now do, in widening their market and making the U[nited] States, instead of Great Britain, the commercial center of the World."[26]

The dream of a railway to the Pacific had centered Greeley's attention upon the economic and political trends in the commonwealth adjacent to Kansas. He had checked Missouri as the pivotal slave state in his plan for peaceful emancipation, and there was reason to be encouraged. Its urban population was increasing with free laborers. To foster this industrial growth and to mitigate sectional economic differences, he was favorably inclined toward a compromise central route, with St. Louis as its probable eastern terminus.[27]

Missouri was already in the midst of a bitter political fracas, which emphasizes the close connection between railway construction and free soil. Junior Senator David R. Atchison had been instrumental in ousting Thomas H. Benton from his senior Missouri post in the senate, and Benton was making a persistent bid to replace Atchison in the 1854 campaign. Both were Democrats, but their attitudes toward the Missouri Compromise were at variance. As a pupil of John C. Calhoun, Atchison maintained that slaves were property which could be introduced into every federal

26 *DTri.*, Apr. 20, 1853. See also *DTri.*, July 29, 1852.
27 Greeley to Colfax, Jan. 18, Apr. 2, 1853, NYPL. *DTri.*, Nov. 21, Dec. 28, 1853. Greeley's railway plan and hope for emancipation in Missouri will be considered at greater length in chapters IX and X.
DTri. on Nov. 24, 1853 declared for a "Northern" route, but this was apparently an effort to smoke out the wildcat scheme of H. B. Stanton and Robert J. Walker for a Texas road. See also *DTri.*, Nov. 21, Dec. 27, 1853; Jan. 5, 1854.

territory, under the protection of troops if necessary. For this reason he had opposed organizing the Platte country as long as the 1820 settlement prevailed. Benton was known to the electorate as "Old Bullion" by virtue of his lifelong antipathy to banks of issue and their paper currency. He had been Andrew Jackson's sword and buckler during the nullification crisis and detested everything that smacked of Calhoun. He was a tough adversary who championed the 1820 adjustment and charged that Atchison's obstinate effort to drive slaves into the west was blocking railroad expansion and stifling St. Louis economically. Benton's argument drove home. Atchison announced to his senatorial colleagues in March, 1853 that since the Missouri Compromise could not be annulled, he was willing to dispose of the Nebraska region in conformity with it.

On returning to Missouri after adjournment, Atchison discovered that his vacillation had given his enemy a distinct advantage. He realized that his political future depended upon a reaffirmation of his earlier stand. He reversed himself and rallied the Calhounites to his cause. Greeley gibed that Atchison was "consistent in nothing but in his fealty to the peculiar institution."[28]

Atchison played his cards poorly and became so involved in an intricate political situation that he never managed to extricate himself. Even the Kansas-Nebraska act was not enough to save the day, although he assumed credit for the legislation and pointed with pride to the fact that it permitted negroes and locomotives to toil together across the plains. Nor was Benton the winner, for during the climax of this factional strife, a third participant grabbed the prize. Old Bullion spent the remainder of his career in the house, where he represented the St. Louis district.[29]

[28] *DTri.*, Dec. 1, 1853.
[29] Perley O. Ray, *The Repeal of the Missouri Compromise* . . . (Cleveland, 1909); "The Genesis of the Kansas-Nebraska Act," *Annual Report* of the American Historical Association, *1914*, I (Washington, 1916), 259-280. Hodder, "A Famous Chapter in American Politics," *Dial*, XLVII (Sept. 1, 1909), 120-122.

Douglas cannot be blamed for Atchison's debacle. Nor can Greeley be censured for the feeble assistance Benton received from the opponents of slavery extension who lived outside of Missouri. Twelve months before Douglas had polished the Nebraska bill, Greeley sought to buttress Benton's position; for he looked upon the Missourian as a bulwark against repeal of the Compromise of 1820, and as a man fostering industrialization in his home state. Apparently Greeley elicited no response. He wrote Colfax in January, 1853: "We ought to run Old Bullion for Speaker of the next House, no matter whether we can elect him or not. Then we ought to go in for the Pacific Railroad on some basis which will avoid the question of rival routes . . ." The *Tribune* carefully explained the national significance of the Missouri contest to its readers, and as that race and the tumult over the Nebraska bill raged side by side, it featured Benton as a man of presidential caliber. This treatment dismayed some of Greeley's readers. Kentucky-born James G. Birney, an ex-gambling Princeton graduate turned abolitionist, urged him to level the *Tribune's* antislavery guns at Old Bullion. Greeley was patient but brief in reply: "I can imagine no good and perceive very much evil likely to result from any attack on Benton through the Tribune. I know his great faults, but I believe he is now doing good, and likely to do more in his adversity than he ever did in his prosperity. He is a Samson falling and carrying down the pillars of the idol temple with him."[30]

Greeley's ringside seat at the Benton-Atchison feud was sufficient to warn him that the Missouri Compromise was in jeopardy, and he had abundant admonition from other quarters. In September of the off-year 1853 campaign, he

[30] Greeley to Birney, Aug. 19, 1854, James Gillespie Birney, *Letters of . . . , 1831-1857*, ed. Dwight L. Dumond (New York, 1938) II, 1165. Greeley to Colfax, Jan. 18, 1853, NYPL.
Ray, *Repeal*, 102-111, 179-182. *DTri.*, Aug. 6, 23, 1852; Apr. 12, Aug. 30, Nov. 12, 21, 29, Dec. 13, 1853; Feb. 6, Apr. 15, July 26, Aug. 16, 1854. Reprint from the St. Charles (Mo.) *Democrat* in *DTri.*, July 13, 1854. *WTri.*, May 13, 1854.

assailed "Prince John" Van Buren, heir of the ex-president and famed as a golden Democratic orator, for asserting that his party wished to lessen the discord between the north and the south. Surely he must know, Greeley scoffed, "that the incipient steps have already been taken toward the legalization by Congress of Slavery in Nebraska—a territory expressly shielded therefrom by the terms of the Missouri Compromise —that Southern Calfornia is still the object of a desperate though covert pro-Slavery struggle—that Northern Mexico is this day the object of slaveholding machination and lust— and that Cuba is incessantly coveted and intrigued for as a weighty addition to the power and influence of Slavery in our Union." Popular sovereignty was said to be the rack on which the Democrats stretched their schemes. Greeley later cautioned Prince John that a more virulent stimulus to friction could hardly be devised, for it would open "every part of the National Territories to a race and a scramble between the Free and the Slave States."[31]

While the bill was still in committee, Greeley was conscious of its import. Once more he blasted those who upheld popular sovereignty, which decreed that *each Territory shall be Free or Slave as the majority of its people shall decide.*" He pointed to the crux of the coming danger: " . . . what shall be its *condition* PRIOR *to any decision of this question by its people?*" The proper solution, he counseled, was to organize the Platte country in accordance with the 1820 agreement.[32]

Shortly after penning this editorial, Greeley folded his red and blue travel blankets and left on his annual Christmas lecture tour. The *Tribune* took little note of the Nebraska measure until after his return toward the middle of January. One exception was a volley from Pike, who had scorned Clay's 1850 proposals[33] and who in Greeley's absence used an argu-

[31] *DTri.,* Nov. 2, Sept. 30, 1853.
[32] *DTri.,* Dec. 14, 1853. Greeley's italics and upper case.
[33] Greeley to Pike, May 16, 1850, Pike, *First Blows,* 62.

ment which the *Tribune* would thereafter shun. Pike suggested that the 1820 compromise had been invalidated by the settlement which came thirty years later. Northern antislavery opinion had been "inundated and overwhelmed in consequence of the succumbing temper and faithlessness of rotten leaders," who had "destroyed the dikes and let the waters flow in and wash away the rich fruits of years." It is likely that he received a lesson in American history when his chief stepped off the east bound train. Pike's interpretation of the 1850 conciliation would weaken the stand the *Tribune* was to take on the Nebraska issue.[34] Never before had editorial unity been so desperately needed. Greeley summoned all his talents and power to face the grave danger which he saw threatening the nation.

A study of the *Tribune's* editorials assailing the Nebraska bill dispels the picture of Greeley as a bouncing little agitator who exulted over slavery discord. Without minimizing either the political opportunities involved or his ever-present anxiety to capitalize on any Democratic blunder, supposed or real, it must be emphasized that he did not set up a scarecrow for the mere joy of knocking it down.

He feared the penetration of the spirit of human bondage, if not the institution itself, into the northwest. His strongest plea against the repeal of the Missouri Compromise was that such a course would suffocate the moral force of liberty and equality within the young republic, and this would end his hope for small farms and industries. Acceptance and continuance of popular sovereignty would open the entire Central American and Caribbean areas to occupation and annexation by filibusters such as Tennessee's one man empire builder, the diminutive and homely William Walker. To give the advocates of slavery extension their Nebraska rope, Greeley believed, would be to strangle democratic sentiment.[35]

[34] *DTri.*, Jan. 6, 1854. Quoted but misdated in Pike, *First Blows*, 188-190. Contrary to Pike's view, Greeley asserted that the 1820 agreement had been strengthened by the Compromise of 1850, *DTri.*, Jan. 14, 21, 23, Feb. 6, 1854.
[35] *DTri.*, Sept. 3, Nov. 26, 1853; Aug. 8, 1854.

He was horrified by the fever for expansion which was besetting the country. His insight into the temper of the southern politicans who were so influential in destroying the Missouri Compromise was keen. It is illuminating to glance at the correspondence of Representative Alexander H. Stephens, ninety-eight pounds of parliamentary finesse and intellectual dynamite from down in Georgia. Stephens was no fire-eater. Formerly a Whig, he now felt "a deep interest in the success of the measure as a Southern man. The issue presented by the bill is one which in the main has arrayed the *free-soilers* in solid ranks against the South. The moral effect of the victory on our side will have a permanent effect upon the public mind, whether any positive advantages accrue by way of the actual extension of slavery or not. The effect of such a victory at this time is important. We are on the eve of much *greater issues* in my opinion. The Cuba question will soon be upon us."[36]

Already Greeley was concerned lest the impulse for freedom had given way to the desire for conquest and a life of leisure amid tropical splendor. John Mitchel, a Dublin revolutionist exiled to America, had just embraced compulsory servitude for the blacks. This dereliction had shocked the kindhearted editor, for he was touched by the Irish independence movement and had applauded Mitchel as one of its outstanding spokesmen. Greeley wondered if Mitchel had not expressed "very nearly the predominant aspiration of the American people when he wished for a good plantation well stocked with Alabama negroes?"[37]

Greeley may have momentarily doubted the basic soundness of the American people, but on the subject of the administra-

[36] Stephens to W. W. Burwell, May 7, 1854, Robert Toombs, Alexander H. Stephens, and Howell Cobb, "The Correspondence of . . . ," ed. Ulrich B. Phillips, *Annual Report* of the American Historical Association, *1911*, II, (Washington, 1913), 343-344. Stephens' italics.
[37] Greeley to Theodore Parker, Mar. 23, 1854 (copy), Parker MSS., MHSL. See also to George N. Sanders, Jan. 7, 185(4), Harvard College Library (hereafter referred to as HCL). *DTri.*, Dec. 10, 1853; Jan. 14, July 14 (unless otherwise noted, all dates for the remainder of this chapter will be understood as 1854).

FREE SOIL, HERITAGE OF LIBERTY

tion he had no hesitation whatever. He was convinced that a more unprincipled set of gangsters had never held sway in Washington. He reminded his readers that appointment of the territorial officials would be made by President Pierce. Freedom would not have a chance under the men sent out by the Democrats. "Everything," he reaffirmed, "turns on the laws which shall prevail in the Territory *prior* to any legal action of the settlers therein." Anyone who talked otherwise "walks in craftiness and lies in wait to deceive."[38]

Greeley admonished his audience not to think that unfavorable geographic conditions would prevent the spread of human bondage into Kansas. Of what value were any such adverse factors against the treacherous growth of aristocratic government, which was already browbeating the common people of the south? Slavery did not flourish, properly speaking, in Delaware, Missouri, Maryland, Kentucky, and Virginia; yet it continued to exist in those states, despite the fact that all five were north of 36° 30′. What other than the Missouri Compromise obstructed the creation of five similar commonwealths beyond the Mississippi? Was not Kansas adjacent to western Missouri? Did it not have the same soil and climate?[39]

He agreed that Missouri by economic dictates should be free, and he hoped that her emancipation was coming. But he believed that the border states were clinging to thralldom because of the social customs it generated and because the cessation of the African slave trade in 1808 had given them a monopoly on the export of human flesh into the cotton and sugar areas. The price of slaves was rising, and Greeley reasoned that the south desired more breeding states, but he vowed he would never let the slavedrivers make a concubine of Kansas.[40]

Greeley was dismayed by the possible abrogation of a compromise backed by thirty-four years of validity; he had

[38] *DTri.*, Feb. 1. Greeley's italics. See also *DTri.*, Feb. 9.
[39] *DTri.*, Jan. 20, Mar. 7, 22.   [40] *DTri.*, Feb. 24, 27, Mar. 13.

51

never granted that the 1850 settlement had withdrawn one iota of strength from the line established along the center of the territory purchased from France in 1803. But his strongest aversion to the bill rose from his dread of the turmoil it would cause. However overwhelming the Pierce victory had been, he believed that the free states would insist upon retaining the compact of 1820.

The *Tribune* gravely pictured the future. The Nebraska bill "inaugurates the era of a geographical division of political parties. It draws the line between North and South. It pits face to face the two opposing forces of slavery and freedom in the national legislature, and gives birth to the most embittered sectional strife the country has ever yet seen."[41]

Events were not slow in sustaining this prediction. The antagonism which burst forth against the Kansas-Nebraska proposal was astounding. Indicative of this eruption were the Democratic papers of Free Soil tendencies which overnight took up cudgels for the Missouri Compromise and proved to be instrumental in starting the Republican party. These were led by the New York *Evening Post*, edited by the venerable William Cullen Bryant. Others were the Hartford *Times*, Utica *Observer*, Rochester *Union*, Buffalo *Republic*, and Cleveland *Leader*, to mention but a few. An angry letter from Charles H. Ray, then publishing the Galena (Ill.) *Jeffersonian* and later one of the directors of the powerful Chicago *Tribune*, underlines the revolution taking place among some northern journalists who had recently been Democrats: "Great God! how I hate and despise the movers of that infamous scheme, and I have just begun to hate them, and to fight it."[42]

Whig editors were just as determined and if anything more vitriolic. Weed began to moralize on the sanctity of contracts in his up-state Albany *Evening Journal*. Able,

[41] *DTri.*, Mar. 17.
[42] Ray to E. Washburne, Feb. 14, Washburne MSS., ii, LC.

52

industrious, and shrewd Samuel Bowles moulded his Springfield (Mass.) *Republican* into the nation's leading provincial paper on the strength of the Nebraska tumult. Sharptongued William Schouler raged against the Little Giant, and politically ambitious Henry J. Raymond, recent founder of the New York *Times,* added his more reserved condemnations to the uproar against the program.[43]

Undisputed in leadership against the supposed evils of Douglas and his allies was Greeley's *Tribune.* Its circulation, spreading throughout the north, spiraled during the first six months of 1854. The *Weekly* jumped from 75,000 to 112,000, while the normal increase would have been a mere 7,000. The aggregate total of all editions vaulted from 115,000 to 157,500, while in less tempestuous days the gain would hardly have been more than 10,000.[44] The *Tribune's* followers "were of the thorough kind, reading all the news, all the printed speeches and addresses, and all the editorials, and pondering as they read. The questions were discussed in their family circles and with their neighbors, and, as differences arose, the *Tribune,* always at hand, was consulted and re-read. There being few popular magazines during this decade, the weekly newspaper, in some degree, took their place; and, through this medium, Greeley and his able coadjutors spoke to the people of New York and of the West, where New England ideas predominated, with a power never before or since known in this country."[45]

Greeley's pen took on classical proportions as he smote the Little Giant "with a club of Hercules."[46] The bludgeoning echoed across the Rock river prairies into the wilds of Wis-

[43] Pro and anti-Nebraska comments are reprinted in *DTri.,* May 24, 25, 26, 29.

[44] Appendices A and B.

[45] Rhodes, "Newspapers as Historical Sources," *Atlantic Monthly,* CIII (May, 1909), 654.

[46] Forest City *Democrat* (after Mar. the Cleveland *Leader*), Feb. 23, *Annals of Cleveland,* 1818-1935, XXXVII, pt. 1 (Cleveland, 1937), abs. no. 1309, pp. 201-202.

FREE SOIL, HERITAGE OF LIBERTY

consin, where "they *all* take the 'Tribune.' "[47] This inexpensive oracle was most needed among the "thick-soled, rag-wearing part of the population" whom Douglas had bewitched.[48] Already "every man, and woman too, of education, culture, and moral feeling" was praising the *Tribune.* Beyond imagination was its hold on "the affections of all the best people."[49]

This view was admittedly exaggerated. Yet it is interesting to observe that Theodore Parker partially judged the quality of a New England town by the number of *Tribunes* delivered to its post office. An even higher tribute came from Senator Ben Wade. He suggested to Pike that the paper omit publication of his orations because it was doing "such execution on the enemies of the republic that it must not be diverted from its course to please any man." But, added the senator hastily, "I can rely on your judgment."[50]

The building on the corner of Nassau and Spruce streets rumbled and groaned as its presses increased their daily load. In the offices above, the members of the staff ground out article and editorial revealing the iniquities of the administration in Washington.

Greeley labored long hours in directing his journal's policy and in writing editorials among the ablest of his career. His strategy was to draw forth such a cry of protest from the free states that the Nebraska bill would be doomed in congress. It had originated in the senate, where administration strength assured its passage; but he hoped to delay it there long enough to enable him to broadcast contrary views. This was Greeley's task, the emission of partisan news reports, editorials, articles, letters, speeches, and pamphlets. He expected the measure to be defeated when it came up for

[47] Bayard Taylor to his mother, Mar. 16, Taylor, *Taylor,* I, 273. Taylor's italics.
[48] Adam de Gurowski to Pike, June 8, Pike, *First Blows,* 253-254.
[49] George F. Talbot to Pike, Feb. 14, Pike, *First Blows,* 205.
[50] Wade to Pike, June 5, Pike, *First Blows,* 246-247. Parker to Convers Francis, Aug. 8, 1855, John Weiss, *Life and Correspondence of Theodore Parker* (New York, 1864), I, 362-363.

consideration in the house, where northern votes predominated. By that time free state representatives would have bowed down to indignant constituents, manifesting their chagrin in no uncertain terms. Above all, the prospective legislation must not be permitted to reach the lower chamber until after the spring campaigns in New England. Good tidings were anticipated. After such a mandate even the most callous Yankee Democrat would spurn the Little Giant's project.

The staff approved this plan. Pike was enthusiastic as he entreated the newly elected Whig senator from Maine, William Pitt Fessenden, to hurry down to Washington: "The bill must be kept in the Senate as long as possible. Meantime hell must be raised in the North. The ear of Congress is open. It must be deafened with a roar of condemnation."[51]

Douglas refused to cooperate and be axed. As the dawn of March 4 broke into the senate chamber, he drove his measure to a vote and victory. He exercised brilliant parliamentary skill, and during the course of the evening gave a masterly oration. But the *Tribune's* reporters handled him roughly, saying that his speech was delivered in a "sneering tone" and with "vulgar grimaces."[52]

Greeley was stunned by this speedy action. In an editorial leader he declared that the country had been shamed and humiliated. He pointed a finger at Senator Edward Everett of Massachusetts, conservative disciple of Daniel Webster. Everett, wearied by seventeen hours of continuous session, had been at home asleep when the final tally was taken. If devotion to slumber was his main excuse, Greeley shouted, "he ought to have remained President of Harvard, and not accepted a position wherewith constitutional drowsiness is incompatible."[53]

51 Pike to Fessenden, Feb. 10, Pike MSS., LC.
52 Pike and "W" from Washington, Mar. 4, *DTri.*, Mar. 7.
53 *DTri.*, Mar. 6. *WTri.*, Mar. 11, carried this editorial along with a letter from several northern Whig senators testifying that Everett was ill and forced to leave the floor at 3:30 a.m.

Sudden though the senate verdict had been, the *Tribune's* strategy was not altered; and wisely not, for it was late May before the Democrats managed to get the legislation through the lower chamber. Every device of propaganda was intensified. Hope was never abandoned. Pike exhorted Fessenden: "Give the boys aid and comfort in the House. We'll give the Neb. rascals hell in the Tribune. They can be licked and we are the chaps to do it."[54]

In any case, the bill had been kept from the house long enough for Greeley to have established effectively a mature policy of opposition; and before it became law, ample time had elapsed to allow his opinions general circulation throughout the north. He had already seized the initiative by accusing the Democrats of deepening antislavery animosity, and he drove his point home by showing that he, for one, was boiling with rage.

Greeley posed as the orderly champion of established government. Substantial citizens were said to agree with him. Mass anti-Douglas demonstrations were encouraged and were reported as having been most respectable in character, "embracing a very large proportion of the conservatism and moral strength of our City." Accounts of similar protest meetings along with speeches delivered throughout the free states filled columns. Whatever the decision might be in Washington, it was conclusively evident to all readers that the sound leaders of the nation, backed by the vast majority of the people, wanted this bill defeated.[55]

Slavery was depicted in the *Tribune* as an institution which made liars and demagogues of its defenders. Such was the character of the slaveholding oligarchy, and this clique obviously directed national policy. The northern masses should no longer trust their sacred liberties to such fiends; but they should arise and throw them out of power, and should then rush to the assistance of their brethren in the

---

[54] Pike to Fessenden, May 15, Pike MSS., LC.
[55] *DTri.*, Jan. 31. See also *DTri.*, Feb. 14, 17, 18, 20, Mar. 2, 9.

south, the non-slaveholding whites, who were writhing under the heel of their aristocratic oppressors.

Politicians like Douglas and Pierce were damned by the *Tribune* as "doughfaces," northern men with southern principles. Such villains made dupes of their constituents. Their one aim was to gain or retain the presidency. The gate to the White House was guarded by a ten-headed monster, slavery. Before trying to enter, it behooved each Democratic contender to gorge these many mouths with concessions.[56]

If the *Tribune* could bring the northern mechanic to realize "the contempt which is thrown on the very nature and life of the laborer, by the slave system"; then "there would be extemporized a spirit of resistance to it that would put an end to its encroachments forever."[57]

"Facts of Slavery" vividly illustrated this point. Southern workers, many "with blue eyes and black hair," who "might easily pass for white if not closely inspected," were being sold on the slave markets and pursued by bloodhounds across pestilent swamps. Women were "felt all over" before they were purchased, and many of the female runaways were "suspected of being in the family way."[58]

The barbarous southerners who engaged in such practices had no souls. Slavery had eaten out their hearts and consigned them to perdition. Their presence could be tolerated as long as they remained to themselves, but now with slimy paws they clutched the common government. Even the navy was "a sort of House of Lords afloat for their sons, and enables them to talk of the stars-and-stripes in the usual flash vein of chivalry."[59] Their state regimes were tyrannical, and now they were launching an offensive against democracy in the north. They ridiculed free state progress as "the grand folly of the age, whence flow inexorably Common Schools, Socialism, Bloomer and all other Isms, Infidelity and Spirit

56 *DTri.*, Feb. 13, 28, Mar. 1, 14.   57 *DTri.*, Mar. 23.
58 *DTri.*, Jan. 18, Feb. 6, 14, 16, Apr. 7, May 1.
59 *DTri.*, Apr. 1.

FREE SOIL, HERITAGE OF LIBERTY

Rappings."[60] Their final mission was crystal clear, "they would rejoice to make of the whole Union a great slave market, for whites as well as blacks."[61]

It was high time that steps were taken to stop this aggression. "Northern Freemen!" the *Tribune* demanded, "shall the vast territory of the North-west, once solemnly consecrated to FREEDOM FOREVER, be converted into a new range for the bloodhounds of future monsters . . . ?"[62]

However abiding an impression the emotional propaganda just analyzed may have had on the northern mind, it was neither as forceful nor as enduring as the *Tribune's* more rational approach. While the paper's vehemence varied from month to month and from election to election, its more mature doctrine was followed with grave perseverance until Greeley found himself in the midst of the Civil War.

The policy was expounded in a composite set of essays, frankly sectional in tone. These articles were designed to appeal most of all to the mechanic and the farmer, and they were carried in each *Tribune* edition. After the last note had been struck, they reappeared "by popular demand" in pamphlet form, selling for only $6 a hundred and 10c a copy.[63]

Greeley's defense of these editorials is essential to their evaluation. About three weeks after the first had seen the light of day, he became annoyed by charges that his journal sought to abolish the constitutional bonds between the sections and was therefore traitorous. His was not a sheet which fostered disunion, he retaliated. It had never counseled or suggested that the north walk out of the federal government, an event which seemed to him most improbable. Nor was the south "a whit *more* likely" to do so, "*unless her politicians fancy that they can bully the Free States by threatening secession—*

60 *DTri.*, Jan. 20. 61 *DTri.*, Mar. 25.
62 *DTri.*, Mar. 7. *Tribune's* upper case. See also *DTri.*, Mar. 8, 10, 13, Apr. 7.
63 *DTri.*, May 25. "The North and the South" (pamphlet) (New York, 1854).

unless they can be allowed to deprive the Union of every characteristic except that of a machine for the propagation and perpetuation of Slavery. Here is the real danger of the Union—that the political leaders of the South, supposing that the North will do anything, submit to anything, to preserve the Union, will so commit themselves in attempting to drag the Federal Government into the execution of their Filibustering designs that they will be ashamed *not* to secede upon discovering that the North refuses, for once, to be dragooned by them. But let us have a fair understanding all around that the North regards the Union as of no special, peculiar advantage to her and can do without it much better than the South can, and we shall have fewer secession capers, and may jog on together quietly and peaceably. We would have the North, whenever the South shall cry out, 'Hold me! hold me! for I'm desperate, and shall hurt somebody!'—coolly answer, 'Hold yourself, if you need holding; for we have better business on hand,'—and this would be found after a little to exert a decidedly sedative, tranquillizing effect on the too susceptible nerves of our too excitable Southern brethren. Instead of bolting the door in alarm, and calling for help to guard it, in case the South should hereafter threaten to walk out of the Union, we would hold it politely open and suggest to the departing the policy of minding his eye and buttoning his coat well under his chin preparatory to facing the rough weather outside . . . "[64]

The argument was shaped as Greeley specified. The entire staff contributed to this series, but a larger part of the spade work was done by Henry C. Carey, a noted Philadelphia economist who was the *Tribune's* expert on the protective tariff.[65] The first article announced that the journal was determined to refute a well known southern pamphlet, first

[64] *DTri.*, May 2. Greeley's italics. For earlier declarations of these views, see *DTri.*, Apr. 12, Oct. 17, 1851.
[65] Abraham D. H. Kaplan, "Henry Charles Carey, a Study in American Economic Thought," Johns Hopkins University *Studies* . . . , series XLIX, no. 4 (Baltimore, 1931).

published in 1850 and recently reprinted, "The Union, Past and Future." Its author had postulated that the north was bound to the south, that secession would cause northern capitalists to lose the yearly use of $140,000,000 in capital and the government at Washington $20,000,000 annually in taxes, but that the economic condition of the slave states would improve with commerce blossoming in Norfolk, Charleston, and Savannah. He had thus concluded that if the Yankees did not continue to send doughfaces to congress, the slave states would withdraw, and the north, especially the workingmen, would suffer.

Southern papers were said to be following this false logic. Recently the Charleston *Mercury* had observed that northern politicians were "hucksters" who were apt to "knock themselves down to the highest bidder" because the free states were economically subservient to cotton, sugar, and tobacco. The *Tribune* thought it deplorable that southerners placed their faith in so spurious an explanation of the political degeneracy of northern congressmen, but it was even more regrettable that an ever increasing number of citizens above the Mason and Dixon line were swallowing this drivel. It was the duty of the country's leading antislavery organ to set matters straight. The facts would be examined and an estimate made of the dangers inherent in disunion.[66]

The second editorial began a direct reply to the southern pamphlet, "The Union, Past and Future." Should secession transpire, the *Tribune* estimated that the southern confederacy would control but twelve states. The border area, including Delaware, Maryland, and Missouri, was economically bound to the north. Kentucky and western Virginia might well be included in this group, but to give the hypothetical confederacy the benefit of every doubt, were not.

Division along the above line, including Minnesota which was soon to enter the Union, would leave the north with twenty states and by far the more abundant natural re-

[66] *DTri.*, Apr. 12.

sources. In addition, her population would be double that of the south, even if the slaves were counted. A fundamental economic law recognized that the strength of a country depended upon its labor, skilled and unskilled. Since southern gentlemen did not work and since slaves were inefficient, there could be no disputing the fact that northern labor was more productive than southern. In the free commonwealths there were superior market and transportation facilities, more diversification of industry and consequently a more rapid turnover in goods. This speed of exchange invalidated the statistics of the 1850 census; yet even on the basis of those calculations, earnings in the south averaged but $60 per capita, while in the north the figure was three times as great. In addition, the southern carrying trade was in the hands of northerners, and would remain there, Union or no Union. Both coast-wise and ocean going cargoes followed a rigid pattern, which could not be altered by a mere political division of the country. Northern harbors handled the great bulk of incoming commodities and would continue to do so because inland communications had converted them into natural entrepôts. For this reason Yankee commercial houses gave cheaper export rates to cotton and tobacco than southern shippers could dream of offering.

Thus, the *Tribune* argument ran, the slave states were far inferior to the free commonwealths in production, and were dependent upon them for trade. These were economic facts which could not be warped by political chicanery. Yet, even granting that the south could supply herself with as much as fifty per cent of her foreign needs, the loss to northern shipping would amount each year to only eighty cents per capita. Let the slave section secede. This trivial sum would be compensated for elsewhere. Northern tariff and trading regulations would be altered so as to admit sugar cheaper and to inaugurate commercial relations with Haiti and

Liberia. At most, southern withdrawal would cost each Yankee forty cents annually.[67]

Such was one side of the ledger. Was it not true that the south cost the national exchequer each year more than it contributed thereunto? That area was constantly leading the country into war, while the north was peace-loving and was striving for industrial and cultural improvements. The proslavery hotheads were expensive fellow citizens and their profligacy had to be borne by the whole nation. The purchase and conquest of Louisiana, Florida, Texas, and California— all either slave states or at the time of aggression expected to become so—had come high. Looming over the present horizon were immense outlays for the Gadsden purchase and the annexation of Cuba. Without the south, there would be no need for an army and navy, so that the upkeep of those oligarchic bodies must be added to the staggering total of the wars fought and to be fought. Perhaps it would be wise to get rid of the slave states. Then Canada could be quietly annexed, and a new union of peace-loving men formed.[68]

It was patent that the south was a fiscal liability; and even worse, that section's political philosophy threatened the industrial and agrarian laborers. The central theme in American history, the *Tribune* contended, was the conflict between the devotees of plantation economy and the northern small land holders. The urban worker was reminded that his wage varied in direct ratio with his ability to migrate westward and take up a quarter section. Southern aristocrats in congress refused to grant homesteads. Just as iniquitously, they blocked internal improvements and prevented adequate protection for American manufacturers, and both of these policies were essential to a self-sufficient nation of independent workers. Although it had been the aim of Franklin and Jefferson to place the mechanic by the side of the farmer, and although each experiment with the tariff had brought pros-

[67] *DTri.*, Apr. 14, 18, 19, May 9.
[68] *WTri.*, Apr. 15. *DTri.*, Apr. 19, 29.

perity to the country, southern politicians had successfully sabotaged the development of factories. Their doctrine of free trade was dwarfing the growth of the northwest and ruining Yankees who tilled the soil by forcing them to ship their produce to cheap markets overseas. And the loudest condemnation of levies against imports came from Virginians, *"whose chief manufacture is that of negroes for exportation,* and who are protected in this department of trade by an absolute prohibition of all competition from abroad."[69]

Every means available for bettering the condition of the free state worker was blocked by the Democratic party, whose one aim was the advancement of slavery. "Can there be no avenue opened for the progress of this great nation," the *Tribune* queried, "that is not first paved with the breathing, bleeding bodies of Slaves? Can no measure of national legislation pass without first paying an exorbitant toll of human suffering and human life? Cannot a free people sit down to eat the fruit of their honest industry without having the foul harpies of oppression enter and pollute their banquet?"[70]

Truly slavery threatened to spread throughout the length and breadth of the land, the series concluded. But the south could never afford to secede. Only the cotton zone was likely even to consider such a course. The border states were compelled to remain in the Union, or the African slave trade would be reopened and their economy, based on the breeding of negroes, would be ruined. Claims had been bandied about that the agrarian northwest would break away from the more industrial east and join a solid south in this fantastic venture; but it was general knowledge that the northwest had been bound by hoops of steel to the east, by railways, canals, and culture.[71] "The South," Greeley promised, "plainly cannot *afford* to dissolve the Union. . . . When the North shall scorn the threats of disunion from the South, and calmly allow the Secessionists to go the whole length of their

69 *DTri.,* Apr. 21. *Tribune's* italics. 70 *DTri.,* Apr. 7.
71 *DTri.,* Apr. 12, 14, 19, 29, May 9, 13, 18.

tether, these chronic threats of dissolution will quickly subside . . ."[72]

Such was the blistering counterattack by which Greeley sought to bring the federal government back to a conservative policy, back to the scheme of gradual emancipation desired, he testified, by the Founding Fathers.[73] Able assistance was rendered him by a majority of the press throughout the free states, and petitions showered upon congress from mass meetings throughout the north. In the New England spring elections, all the states voting turned radically from the triumphs they had given Pierce in 1852.[74] As the Nebraska question was of paramount national importance, Greeley hailed victories in New Hampshire, Rhode Island, and Connecticut as death blows to Douglas' measure. Personal pride may have been responsible for some of his rejoicings, since about one in every ten voters in those states subscribed to the *Tribune*.[75]

A wave of optimism swept through the *Tribune* building. Greeley assured his reading family that antagonism had killed the bill. He found himself unable to repress his "joyful, confident hope that the Nebraska Iniquity" was doomed. It might "flounder and struggle, in a dying way, for some weeks yet," but it would be "kicked out of the House . . . if there be any trust in the signs of the times." The destroyers of liberty had failed to disgrace the country. But their power remained great, and they would try again. Excitement should be maintained, for only at the polls could the contest be positively settled. All the demagogues who were plotting to spread slavery must be ousted from Washington.[76]

[72] *DTri.*, May 13. Greeley's italics.
[73] *DTri.*, Jan. 17, Feb. 4, 8, 11, Mar. 10.
[74] Andrew W. Crandall, *The Early History of the Republican Party . . .* (Boston, 1930), 20-22.
[75] Appendix A. *DTri.*, Mar. 8, 17, 20, 28, Apr. 4, 5.
[76] *DTri.*, Apr. 27. See also *DTri.*, May 8. Greeley's blunt declarations may have had a more solid basis than mere anti-Nebraska sentiment. Weed, Seward, Senator Thomas J. Rusk of Texas, ex-Governor Charles Paine of Vermont, George Law, Richard M. Blatchford and Simeon Draper of New York City, Philip Greely, Jr., of Boston, and most important,

Greeley's optimism was ill-founded. Inter-party feuds were giving the Democratic whips some trouble with the bill in the house, but it remained very much alive. When introduced on March 21, by Douglas' friend, Representative William A. Richardson of Illinois, the motion of Francis B. Cutting, New York Democrat, that it be assigned to the committee of the whole carried by a 110-95 tally. Its passage was imperiled by this maneuver, since that body considered measures in the order of their references, and it was already swamped with business; but party discipline and the driving parliamentary skill of Douglas and Alexander H. Stephens rescued the proposal on May 8 by having it voted out of committee. Within three weeks it was the law of the land.[77]

The *Tribune* underwent daily explosions during this trying period in May. The opposition minority was entreated to obstruct enactment by any method possible. Pike warned that Democratic success would stir up a political cyclone: "We see the gigantic array gradually approach, closing its thick ranks, and moving onward with a force that no merely human power or human institution can resist. It sweeps along with the force of the tempest and the tornado. The spirit of liberty animates, the spirit of progress impels, and a spirit

Erastus Corning and Dean Richmond, N. Y. Democrats and president and vice-president respectively of the New York Central Railroad, were at this time interested in a transcontinental line through Texas, and may be presumed to have opposed the organization of Nebraska for this reason, among others. The split of the New York Democracy into "Hards" and "Softs" gave these men an opportunity to defeat the Nebraska bill. A strange thing happened when the legislation was presented to the house. Francis B. Cutting, a Hard Democrat, moved it to the committee of the whole with the apparent intention of killing it. The vote on this motion shows only one New York Democrat voting with the administration forces. See Weed MSS., RRL, all letters to Weed: from Philip Greely, Jr., Sept. 20, 1853; Blatchford, Nov. 19, 1853; Seward, Jan. 7, 8; Orville Clark, Mar. 18; and Orsamus B. Matteson, Mar. 30, Apr. 22. See also *Congressional Globe*, 33rd Congress, 1st sess. (Washington, 1854), pt. 1, 97, 701-703.

Greeley knew of the Texas project. William Schouler to Greeley, Aug. 19, 1853, Greeley MSS., NYPL. Also of interest are Greeley's observations in *DTri.*, Nov. 21, 24, Dec. 27, 28, 1853; Jan. 5, June 24, 1854.

[77] *Congressional Globe*, 33rd Congress, 1st sess., pt. 1, 701-703, pt. 2, 1128-1133.

of solemn religious duty inspires and leavens the whole mass. This invincible army bears aloft the motto,'GOD WITH US!' "[78]

Greeley was in rare form as he battled his way through the final days of the struggle. With a touch of pathos, he announced that his office would fly the stars and stripes until the bill had passed the house. He hoped never to strike the colors. If he did, that act would "herald the capitulation and dishonor of the Northern Representatives . . . "[79] He headed the editorial page with a box shrouded in a thick black border and captioned [80]

THE ROLL OF INFAMY

On this scroll of political suicide were engraved the names of all the free state representatives who had joined Richardson and Stephens in recalling the bill from committee. The heavy hand of corruption was said to have been responsible for this foul deed: "If *some* Members don't secure good offices or fat contracts . . . then there will be outrageous cheating around the board somewhere."[81]

No praise was too great for the enemies of this pernicious bill, for in its defeat lay the salvation of the country. Greeley looked toward Benton in adoration. That noble Missourian was the one statesman fitted to be "an indomitable leader of the minority. . . . Let him but exhibit on this occasion those rare qualities of resistance possessed by him over every other public man of our time and defeat this measure, and he will insure to himself the highest honors of a grateful people, and fitly crown his long political career with an act of high historical grandeur and enduring fame."[82]

By contrast the Pierce administration showed itself in a most sinister aspect. "Here we are at this moment," the *Tribune* shouted, "driven to the brink of civil revolution by

[78] *DTri.*, May 10. *Tribune's* upper case. Quoted but misdated in Pike, *First Blows*, 230-232.
[79] *DTri.*, May 13.   [80] *DTri.*, May 12 through May 23.
[81] *DTri.*, May 10. Greeley's italics.
[82] *DTri.*, May 11. See also *DTri.*, May 13, 17.

insane legislative proceedings in behalf of Slavery, backed by the Administration. . . . It does seem as though it were high time for the people to rise *en masse* and demand of the executive branch of the Government to cease to worry the public mind and vex the public ear with its slavery projects . . ."[83] Otherwise, the journal warned: "The passage of the Nebraska bill will [be], and must be regarded out of Washington, as precisely what we have already stated—a declaration of war on the part of the slaveholders against the northern section of this Union and its most cherished feelings, institutions and principles. Let those who have chosen to commence this war take the responsibility of all its consequences. From the moment of the passage of the Nebraska bill such a war will exist. Where it will end who can tell?"[84]

These last minute blows were felt in Washington, but in vain. Try as they might, the paper vendors in the capital could not satisfy the great demand for *Tribunes*. Representative Elihu B. Washburne of Illinois explained why. Greeley's journal was "the terror of all the traitorous scoundrels here. . . . The rascals stand about the hotels trembling when the newsboys come in with the *Tribune*. They are all taken in a 'jiffy.' "[85]

The flag over the *Tribune* building was struck on the night of May 22. The mourning box inscribed with practically the same list of congressmen was headed[86]

BE IT REMEMBERED

The first editorial leader after passage was Pike's "THE REVOLUTION IS ACCOMPLISHED and Slavery is King!—How long shall this monarch reign?" It should not be long. A sectional party must be formed which would march forward in blazing glory until the doughfaces were "vomited forth

83 *DTri.*, May 15.   84 *DTri.*, May 20.
85 E. Washburne to Pike, May 24, Pike, *First Blows*, 233. See also an unsigned letter from Washington, May 16, *DTri.*, May 17.
86 *DTri.*, May 27 through June 1. *WTri.*, June 3.

from the free States." Happily, he reflected, bayonets were unnecessary. Ballots would gain this end.[87]

Oddly enough, Greeley was more restrained. Conservatively he said: "There never before was a Congress—we believe there will not soon be another—in which this measure could have prevailed." He had vigorously withstood the bill while there was a chance of defeating it, but now was the time for calm action. The north must seek a *"perfect union of all earnest opponents of the Nebraska Iniquity to procure its repeal,"* and there must be *"immediate, energetic and comprehensive organization to aid the migration of freedom-loving settlers to Kansas."*[88]

This restraint was not without cause. The Nebraska storm struck Greeley when he was already depressed by the antislavery rout of 1852, and his energetic advocacy of free soil had failed to block Douglas' maneuvers. The editor's spirit was deflated. The Little Giant had been able to pilot his project through congress in spite of every salvo the *Tribune* could bring to bear.

Greeley was disillusioned with the American people. They seemed willing to sacrifice their liberties on the altar of slavery. He had exhibited this trend when writing Colfax in March: "I have little faith in the principle of the North, but some in its pride. To be overreached in a bargain is not pleasant to Yankees, and I shouldn't wonder if they were to kick. At all events we shall get a good drive out of them this time."[89] The intensity of that drive had been beneath his expectations.

It was well for Pike to demand a new party, but Greeley was not then a free political agent, nor did he care to be. Since his entrance into partisan journalism, he had been associated in the public mind with Weed and Seward. To Greeley, this "partnership" had ties firmer than mere alle-

[87] *DTri.*, May 24. *Tribune's* upper case. Quoted with different punctuation in Pike, *First Blows*, 235-237.
[88] *DTri.*, May 24. Greeley's italics.
[89] Greeley to Colfax, Mar. 12, NYPL.

giance to the Whig organization. Furthermore, the hard-
working editor was a man of almost engrossing political
ambition. The dream of being governor of New York compelled him, in the summer of 1854, to turn warily toward
Albany and seek consultation. What did Weed and Seward
think of the situation? Were they ready to abandon the
Whig hulk as he had done, and, with Greeley temporarily at
the helm, launch a new craft upon uncharted waters?

CHAPTER 3

POLITICAL
INDEPENDENCE

I was a pack-horse for Weed and Seward for the first half of my career. I revolted at last, and was not ruined.—Greeley to Justin S. Morrill, March 12, 1872.

WEED and Seward were not ready to leave the Whig party, and this reluctance led to a disruption of their long standing relationship with Greeley. There was a fundamental political difference between them and the editor, and the mystery is not that the partnership should have been dissolved, but that it held together so long.

Greeley's was the more emotional outlook. It was a blend of his political ideals and his personal ambitions. He insisted that a party was of value only when it advanced the progressive aims of the people, and he eagerly desired a public office which would accomplish the task. Weed and Seward were more practical. Their position depended, not upon a mass of newspaper subscribers, but upon the smooth functioning of a well-oiled political machine which could not be retooled overnight. While in 1854 Greeley saw in the antislavery movement a means for limiting the spread of bondage and simultaneously elevating himself to the governorship, Weed and Seward clung to the state Whig organization as the one instrument capable of controlling the legislature and returning Seward to the senate in 1855. On the party's national prestige they pinned their hopes for Seward's presidential effort in 1856.

70

POLITICAL INDEPENDENCE

There had been a time when Seward, Weed, and Greeley considered themselves guardians of the common man. Indeed, Seward's repute as a radical lasted almost as long as Greeley's. Soon after his inauguration as governor in 1839, Seward became an official champion of the underdog by refusing the extradition to Virginia of three New York sailors who had helped a slave escape from Norfolk. During the next twenty years, his antislavery leadership became nation-wide. To his career as a politician he brought a superior intellect, a keen understanding of the law, and an engaging oratorical ability fashioned about a close study of Edmund Burke's parliamentary utterances. Seward was a spokesman for homesteads and protection, and his appeal was directed toward the working class. Consistently he opposed discrimination against the foreign born, a stand the more remarkable since his party, the Whig, was more nativist in character than the Democratic. Greeley was drawn to such a staunch ally for freedom. Desiring to see the name of a progressive on the 1848 Whig ticket, he testified that Seward was "the only man alive whose nomination as Vice President could convert a probability into an assurance of victory."[1]

Weed never figured so prominently before the public eye, but there is reason to conclude that Greeley admired him even more than he did Seward. The bonds of friendship between Greeley and Weed's family were stronger than those with Seward's. Greeley and Weed entered into business ventures together. In addition, Greeley had utmost respect for Weed's ability as a politician. He envied Weed's versatile supervision over men, groups and interests. As he observed in 1846, "Weed is confident, and I have great faith in his knowledge and sagacity."[2]

[1] Greeley to Colfax, Apr. 3, 1848, NYPL.
Frederic Bancroft, *The Life of William H. Seward* (New York, 1900), i.
[2] Greeley to Colfax, Feb. 28, 1846, NYPL. See also Seward to his home, Mar. 31, 1847, F. Seward, *Seward*, 42. Greeley to Weed, Apr. 18, 1852, Barnes, *Weed*, i, 216-217.

71

During the early days of the partnership, Greeley expected the Albany journalist to enter the reform movement. In 1843, he tried to influence Weed's literary habits: "Do oblige me by reading Carlyle's *Past & Present*! Best this century. If wearied skip Book II." Three years later, he became more forthright: " . . . I hope you will take a less gloomy view of the state of affairs respecting Reformers and a Reform spirit generally. . . . I thank you for your article in favor of Labor Reform. You will find it impossible to resist the current within as well as around you in favor of Reforms. . . . I do wish you could . . . exert your influence with the great Manufacturers in favor of a reduction of the Hours of Labor. I only ask them to come down to twelve hours solid work for five days in the week and ten on Saturday. Surely, this is enough. Try to help carry this reduction."[3]

Nor was Greeley barking up the wrong tree. Weed had been interested in trade unionism, and thanks largely to him the New York Typographical Society had been able to obtain a state charter as a benevolent organization.[4] But as he became older, he put idealism behind him and emerged a powerful political boss. His sway over economic measures reached from Albany into Washington. Few men in American history have rivaled his string of political marionettes.

This change in Weed's character was apparent to his close associates. John L. Schoolcraft wrote him in 1853 about an important bill then pending before the New York legislature: "I have often differed from you when laws are to be Enacted for the benefit of Corporation. . . . Consolidation will pass. [Y]ou and I know the Rail Roads have the power to pass any law with your advise [*sic*] and counsel, it does not admit of a doubt, my opposition ceases from to day. You know my attraction to you and whenever I differ with you on a question of policy, I always do it with regret. Your mind for a year past has been active to accu[mu]late. You see the

³ Greeley to Weed, May 14, 1846; May 14, 1843, Weed MSS., RRL.
⁴ Stevens, *New York Typographical Union, No. 6*, 98.

Golden Dollars in the distance and the energy of your mind is to enter for the race. . . . How different it was with you for the past ¼ of a Century. Your happiness was to do good to others."[5]

It was in the midst of Weed's more benevolent era that he had journeyed down to New York City to engage Greeley as Seward's press agent, and it would have been difficult to locate a journalist better qualified to sell Whig economic principles to the working class. Everything went nicely as long as Greeley was content with an inferior status,[6] but he soon wanted to become a policy-forming executive within the firm. As he wrote Colfax, "I am quite enough accused of being under Albany influence."[7]

This dissaffection became clear to Weed and Seward as the New York state constitutional convention of 1846 approached. Greeley suggested that such liberal measures as black suffrage and direct appeals to laborers would make sound Whig policy. His personal aspirations were simultaneously revealed. He gave Weed to understand that he was disappointed at having failed to attend the constitutional conclave as a delegate, and hinted at his intense desire for elective office—anything from the governorship down to a seat in party councils.[8] It was not his nature to demand outright that his political thirst be quenched, but certainly Weed and Seward were aware of his ambitions.

By 1848 Greeley was firmly convinced that he was an equal member of the triumvirate. He felt that Whig leadership was destroying the party by refusing to take a stand against slavery extension and by nominating Zachary Taylor, but

[5] Schoolcraft to Weed, Feb. 3, 1853, Weed MSS., RRL. See also Van Deusen, "Thurlow Weed: A Character Study," *American Historical Review*, XLIX (Apr., 1944), 427-440.
[6] Greeley to Seward, Nov. 16, 1839, *Collector*, XVI (Mar., 1903), 52. To Weed, Dec. 7, 15, 1841; Feb. 8, 9, Aug. 13, 1842; July 9, 1844, Weed MSS., RRL.
[7] Greeley to Colfax, Apr. 22, 1846, NYPL.
[8] Greeley to Weed, June 29, Sept. 11, 28, 1846, Weed MSS., RRL. To Weed, Jan. 22, 1846; Oct. 3, 1847; Jan. 31, 1848, NYHSL. To Colfax, Apr. 22, 1846, NYPL.

he cast no blame on his partners. Weed helped hold him in line by sponsoring his nomination on the Whig ticket for an unexpired congressional term. Greeley told Colfax only a part of the story when he contended that respect for Weed and Seward prevented him from tearing the Taylor campaign apart in the *Tribune*. He described his personal sacrifice as great: "I could have been the oracle of the Free Soil Party, with any extent of circulation, had I chosen. Party fidelity— or rather, fidelity to men I love who still cling to the putrid corpse of the party . . . has withheld me. . . . I could shake down the whole rotten fabric by a bugle-blast, yet will not sound it, because some good men I love would be crushed beneath its ruins."[9]

However much Greeley may have effaced himself, Seward was unappreciative, for he injured Greeley's personal pride that same year. The *Tribune's* prodding editorials often involved Greeley in libel suits, and one of these was removed from the courts by making Seward the arbitrator. Greeley's radical ideas, Seward told Weed, "have led him into an error, in which he has deeply injured men worthy of all respect and confidence, and even generous men." Seward's decision was published by requirement in both New York City and Albany. Greeley remembered it as a "most humiliating lecture" in which Seward exalted his "judicial sternness and fearlessness unduly . . . "[10]

[9] Greeley to Colfax, Sept. 15, 1848, NYPL. A week later, trying to hedge on his bargain with Weed to support Taylor, Greeley thanked Weed for his "powerful aid" in the congressional matter and asked his Albany friend to go to no further trouble. Greeley said he would not withdraw his name from the congressional contest and would work for the Whig ticket, but "that I yield no further support to Gen. Taylor than is dictated by an imperative sense of duty and my pledge publicly given the day after the Philadelphia nomination. . . . I will not have it said that I was enticed to support him." Greeley was elected to congress. Greeley to Weed, Sept. 22, 1848, NYHSL.

[10] Greeley to Seward, Nov. 11, 1854, Greeley, *Recollections*, 315-320. Seward to Weed, July 12, 1848, F. Seward, *Seward*, 71. His partners failed to moderate Greeley's radicalism. Publishing his first edition of *Hints* in 1850, he observed to Colfax that the world had progressed since the lectures constituting the text were delivered, and his Fourierist talks would "seem quite tame now." Greeley to Colfax, Mar. 31, 1850, NYPL.

The rupture was only temporary. Greeley was soon predicting that Seward would be elected president in 1856 on a progressive, antislavery platform, "winning a victory that is good for something."[11] He cooperated well until after the nomination of Winfield Scott in 1852; but then, possibly because he was denied the gubernatorial candidacy, he again became critical of Whig management.[12]

At about the same time, a new explosive dropped upon the scene. In 1851, Henry J. Raymond founded the New York *Times*, and Greeley began to feel the pressure of another cheap morning Whig paper in the city. Raymond launched his journal with Albany backing; and although at first Greeley may have been unaware of this fact, he soon perceived the truth, for Raymond began to assume Greeley's duties within the partnership. The jeopardy in which this situation placed the Weed-Seward-Greeley combination can hardly be exaggerated, for Greeley was a sensitive and jealous man. More important, Raymond's relations with the Albany machine assumed, in Greeley's mind, the colorings of an attack against the *Tribune*. To intend or to do injury to his paper was to knife at Greeley's soul.[13]

Raymond had entered the newspaper profession as Greeley's assistant, but the two men failed to get along together. Greeley disliked Raymond, termed his work "clever but careless," and said he failed to grasp "the grave importance" of the editorial vocation, or to realize "the necessity of throwing earnestness, power into every thing." Greeley considered him a political reactionary.[14] Raymond soon left the radical *Tribune* for James Watson Webb's conservative *Courier and*

11 Greeley to Colfax, Mar. 17, 1850, NYPL.
12 DeAlva S. Alexander, *A Political History of the State of New York* (New York, 1906), II, 173.
13 When referring to Raymond in the *Tribune*, Greeley sometimes managed to overcome his antipathy toward his rival. No evidence has been found to support the claim that Greeley subscribed $10,000 to the *Times* as it was launched, "Fun From Under the Old White Hat" (pamphlet) (New York, 1872), 24-25.
14 Greeley to Rufus W. Griswold, Jan. 15, 1841, Greeley MSS., LC.

Enquirer, where as managing editor he berated Greeley's Fourierism. That socialist doctrine, Raymond vowed, would crumble civilization's bulwark, which was the sanctity of property. It would dissolve the family and flood the country with immorality.[15]

After such scurrilous attacks, Greeley's heart could hold nothing for Raymond but hatred, which was aggravated as he saw his rival scramble up the political and journalistic ladders. Raymond was as ambitious for elective office as Greeley, but he was not imbued with the idea of politics as a means of spiritually elevating the people through reform. Weed naturally looked upon Raymond as the more reliable of the two, and the same year that the *Times* was established, its founder was elected speaker of the New York assembly.[16]

Greeley gave clear warning of a storm in the offing soon after the *Times* was launched. Since his elevation to the senate in 1849, Seward had frequently favored Greeley by sending his speeches for publication to the *Tribune,* allowing that office to distribute them to the other metropolitan papers. This token added to Greeley's prestige among his fellow editors.[17] Suddenly it seemed that the courtesy was transferred to Raymond. When Greeley complained, the senator replied that the *Times* Washington correspondent could not be denied because he was far more active than Pike. Greeley's rejoinder blazed with indignation. The public was beginning to look upon the *Times* as Seward's special journal, and to believe that "its filibustering editorials and the general negation of principle" were inspired by Washington. "I do not dispute your right to *make* it your organ—I would just as soon that were the case as not,—but unless you intend that, I object to whatever gives a false appearance of it." Greeley

---

15 Parton, *Greeley,* 172-183. This attack came early in the fall of 1846.
16 Augustus Maverick, *Henry J. Raymond* . . . (Hartford, Conn., 1870), 13-119. There is no adequate life of Raymond. Mr. Francis Brown, of the *New York Times,* is now working on such a study; he has kindly read this chapter and offered a number of suggestions.
17 Seward to Greeley (1850?); Mar. 8, 1852, Greeley MSS., NYPL.

asked only for "such treatment as you would cheerfully accord to your bitterest enemy . . . "[18]

Greeley soon calmed down again, but worse trouble was ahead. He had solicited patronage or state-sponsored advertising since the early days of the partnership. His request was indirect, but none the less unmistakable.[19] Raymond, soon after his tour as speaker, obtained a lucrative contract from the state. Greeley's anger seethed. He was sure that his rival had indulged in political artifice, and the circumstances seemed to sustain his conviction; but despite his urging, Weed took no positive step to rectify matters.

The advertising Raymond received was considerable. In the spring of 1853, the Albany legislature passed a bill requiring the weekly publication of business transacted in the New York City banks. These reports, along with a brief summary of the whole, were to be carried at bank expense in a morning city journal. The measure had originated in the assembly, where Raymond's influence as its recent speaker remained great; and the state superintendent of banks, who was delegated by law to choose the lucky paper, was Raymond's friend and had at one time been a *Times* stockholder.[20]

Greeley saw which way the wind was blowing, and offered to print the summary free. To no avail. The contract went to the *Times*, and Raymond, "the little villain," gloated editorially over his paper's increased prominence. Adding insult to injury, he penned a sarcastic note to Greeley, promising to allow delayed publication of the important bank news if the *Tribune* proved "worthy" of the favor. Greeley raged

[18] Greeley to Seward, Feb. 6, 1853, Greeley Transcripts, LC. Seward to Greeley, Feb. 1, 1853, Greeley MSS., NYPL. Raymond's energetic Washington correspondent was James W. Simonton, later a successful California editor and politician.
[19] Greeley to Weed, Dec. 7, 1841, Weed MSS., RRL.
[20] D. B. St. John to Raymond, Harper & Co., July 25, 1853, reprinted from the *Daily Times* of Feb. 23 in *DTri.*, Feb. 24, 1855. Weed to Greeley, Aug. 10, 1853; St. John to Greeley, Aug. 10, 13, 17, 1853, Greeley MSS., NYPL. *Laws of the State of New York*, 76th sess., 1853 (Albany, 1853), 539.

as he forwarded the letter to Weed: " . . . see the insolence with which the little viper talks to me . . . "[21]

The bank incident reveals the waning strength of the Weed-Seward-Greeley combination, but Raymond's offenses struck deeper. By 1853 competition with the *Times* had driven the *Tribune* into embarrassing fiscal straits, and in the next year, as will be seen, the honors of a state Whig party nomination went not to Greeley but to Raymond.

The financial worries which Greeley experienced were not fundamental. The *Weekly* was a bulwark against any collapse of the *Tribune* Association. The *Times* was curtailing the circulation of the *Daily Tribune* alone. In attempting to offset this inroad, Greeley overstepped himself. In his defense, it may be said that a well-run *Daily Tribune* was essential to a first-rate *Weekly*, but by no means was Raymond threatening to stifle the *Daily* altogether.

Greeley was confessing privately early in 1853 that Raymond had cut his *Daily Tribune's* subscription list two thousand within the year. The *Daily Times* was—to Greeley's way of thinking—"conducted with the most policy and the least principle of any paper ever started," and invariably seized the more popular side of every question, thus making "lots of friends by ultra abuse" of things progressive. Rather than lose all as Greeley feared he might do by standing still, he had insisted that the *Tribune* be transformed with a new type on a larger page; but he had been forced to promise McElrath, his business manager, that the price of the *Daily Tribune* would be raised to three cents if expenses were not being met within the year. He was confident that such a contingency would not arise, and challenged: "Now let any body print as good a two-cent paper if he can."[22]

21 Greeley to Weed, Aug. 16, 1853, NYHSL. To St. John, Aug. 8, 11, 16, 1853, reprinted from the *Daily Times* of Feb. 23 in *DTri.*, Feb. 24, 1855.
22 Greeley to Colfax, Apr. 2, 1853, NYPL. See also Greeley to Colfax, Dec. 9, 1853, NYPL.

The enlargement was made in April, 1853. It covered not the *Daily* alone, but all three *Tribune* editions. The paper was revitalized,[23] and during the Nebraska struggle there were torrents of new subscriptions; but this only aggravated the financial perplexity, for the alteration had increased the cost of each issue above its subscription return. Additional advertisements were critically needed; but these came in slowly, since New York City merchants preferred other papers. They disliked the *Tribune's* antislavery crusade, and the reputation for socialism which attached to the editor. Only when the range and volume of his readers left them without choice did they give Greeley their business. The *Daily* and especially the *Semi-Weekly* seemed to experience difficulty in selling space.[24]

As the *Tribune's* reading family grew, its financial returns decreased. Greeley, little heeding fiscal matters, was delighted with his enlarged audience and the improvement in his services. Other members of his joint stock company were not so happy. A fight as to price ensued, with the business manager, McElrath, insisting that the *Daily* be raised to three cents.[25] Apparently planning to buy him out, Greeley turned to western friends for capital,[26] but evidently could not command it. A compromise in September, 1854, reduced the folio to its former size and retained the low price of two cents. But the strain had been too great. Affairs were in such straits that the shareholders deemed an increase to three cents advisable. Greeley assented, but only on the condition

[23] The *Daily, Semi-Weekly, California,* and *European* editions were issued with longer and wider columns, representing an increase of roughly one-third in printed area, on and after Apr. 11, 1853, the day which ushered the *Daily* into its thirteenth year. The *Weekly* was similarly enlarged as it entered its thirteenth year, on Sept. 3, 1853. The claim was publicly made that these enlargements, based on current circulation, cost $70,000 annually; and Greeley privately stated the additional outlay yearly was at least $65,000. Greeley to George N. Sanders, Jan. 7 185(4), HCL. *DTri.,* Apr. 11, Aug. 3, 1853.
[24] Greeley admitted in *DTri.,* Nov. 23, 1854, that his advertisements were not keeping pace with his circulation.
[25] Dana to Pike, July 10, 17, 1854, Pike MSS., Calais (Me.) Public Library.
[26] Greeley to Reavis, June 29, July 7, 1854 (clipping), Greeley MSS., LC.

that Raymond and James Gordon Bennett of the New York *Herald*, the third of the prominent morning dailies, would do likewise. Bennett acceded, but Raymond held out.[27] One explanation of his ability to refuse possibly lies in the fact that Weed was at the time lending him money.[28]

With such rough going the Weed-Seward-Greeley chariot was gradually shaken apart. Upon reaching the critical juncture of the New York state campaign in the fall of 1854, it collapsed, the fatal jolts administered by Weed's refusal to sponsor the Republican party at that early date and by Greeley's failure to obtain a Whig nomination.

This New York state election was one of the most complicated America has ever witnessed. A plethora of candidates, named by four distinct political groups, confused the voter. The campaign menu was so diverse that it frightened the professional politician, but the amateur thought it promised a picnic. Greeley groomed himself for a delightful outing.

Four separate tickets reflected peculiar political circumstances. The country's major parties, Whig and Democratic, had been disintegrating under the impact of the slavery controversy since the acquisition of new territory after the Mexican War, and this tendency was particularly marked in New York. In 1848 the Democrats split into the "Regulars" and the "Free Soilers," the first faction commonly called "Hards" and supporting Lewis Cass of Michigan for the presidency, the second opprobriously termed "Softs" and voting for Martin Van Buren. Two years later the Whigs divided over the Compromise of 1850. The "Silver Greys" or "Hunkers" claimed it was the last word in the slavery dispute and condemned the opposition by Seward in the senate; but the progressive leaders, appealing to those voters who resisted the finality resolution, were the more powerful. Directed by Weed, they quickly destroyed the Hunker organization,

[27] The increase in price would have realized around $62,000 annually for the *Tribune* Association. Dana to Pike, Sept. 1, 25, Nov. 22, 1854, Pike, *First Blows*, 260-262.
[28] Raymond to Weed, Apr. 28, Aug. 5, 8, Oct. 28, 1854, Weed MSS., RRL.

although its spirit lived to plague the party in 1852 and 1854.

Issues other than slavery were pulverizing the parties. Reform movements launched in the 1840's were converging to demand prohibition of the sale of intoxicants, and nativism was coagulating into the so-called American party to battle the presumed menace of thousands of Catholic immigrants from Ireland and the German states.

A confirmed teetotaler, Greeley had entered the lists against drink early in his career. Convinced that the practice was conducive to crime, prostitution, and pauperism, he kept up a constant fire of dry propaganda. Irritated by lax enforcement of excise regulations and stimulated by the Maine law of 1851 forbidding trade in liquor, Greeley turned toward uprooting the commerce permanently.[29]

Concerted efforts to get prohibition accepted in Albany twice failed, and the controversy became acute in the 1853 local elections. The *Tribune* and its cohorts were determined to obtain a pliable legislature. Greeley acclaimed the proposed measure as "a necessary result of the progress of the age—a world's law, which broke out in Maine. . . . Those who would stay its progress might as well undertake to abolish the fundamental truths of Mathematics and Chemistry."[30]

No one rose to dispute this proposition effectively, and enthusiasm brought victory. Under the guidance of State Senator Myron H. Clark, the reformers pushed through their bill, but it was vetoed by Governor Horatio Seymour, a Soft Democrat, on March 31, 1854.[31] Branding Seymour a political charlatan, Greeley threw the issue squarely into

[29] John A. Krout, *The Origins of Prohibition* (New York, 1925), esp. 227, 240, 278-280. Ingersoll, *Greeley*, 631-632.
[30] *DTri.*, Oct. 8, 1853. Prohibition was the chief *Tribune* topic throughout the fall of 1853.
[31] *State of New York Messages from the Governors*, ed. Charles Z. Lincoln (Albany, 1909), IV, 752-771. Krout, "The Maine Law in New York Politics," *New York History*, XVII (July, 1936), 260-266. Stewart Mitchell, *Horatio Seymour of New York* (Cambridge, 1938), 154-158.

81

the approaching gubernatorial campaign. "We *may* be beaten—we *must not* be betrayed," he wrote. "Let this year witness the putting forth of our mightiest efforts, in the firm conviction that, with the blessing of God, we can rid our State of the curse of legalized rum-selling by this one gigantic struggle. Forward!" The critical test for selecting a new chief magistrate should be his attitude toward the Maine law. [32] Greeley as its loudest advocate was certainly the movement's logical candidate.

Nativism was cutting an even wider political swath. Emotional patriotism claiming "America for the Americans" had been a potent force in the nation's culture since Revolutionary days. Simmering in the 1830's, it boiled into riots and local political successes during the next decade; but only the increased Catholic immigration following the Irish famines and the economic hardships and 1848 revolutionary failures in Europe gave this sentiment the nourishment necessary to bring it to full strength. An obsession that popery was destroying the nation gained wide currency. To this fear were added those of a more tangible nature. Immigrants appeared to be getting the best jobs, or to be lowering the wage standard by working for a pittance; and to the biased it looked as though demagogues were controlling the government by herding "foreigners" out of the groggeries into the polls. Against these imagined perversions of American institutions, the "Order of the Star-Spangled Banner" and the "Order of United Americans" coalesced with similar societies to form the American party. [33]

The followers of this new party were disciplined into lodges, where secret rituals, captivating the gullible, were performed. A stranger met on the street was tested with the

[32] *DTri.*, Apr. 3, 1854. Greeley's italics. See also *DTri.*, Mar. 31, Apr. 1, 1854.
[33] Ray A. Billington, *The Protestant Crusade, 1800-1860* (New York, 1938). Louis D. Scisco, "Political Nativism in New York State," Columbia University *Studies in History, Economics and Public Law*, XIII (New York, 1900-1901), no. 2, 203-457.

query, "Have you seen Sam?" If one of the select, he would
return the password. All assemblies were closely guarded, the
better to keep away sinister influences; and if a non-member
became curious and tried to pry into the forbidden, he was
frozen with a cold, "I know nothing." This bewildering
response bestowed upon these misguided patriots an appropriate appellation, "Know Nothings."

Greeley exhibited a deep-set hostility toward the spirit of
Know Nothingism from the first, but there were reservations
in his attacks which would later prove beneficial to the
Republican party. To his mind additional manpower, hence
immigration, was essential to the exploitation of the country's
wealth; and though Protestant to the core, he believed that
an assault against the Catholic Church would only strengthen
it. He observed in the *Tribune* that "the 'Know-Nothing'
organization is but a new dodge of Protean Nativism—is
essentially anti-Foreign, especially anti-Irish, and anti-
Catholic. How can we regard any movement of this sort as
other than hostile to the vital principles of our Republic?"[34]

But Greeley had long been irritated by the general
tendency of the foreign born to vote the Democratic ticket.
As the Know Nothings grew in numbers, he advised immigrants to cease forming clubs in order to maintain contact
with the homeland.[35] He admitted that the newcomers were
"deplorably clannish, misguided, and prone to violence," and
that a registry law was needed. But he regarded as dangerous
all secret political combinations, such as Tammany Hall and
the American party. He would not fight a wrong with a
wrong. The *Tribune* stood for "Equal Rights for All Men,
regardless of nativity, creed or color."[36]

So thin had northern political bonds been worn by
nativism, agitation for prohibition, and the slavery controversy, that the Kansas-Nebraska bill broke them altogether.

[34] *DTri.*, Nov. 16, 1853.
[35] *DTri.*, Mar. 28 (unless otherwise noted, the year 1854 will be understood
for the remainder of this chapter).
[36] *DTri.*, June 15. See also *DTri.*, July 31.

Slowly various groups were welded into a compact and forceful demand for a single object, the restriction of human
bondage. Had Greeley not been a partner in the firm of
Weed-Seward-Greeley and a prospective governor of the
Empire State, he would have been among the first to hail
such a fusion; but under the circumstances, he faltered and
failed to give the new party the full backing of the *Tribune*
until after the fall elections of 1854.

As Douglas reported his Nebraska bill out of committee,
sympathy for a party to quarantine slavery began sweeping
the north. Its early supporters turned to Greeley for leadership, but he disappointed them. He sent a most uncharacteristic reply to an entreaty from Ripon, Wisconsin, that he
unfurl the "Republican" banner from his paper's masthead.
Editors, he hedged, "can only follow where the people's
heart is already prepared to go with them." Theodore Parker
requested that Greeley assist in inaugurating a sectional
party, and he responded that he had "never been able to
discover any strong, pervading, overruling Anti-Slavery
sentiment in the Free States. . . . Hence I have never seen
the way clear for an independent Anti-Slavery party. I
believe a large majority of the voters are impelled by interest
rather than principle, and that any political movement which
appeals wholly to mind, ignoring material considerations, is
doomed to failure."[37]

When Greeley wrote Parker, he had just finished a western
lecture tour, and had been none too impressed by the antislavery current he had found. At the time, he did not antici-
pate Democratic success with the Nebraska measure; in fact,
he thought it could not be carried. Its passage put a new
light on matters. Confidence in the possibility of a new
political organization rocketed. Members of the staff were
affected, and Greeley let them voice their views. He and his
assistants were caught in the momentum of the anti-Nebraska

[37] Greeley to Parker, Mar. 23 (copy), Parker MSS., MHSL. Greeley to
Alvan E. Bovay, Mar. 7, Seitz, *Greeley*, 156-157.

crusade. To launch a sectional party was the next logical step for the *Tribune,* and it opened an uncharted channel for Greeley's personal ambitions. It is hard to say exactly when he sensed this aspect, but certainly he came to believe that the demand for discarding the Whig party would elevate him in the esteem of Weed and Seward.

The *Tribune* intensified its blistering attack against slavery in the hot summer months following the passage of the Nebraska bill. An editorial satirically asked that the African slave trade be reopened now that the institution was to be spread over the free lands of the west. The monopoly held by the Old Dominion over the domestic trade must be broken, for Virginia slaves were too civilized to do hard work. Many were the children of senators, bankers, and landowners, and had "inherited largely the pride and ambition proper to the first families of an ancient community . . . "[38]

The staff felt that the repeal of the 1820 compact had invalidated all compromises, and opened an assault against the fugitive slave act, a part of the 1850 adjustment which compelled federal marshals and courts to return runaways to their southern owners. In complying with this law, government officials created a number of incidents which made splendid copy. The *Tribune* featured the Tony Burns and Joshua Glover affairs for days.[39] Bondsmen in flight, Greeley judged, were merely following a universal impulse for freedom, and they had the full sympathy of the north. Public tranquillity, he wrote, demanded a modification of this repulsive legislation, "at least to the extent of giving to the alleged fugitive the right of *trial by jury* in the place where he is arrested." Unless this concession were granted, it could "hardly be doubted that systematic, organized, revolutionary resistance to the business of kidnapping men from the soil of the Free States will sooner or later be resorted to . . ."[40]

[38] *DTri.,* May 26. [39] *DTri.,* late May, June, and July.
[40] *DTri.,* May 31. Greeley's italics.

85

Other editorials claimed that the law as it stood had no moral force; it was merely a slavedriver's device for humiliating the north. The Pierce administration was out to suppress freedom with the sword.[41] A *Tribune* poet cried that the stars and stripes had been disgraced[42]:

> Tear down the flaunting lie!
> Half-mast the starry flag!
> Insult no sunny sky
> With Hate's polluted rag;
> Destroy it, ye who can!
> Deep sink it in the waves!
> It bears a fellow man
> To groan with fellow slaves.

There was ample nourishment for a sectional party. By June, Greeley had warmed to the point of expressing himself openly. His paper would continue to uphold the Whig policies of national economy, he promised; but since he agreed "substantially with the Free Democratic party in all it affirms with regard to Slavery," he wished "to see a union of all those members of the two parties who believe resistance to the extension of Slave Territory and Slave Power the most urgent public duty" of the day. He was not particularly concerned about a name for the new party, but he thought "some simple name like 'Republican'" would fitly apply to those who united to restore the Union "to its true mission of champion and promulgator of Liberty rather than propagandist of Slavery."[43] He wanted as the sole requirement of a congressional candidate the pledge that he "*earnestly and in good faith do his utmost to reëstablish the Missouri Restriction, and secure Kansas and Nebraska for Free Labor and Free Men*. We ask him to postpone or subordinate other questions (as we do) until this end is attained ... "[44]

[41] *DTri.*, June 1, 6. *WTri.*, June 10.
[42] *DTri.*, June 13. Also carried, with different punctuation, in Greeley, *The American Conflict* ... , I (Hartford, Conn., 1864), 220.
[43] *DTri.*, June 16.
[44] *DTri.*, June 28. Greeley's italics and parentheses.

Irrespective of this promise to concentrate on the slavery question, the *Tribune* continued its war against drink. The first was a national and the second a local issue. Greeley was seeking to join prohibition with slavery restriction and produce a winning party. To the anti-Nebraska appeal in congressional districts, he would add the attraction of the Maine law in the state elections. Success would carry him into the governor's chair on a wave of popular enthusiasm which no politician could check. For once Weed would have to knuckle under to his fearless leadership.

What was in the back of Greeley's mind may be seen in his letters to Schuyler Colfax, who was then publisher of the South Bend (Ind.) *St. Joseph Valley Register.* Greeley advised his friend to accept a nomination for congress if it came to him unsolicited. "I don't think it much object to be elected," he continued, "but running at such a time will enable you to extend your acquaintance, your influence and your circulation. I decidedly would do it if I were asked to do so. . . . Anti-Nebraska and anti-Rum ought to unite Whigs and Free Soilers and carry your State this Fall."[45] With mounting enthusiasm, he repeatedly praised the anti-drink and anti-Nebraska platform. It would sweep the free states. New York, Pennsylvania, and Indiana were certain. "You don't yet know how strong you are," he chided Colfax.[46]

As nominations for the fall campaigns began throughout the country, the *Tribune* encouraged the fusion of various anti-Nebraska groups. Particular praise went to the "free-men" of Michigan, who met at Jackson on July 6 and drew up a state ticket. Members of all the old parties had attended; and Greeley found it proper that two former Democrats, three Free Soilers, and five Whigs had been selected. "The name under which the opponents of the Nebraska Iniquity

[45] Greeley to Colfax, Mar. 12, NYPL.
[46] Greeley to Colfax, July 7, NYPL. See also Greeley to Colfax, Mar. 19, June 5, 20, 28, NYPL.

have enlisted for the war," he noted, "is simply REPUBLI-CAN, and this, we think, will be very generally adopted."[47]

Greeley was determined that New York should follow in Michigan's footsteps. On July 4, the *Tribune* carried an announcement that the anti-Nebraskans would hold a convention at Saratoga on August 16. The character of the gathering was such as Greeley had long advocated. No local political machinery would grind out delegates. All who desired could come and talk and vote. And, by strange coincidence, a mass temperance rally was scheduled for the same place on the following day, with Horace Greeley as its chief speaker.[48]

Objections to this procedure were voiced by Whig conservatives, and Greeley countered with a lashing editorial leader. He knew "no legitimate use of Party except to embody and give effect to enlightened Public Sentiment." A political revolution was taking effect in the north, and new implements were needed to enforce its ideas. On two important points, "a majority of the People of this Country are agreed —first, that Slavery shall have no further extension under the flag of our Union, but shall be constrained to release the dubious hold it has lately acquired on . . . Kansas and Nebraska; secondly, that men shall no longer enrich themselves by the injury and ruin of others through traffic in Intoxicating Beverages. The former is a subject of Federal, the latter of State legislation; and, while they have no necessary connection, they certainly have strong natural affinities." Greeley spoke straight from the shoulder. All the old political machinery should be junked. "Those who fear their party standing, so laboriously achieved, will suffer by any disruption . . . will of course labor to keep things as

[47] *DTri.*, July 11. Greeley's upper case. Proceedings of the convention are abstracted from Detroit papers.
[48] *DTri.*, July 4, 7. See also dispatches and editorials, *DTri.*, Aug. 16, 17, 19, 22.

nearly as may be in the old ruts, and make the Saratoga
movement as aimless and insignificant as possible."[49]

Greeley was talking about Weed and Seward. He knew
what his partners were thinking. Seward was looking toward
1856 as the year in which he would be honored with Whig
presidential laurels, an event which Raymond was heralding
in the *Times*.[50] Seward regarded the fusionists with increasing discomfort. The cohesive force of this group was a
conservative anti-Nebraska sentiment, tempered by a desire
on the part of their practical men not to alienate the south
too intensely. Their tendency was to draw together dissatisfied Whigs, Free Soilers, Independent Democrats, and those
Know Nothings who detested the Nebraska act, to smash the
Whig structure, and to brand Seward unavailable for the
presidential nomination because of his radical antislavery
and antinativist declarations.[51] Letters seeking advice about
"disbanding and reorganizing" annoyed him. He complained
to Weed after Greeley had asked him to cooperate with other
congressmen in publicly recommending union and frater-
nization of all the anti-Nebraska elements: "How would such
an address look, signed by *me*? How would it look signed
by others and not by me—Can[']t you give us a good
stirring appeal to the people to look away from Washington
and settle these things practically at home—I shall forbear
at at [*sic*] all events—" Nor had Seward signed the antislavery congressional call "To the People of the United
States" when it was published in the *Tribune* late in June.
For him, all might be lost and nothing gained by beginning a
new party.[52]

[49] *DTri.*, July 18.   [50] Bancroft, *Seward*, I, 364-368.
[51] Seward to Weed, Jan. 7, 8, May 29, June 12, Weed MSS., RRL. Seward
to his home, May 31, F. Seward, *Seward*, 230-231. George Bailey to Pike,
May 30, Pike, *First Blows*, 237-238.
[52] Seward to Weed, June 24, Weed MSS., RRL. Seward's italics. The
address appeared *DTri.*, June 22, over the signatures of Solomon Foot,
Daniel Mace, and Reuben E. Fenton, with the notation that it was "indorsed
by all the Anti-Nebraska members of Congress." See also Seward to Weed,
July 30, Weed MSS., RRL.

Weed had been oiling his Whig machine for years, and had no desire to junk it. In fact, the Saratoga movement and the possibility of Greeley's receiving a gubernatorial nomination from that gathering threatened the Albany politician's supremacy in the Empire State. Greeley's paper was an asset to the machine, but not worth the price his term as governor would exact. In Weed's eyes, Greeley took on the attributes of a maniac when in an elective office. He was so unreliable that he could conceivably wreck the smoothest running organization. He was too domineering and dictatorial to get along with other politicians. He refused to give and take. He had been tried and found wanting. With Weed's aid, Greeley had been sent to the house of representatives in 1848. Immediately, he utilized his prerogative to antagonize his colleagues by publicizing their mileage graft in the *Tribune*.[53] One of his first objectives seemed to be newspaper copy, and he was delighted with the hornet's nest he had stirred. "I have divided the House into two parties," he boasted to a friend, "one that would like to see me extinguished and the other that wouldn't be satisfied without a hand in doing it." Seward, anguished by his partner's capers, decided that Greeley was out to reform congress overnight. "He won[']t let them adjourn until three o'clock," Seward wrote Weed, "and martyrizes himself five or six times a day, by voting against the whole House. I am sorry, but who can reason with him?"[54]

Already clogged with the dry rot of nativism and slavery agitation, the Albany machine could hardly undergo the additional strain of Greeley as a candidate for governor. Weed's political cronies looked upon the man in horror. One of his better lobbyists, clearly referring to such as Greeley, pleaded that the state ticket be one "the boys can go for[,] men whom we can call on and pass those long winter evenings

---

[53] Seitz, *Greeley*, 291-294. *Congressional Globe*, 30th Congress, 2nd sess. (Washington, 1849), 371.
[54] Seward to Weed, Dec. 7, 1848, F. Seward, *Seward*, 92. Greeley to Griswold, Jan. 21, 1849, Boston Public Library.

at C[ongress] Hall[,] men willing that we should take a trifle of that old rum and *a* oyster—and men finally who have no idea that office confers any spiritual power—"[55]

Greeley knew he could not fit the bill, and did not expect the Weed clique to back him.[56] For this reason, among others, he was outraged by party conventions, held under the collective thumb of professional politicians. He had countered with a widely publicized scheme for doing away with such conclaves altogether. He would have the citizen mark the ballot with the party of his choice, and then write in the name of a prominent man favored for each office. Success would go to those who obtained a plurality of the votes given to the majority party.[57]

His was an unfortunate position, Greeley thought. He could not push himself on the electorate. Beating his own political drum was too much akin to advertising himself in his own paper. He later explained to his readers in general terms the predicament in which a politically ambitious editor found himself. He was unable, with propriety, to solicit a nomination, but should one come to him unsought, "not because he would like the office, but because his party thinks it cannot get on without the use of his name, or at best has no one else who can run so well, let him accept and make the best of it."[58]

Greeley's yearning seemed to be materializing. So powerful were anti-rum and anti-Nebraska, and so much had the *Tribune* contributed toward making those issues outstanding, that he believed himself the one man for the post of governor.

[55] D. H. Abell to Weed, Sept. 10, Weed MSS., RRL. Abell's italic. Congress Hall was an Albany tavern.
[56] Greeley to Seward, Oct. 25, Seward MSS., Auburn. To Seward, Nov. 11, Greeley, *Recollections*, 315-320.
[57] *DTri.*, Jan. 7, Sept. 26, Oct. 19, Dec. 28, 1855; Nov. 13, 18, 23, 30, Dec. 18, 1858.
[58] *DTri.* ("political" column), Aug. 5, 1858. This comment and an editorial on the same topic appearing in *DTri.*, Apr. 27, 1855, while Greeley was en route to Europe, were distorted by the Regular Republicans when Greeley ran for the presidency in 1872. "The Greeley Record" (pamphlet) (Washington, 1872), and "Horace Greeley jugé par lui-même" (pamphlet) (Washington, 1872).

Of course, Weed did not care to honor him, but already the Albany machine was clanking and sputtering. Weed might hop on Greeley's new bandwagon and be thankful for the lift. Out of deference to the partnership, Weed would surely not defy public opinion and prevent the drafting of Greeley at Saratoga on August 16.

Weed knocked this dream into a cocked hat. His fist was covered with a velvet glove, because he hoped to retain *Tribune* backing, but the blow was none the less powerful. This was no time to pull punches. Even had he wanted Greeley as his gubernatorial candidate, Weed had no choice. Saratoga jeopardized his predominance in New York state; it threatened to collapse his Whig organization before he could prepare a transfer. Under these circumstances, the finesse with which he handled Greeley and turned Saratoga from a nominating convention into a mass anti-Nebraska rally marks him as a political genius.

Toward the end of July, Weed became concerned over the movement for a new party. He called Greeley to him for a conference in his New York City office, room 11 in the Astor House. Gracefully he explained that Greeley's estimate of the political situation was shortsighted. Seward's return to the senate by the legislature that would be elected in November was rightly the prime mission. Every Democrat in the country would greet Seward's defeat with glee. Weed was not sure that Seward could be reelected. He pointed out to Greeley that the Know Nothing menace was frightening. Seward's bitterest opponents, Hunker Whigs and Hard Democrats, were flocking into its lodges. Its secret manipulations would give it control of many local conventions. The Know Nothing party would not make nominations, he supposed, but it would doubtless support and elect its favorites. Greeley must know, he continued, that Know Nothing strength grew daily. Weed could see no escape. The nativists must be appeased. Seward himself was a hindrance to that task. He was hated by the Know Nothings because as governor of New York several years back he had favored autonomous Catholic schools, and throughout his career he had looked with sympathy upon the foreign born, particularly the Irish.

On the other hand, Weed elaborated, Greeley realized that many of the Know Nothings were also anti-Nebraskans. With these as a nucleus the Weed machine would have to enter the lodges, battle the anti-Seward element, and try to emerge with a state legislature favorable to Seward; but the anti-Nebraska nativists must have a *quid pro quo.* Weed's plan had no chance of success unless the antislavery Know Nothings were placated with a Whig gubernatorial candidate who belonged to one of their lodges. Weed reminded Greeley that he could not humiliate himself by taking such a step, and even if he were to do so, he would likely spoil the whole scheme since he also was disliked by the Know Nothings.

Weed agreed with Greeley that his temperance and anti-Nebraska agitations gave him a valid claim to the governorship, but unfortunately another aspirant had stolen the Maine law political thunder. The American Temperance Union had recently requested that the Whig party nominate Myron H. Clark, who as a state senator had been instrumental in piloting through the bill which Seymour had vetoed. But then, Weed concluded, it was too early to predict what would happen at the Whig convention. Was it not possible that Greeley himself would be selected? In any case, the gubernatorial race was a secondary consideration. Weed drove his point home. The Weed-Seward-Greeley partnership must work harder and cooperate better than ever before, or Seward's place in the senate would be filled by a proslavery Democrat or at best by an ex-Hunker Know Nothing. Saratoga must not make nominations. In this great crisis all the

93

anti-Nebraska sentiment in the state must be thrown behind the Whig party and Seward.[59]

Weed's argument worked like a charm. Greeley fell in line, altering the *Tribune's* policy. In an editorial he announced that while he believed Michigan's example in forming a state ticket from members of all the old parties "under the common appellation of REPUBLICAN," might wisely have been followed, he had failed to observe any indications that antislavery opinion in New York was that far advanced. He was very sure that it had not been contemplated by a majority of the signers of the Saratoga call.[60]

Greeley opened his heart to Colfax. "We shall have no nomination at Saratoga," he wrote regretfully, "and, alas! no fusion at all, which will do harm in all the 'fusion' States. It will tell heavily against us that we carry all the States Whig that we can, and go 'fusion' where we can do no better. Schuyler, this won't work, and you'll find it so."[61] Unfortunately, there was no alternative in New York, he said, repeating Weed's argument: "In this State, Know-Nothingism is notoriously a conspiracy to overthrow [']Seward, Weed and Greeley,' and particularly to defeat Gov. Seward's reëlection to the Senate."[62] Greeley promised the scheme would be frustrated. "We are going to do badly here—carry the State strong enough, but on a 'Know-Nothing' platform, with Silver Greyism the cat under the meal . . ." Seward would win, but it made Greeley sad to contemplate the low-caliber ticket necessary to that end. "I am going up to Albany on Monday, to see what can be done," he concluded, "but I guess it's too late. We shall have the meanest kind of candidates for 'most everything imposed on us by Know-

[59] *DTri.*, May 7, 1860. Greeley to Seward, Oct. 25, Seward MSS., Auburn. Greeley, *Recollections*, 311-322. Barnes, *Weed*, II, 225-226, 282-289. F. Seward, *Seward*, 457. Seitz, *Greeley*, 157-166. Bancroft, *Seward*, I, 364-374. Scisco, "Nativism," 111-112. Alexander, *New York*, II, 194-198. See also notes 60-63, 65-70, 75-79, below.
[60] *DTri.*, July 24. Greeley's upper case.
[61] Greeley to Colfax, July 26, NYPL.
[62] Greeley to Colfax, Aug. 20, NYPL.

Nothings—if we don't rebel, as we ought to, but probably sha'n't."[63]

He journeyed up to Albany to see Weed and take a second lesson in practical politics. His personal hopes were high, and on arrival he relieved his mind of a burning question. Could he run for lieutenant governor? That post, he explained, was desired by few, and if it were lost, it would injure neither the Whigs nor Seward's chances for reelection. By making the campaign, he believed he could advertise his paper, assuage his political ambitions, and meet his enemies face to face.

Weed listened patiently. It was hard to predict, he replied, but he feared the answer was no. A prohibitionist must be run for governor, and to anchor the other end of the ticket with an ardent dry might bring disaster. Weed explained he was not sure he could control the Whig gathering, and it was decided to mark time and wait for future developments.[64]

Greeley was not trusted to block the formation of a new party at Saratoga. Weed took matters into his own hands. His assistants reported on the prospective members of the conclave, and aided in selecting proper men to represent Whig interests on August 16.[65] He assured ex-Governor Washington Hunt that a call for an antislavery Whig convention would go out before the fusionists met, and this would help the Whigs monopolize the anti-Nebraska issue. Hunt was pleased, and in relaying the glad tidings to Senator Hamilton Fish, testified that Weed "too fears the result of the Saratoga performance. He says Greeley is for making nominations, and hopes to be presented for Governor. On the other hand Weed is apprehensive that the Knownothings & Silver Grays will control our State [Whig] Convention. This will be so if nominations are made at Saratoga—not otherwise."[66]

[63] Greeley to Colfax, July 26, NYPL. [64] See note 59, above.
[65] Elbridge G. Spaulding, Aug. 8; Raymond, Aug. 8; O. Nicholson, Aug. 11, all to Weed, Weed MSS., RRL.
[66] Hunt to Fish, Aug. 2, Fish MSS., LC.

There was not much danger of Greeley's breaking over. He too feared the threat against Seward. And Weed had left him room for hope. Greeley followed the advice of the Albany boss praying that circumstances would so adjust themselves as to allow him to make some race.

The *Tribune* continued its endeavors for anti-Nebraska fusion in other states,[67] but it was discreet when mentioning Saratoga. Nothing of editorial importance on the subject was said during August—until the day before the meeting. This editorial is the more notable since the timing was such it could not well appear in the *Weekly*. Greeley did not want his home state timidity observed by his western friends.

For the benefit of his restricted *Daily* audience, Greeley put on a side-show. The *Tribune* had been criticized for not demanding nominations at Saratoga: "Our justification is simply that we did not think the people needed any spurring on the subject. We have said all that we thought necessary in making the objects of that Convention generally known and repelling the calumnies of its opposers." Were the people really ready for a new party? "If they are then the time for it has come. But while nobody doubts that a great majority of our voters are immovably hostile to the principles and aims of the Nebraska bill, in so far as it affects the Missouri Restriction, yet it is not so clear that any majority at all are ready to abandon their old associations, forget their chronic differences, and unite on this one issue."[68]

Greeley penned these sterile sentences for the *Daily* with relative ease, but he sickened at the idea of superintending the prospective funeral in Saratoga. He would rather someone else would bury his baby. He forwarded a list of proposed resolutions to Weed, whom he thought would be on hand, adding: ". . . I am unwell, and may possibly not be able to attend. . . . Know Nothingism is all the go this way, and threatens to sweep the deck."[69] Yet when the fatal hour rolled

[67] *DTri.*, July 26, 31, Aug. 12.   [68] *DTri.*, Aug. 15.
[69] Greeley to Weed, Aug. 10, Weed MSS., RRL.

around, Greeley was in Saratoga. Weed was indisposed. A
friend commiserated with the ailing Albany boss: "Of course
you do not wish to be at Saratoga today—if you are no more
ill than *that*, I shall feel rejoiced[.]"[70]

Upon Greeley's shoulders had fallen the burden of turning
Saratoga into an anti-Nebraska rally, and on August 16 he
finished the job without an audible murmur of dissent. He
drew up the resolutions, couching them in strong antislavery
phrases. The next day he addressed the temperance meeting,
and then returned to New York City. His dispatches to the
Tribune lacked his usual sincerity. "The number of Delegates
to the Freemen's Convention," he wrote, was "very large";
and less than one-third desired to nominate. Weed could not
have handled the situation better. The Saratoga group had
called for a reconvocation in Syracuse late in September.[71]
That timing was perfect. It would follow on the heels of the
Whig convention to be held in the same city, and everybody
knew that the anti-Nebraskans would echo the Whig ticket.

Greeley deserves sympathy during this trying period.
Beset as he was with other trials and tribulations, he had to
surmount a major editorial obstacle in supporting the Republicans outside of New York and the Whigs inside. It irked
him to have his paper border on inconsistency. In this
instance he had to walk a very tight rope. He did so by skip-
ping gingerly over the fact that no nominations were made
at Saratoga, and considering it as the chief political event of
the year. He damned as a "liar" the journalist who branded
the conclave a Whig plot.[72] That party had collapsed everywhere but in New York, he testified. Believing the Iowa
election in August constituted the acid test for the Republicans, he hailed their triumph there joyously. It was not, as
some claimed, a Whig victory. Rather, he informed his
public: "It was achieved by a fusion of all honest parties,—
by the combination of men previously entertaining different

70 Alvah Hunt to Weed, Aug. 16, Weed MSS., RRL. Hunt's italics.
71 Greeley's dispatches and editorials, *DTri.*, Aug. 16, 17, 19, 22.
72 *DTri.*, Aug. 19.

or antagonistic sentiments on political questions, who came together on the common ground of Slavery Restriction and Liquor Prohibition, and fought the glorious battle of Freedom as one man . . . "[73] Yet, much as he might wish the inauguration of a new party, he cooperated fully with Weed in the Empire State, reinforcing his Saratoga accomplishment with a successful effort to prevent the drys from nominating independently before the Whigs.[74]

Explanation of this dexterous editorial policy lies in Greeley's political ambition, although he was also worried about Seward. Weed kept him on tenterhooks, dangling before his sensitive nose a choice Whig morsel. For this reason, Greeley emerged from the Saratoga ordeal with a faint gleam of hope still present. " 'Seward, Weed and Greeley' are in the popular conception inseparable," he bragged to Colfax only two weeks before the Syracuse convention. "Things look pretty well here," he continued. "Any body" could be elected governor. At about the same time, Dana told Pike: "The Whigs have got to nominate Greeley for Governor and fight the Know-Nothings. . . . Weed and the other leaders admit that Greeley is the only man who will do at all for the battle. The Softs will run Seymour on the rum tack, and it will be an interesting contest."[75]

Whatever Greeley may have been led to believe, Weed had his eye on Myron H. Clark, who had been admitted to a Know Nothing lodge at his home in Canadaigua.[76] Although Weed's supervision of the approaching gathering at Syracuse may have been weaker than it had been on previous occasions,

[73] *DTri.*, Aug. 23. See also Greeley to Colfax, July 7, NYPL. While Greeley was in Saratoga, the *Tribune* itself had referred to the outcome in Iowa as a Whig triumph, *DTri.*, Aug. 17. Reasons in addition to those of the *Tribune* for the Democratic defeat in Io. may be found in Milton, *The Eve of Conflict*, 173.
[74] *DTri.*, Sept. 1. The true position of the drys was said to be one of "armed neutrality"—which in the 1854 New York canvass meant Whig support.
[75] Dana to Pike, Sept. 1, Pike, *First Blows*, 260-261. Greeley to Colfax, Sept. 7, NYPL.
[76] Blatchford to Weed, June 24; Spaulding to Weed, Aug. 20, Weed MSS., RRL. *DTri.*, May 7, 1860.

events transpired much as he had planned. The Know Nothings, for the time being, followed their normal procedure of boring from within, dispatching members from local conclaves which they controlled to the larger convention; and Weed learned that some of the nativists, at least, were pliable.[77] Clark knew on which side his bread was buttered. On the eve of the convocation at Syracuse, he wrote Weed that he had been reflecting on "the subjects of our interview this evening,—I am in your hands,—I know you can defeat my nomination if you see fit to do so."[78]

Greeley was in the dark as to what would happen until after the Whigs met on September 20. An editorial in the *Tribune* four days previous indicates that he had by then lost all hopes for governorship, but Greeley noted that the office of lieutenant governor "did not seem to be in much request."[79]

Clark was nominated for governor on the 20th, but that was not the worse blow to Greeley. That detestable publisher of the *Times*, Henry J. Raymond, got the nod for lieutenant governor.[80] The Whig platform was as strongly antislavery as Saratoga had demanded, and included a plank asking for internal improvements. It said nothing against the sale of intoxicants, but Clark was enough for the drys. Supporting conventions of anti-Nebraskans and prohibitionists at Syracuse and Auburn parroted the Whig ticket. The anti-Nebraska group fell into line with little more than a rasp; but Raymond, who had excused Seymour's veto of the 1853 anti-liquor legislation in the *Times*, was forced to write a letter to the temperance convention promising to support the Maine law before winning approval. There was but one hitch, and it was trivial. The Free Soil element of the Soft

[77] John P. Cummings to Weed, Sept. 18, Weed MSS., RRL.
[78] Clark to Weed, Sept. 19. See also Clark to Weed, Oct. 17, 21, Nov. 18, 30; and J. J. Chambers to Weed, Oct. 31, Dec. 3, Weed MSS., RRL.
[79] *DTri.*, Sept. 16.
[80] Weed stated that he had not thought of Raymond in connection with this nomination "until his name was suggested to me at Syracuse." Barnes, *Weed*, II, 227.

Democrats insisted on real fusion, and named one of their men, Bradford R. Wood, alongside Clark.[81]

Greeley was heartbroken as he wrote a long editorial leader, but under the circumstances he was most restrained. He had made a bargain and would stick by it. Clark must be elected, he stated, for otherwise slavery restriction and temperance would be defeated. The real convention, he reiterated, had been held at Saratoga, not Syracuse. He believed the Whig party "a thing of the past," but was still glad that the anti-Nebraskans at Saratoga had not confused the campaign by making nominations. Fusion of the antislavery elements had not failed at Saratoga, he continued, but at Syracuse when Raymond was selected. The nomination for lieutenant governor should have gone to Wood, who as a former Democrat was "pure and unexceptionable." Why, he wondered, had the drys chosen Raymond and not Wood? Could Raymond turn into a Maine law man however much he tried? Greeley then asked not to be accused of "jealousy or hostility toward the Editor of a rival journal." He pledged the Whigs his backing, "in the firm belief that Mr. Raymond . . . will prove a faithful and efficient champion as well of Liquor Prohibition as of Slavery Restriction."[82]

There were three other tickets in this bewildering campaign. Both Democratic factions nominated before the Whigs. The weaker and more traditionally proslavery Hard element backed Green C. Bronson for governor in July, and the Softs renominated Seymour during the first week in September. The policy of the Softs towards slavery restriction only outwardly resembled their 1848 stand; their platform opposed the Kansas-Nebraska act on principle but accepted it in practice. Such duplicity gave rise to a slight dissension, a few enthusiastic Free Soilers bolting under the leadership of Preston King to nominate Clark and Wood, the latter being subsequently withdrawn in favor of Raymond.

[81] Dispatches from Syracuse and editorials, *DTri.*, Sept. 20, 21, 27, 28.
[82] *DTri.*, Oct. 3.

The Softs were not materially upset by this event. They gave clear warning that with the support of the wets and the liquor interests they would make prohibition the major issue of the canvass.[83]

The fourth slate was drawn up by the Know Nothings, who departed from their Trojan horse tactics and set out for themselves. This innovation was largely caused by the success of Weed's undercover activities in the lodges. The Albany machine smoked out the Hunker Know Nothing group, which had been caught unawares by the Whig nomination of an antislavery nativist for governor. To retaliate, the Silver Greys seized control of the Know Nothing state organization and voted the Canadaigua lodge, to which Clark belonged, spurious. They then proceeded to name Daniel Ullman, Seward's arch foe, as a candidate for chief magistrate. Weed, the master politician, had scored again. This step divided the society. A batch of Sewardites withdrew from the American party convention, established a separate executive board, and formally sustained Clark and Raymond.[84]

Such success was small comfort to Greeley's injured soul, but he stuck to his guns during the ensuing canvass. The *Tribune* rendered outstanding, if sometimes grudging, service to the Whig cause. Foremost was the liquor issue. Letters, addresses, and statistics on crime, health, and slums were published to prove the beneficial results of prohibition. Editorials promised it would lessen the taxpayer's outlay. Greeley saw the Maine law sweeping the country, and cried "Shall NEW-YORK lag behind?"[85] A drought was curtailing the fall harvest, and he clamored that the country was imperiled with famine while distilleries were "converting the staff of life into a deadly and crime-inciting poison."[86] With

[83] Alexander, *New York*, II, 195-198. Dispatch from Syracuse, Sept. 6, *DTri.*, Sept 7.
[84] Scisco, "Nativism," 117-125.
[85] *DTri.*, Aug. 24. Greeley's upper case.
[86] *DTri.*, Aug. 25.

amazing energy he not only directed editorial policy, but also lectured on temperance throughout the state.[87]

The *Tribune* managed to link the perils of slavery to the prohibition question. Slaveowners, it contended, wanted free laborers to drink in order to demoralize them; for in such a condition they were powerless to remove the doughfaces from office. These northern demagogues, in turn, were pointed to with scorn as the true advocates of disunion, out to suck the north dry of all its strength and thereby allow the south to set out alone and extend slavery over the hemisphere.

The *Tribune* also gave its attention to the tariff. The north was being weakened, it argued, by slaveocracy's policy of free trade, which was rapidly turning the United States into an appendage of British manufacturing and commerce. America was becoming an agrarian nation, forced to ship its output abroad at prices set by the English. Would it not benefit the country to develop its own factories behind a wall of protection, thereby giving the farmers a market nearer home and lowering the transportation charges against their produce?[88] "The Southern policy—slavery, aggression, annexation, war, debt, commercial incertitude and periodical bankruptcies," the *Tribune* snarled, "has always been opposed by the respectable reading, thinking, sober portion of the North; while rum-hole politicians, and all that part of the population whom they control, have coalesced with the negro-drivers."[89]

There was caustic comment in abundance for the Know Nothings. On the editorial page was carried their traditional query,

"HAVE YOU SEEN SAM?"

"Yes, *we* have," the *Tribune* replied. "He isn't good-looking, either."[90] A news story fixed on the members of the Ameri-

[87] Dispatch and a speech, *DTri.,* Nov. 3, 6. Dana to E. Washburne, Sept. 25, Washburne MSS., II, LC.
[88] *DTri.,* July 27, 28, Oct. 4, 5, 23.   [89] *DTri.,* Sept. 15.
[90] *DTri.,* Nov. 8. *Tribune's* italics.

can party an additional nickname, "Hindoos." Ullman, it was said, was not a native of the United States, but had been born in Calcutta, the son of German Jewish parents. To substantiate the accusation, letters, signatures in old college books, and personal affidavits were published.[91]

As the day of balloting approached, Greeley was pleased with the promising outlook in the congressional districts,[92] but neither the state ticket nor the support it received from old line Whiggery satisfied him. Fearful of defeat, he did not conceal his criticism. In mid-October, he declared that a new party should have been launched, but that New York's Whig politicians had blocked the formation of "a new organization on the simple Republican platform." If the state did not show at least a 100,000 majority against the Democrats, the sole reason would be that the people had not been permitted to vote distinctly on the issue of compromise repeal.[93]

As October passed, it became clear that the firm of Weed, Seward, and Greeley was doomed. The crux of the matter was simple. Greeley believed that his career and his paper were being held back by a set of provincial politicians in Albany. He was more than a New York journalist, his prestige covered an entire section. The *Tribune* was, in 1854, reaching roughly eight per cent of the free state voters, with a higher per capita circulation in Wisconsin and Vermont than in the Empire State.[94] The task of supporting the Republicans elsewhere and the Whigs at home strained Greeley's nerves and hurt the circulation of his paper.

Reviewing the pre-November elections in the north, Greeley noted that every commonwealth thus far had condemned the administration. Rhode Island, New Hampshire, Connecticut,

[91] *DTri.*, Oct. and early Nov. Scisco, "Nativism," 122-125.
[92] *DTri.*, Oct. 27. There are indications that Weed was sponsoring fusion in some of the congressional districts. Preston King to Weed, Oct. 4; Samuel Dickinson to Weed, Oct. 11, Weed MSS., RRL.
[93] *DTri.*, Oct. 16. Greeley disliked both Whig candidates. Raymond got an apologetic press, *DTri.*, Sept. 21, Oct. 4. Greeley waited until after election to censure Clark, *DTri.*, Nov. 9.
[94] See appendix A.

Iowa, Maine, Vermont, Pennsylvania, Ohio, and Indiana had balloted. In 1852, all had been Democratic but Vermont, and now all were in opposition. The house of representatives had been revolutionized, the delegations from those states changing, roughly, from 50-25 pro-Pierce to 63-12 anti-Pierce. The four states voting in November, he continued, Michigan, Illinois, Wisconsin, and New York, were with a single exception sure to follow. Why should there be doubts of New York? Was she not overwhelmingly anti-Nebraskan?

In spurring his readers toward greater endeavors, Greeley became more optimistic as election day, November 7, approached. Clark, he predicted, would win by 50,000 plurality, and again on the eve of the election, by a handsome majority.[95]

In his private correspondence Greeley was anything but confident. He feared that Ullman would draw strength from Clark, giving the victory to Seymour. Curbing his anger, Greeley penned a letter to Seward. Relative to the states which had adopted Republicanism, he began, New York was destined to be disgraced, "simply for the want of courage and common sense." He would like a discussion with Weed, but that was out of the question: "Weed likes me, and always did—I don't think he ever had a dog about his house that he liked better—but he thinks I know nothing about politics. . . . I won't try anymore to overcome his fixed prepossessions on this point."

Greeley was more explicit when writing to Colfax. Prospects were "infernally black." Weed would secure a Seward legislature, but at the expense of "letting every thing else go as it might." Nor were Weed's methods laudable, for some of those upon whom he relied were "red-mouthed Know-Nothings." Greeley was disgusted: "This is just the most scoundrelly canvass that I was ever engaged in. I feel a crawling all over on account of it. It is a glorious reflection

[95] *DTri.*, Oct. 21, 23, 26, Nov. 2, 4, 6.

that it is so nearly over. There weighs on my heart a feeling of misery—a premonition of disaster,—which I cannot shake off." And he signed himself, "Yours, with a sore head . . ."[96]

Greeley knew whereof he spoke. Ullman was surprisingly popular, and Seymour came close to victory. Clark finally won by a narrow plurality of 309; but the results were as complicated as the campaign had been confusing, and almost a month elapsed before the outcome was positively known. During the tallying, first Seymour and then Clark led; but even more unpleasant for Greeley, Raymond's success was early assured. "The little villain" outran his ticket.[97]

It was too much to expect Greeley to maintain his mental equilibrium during the period of reckoning. His readers were quickly informed of his views. He damned the canvass as a disaster for the prohibitionists and the anti-Nebraskans before the ballots were out of the box.[98] Bad leadership was blamed. The Republican party should have been launched: "In short, both the old parties were dead, and needed to be shoveled under, whether from regard to the purity and salubrity of the atmosphere or to having the ground clear for such action thereafter as circumstances might demand." New York wanted to join the Republican movement, but "too many of her politicians were not ready." The Whig convention had been a farce. It should have provided for united action with the Free Soilers, but it "passed capital resolves all pointing to Fusion, and proceed to nominate an entire Whig ticket! This was like asking your friend to join you in a pic-nic and yourself eating up all the mutually supplied viands before he could arrive." The Albany machine, and

96 Greeley to Colfax, Nov. 6, NYPL. To Seward, Oct. 25, Seward MSS., Auburn.
97 The final count was Clark 156,804; Seymour, 156,495; Ullman, 122,282; Bronson, 33,850. Raymond polled 362 votes more than Clark, but had a plurality of 28,333 since the Soft nominee for lieutenant governor ran behind Seymour by a total of 27,662. This would seem to indicate that the temperance men supported Raymond, but that the liquor interests were concerned only with Seymour. *Whig Almanac . . . 1855* (New York, 1854). 54.
98 *DTri.*, Nov. 8.

especially Seward, was censured for this injustice and for the disappointment which followed at the polls. "The man who should have impelled and guided the general uprising of the Free States," Greeley complained, "lives in Auburn, and his name is William H. Seward. Instead, however, of taking the position which circumstances and his own antecedents seemed to require, Mr. Seward, adhering to the vacant shell of Whiggery, has stood aside and allowed the great movement of the Free States to go forward without a word of bold and hearty encouragement or sympathy from its national leader."[99]

On November 9, two days after the polls had closed, Greeley marked time, awaiting more returns. The following evening he excused himself editorially. "How tame and spiritless was the canvass!" He was not at fault. He had "earnestly appealed for a union of the friends of Freedom, without regard to old party names, which had long ceased to indicate real differences of principle."[100] On Saturday the 11th, despair overwhelmed him. A false report had come into the *Tribune* office. It was believed that Clark's total had been padded, and that Seymour was "certainly chosen governor."[101] That evening Greeley wrote a long letter to Seward.

It was high time, he announced, to dissolve "the political firm of Seward, Weed, and Greeley . . . " He asked Seward not to get upset. He would not make a fanfare of his departure, and he would support Seward's return to the senate in February; but he hoped the public would, after a time, cease to think of the three men as a team.

He told Seward why he was pulling out. Time had been ripe that fall for his election as governor, but Weed had cut him down from behind with reasoning that was timid and faulty. Fearlessness alone would have assured both Seward's return to Washington and a Democratic reversal in the state. Now Douglas' political horse had won, with Seymour remaining in the Albany saddle. "I suspect it is true," Greeley

99 *DTri.*, Nov. 9. 100 *DTri.*, Nov. 11.
101 *DTri.*, Nov. 13.

confessed, "that I could not have been elected Governor as a Whig." That was not his argument. Had his partners been willing, "there *would* have been a party in the State, ere this, which could and would have elected me to any post, without injuring me or endangering your reëlection." Still unsatisfied, Weed had forced the bitterest dregs down his throat. Greeley would have "gloried" in running for lieutenant governor on the Whig ticket, but the "nomination was given to Raymond,—the fight left to me. And, Governor Seward, *I have made it*, though it be conceited in me to say so." He felt that neither Weed nor Raymond had worked heartily for Clark. What compensation did he get for toting this tremendous burden alone? He was throwing up his interest in a concern which paid no dividends.[102]

This letter reached Seward after some delay, for he was taking the waters at Saratoga Springs. On November 21, Seward wrote Weed. Misjudging the alienation as temporary, he promised that Greeley had "no idea of saying or doing any thing wrong or unkind, but it is sad to see him unhappy, I hardly know how he is to be approached just now?" Seward knew the source of the trouble: "Raymond[']s nomination and election is [*sic*] hard for him to bear . . . " How could a reconciliation be brought about? Could Weed not find some harmless appointive office for their estranged companion? "I think this is a good letter to burn," Seward concluded. "I wish I dared do Greeley so great a kindness as to burn his."[103]

Apparently Seward wrote Greeley on the same day, but this communication has not been found. Greeley's response to it, however, is revealing: "My Political life is ended. Do not regard me as dissatisfied with what has been. There was a time when it would have been precious to me to have had some public and palpable recognition that I was accounted

102 Greeley to Seward, Nov. 11, Greeley, *Recollections*, 315-320. Greeley's italics.
103 Seward to Weed, Nov. 21, Weed MSS., RRL.

107

worthy among others. But my mother, for whose sake I should have valued this, is now paralytic, almost unconscious, and can hardly live through the winter. I have no other relative for whom I care much to whom my elevation would be a triumph, and I only ask to be permitted to glide out of the arena as quietly and as speedily as may be." He wished to retire to his little farm up the Hudson valley at Chappaqua. He had partners to whom the *Tribune* was merely a piece of property, and he thought it could be rendered more valuable in hands other than his own. Seward need not worry, the *Times* could serve the Albany machine in the future.

Seward must have vigorously defended Weed, for Greeley closed with a glowing tribute: "I do not think I ever could have stood so long and so steadily before the cannon's mouth by your side as by Weed's; for Weed, with all his faults and all his unintended harshness toward me (the more severe *because* unintended) is still in my judgment *the* man of New-York."[104]

As Seward journeyed from his home in Auburn to Washington for the last session in his first senate term, he stopped off in New York City and walked around to the *Tribune* building. The conversation lasted for an hour. The editor's frame of mind was low because of fiscal troubles, Seward reported to Weed: "But below this is chagrin at the failure to obtain official position which he now admits could not have been secured if he had been nominated."[105]

Doubtless Seward's chief worry at the moment was his reelection. The menace of the Know Nothings was omnipresent. A close friend "never saw Weed feel quite so bad."[106] Could Weed be sure that his Know Nothing Whig assembly-

[104] Greeley to Seward, Nov. 24, Seward MSS., Auburn. Greeley's parentheses and italics. See also to George E. Baker, Feb. 8, 1855, Barnes, *Weed*, II, 232.

[105] Seward to Weed, Dec. 2, Weed MSS., RRL. Seward apparently did not fully understand the financial plight of the *Tribune* Association, for he told Weed that Greeley was concerned, among other things, over "the loss of subscribers."

[106] Blatchford to Seward, Dec. 7, Weed MSS., RRL.

men would keep their pledge? The legislature met early in 1855, and Weed kept a constant watch over the doubtful members. Seward was returned to the capital with a surprising majority.[107]

There was no cause for alarm over Greeley's immediate behavior. The *Tribune* upheld Seward until after his 1855 triumph; but in an editorial that followed close upon this event, Greeley openly, if indirectly, declared his political independence. New York, he began, was proud to be represented in the senate by so outstanding a statesman. Seward's position was now assured until 1861, and Greeley knew Seward would "discountenance any efforts to make him a candidate meantime for a higher station." Then, for the first time, Greeley pointed a finger of scorn at the supposed corruption within the Albany machine. He explained that should this be Seward's last public trust, his aspirations would not thereby be baffled. Unfortunately Seward had been too pliable to the "influences which bear sway in the tainted atmosphere of the Senate. The vice of the time is Complaisance, and from this vice Gov. Seward has not been wholly free. Noisily accused of sacrificing the interests of his constituents by ultraism and fanaticism, his real shortcoming has been the very opposite of that attributed to him. In an age of overwhelming peculation, we cannot remember that he has once denounced in the Senate an act of public robbery ... we do not recollect he has once raised his voice decidedly against the Senatorial stealing ... "[108]

It had been a hard campaign, and Greeley was a sick man when it was finished. It would be foolish to follow his reasoning, and assign to Weed and Seward the blame for his neurotic condition. The fact is that he and Weed came to a parting of their ways when the *Tribune* outgrew its swaddling clothes. Greeley then became too ambitious and too meddlesome. Raymond was better suited to maintain a Manhattan journal for the Albany machine, for he alone appreciated

[107] Bancroft, *Seward*, I, 374-379. [108] *DTri.*, Feb. 7, 1855.

Weed's position, his lobbying activities, his contacts with men of all political opinions, his conservative political views. Raymond understood, finally, the basic source of Weed's strength, control of the legislature; for it mattered little to Weed who filled the governor's mansion, so long as he was a reliable fellow fully cognizant of the practical aspects of politics. Only with the backing of the legislature could Weed hope to exert state and national political pressure. Raymond accepted this situation.

Greeley's prestige rested on moral foundations, its structure consisting of section-wide propaganda. Practical politics stood in the way of his personal dream, gaining an elective office. For these reasons he hated the professional politician. To speculate as to when the partnership would have collapsed if Greeley had not sought the governorship in 1854 is useless. It could not have lasted much longer. The chief ingredients of Greeley's complex character, his preoccupation with the reform movement and his personal ambition, combined to end forever his subordination to Albany.

Seward held presidential hopes, and his case differed slightly from Weed's; but, being a wise man, Seward based his aspirations chiefly on Weed's power, and only in the final instance on newspaper propaganda. Both he and Weed rightly refused to jeopardize home state strength in 1854 merely to satisfy the political appetite of a journalist. Within a few years they would seek Greeley's support, and doubtless they foresaw this contingency. They thought Greeley could be brought around when the time was right. They miscalculated. Only after they had failed in this endeavor in 1860 would they take advantage of the simple honesty of Greeley's disappointed letter and attempt to damn him as a sneaking little office-seeker.

Had Greeley approached his problems with more logic and less emotion, he would never have tangled himself into a neurotic knot. He would have realized that his career as an editor and as a politician depended on his ability to play a

110

lone hand in New York state, otherwise his talents would be restricted or even suppressed. But he had grown up, journalistically, with Weed and Seward. He should not be judged too harshly.

At last he was free, politically independent. Relieved of a great burden, he was for the moment miserable. He needed a vacation, as he said, "to cool my fevered brain and renovate my overtasked energies."[109] Temporarily he turned his paper over to Dana and Pike, and joined his hypochondriac wife and their ailing children in Europe. While he jaunted about the Continent, his substitutes were given the important assignment of unfurling the Republican banner from the *Tribune* masthead.

[109] Greeley to Seward, Nov. 11, Greeley, *Recollections*, 315-320.

111

CHAPTER 4

KNOW NOTHING OR KNOW SOMETHING?

"Sam" is *every where*, is directed by his Anti-Slavery friends, & is a good fellow. . . . Seward *must* see *Sam,* as soon as he can, or he *cannot succeed*—at any rate, *in the West.*—A. M. Hackley of the Dubuque (Iowa) *Tribune* to Weed, February 16, 1854.

ENMESHED as he had been in the snarls of machine politics, Greeley never had a chance to launch the Republican party formally in the columns of the *Tribune.* He left this task to Dana and Pike as he prepared to sail for Europe, and they were fully capable of handling so grave a responsibility.

Republicanism had been born with the introduction of the Nebraska bill into the senate, but it faced a dire peril in its infancy. The Know Nothings menaced it with strangulation. This threat had to be removed before the *Tribune* could nourish the Republican party into full manhood.

In 1854 the Americans had elected numerous local tickets, many congressmen, and nine governors. It is safe to say that a tenth gubernatorial candidate, Daniel Ullman, would have been successful but for Weed's manipulations in New York. What Weed had done locally for the Whigs must be repeated nationally for the Republicans, or else the Know Nothings would emerge the outstanding opposition party to the Democrats.

Greeley had from the first believed that the Americans were kidnapping potential Republicans and burying them away behind the secret rituals of their lodges. As he put it: "Know-Nothingism is but the outworking of an idea. It is but one of the many forms of protest against the corruptions of party politics, and especially against the deep treachery of the leaders of the Nebraska party to the vital principles of Democracy."[1]

Firmly believing that many Hindoos could, with proper inducement, be ushered into the ranks of the Republicans, Greeley set the policy of his paper before he embarked for Europe. He examined the Know Nothing doctrine and noted that its chief principle was a suffrage requirement of twenty-one years residence for all foreign born citizens. Voting regulations are supervised by the states. The organization had no nation-wide platform, and Greeley concluded that it was as "devoid of the elements of persistence as an anti-Cholera or anti-Potato-Rot party would be."[2]

The objective which Greeley left behind as he sailed for Europe early in April, 1855, was simple but drastic: Dana and Pike must smoke out the anti-Nebraskans from the Hindoo camp and groom them for entry into the Republican fold.

Know Nothing leaders were aware of danger from such men as Greeley. Since they were bent upon building a national and not a sectional party, it was clear that the slavery controversy loomed as their greatest hazard. They expected to surmount it by strict discipline, for theirs was a political army pyramided for unity of action. Its base was rooted in mass lodge membership all over the country and it rose through district and state control centers into the Grand National Council, loadstone of the lot. The native born were to be inspired with hatred for everything "foreign," and were to be taught to love George Washington, the "American way of life," and the constitution as it was, slavery included.

Those who drew up this plan and began to construct its edifice of solidarity were doomed to failure. In order to take a stand against sectional antagonism, it was necessary that they agree on what the constitution said about slavery in the

[1] *WTri.*, June 24, 1854. [2] *Whig Almanac . . . 1855*, 23.

territories, and this they were unable to do. That the subject should have given rise to differences of opinion is not surprising, but the important fact is that their debates were fatal. Bickering opened wide seams of discord. Soon the "Know Somethings," northerners who wanted above all else the restriction of slavery, swarmed into the parade of the *Tribune* and its cohorts. The remainder continued to argue until they were split into "South Americans" and "North Americans," pro and antislavery, and these found refuge in the major parties. By 1860 only a remnant rummaged amidst the pulverized mortar of what had been a grandiose undertaking.

Weed began the decomposition of the American party by compelling its leaders to take notice of the slavery issue. His maneuver securing the anti-Nebraskan Whig gubernatorial nomination for a Know Nothing, Myron H. Clark, had split the Hindoo following in the Empire State. Shortly after this event, the Grand National Council, meeting in Cincinnati, undertook a revision of the ritual in an effort to mitigate antislavery friction. The oath for those of highest standing within the order, the third degree, was modified. These were the members judged fit for public office, and they must thereafter swear to stamp out controversy over slavery. Those simply affiliated, the first degree, and those deemed worthy of trust within the local lodges, the second degree, were not affected.

It was wrongly hoped that this limited change would circumvent trouble. The new pledge supported the Kansas-Nebraska act, for to repeal it would augment antagonism. Many northerners refused to play the game. Purges followed as the revised formulary produced disaffection throughout the free states.[3] In Ohio the Know Somethings published

---

[3] Scisco, "Nativism," 100-104, 133-144. Billington, *Crusade,* 380-388. Henry Wilson, *History of the Rise and Fall of the Slave Power in America,* II (Boston, 1874), 421-422, says that the third degree was sponsored by southern unionists who wished to stamp out secession sentiment in their section.

their opposition to slavery extension and popery alike, and soon this faction was disrupting parent lodges in the west.[4] Antislavery sentiment was so predominant in many New England states that the order from Cincinnati was flouted. Under ex-cobbler Henry Wilson's guidance, the Know Nothing machinery of Massachusetts was slowly converted to an engine of Republicanism.[5] On the side line the *Tribune* cheered.

Wilson's career as a Know Nothing must be reviewed briefly, for it was in cooperation with him that the *Tribune* helped to produce the first nation-wide split in the American party. He had been early to enter the Hindoo cavalcade although he was an antislavery enthusiast. He said that hundreds of thousands who had little faith in Know Nothing principles joined up in order to serve "the higher claims of justice and humanity," which these individuals were able to do since they "were willing to use its machinery to disrupt the Whig and Democratic parties, in the confident hope that, out of the disorganized masses, then would come a great political party antagonistic to the dominating influences of the Slave Power." Wilson's aim was to build a national free soil organization. Testimony from both conservative Edward Everett and radical Thomas Wentworth Higginson—fellow citizens of Massachusetts who agreed on little else—relates that Wilson was out to gain this end by inducing the southerners to send men of northern sentiments to Washington. In short, Wilson wanted to breed a few slave state doughfaces.[6]

[4] *Tribune* correspondence from Cleveland, Mar. 20, *DTri.,* Mar. 24, 1855. John P. Hale to Weed, Feb. 2, 1855, Weed MSS., RRL. C. H. Ray to E. Washburne, Apr. 21, 1855, Washburne MSS., II, LC.
[5] George H. Haynes, "The Causes of Know-Nothing Success in Massachusetts," *American Historical Review,* III (Oct., 1897), 67-82.
[6] Wilson, *Slave Power,* II, 419-434. Higginson to Pike, Feb. 9, 1857, Pike, *First Blows,* 360. Everett to Mrs. Charles Eames, June 4, 1855 (copy), Everett MSS., MHSL. Wilson to Israel Washburn, Jr., May 28, 1854, Washburn MSS., I, LC. To Charles Sumner, Feb. 26, Mar. 15, 16, July 2, 1854, Sumner MSS., HCL.

115

The Americans in Massachusetts sent Wilson to the senate late in 1854, and as he entered that august body the southern Know Nothing press is said to have affirmed his "soundness" on the slavery question in "one united voice." Hindoo papers below the Potomac were especially anxious to convince their readers that their party was not antislavery. The crucial slave state test for their political team would come on May 24, 1855, when they would contest Democratic control of Virginia. Inopportunely that spring, Wilson spoke against slavery, and his remarks were featured in the Democratic press of the Old Dominion to prove that the northern lodges were abolitionist. The American nominee for governor was beaten by a narrow margin, and Know Nothingism started its decline as a power in the south.[7]

This defeat cast a pall of dissension over the Grand National Council which convened two weeks later in Philadelphia. Wilson was on hand as a delegate. He later said that he had decided to break Americanism apart unless it took a "moderate but positive" antislavery stand.[8] Before he finished he had knifed Know Nothing unity.

Here the *Tribune* entered the picture. Dana hired Samuel Bowles, influential editor and publisher of the Springfield (Mass.) *Republican*, to cover the meetings of the council. Bowles could not get on the floor of the conclave. He was not a delegate, not even a member of a lodge; in fact, he detested Know Nothingism. He went to Philadelphia, and as the *Tribune's* anonymous correspondent blazoned the council's controversies on slavery before the world.[9] His exposés had their comical side, for all lodge members were pledged to secrecy—and were particularly instructed to guard the delib-

[7] James P. Hambleton, *A Biographical Sketch of Henry A. Wise* . . . (Richmond, 1856), 236-245. See also, Barton H. Wise, *The Life of Henry A. Wise* . . . (New York, 1899), 165-205.
[8] Wilson to Parker (June ?, 1855), Elias Nason and Thomas Russell, *The Life and Public Services of Henry Wilson* (Boston, 1876), 130-132.
[9] Bowles also reported for his paper and the Boston *Atlas*. George S. Merriam, *The Life and Times of Samuel Bowles* (New York, 1885), I, 137-139. Richard Hooker, *The Story of an Independent Newspaper* (New York, 1924), 70-75.

erations of the governing body from the eyes of the press. Just who Bowles' informers were is hard to say, but there are indications. Greeley's comrade Schuyler Colfax figured prominently in the Indiana delegation, and Wilson himself later praised Dana, Pike, and Hildreth for their unrelenting endeavors in the early phase of the antislavery crusade.[10] The angry Know Nothings failed to locate the *Tribune* scribe, and Bowles enjoyed baiting them on this point. "A live Jesuit is here," he wrote soon after his arrival in Philadelphia. The next day, he observed that "Father Galand the Jesuit is still around and is suspected of being the Reporter for THE TRIBUNE. Is he a spiritual medium?"[11] Perhaps not, Bowles suggested: "It is believed that a Catholic spy has been discovered in the Council in the person of one of the members from an extreme Southern State. He is observed taking full notes of all its proceedings, is exclusive in his devotions to silence and non-action save when the Catholic question is up, when he is quite on his tops; has been seen going to the room of the Jesuit Father Galand, who is stopping at one of the principal hotels; and finally and conclusively in the eyes of those who are watching him, he was observed to make his dinner exclusively of fish on *Friday*. There is a good deal of burning indignation getting up in bigoted Protestant hearts on the subject, and threats of an explosion in the Council over it are muttered in various quarters."[12] Finally, Bowles took compassion on the bewildered searchers, and vowed to unmask the *Tribune* correspondent. He could be easily spotted the next day on the Camden and Amboy ferry, for he would be "The Man with the Carpetbag."[13]

In addition to the understanding with Bowles, the *Tribune's* staff was ready to sustain Wilson's tactics with edi-

---

[10] Wilson, *Slave Power*, II, 407-408.
[11] From Phila., June 7, 8, *DTri.*, June 8, 9 (unless otherwise noted, all dates for the remainder of this chapter will be understood as 1855). *Tribune's* upper case.
[12] From Phila., June 9, *DTri.*, June 11. Bowles' italics.
[13] From Phila., June 14, *DTri.*, June 15.

torials. George E. Baker, one-time *Tribune* Washington correspondent and biographer of Seward, was confused and frightened by plans underway. He made haste to write Seward, whose *bête noire* was Americanism, that "Pike is disposed to make terms with Satan I think—He says, *combined*, K[now] N[othing]ism & Anti Slavery can sweep the country—divided Slavery must triumph."[14] Pike was out for fusion, but only on Republican grounds.

During the spring and early summer of 1855, the *Tribune* had taken the same position on the slavery question that Wilson would occupy in Philadelphia that June. Pike wrote most of these editorials, their temper differing from his employer's earlier stand. Late in 1854, Greeley had rejected as insufficient a mere redrawing of the Missouri Compromise line. His Republican party would insist that slavery be excluded from all territories. This alone, he stated, was "a reparation, broad and full enough to satisfy the deceived and outraged North, and allay the indignant feeling of the truly democratic masses of the free States."[15] Pike now evaded the use of the word "Republican" and indorsed the 1820 settlement as the *Tribune's* goal. "We are two peoples," he exhorted. "We are a people for Freedom and a people for Slavery. Between the two conflict is inevitable. A victory will be won against Freedom, or Slavery will be driven back over the ruins of its gross usurpations and confined within its legitimate limits under the Constitution." It was time to wake up, he protested. While the south worked to extend chattel labor, "the North—the money-making, busy, outraged North —secure in its own tranquillity and prosperity . . . gives symptoms of relapsing into a mere armed neutrality, or what is worse, of expending its zeal, energy, and virtuous indigna-

---

[14] Baker to Seward, Apr. 19, Seward MSS., Auburn. Baker's italics. To this letter Baker added a marginal note: "Greeley told me a few days before he left that the Democrats should triumph in preference to allowing the KN[']s any success."

[15] *DTri.*, Dec. 16, 1854. Greeley would bring the *Tribune* temporarily back to this position on his return from Europe, *DTri.*, Sept. 24. See also notes 2-3, chapter x.

tion in disputations and quarrels over the growth of one among fifty religious denominations, and the dangers of an increment, by immigration from foreign States, of our free population."[16] The *Tribune* was willing to lay aside all other questions and work for the restoration of the Missouri Compromise, an issue on the decision of which hung "the character of the Government for many years. We shall remain a Union of balanced powers, or we shall become, in effect, a consolidated Government in the hands of the slave oligarchy, to whom the free states must be tributary and obedient in every political relation, or whose domination they must rebelliously spurn."[17] The free states must unite in this critical hour. Should the Philadelphia council avoid the discussion of slavery, it could only mean that free labor was being duped, that the Know Nothings were creating a monster of evil, the head of which was "to be Southern, and the tail Northern."[18]

On the eve of the gathering in Philadelphia, Pike predicted that "it will make a vain effort to cover with a little ashes the great smouldering volcano of Northern sentiment." As a result, the Know Nothing rank and file would revolt. There was no neutrality on the slavery question. "The moment the new party begins to act in the domain of National politics it must be on one side or the other." Pike had no patience with the "Boo-hoos," men who sobbed that the Union would be dissolved. He had something else to do "besides attending to the tears and moans of a few political old women and effete office seekers." The *Tribune* agreed with the rabidly southern Charleston *Mercury*: there was but one controversy and that was human bondage.[19]

So it developed that the Know Somethings were ready to divide their party when the delegates assembled on June 5, and the *Tribune* was prepared to advertise the break to the world. Friction soon arose over the slavery issue, and Dana

16 *DTri.*, Apr. 12.   17 *DTri.*, Apr. 19.
18 *DTri.*, May 8. See also *DTri.*, Apr. 28, May 7, 15, 16, 18, 24, 26, 28, 29, 31.
19 *DTri.*, June 2, 4.

asked with satire as lacking in subtlety as a sledge-hammer: "When will men allow this subject to rest?"[20] Bowles reported that southern delegates favored seating certain avowed Catholics from the deep south, which proved that these Americans were proslavery and not anti-popery. Southern rage, he added, was intense against the Massachusetts delegation, and especially against Wilson.[21]

For six days the preliminaries continued, each side looking for an opening and many delegates amazed at the accurate publicity their convention was receiving. Then came the crisis with the majority report from the committee on resolutions. Dana knew what was transpiring. On the day before he had written that the slavery problem must be faced: "The secrecy of the Council cannot hide from popular indignation and overthrow men who betray free constituencies. A war of extermination against Northern doughfaces will be waged this year and the next in the Free States that will know no mercy and be fatal to the whole race."[22]

Southern delegates, aided by those of New York, the Minnesota Territory, and the District of Columbia, dominated the committee on resolutions. It proposed that agitation be smothered by sustaining popular sovereignty, that the existing laws upon the subject of slavery were final and conclusive. The minority report, signed by Colfax among others, demanded repeal of the detested Kansas-Nebraska act.[23]

Know Something hopes soared. The slavery forces were taking such extreme ground that even the northern moderates must revolt. There had been a possibility that Governor Henry J. Gardner of Massachusetts would head the northern opposition to a sectional party. Now his conformity could be

20 *DTri.*, June 6. See also *DTri.*, June 7.
21 From Phila., June 6, *DTri.*, June 7.
22 *DTri.*, June 11. Pike's editorials ceased temporarily around June 1. He was married on June 5, and presumably went on a honeymoon. *WTri.* ("Married" column), June 23.
23 From Phila., June 11, *DTri.*, June 12.

expected. "Do you seek to wear a martyr's crown?" he was asked. No more was said.

But Gardner refused to go all the way with the antislavery faction. Bowles and others had already drafted a tentative secession address which was a Republican rather than a nativist document.[24] It praised the constitution, pronounced bondage a moral wrong, affirmed congressional jurisdiction over the territories, demanded the unconditional restoration of the Missouri Compromise, and asked for a fusion of all freedom loving men, irrespective of religion or place of birth. Gardner read it over and fumed he *"would be d----d if he would be abolitionized, anyhow."* It was necessary to let him write the call which was later used, and he told Wilson he would remain in the council if the convention voted down the proposal of the committee on resolutions and followed a neutral course.

Bowles and his boys were discouraged. Their call for Republicanism was stalled, and a conciliatory trend might take the game away from the radicals who were few in numbers and weak in prestige.[25]

The *Tribune* gave the Know Somethings a shot in the arm. Dana praised them for the "brave and manly way in which they carry the war into Africa." The next day he published a dispatch from Milledgeville, Georgia. The Democrats in convention assembled had occupied an extreme proslavery position. "Let the North take her ground as distinctly and firmly as the South," he requested, "and a speedy end will be put to the dispute. We have not the slightest fear that this settlement would lead to disunion."[26] Bowles, reporting from Philadelphia, asserted that there was no middle ground; the least the north would accept was the repeal of the Nebraska legislation: "If the South cannot grant that, the

24 Merriam, *Bowles,* i, 138-139.
25 (Bowles) to the *Tribune* from (?), dated Oct. 27, and signed "The Tribune's Correspondent at the Philadelphia Council," *DTri.,* Oct. 31. Copied as printed. See also Wilson, *Slave Power,* ii, 422-432.
26 *DTri.,* June 14, 13.

organization better divide. That issue is to be fought out— Freedom to Kansas, the restoration of the Missouri Compromise—and the party . . . which falters on it will be crushed to atoms in the surging, swelling tide of popular feeling which the trial of that issue will evoke."[27]

Bowles was doing his job almost too well. He became anxious lest the doughface stories he had spread so widely force the New York delegation to reject the majority plank sustaining the Kansas-Nebraska act. This move would swing the entire convention toward a reconciliation with Gardner and the moderates. New York's representation on the resolutions committee had supported the southerners. The lodges in the Empire State had been cleared of their antislavery enthusiasts when the Sewardites had withdrawn during the Clark election, and among the free state delegations the New Yorkers were unique, and none too happy, in their strong proslavery attitude. In the end they held firm, and the Nebraska plank was adopted.[28]

Conciliation having failed, the Know Somethings withdrew and released Gardner's "Address to the People." It asked for restoration of the Missouri Compromise, a more rigid naturalization law, and appointment of none but native born to diplomatic posts. It was signed by all the delegates from Massachusetts, Maine, and Ohio, a majority of those from Indiana, Illinois, and Vermont, and a minority from New Hampshire, Connecticut, Rhode Island, Michigan, Wisconsin, and Iowa.

The refusal of the majority to compromise had made possible Know Something success. Bowles rejoiced: "Thank God! *There is a North* at last."[29] Dana praised the conduct of the Know Somethings, who "went out of the Convention because they were high-souled men, and not cringing, heart-

[27] From Phila., June 13, *DTri.*, June 14.
[28] From Phila., June 13, 14, *DTri.*, June 14, 15.
[29] Some of the Pennsylvania and New Jersey delegates also seceded, but signed a second address. From Phila., June 14, *DTri.*, June 14, 15. Bowles's italics.

less doughfaces." Their address showed no "bitterness" toward foreigners. Its purpose was "simply to Americanize America."[30] Bowles later explained why he and Dana were so happy: "The leading northern delegates . . . agreed to go home, and throw up the American organization as an organization, in order to unite the North in an all-powerful and effective party against the aggressiveness of Slavery."[31]

The time had come for the *Tribune* to speak freely of the Republican party. An editorial observed that a "disposition will now naturally be felt in many quarters to abandon the secret devices of the Know-Nothings and to take the field for future contests with the honest Republican system of free discussion and open, independent voting." The way had been cleared for "that Northern Republican party which may yet give peace to the nation and redeem it from the cankers and shames that have been growing upon it for many years."[32] Another editorial announced that while former Whigs such as Robert Toombs of Georgia were dreaming of calling the roll of their slaves on Bunker Hill and for that reason were rushing into the Democratic camp, it was cheering to note that "the same process of the dissolution of parties has produced a corresponding movement in behalf of Freedom at the North."[33]

Dana and Pike were more sectionalistic than Greeley. On his return from Europe, he would attempt to introduce Republicanism among the lower economic groups in the south, but even to Greeley this end would be secondary to the consolidation of a strong antislavery party in the north.

On August 8, Greeley stepped briskly down the gangway of the good ship *Baltic* out of Liverpool. He was refreshed

[30] *DTri.*, June 15.
[31] (Bowles) to the *Tribune*, Oct. 27, *DTri.*, Oct. 31. A collection of the Bowles papers has been promised to the Princeton University Library in 1950.
[32] *DTri.*, June 15.
[33] *DTri.*, June 25. See also, *DTri.*, June 16, 18, July 2, 4, 12, 19, 20, 28, Aug. 7.

and eager to reenter the slavery controversy,[34] but bad news awaited him. His mother had recently died, and he hastened along on a sad journey to the family home in northwestern Pennsylvania. His heart was heavy with grief, but as he went back to New York City, he stopped off at least once to lecture at a county fair.[35] His hold on the public seemed firmer than ever, and he took new courage. More and more of his fellow citizens were learning of and admiring his mission in life, and he must not disappoint them. Book stands along the way were featuring one of the popular biographies of the decade, James Parton's *The Life of Horace Greeley*. It was about this time that Thomas Wentworth Higginson encountered Greeley, who was "observed by all, and people tried to make the newsboys sell him his own life."[36]

After an absence of four months, Greeley again mounted the stairs of the *Tribune* building, and listened to the reports of his assistants. Everything seemed to be going well. He seized a quill and wrote an editorial: "To our mind, Justice, Policy, Patriotism, Consistency, imperatively require that every Whig should hold out the flag of amity to every Democrat who agrees with us on the great issue of the day. If we really believe the passage of the Kansas bill the outrage we have so often proclaimed it, we ought to be foremost in forgetting all past differences, in exhorting all to one common effort for the redress of this gigantic wrong." Nothing— protection, internal improvements, not even temperance— would be allowed to obstruct this course. "Thenceforth, the Republican movement, judiciously conducted, will go forward conquering and to conquer."[37]

[34] Greeley to Samuel Sinclair, July 5, Greeley MSS.; NYPL.
[35] Lecture MS., Bucks County Historical Society Library, Doylestown, Pa.
[36] Higginson to his home (Aug. ?), Mary T. Higginson, *Thomas Wentworth Higginson* . . . (Boston, 1914), 133. See also T. W. Higginson, *Contemporaries* (Cambridge, 1900), 49.
Parton's work sold 30,000 copies within a few months. Constance M. Rourke, *Trumpets of Jubilee* (New York, 1927), 313. James C. Derby, *Fifty Years Among Authors* . . . (New York, 1884), 220-224.
[37] *DTri.*, Aug. 24.

CHAPTER 5

IN WHICH MR. GREELEY
IS CANED

Charge Dana not to slaughter anybody,
but be mild and meek-souled like me.—
Greeley to Pike, February 15, 1856.

THE TRIBUNE office was filled with overconfidence when Greeley got back from Europe. Dana was starry-eyed from visualizing Republican prospects, and he could hardly contain himself as he related the details of the American party fiasco in Philadelphia the previous June: "The Knownothings, thank God, are in their graves. What a short life they had of it!"[1]

Dana was wrong, and Greeley learned better the hard way. Pitched battles were ahead before the American party was ready for burial. All the ammunition in the *Tribune's* arsenal, which by this time included the dumdums of a "Bleeding Kansas," failed to repulse the Know Nothings and prevent their carrying the off-year 1855 campaign. On they charged, but by arduous efforts the Republican leaders managed to isolate their left flank and throw confusion into their headquarters by electing a Know Something speaker of the 34th House of Representatives. Greeley was armed to the teeth and much in evidence at Washington as his own chief *Tribune* correspondent during this long and bitter contest for the speakership, but he conducted himself none too brilliantly in the front lines. He was too aggressive, an easy target for enemy sharpshooters.

[1] Dana to Pike, Aug. 23 (unless otherwise noted, all dates in this chapter will be understood as 1855), Pike, *First Blows*, 297-298.

These tactical errors were of little importance in the final analysis. Greeley was drawing up plans for a larger campaign, and in outlining Republican strategy for the coming presidential engagement, he was more adept. Battlefield experience in Washington was a contributing factor to his later success. He was under fire from December, 1855 until mid-April, 1856. He suffered bodily fear, physical violence, and mental anguish. He withdrew from Washington a more practical warrior who would better serve his party's cause in 1856.

Greeley entered the political fracas directly on his return from abroad. The Republican outlook for the off-year elections was good. In New York the Know Nothings put up the historian Joel T. Headley for secretary of state, key post in the race, but their convention bogged down when it reached the slavery question. Despite the stand their delegation had recently taken in support of the pro-southern element at Philadelphia, they finally adopted a compromise resolution, upholding the Kansas-Nebraska act but declaring against the extension of slavery.[2] Greeley scoffed that the Philadelphia brokers had been unable to deliver the goods. He grinned as he labeled their platform "THE HINDOO BACK-OUT."[3]

Within the Democratic fold, the Hards and Softs remained at odds, the latter making a futile attempt to placate the Free Soilers by mildly censuring the administration's activities in Kansas.[4] William C. Bryant thought the gesture a hollow one and kept his erstwhile Democratic paper, the *Evening Post,* squarely behind the anti-Nebraska cause.[5] "A large mass of the Democratic vote," Greeley exulted, "is afloat."[6]

Prospective Republicans radiated harmony as they set about their salvage operations. Weed was ready for fusion,

<hr/>

[2] Alexander, *New York,* ii, 209-211, 214-216. [3] *DTri.,* Aug. 31.
[4] Dispatches and editorials, *DTri.,* Aug. 24, 29, 30, 31, Sept. 1.
[5] As summarized from the *Evening Post, DTri.,* Sept. 1.
[6] *DTri.,* Sept. 5.

not because of Greeley's influence, but as he wrote Seward: "The necessity of getting in line with other states is imperative."[7] Weed managed things neatly, lessening what resentment the Free Soilers might have carried over from 1854, when Raymond had been given preference over their choice for lieutenant governor. The Whig and Republican conventions met in Syracuse on the same day, September 26, when they organized separately, nominated identical tickets, and adopted the same platform. Then the Whigs marched amid jubilant shouting into the Republican hall. Preston King, a former Soft, was placed at the top of the slate. Greeley had a hand in the resolutions, which objected to the formation of additional slave states, denounced the administration's Kansas policy, repudiated the "anti-republican" secrecy of Know Nothingism, and echoed Jefferson's inaugural principle of 1801—" 'Equal and exact justice to all men . . .' "[8]

In the ensuing campaign, the *Tribune* exhibited a tendency which was unfortunate for the incipient Republican party. Greeley accepted Dana's impression that all the anti-Nebraskans had been carved from the American carcass, which was true neither in New York nor elsewhere. With this exception, the *Tribune* was a model of melodious pleading as it urged all comers to hop on the Republican bandwagon. It worked for success in local elections throughout the north, its staff aware that a solid foundation must be laid for the next year.

Greeley's anxiety for full accord is evidenced by his work in killing a separate prohibition ticket. Victory for the New York drys in 1854 had given them a blank check, and they cashed in with a rigid statute soon after taking office. The law, however, was poorly drawn, allowing its adversaries not only to brand it unconstitutional but also to sabotage its

[7] Weed to Seward, July 23, Seward MSS., Auburn.
[8] A Know Something group also fused at this time. Dispatches, correspondence, and editorials, *DTri.*, Sept. 24, 26, 27. Platform reprinted in *DTri.*, Oct. 2.

enforcement. Going into effect on an inauspicious day, July 4, 1855, it was respected only in some of the rural communities.[9] Validity of the law depended upon the verdict of the Court of Appeals, the highest in the state. The electorate was to pick a judge for that bench in the fall canvass, and the liquor interests had, in this instance, united the Hards and Softs behind their favorite, Samuel L. Selden. The prohibitionists had much at stake.

The Republican party, Greeley realized, could ill afford to be dry, for some members liked their legal drinks.[10] He decided to remove the issue from the political field in order to strengthen the crusade against human bondage. As a member of the State Temperance Committee, he was diligent in gaining the adherence of Maine law men to much of the anti-Nebraskan ticket.[11] The choice at Syracuse of a well known dry, Bradford R. Wood, for the Court of Appeals assisted him in swinging the prohibition convention behind the Republican party. Wood was defeated, and the *Tribune* scarcely noticed the verdict against prohibition in the spring of 1856.[12] Greeley's course was set. It was necessary to limit slavery before any salutary reform, local or otherwise, could be attained.

Likewise Greeley pulled in the *Tribune's* economic horns, which were so patently Whig that the Free Soilers might otherwise have been gored. Fewer editorials on protection and internal improvements appeared than in former years, and those carried were modified in tone. Free trade, he wheedled, was not all what these radical advocates of democracy thought. It did not benefit consumers, but was merely an outgrowth of slavery. As proof, he asked them to look to the

[9] *Laws of the State of New York*, 78th sess., 1855 (Albany, 1855), 340-356. *DTri.*, esp. Mar. 16, 23, Apr. 3, 7, 10, 20, 23, 25, 30, May 2, June 26, July 3, 6, 9, 11, 13.
[10] *DTri.*, Aug. 29, Sept. 10, 19, 29, Oct. 1, 20.
[11] Dispatches and editorials, *DTri.*, Sept. 10, 29, Oct. 1, 4, 5, 13.
[12] *DTri.*, Mar. 27, 29, 1856. 3 Kernan (New York), 378. Two vacancies on the Court of Appeals had been at stake in the 1855 election, but interest had centered on the important long-term race between Selden and Wood.

south, where such a policy denied railways, factories, and diversified labor to an entire section. Was not its sole purpose the maintenance of slave culture by assuring plantation owners ample foreign exchange for their staple crops?[13]

The *Tribune* welcomed former Democrats into the new party. Wishing them to feel at home while warming their hands over the Republican hearthstone, an editorial proclaimed: "We hope . . . the Republican party, which promises to be so strong in the coming contest, will take the pains to expose the extraordinary invasions of the rights of the States, which their enemies have committed and still menace. Let them plant themselves on the ancient and true republican grounds, on the original landmarks of the Constitution, and let them rally the nation, as Jefferson rallied it, to the support of local self-government and the rights of man."[14]

No flourish of fellowship was made toward the Know Nothings. Greeley vowed that he would never truckle to their bigoted spirit and that he would always defend the right of a citizen to the ballot. The American party, he repeated, was but a subterfuge of the Silver Greys, who sought to keep the north humbled under the heel of the south; for this reason, the Sham Democrats secretly supported that clique. There was but a single question, and it had only two sides, one for and the other against the spread of slavery. Know Nothingism had already faded into the darkness of the night where all hypocrisy belongs, so thought the *Tribune*.[15]

The charge that the Republicans were out to succor the negro was becoming current, and the derisive term "Black Republicans" was being used too generally for Greeley's comfort. He refuted the accusation with telling blows, saying that his party was the white man's hope, the only safeguard free labor knew; its aim was not emancipation and the elevation of bondsmen to equal rights with persons of lighter

[13] *DTri.*, Aug. 18, Sept. 5, 11, 12, 29, Oct. 2, 23, 25.
[14] *DTri.*, Aug. 1.   See also *DTri.*, Aug. 10, 18, 20, 28, 29, 31.
[15] *DTri.*, Aug. 24, Oct. 8, 13, 15, 19, 29.

complexion, but rather a restriction of slavery so as to prevent the government from becoming oligarchical.[16] From his *Tribune* rostrum he gave some "UNPALATABLE COUNSEL" to abolitionists of all colors. Personally he favored civil rights for negroes in the free states, he said, but agitators should cease holding conventions and screaming at the top of their lungs. He had no hope that even their immediate aim of removing the property qualification for negro voting in New York state could be attained "for many weary years." Meanwhile could they not keep quiet and avoid exposing to "popular odium" men such as himself who agreed with them? "One negro on a farm which he has cleared or bought, patiently hewing out a modest, toilsome independence," Greeley judged, "is worth more to the cause of Equal Suffrage than three in an Ethiopian (or any other) convention, clamoring against White oppression with all the fire of a Spartacus." Blacks should enjoy "the common Rights of Man," but they stood in need of the spirit with which those liberties had been gained by other races. They would never win them as "white men's barbers, waiters, ostlers and boot-blacks." Let them first secure "an intellectual and essential enfranchisement" through "toil, privation and suffering."[17]

Disassociating himself from the abolitionists was but an introduction to Greeley's major task. He must get conservatives to join the Republicans. His guidepost for this mission was "Bleeding Kansas." Domestic tranquillity was then as always the chief aim of the conservatives, and he wondered if popular sovereignty would give it to them: *"Is it possible to have peace if every foot of our common Territory is to be henceforth a battle-ground between Freedom and Slavery?"*[18] Greeley's answer was a resounding no; and for three years Kansas served as his greatest argument in winning advocates for the doctrine of restricting slavery.

16 *DTri.*, Aug. 24, Sept. 29, Oct. 8, 15, 25.
17 *DTri.*, Sept. 22. Greeley's parentheses. See also *DTri.*, Sept. 26, 29.
18 *DTri.*, Nov. 3. Greeley's italics.

Greeley tried to be a fair-minded man, but he was sometimes carried far from cool reason by the passions of the
hour. Certainly this was true when the Kansas issue was
flaunted. Like the proverbial bull, he snorted and raged and
kicked dust into the eyes of his readers.

The basis for his editorials on Kansas was letters received
from agents in that much abused territory. He would doubtless have discharged anyone who tried to refute his fixed
prejudices, yet it is regrettable that he did not employ less
emotional reporters.

He was determined to populate Kansas with men who loved
freedom. While the Nebraska bill was pending before the
senate, he began looking for articles on emigration prospects,
making it, as he said privately, his "first business" to publish
them in the *Tribune*.[19] Soon it was necessary to engage
correspondents on the scene, and the crew Greeley assembled
went forth with hatred in their hearts to battle slavedrivers
across the western plains.

Chief among them was William A. Phillips of Illinois, a
friend of Dana's. Intensely abolitionist, irritable, and finan-
cially interested in the free state cause, few equaled him in
bias. Others included the energetic Thomas Wentworth Higginson, disunionist minister from Worcester, Massachusetts;
John Henry Kagi, who was with John Brown at Harper's
Ferry; and James Redpath, later of Chautauqua fame, who
concluded in 1859 that slavery was war and that he would
"fight and kill for the sake of peace."[20]

[19] Greeley to Colfax, June 28, 1854, NYPL. See also to James Hall,
Feb. 24, 1854, Greeley MSS., NYPL.
[20] Redpath, *The Roving Editor: or, Talks with Slaves in the Southern
States* (New York, 1859), v-vii. Charles F. Horner, *The Life of James
Redpath* . . . (New York, 1926), 7-46, 50-110.
Oswald G. Villard, *John Brown* . . . (Boston, 1910), 679. *DTri.*, Oct. 24,
26, 27, 28, 1859.
Higginson, "A Ride through Kansas" (pamphlet) (New York? 1856?);
Letters and Journals of . . . , ed. Mary T. Higginson (Boston, 1921), 137-
144; M. Higginson, *Higginson*, 166-189.
Phillips, *The Conquest of Kansas, by Missouri and Her Allies* . . .
(Boston, 1856). Phillips to Lyman Trumbull, Feb. 12, 1856, Trumbull MSS.,
I, LC. *Transactions* of the Kansas State Historical Society, *1889-1896* . . . ,

The theater of operations for these opinionated journalists grew more intense every day. Plans to settle Kansas and Nebraska with antislavery stalwarts had been drawn up early in 1854. Eli Thayer, a Massachusetts firebrand for freedom, then launched the New England Emigrant Aid Company, with a widely heralded paper capital of $5,000,000, although only some $140,000 was collected. This society dispatched few settlers, but it was of great importance. It stimulated the organization of similar groups and committees throughout the north, and its officials in Kansas became leaders in the free state movement.[21]

Greeley had long contended that western lands should be colonized under the sponsorship of eastern funds. He felt that such a scheme offered opportunities to erect compact communities by providing liquid capital for schools, mills, and churches. To these expected advantages was now added the political compulsion inherent in the Nebraska legislation. Of course the *Tribune* backed Thayer's program.[22]

Southerners were impressed with the supposed wealth of the New England corporation. Directed by ex-Senator Atchison and Benjamin F. Stringfellow of Missouri, they in turn set out to prevent the so-called steal of Kansas by "abolition fanatics" from the north.[23] As Greeley had warned,

v (Topeka, 1896), 110-113. Wiley Britton, *Memoirs of the Rebellion on the Border, 1863* (Chicago, 1882), 89. *Kansas, a Cyclopedia of State History*, ed. Frank W. Blackmar (Chicago, 1912), II, 471-472.

[21] Samuel A. Johnson, "The Genesis of the New England Emigrant Aid Company," *New England Quarterly*, III (Jan., 1930), 95-122; "The Emigrant Aid Company in the Kansas Conflict," *Kansas Historical Quarterly*, VI (Feb., 1937), 21-33. Ralph V. Harlow, "The Rise and Fall of the Kansas Aid Movement," *American Historical Review*, XLI (Oct., 1935), 1-25. Edgar Langsdorf, "S. C. Pomeroy and the New England Emigrant Aid Company, 1854-1856," *Kansas Historical Quarterly*, VII (Aug., Nov., 1938), 227-245, 379-398. For the numbers sent by the New England organization, see Louise Barry "The Emigrant Aid Company Parties of 1854," and "The New England Emigrant Aid Company Parties of 1855," *Kansas Historical Quarterly*, XII (May, Aug., 1943), 115-155, 227-268, esp. 228.

[22] *DTri.*, May 29, 30, 31, June 22, 30, 1854.
Greeley, *Hints*, 42-47. Thayer, *The New England Emigrant Aid Company* . . . (Worcester, 1887), 20; *A History of the Kansas Crusade* . . . (New York, 1889), 36-51.

[23] Edward Channing, *A History of the United States*, VI (New York, 1925), 159-166.

the popular sovereignty race began under ominous circumstances.

For several months after the passage of the Nebraska measure, the *Tribune* remained pessimistic about the chances for freedom in the coming struggle. It reprinted strong proslavery pronouncements found in the southern press to prove that Kansas could be, and that the slaveowners expected it to be, turned over to enforced labor.[24] Monstrous ruffians from Missouri, rifles and whips in their hands, were depicted as flowing into the new territory, while only a trickle of northerners, blessed with "energy and native intelligence," found its way across the border.[25] Greeley pointed to Kansas as evidence of a grandiose effort to flood the continent with bondsmen. The Douglasites saw that "future acquisitions of territory south and west of our present limits are morally certain, and they want a principle established which will enable them to deal with all these as they did with Texas in her settlement, illegal introduction of slaves, revolution and annexation."[26]

A subtle purpose underlay this attitude of defeat. No large-scale emigration to Kansas could be expected before spring, and the *Tribune* was, in the meantime, bent upon rousing Yankee ire. Early in 1855, Pike began encouraging the settlement of Kansas by northerners. If the land was to be saved from the "Cossacks of civilization," a mighty emigration must be organized under resolute leaders and backed by abundant means.[27] Thereafter the *Tribune* urged anti-

24 *DTri.*, June 1, 3, 19, 24, 26, 28, July 6, 14, 1854.
25 *DTri.*, July 31, 1854. See also all correspondence from and editorials on Kansas, *DTri.*, summer, 1854.
26 *DTri.*, Aug. 22, 1854.
27 From Washington, Feb. 10, *DTri.*, Feb. 13. Reprinted in Pike, *First Blows*, 274-277.
Thayer had misunderstood the *Tribune's* tactics and had been disturbed by its pessimism. He informed Greeley that he knew of thousands who were going to Kansas in the spring, concluding: "The Slave power has no strength to contend against a monied organization which will be sure to pay its stockholders twenty five per cent per annum & enrich the emigrants which it controls in an [equal] ratio—" Thayer to Greeley, Feb. 2, Greeley MSS., NYPL.

slavery heroes to face the widely advertised southern hordes in Kansas and win the day for freedom.

The *Tribune* accused the administration of using undercover tactics in order to make Kansas slave, but there is nothing to sustain this charge of bad faith. As a matter of fact, the first territorial governor appointed, Andrew H. Reeder of Pennsylvania, is notable only for his ineptitude. He sowed seeds of trouble, leaving the Democrats to reap a whirlwind.

Appointed in June, 1854, Reeder did not manage to get out to Kansas until October of that year. Then in place of ordering a census and a territorial election, he went on a tour of inspection, on which he is said to have purchased likely parcels of real estate. He postponed the census until late winter, when there was snow on the ground, and scheduled the first election for March 30, 1855. Proslavery advocates were infuriated by these delays. They reasoned that Reeder wanted to give the mighty New England company time to overrun Kansas with abolitionists. On the day of balloting, armed men from Missouri, led by Atchison and Stringfellow and incited by whiskey, marched into the new territory. The resulting legislature was overwhelmingly pro-southern.[28]

This novel technique of winning a political contest caused the antislavery press to shake with rage. The *Tribune* was vigorous in denunciation. Pike roared: "An inevitable collision is before us, between the North and the South, on the question of Slavery Extension."[29] His colleagues joined the chorus. The free states must control Kansas; otherwise "their degradation is unspeakable, and they are fit only to live as the slaves of slaves";[30] otherwise, the prairies would eventually be hoary with sin and shame. Yankees should take courage. Kansas was wanted by the slaveholders as a manifestation of their "universal control on this Continent" and

---

[28] Albert J. Beveridge, *Abraham Lincoln, 1809-1858* (Boston, 1928), II, 310-313.

[29] *DTri.,* Apr. 13. [30] *DTri.,* Apr. 27.

as a place for the reproduction of bondsmen: "But a new
State cannot be a slave-breeding State. A virgin country
revolts, through an instinctive rigor of nature, against all
attempts to devote it to such loathsome uses. The infamous
occupation of breeding men and women for sale, flourished
only in the feculent muck accumulated from the corruptions
of whole generations of squalid servitude and incompetent
and slothful cupidity; such, for example, as the foul currents
of Slavery have deposited over the moral and physical wastes
of Maryland and Virginia."[31]

Little disturbed by these blasts from the east, Reeder kept
plodding along in Kansas. He avoided the question of
spurious votes by issuing certificates of election to almost all
those chosen, but he still had trouble with the legislature. One
reason was that he convoked the body early in July in Pawnee
City. This was an isolated town, existing on paper only, one
hundred and forty miles west of Missouri; but in his opening
message, the governor indicated that he expected it to become
the territorial capital. He had invested some money in adjacent lands. Over his protest, the members adjourned to a
more convenient locality and began their work. Reeder called
the sittings illegal and rejected their measures. Passing them
over his veto, the legislature established local governments
and laid the framework for statehood. The laws reflected a
marked proslavery bias, being modeled upon Missouri statutes but with harsher regulations governing negroes. The
legislature was out to stifle antislavery sentiment, one enactment specifying the death penalty for aiding a bondsman to
escape and another decreeing it a felony to attack the institution verbally.

The free state men were not caught unawares. Led by
Charles Robinson, experienced frontiersman and the Emigrant Aid Company's chief Kansas official, they held a
conclave at Big Springs. There they swore not to obey the
"bogus" laws passed by the territorial legislature. Late the

[31] *DTri.*, Apr. 18.

following October, they drew up a constitution at a convention in Topeka. They then held a private election, adopting the Topeka instrument and choosing state and local administrators.

By August the Pierce administration was sufficiently disgusted with Reeder's conduct to replace him with Wilson Shannon, former Democratic governor of Ohio. When Shannon arrived in Kansas, he found problems of the first magnitude to test his meager executive abilities. Two rival governments were functioning and there was threat of civil strife.[32]

Greeley could hardly have created a better background for Republican propaganda had he been the angel Gabriel. He made long use of Kansas, at the moment adapting the news from that territory toward trying to win the off-year campaign. He stressed his paper's predictions that the Democrats would sweat until slavery had been established on the western plains, utilizing Reeder's dismissal to illustrate his contention that popular sovereignty was but a cloak for the forces of evil. A *Tribune* somersault was necessary to make this point, but in such small matters Greeley was every inch an acrobat. Reeder had been damned roundly until his break with the administration, then overnight he was pictured as a shining knight unsheathing a broad Republican sword. His speeches exposing "ruffianism" in Kansas were briefed with ardor. He had been removed, the *Tribune* said, because he was too fearless and honest to implement Pierce's orders to make Kansas a slave state. The administration alone, it argued, was responsible for the impending chaos.[33]

No *Tribune* reader could believe that the free state men would start trouble. They were sketched as peace-loving, law-abiding citizens; but even their limit of endurance had been surpassed by "ruffian" atrocities, and they were urged to

[32] Nichols, *Franklin Pierce* (Philadelphia, 1931), 416-418. Milton, *The Eve of Conflict,* 187-196. Beveridge, *Lincoln,* ii, 316-324.
[33] *DTri.,* esp. Apr. 27, May 1, 24, 26, June 8, July 6, 13, 21, 24, 26, 31, Aug. 2, 11, Sept. 11.

defend their lives and their property. While insisting that no opposition be shown the officials of the federal government, Greeley demanded that the "bogus" laws and legislature be resisted to the last ditch.[34] He did not at the time admit it in the *Tribune,* but he was a member of a New York City arms committee which was assisting the New England Emigrant Aid Company in sending Sharps rifles out to Robinson.[35]

Greeley was certain that only the Republicans could be trusted to do justice to Kansas. The 34th Congress would convene in December, he reminded his audience, and it must be impressed with antislavery victories throughout the north that fall. The house would face a grave decision. Would it seat Reeder, chosen by the free state men as their delegate to congress, or General John W. Whitfield, whom the proslavery legislature had sent to Washington? Without interference from any quarter, Greeley continued, the respectable settlers had almost unanimously selected Reeder; whereas Whitfield's support came from Missouri. Greeley thought his party so firmly in the Kansas saddle that he quietly accepted the workings of popular sovereignty. Reeder would be the representative of the majority, and should be upheld. Likewise congress should accede to the Topeka document, for it fulfilled the freedom-loving aims of the real emigrants into the territory. California, Michigan, and Iowa, Greeley wrote, had entered the Union with constitutions drawn up under similar circumstances.[36]

It was too early for Greeley to blast forth his campaign call for 1856, but he was tuning his horn. The Republicans must triumph in the 1855 elections. That success would deliver an ultimatum that the northern Know Nothing congressmen elected in the fall of 1854 support the antislavery cause in Washington. These fence-sitters were essential. They

34 *DTri.,* all Aug., Sept., and early Nov. issues.
35 Greeley to Weed, Oct. 23-24, Weed MSS., RRL. William H. Isely, "The Sharps Rifle Episode in Kansas History," *American Historical Review,* XII (Apr., 1907), 546-566.
36 *DTri.,* Sept. 11, 19, 21, 25, Oct. 6, 17, 19, 22, 23, 25, 31.

must join the Republicans, and assist in organizing the house, seating Reeder, and admitting Kansas to statehood under the Topeka instrument. The senate would of course remain Democratic. Congress would thus hang itself on the Kansas issue, and Greeley could toot his Republican trumpet to the heavens as he sought victory in the presidential canvass of 1856.

Events did not transpire as smoothly as he had hoped. The Americans won the 1855 election in New York. Greeley was upset, but he realized that local contests were a Know Nothing forte. The *Tribune* blamed the outcome on a lack of Republican machinery and upon Hindoo treachery.[37] Just three days before the ballots were cast, Greeley had publicly complained: "Many thousands of thoroughly Free-Soil men are ensnared by the lodges and made to grind in the prison-house of Slavery." He afterwards told Colfax: "We have 20,000 more Republicans than K[now] N[othing] votes in our state to-day; but our active men for the polls had nearly all 'seen Sam,' and we could not get our votes to the polls. That is the whole story."[38] The disturbances which Wilson, Bowles, Dana, and Pike created in Philadelphia had failed to destroy the appeal of nativism. Nor had the Kansas propaganda been sufficient, by the fall of 1855, for that work, although the society was weakening. Six months before the election, it is estimated that there were 1060 lodges in New York with a total membership of 178,000. Their ballots in November totaled less than 150,000.[39]

Results throughout the north disturbed Greeley. Only in Vermont was anything like a clean-cut Republican victory gained. Massachusetts remained American, Gardner having been favored over Republican Julius Rockwell. The Know Nothings were generally successful, although they had taken a stand against the Kansas-Nebraska act in one fashion or

37 *DTri.*, Nov. 7, 8, 9, 10, 12, 19, 20.
38 Greeley to Colfax, Nov. 13, NYPL. *DTri.*, Nov. 3.
39 Scisco, "Nativism," 142, 161.

another in each of the free states.[40] This fact gave Greeley some comfort. He was sure the American party would dissolve when confronted with those questions which on a state and national plane had divided and disintegrated the older parties. "The effect on their despotic organization remains to be realized," he predicted confidently.[41]

Greeley knew that the Know Nothings must be steered skillfully or they would run amuck in Washington. He had told Colfax before November that congress could be organized by sheer Republican strength. He had favored Israel Washburn, Jr., of Maine for speaker, and had refused to consider an anti-Nebraskan who followed the American party line. The elections changed Greeley's mind. Colfax had been chosen to the house of representatives the previous fall, and to him Greeley confessed: "You see I am weak; I don't object to any thing. . . . Don't hesitate to run with the K[now] N[othing] machine."[42]

The *Tribune* dropped its harsh attitude toward the Know Nothings and moved into line with Greeley's advice to Colfax. If once again it became necessary to treat the rank and file Hindoos more kindly, to give them the same considerate press they had received before the June assembly of the Grand National Council in Philadelphia, Greeley entered into no compromise with their leaders. Rather, he undermined them by appealing to their followers. With language sharpened to the event he cut athwart the issues he judged superfluous into the core of the slavery controversy.

Gentle invitations for fusion were whispered into Know Nothing ears. Greeley pleaded that justice to Kansas was the only concern of his party and the one problem facing the northern people.[43] To his mind, freedom in the west was "the pillar and ground of the true 'American policy.' "[44] The Silver Greys were the real enemies of liberty. They controlled

40 Crandall, *Republican Party*, 31–38.   41 *DTri.*, Nov. 7.
42 Greeley to Colfax, Nov. 13, Sept. 7, NYPL.
43 *DTri.*, Nov. 10, 13, 14, 17, 19, 20.   44 *DTri.*, Nov. 9.

the lodges and were sacrificing the Revolutionary heritage of democracy by claiming to protect white men from a foreign and papal invasion. Meanwhile the nation was really becoming enslaved. He was sure that the masses would refuse to follow such tragic direction: "The Republican Movement can only be beaten by adopting its principles and promising to do its work. . . . We Republicans, who are utterly opposed to the essential idea of Nativism, are willing to waive all differences between us and other opponents of Slavery Extension, if we may thereby save Kansas from the clutch of the Slave Power. So that the new Speaker and Clerk are clearly hostile to Atchison, Stringfellow and Whitfield, we do not care to ask what they think of 'Sam.' And now, should the organization of the House be thrown into Pro-Slavery hands, the People will know why and by whom, and will pass judgment accordingly."[45]

Having struck his blow at the Know Nothing hierarchy, Greeley went down to Washington late in November to report its effect. As he boarded the train, happenings in Kansas promised to assist him greatly. This time it was the so-called Wakarusa War, and the *Tribune* employed it to the full in helping elect a Republican speaker.

From the vantage point of history, the Kansas of November, 1855 resembles a comic opera. The free state men had, under Robinson's supervision, developed the center of their activities, Lawrence, into an armed camp. A hotel served as a fortress, and Yankees with Sharps rifles drilled over the countryside.

Only a short distance away was Lecompton, which was the provisional capital of the territory and headquarters for the proslavery forces. Both Lawrence and Lecompton were in Douglas county, which was near the sources of supply in Missouri. The legal legislature had formed a local government to maintain order in this community, but the antislavery

[45] *DTri.,* Nov. 21.

enthusiasts had pledged disobedience to "bogus" laws enacted by a "Missouri mob." There was the rub.

In November a young man from Ohio was said to have been cruelly murdered by a Virginian. Samuel J. Jones, "bogus" sheriff of Douglas county, refused to arrest the assassin, so the story goes; instead he took into custody as a material witness one of the victim's close friends, also a person of northern sentiments. The free state men were incensed. They rescued the prisoner and carried him in triumph back to Lawrence.

Jones ran to Governor Shannon for support, and the two gathered up a posse, marched upon Lawrence, and invested the village. No shooting occurred. Shannon entered the town for a parley, and the charge is made that he got drunk and signed a humiliating treaty, giving Robinson police power for Lawrence and its vicinity. The proslavery cohort dispersed, and for a time peace was assured by cold winter winds which swept across the prairie.[46]

The *Tribune* account of this conflict is more fascinating, if less accurate. Editorials explained that the long dreaded civil war was inevitable. The people of Kansas could hardly be expected to submit to the dictatorial rule of Missouri "ruffians."[47] The administration was responsible for the trouble. "What is true and what is proper in a State actually enjoying a republican Government, has no application to a State [*sic*] like Kansas, already overrun, and again threatened by an insolent invasion from abroad."[48] The Christians of Kansas had only protected their wives and children. An editorial declared, ". . . we judge that the Sharp's [*sic*] rifles have served a good purpose, and that there has been no more fighting. Sharp's rifles, after all, are your true peacemakers, at least when one has to do with border ruffians."[49] Greeley crisply remarked: "The discomfited and lop-eared invaders

46 Villard, *Brown*, 112-131. Beveridge, *Lincoln*, ii, 306-307, 319-329.
47 *DTri.*, early Dec. issues. 48 *DTri.*, Dec. 7.
49 *DTri.*, Dec. 12.

pretend that against their wish they were kept from fighting by the pusil[l]animity of Governor Shannon," but the editor knew it was really the sight of antislavery weapons plus the bitter cold and the failure of the posse's whiskey supply.[50]

Tranquillity may have descended upon the plains of Kansas after this incident, but the *Tribune* failed to mention it. Bellicose letters from Stringfellow and Atchison were reprinted from southern journals,[51] and the need of preparing for future struggles was stressed. Men and arms must be sent into the embattled region immediately, else the *Tribune* feared for the nation's safety. Further outrages in the form of attacks on free state men who were merely carrying on their honorable occupations and orderly government were described by the Kansas correspondents. Throughout the lengthy speakership contest in Washington, they told of devils shuttling back and forth from Missouri, in and out of the supposedly wicked town of Atchison, to rob and to murder.[52]

Greeley and Dana used this propaganda to the limit in promoting Nathaniel P. Banks, Jr., a Massachusetts antislavery Know Nothing of former Democratic affiliations, for speaker of the house. Greeley's dispatches and letters from Washington and Dana's editorials reiterated that justice to Kansas would come only if the lower chamber were controlled by Republicans. Their audience learned that while recalcitrant representatives prevented such organization, Shannon and Stringfellow were mustering "Federal Soldiery and the Missouri ruffiancy to dragoon and slaughter the Free Settlers of Kansas."[53] Northern congressmen, whom the *Tribune* specified as having been elected on an anti-Nebraska pledge, were singled out and castigated editorially for not supporting

[50] *DTri.*, Dec. 25.   See also *DTri.*, Dec. 28.
[51] Copied from the Montgomery (Ala.) *Advertiser* and the Atlanta *Examiner* in *DTri.*, Dec. 4; Jan. 19, 1856.
[52] Correspondence in *DTri.*, Dec.; Jan., Feb., and Mar., 1856 issues.
[53] Greeley from Washington, Dec. 4, *DTri.*, Dec. 6.

Banks. The blame was placed on Know Nothingism, its leaders were delaying the forward march of freedom. Constituents of these congressmen read that Kansas bled *"because men elected expressly to oppose and defea[t] the principles and policy with regard to Slavery of which Senator Douglas's Nebraska bill affords the fullest and fairest expression, have proved recreant to their solemn trust."*[54] They were preventing the exercise of adequate pressure on the Pierce administration to ensure humane treatment for the free state settlers. The house should curtail army appropriations and send out an investigation committee, under Republican domination of course, to report on actual conditions in the territory. Dana's rage seemed boundless. He wanted to throw the culprits bodily out of the capital.[55]

Such an approach was hardly the way to win Republicans and influence Know Nothing congressmen. American party leadership had as much to gain in Washington as did the Republican, and the situation called for diplomacy, not arrogance.

The job to be done in Washington was similar to that the *Tribune* had been so instrumental in accomplishing the previous June in Philadelphia. A sufficient number of Know Nothing representatives must be weaned away from their society's influence to elect a man of Republican convictions as speaker. Once again the Know Something technique performed well, but this time the task was more difficult. Two full months of wrangling ensued before the house was organized.

Of the 154 opposition representatives in the 34th Congress, roughly one-half were Americans of one shade or another. Administration supporters totaled around 79. The first ballot for speaker on December 3, 1855 indicated five lines of cleavage, with as many groups looking toward the 1856

54 *DTri.*, Dec. 29. *Tribune's* italics.
55 Greeley's Washington dispatches and letters, and Dana's editorials, *DTri.*, Dec.; Jan. and Feb., 1856.

campaign. A compact Democratic minority of 74 stood behind the Kansas-Nebraska act and voted for Douglas' friend, William A. Richardson of Illinois.

The anti-administration majority split four ways. The Republicans began pulverizing the Americans by stressing the slavery issue. Candidate Banks, however, opened weak with 21 tallies. Lewis D. Campbell of Ohio, a moderate Know Nothing who had favored a compromise platform at Philadelphia, totaled 53. The regular Hindoos, led by ex-President Millard Fillmore's law partner, Solomon G. Haven of Buffalo, cast 17 votes for Henry M. Fuller of Pennsylvania. Humphrey Marshall of Kentucky drew the support of 30 southern Know Nothings, most of whom would rather elect a Democrat than accept an antislavery nativist such as Campbell or Banks.

Greeley disliked Campbell and feared that his success would allow the moderate Know Nothings to dominate the Republican party.[56] This would mean a platform in 1856 similar to that formulated by Governor Gardner in June, 1855 for the Philadelphia secession faction. Banks was Greeley's man, representing as he did the American element which wished to fuse with the Republicans on the single plank of slavery restriction, thereby making possible a broad call such as Bowles had drawn up.

Voting continued along the lines of the first ballot for five days, when Republican leadership prevailed. Campbell's backers were shifted to Banks. There was a proviso in this deal, that if the Massachusetts congressman failed to win within a reasonable period, then middle-of-the-road nativist Alexander C. M. Pennington of New Jersey would receive the support of both Campbell and Banks. The refusal to carry out this understanding indicates the determination of the Republicans.

They were assisted in maintaining Banks by the fact that he quickly jumped within an ace of victory. He was polling

[56] *DTri.,* Nov. 17.

107 votes by December 19, only six short of a majority. But he seemed unable to make the grade. The Republicans sought recourse to the plurality rule, which had broken a similar deadlock in 1849; but unable to see any advantage in such a procedure, the Democrats and Americans refused to supply the majority necessary for its acceptance.

The Democrats had a scheme of their own. They worked for the alliance not only of the southern Hindoos but also of the Fuller remnants, which bloc held the balance of power. Thinking their efforts successful, the Democrats helped push through the plurality rule on February 1; but the strait-laced Hindoos held back. They saw that if they voted for a Democrat their 1856 position would be hopeless. The final tally came on February 2. Banks won with 103, while the Democratic total was 100. Fuller got 6 votes, and Campbell was backed by 4 die-hard moderates.[57]

By this narrow margin was the leadership of the Republican party retained in the hands of Greeley and his associates. Banks' defeat would have delayed, although it could hardly have prevented, Republican maturity.

Greeley recognized the grave importance of the contest, and in his own way cooperated with other Republican leaders. It was largely from them that he received much inside information, or misinformation. At any rate, he maintained a steady flow of optimistic dispatches and letters to the *Tribune*. Every day he predicted that a Republican victory was just around the corner. Early in December he announced that he would be "mortified" if the choice were not made within forty-eight hours.[58] As nine weeks and one hundred and thirty-two ballots gave no result, he had reason to be embarrassed. At least Hamilton Fish thought so when he concluded that Greeley's reporting showed how "even a shrewd & intelligent politician may be deceived, or deceive

[57] Crandall, *Republican Party*, 53-59. *Congressional Globe*, 34th Congress, 1st sess., pt. 1 (Washington, 1856), 2-337.
[58] From Washington, Dec. 3, *DTri.*, Dec. 5.

himself."[59] Greeley apologized to his readers by claiming that his timetable was disrupted because there was so little love for straightforward, manly dealing among human beings, yet he was not hesitant in taking some of the credit for Banks' triumph. He wrote a good friend that the speakership battle had been arduous, but "by science, by engineering, by industry, and wholesome discipline, we managed to beat them all."[60]

There is reason to doubt that Greeley was as helpful as he presumed. Other men found it difficult to collaborate with so nervous and high-strung an individual. He brooked little opposition to his views and was reluctant to argue a question on its merits. The *Tribune* was even less understanding. Its appeals to the lodge membership probably had an influence in swinging Know Nothing congressmen into line, but some of this effect was dissipated by its presumptions. Greeley, and especially Dana, looked upon the *Tribune* as the nation's oracle, and sought to impose its will upon congress.[61] Frequent condemnations of men who did not see fit to vote for Banks although they were elected on an anti-Nebraska platform caused certain representatives to rise to a point of personal privilege and denounce Greeley before the assembled house.[62]

Of course Greeley did not blame himself for this ill will, and only after harsh experiences did he think it advisable to soften the tone of his paper. "I hate this hole," he complained to Dana soon after his arrival in Washington, "but I am glad I have come. It does me good to see how those who hate The Tribune much fear it yet more. There are a dozen here who

[59] Fish to R. A. West, Jan. 30, 1856, Fish MSS., LC.
[60] Greeley to O. A. Bowe, Feb. 9, 1856, Greeley MSS., NYPL. From Washington, Feb. 4, *DTri.*, Feb. 6, 1856.
[61] *DTri.*, Jan. 31, Feb. 22, 1856. Greeley from Washington, Jan. 29, *DTri.*, Jan. 31, 1856. Colfax, on the other hand, credited Banks' success largely to Greeley and the *Tribune*. Ovando J. Hollister, *Life of Schuyler Colfax* (New York, 1886), 87.
[62] *Congressional Globe*, 34th Congress, 1st sess., pt. 1, 31-32, 174-176, 230-231, 304-310.

will do better for my eye being on them." Later he raged that "every traitor and self-seeker hates me with a demoniac hatred which is perpetually bursting out."[63]

These "traitors" and "self-seekers" had the power to thwart the selection of Banks, and the compelling necessity of gaining their adherence to the Republican bloc taught Greeley a good lesson. As the ballots followed one another without result, he began modifying his reports and urging Dana to restrain himself editorially. He even admitted privately that the *Tribune* on several occasions prevented a full Banks vote. He tried to lay the blame on Dana, but in doing so he went far in controlling his own temper.[64]

The value of circumspection was finally beaten into Greeley's head with a cane. This time the congressman decried in his Washington letter to the *Tribune* was Albert J. Rust, a Democrat from Arkansas. Unlike the northern Know Nothings, Rust was not a person to take Greeley's language lying down. Nor was it easy for the southerner to decide what to do. According to his standards, the affair should have been settled with pistols at twenty paces, but it was well known that Greeley abhorred the barbaric custom of dueling. Rust was irritated by this hindrance to full satisfaction, and shortly after the strictures were published, he spied Greeley walking down Capitol Hill toward Pennsylvania Avenue. Rust moved to the attack. To Greeley's nearsighted eyes it appeared as if a drunken stranger were bearing down upon him, and his spine began to tingle as the irate figure came up to him and asked, "Would you resent an insult?"

"I don't know, Sir," Greeley responded. Rust then inquired if Greeley were a dueling man.

The reply parried, "That is according to circumstances."

The exasperated southerner lifted his fist and struck Greeley across the side of the head with a blow that sent him

[63] Greeley to Dana, Jan. 17, 1856, Greeley, *Letters*, 97-98. To Dana, Dec. 1, Greeley MSS., LC.
[64] Greeley to Dana, Jan. 25, 28, 30, Feb. 1, 3, 6, 1856, Greeley, *Letters*, 100-117.

reeling against a nearby fence. Rust turned abruptly and went down Pennsylvania Avenue, while Greeley shook the daze from his brain, and then followed in hot pursuit.

The furious editor overtook Rust a few blocks away, just in front of the National Hotel. The gentleman from Arkansas seemed cooler, but Greeley's Yankee blood was boiling. A crowd collected as Rust described what he would do if his adversary would only abide by the dueling code, to which Greeley retorted, "I don't shelter myself under that plea."

The words and the manner in which they were spoken were too much for Rust. He lifted his heavy cane in a wide sweep toward Greeley's head. Seeing the stick whirl through the air, Greeley raised his left arm to fend it off, and grappled with his right toward his enemy. The cane fell with a bruising thud, and the audience moved in to stop the struggle.[65]

Greeley regretted that he had not knocked Rust down. He wrote the *Tribune* that he was apprehensive of other attacks, but: "I came here with a clear understanding that it was an even chance whether I should or should not be allowed to go home alive; for my business here is to unmask hypocrisy, defeat treachery and rebuke meanness, and these are not dainty employments even in smoother times than ours." In his private correspondence, Greeley seemed to relish the thought of sacrificing himself on the altar of freedom and the Republican party. He was determined to stay in Washington until after the question of the Kansas delegate to congress had been settled. "And if any want to kill me meantime," he remarked privately, "let 'em. I am very tired, and not likely to get any rest in this world. . . . As to Rust and such cattle, I am not afraid of them. I have been sick and lame on

---

[65] Based on Greeley's and Rust's accounts, found in *DTri.*, Jan. 30, 31, 1856. The remarks to which Rust took exception, dated at Washington, Jan. 24, were published in *DTri.*, Jan. 28, 1856. Greeley later admitted these remarks were harsh and provoking, from Washington, Jan. 29, *DTri.*, Jan. 31, 1856.

account of my injuries, and was not able to be at the Capitol the day Banks was elected. But I am now nearly well."[66]

The brutal and inexcusable assault upon Greeley upset him, but he acted his part bravely. Senator Fessenden reported dining several times with Greeley, "and a character he is, to be sure. His beating does not seem to have affected him much. He struck back as well as he could. I do not think he would run to save his life, and such is the general impression."[67]

Greeley enjoyed standing his ground and defying all comers; but unfortunately for him, many non-Democrats in Washington failed to share Fessenden's admiration for the battered editor. Senator Fish observed: "It has been with difficulty that several members who have received his abuse, have been restrained from a personal attack upon him for some time past. While I condemn the violence upon him, it cannot be denied that his 'personalities' have been excessively offensive."[68] Of course, dyed-in-the-wool Know Nothings agreed with Fish, who remained a rock-ribbed Whig; but the same sentiments were also prevalent among some Republicans. Before the Rust attack, Weed had taken time off from his Albany duties, where a speakership race similar to that in Washington was going full tilt, and had journeyed down to the capital in order to assist Banks. In disgust he told Seward that he could have done more if "Greeley and I had paired from the beginning . . . " Just after the caning episode, Seward rejoined: "I don[']t know much about the matter but I think our friend of the Tribune is wanted more at Albany than here—"[69] Nor, it seems, was Seward discreet enough to keep his satisfaction with Greeley's mishap a secret. New York's famous statesman reportedly spoke in

66 Greeley to Bowe, Feb. 9, 1856, Greeley MSS., NYPL. Greeley from Washington, Jan. 29, *DTri.*, Jan 31, 1856.
67 Francis Fessenden, *Life and Public Services of William Pitt Fessenden* . . . (Boston, 1907), I, 78-79.
68 Fish to West, Jan. 30, 1856, Fish MSS., LC.
69 Seward to Weed, Jan. 29, 1856, Weed MSS., RRL. Weed to Seward, Jan. 24 (1856), Seward MSS, Auburn.

deference to Rust, and referred to Greeley contemptuously as "an editor of a newspaper."[70] But the worst reprobation of Greeley came from the Indianapolis *Indiana State Journal*: "We have no doubt that his letters have created more ill-feeling, hardened indifference into absolute estrangement, and widened the breach between recusants and the party more than any other influence operating at the Capital. . . . If he owned the Republicans in Congress, he could hardly be more imperious."[71]

Greeley could have undergone martyrdom, but he was cut to the quick by a lack of sympathy from his comrades in arms. He admitted to Dana that he was underfoot in Washington: "When a man's friends are set against him, he stands a hard chance with his enemies." Hotheads all about the city were threatening him. A few days later he revealed a severe nervous strain: "I am too sick to be out of bed, too crazy to sleep, and am surrounded by horrors."[72]

He came out of this ordeal a more practical man, a more efficient organizer and propagandizer for the Republican party, and the crucial presidential campaign of 1856 was just ahead.

[70] *DTri.*, Jan. 15, 1857; May 26, 1860. These remarks do not appear in the *Congressional Globe*.
[71] Quoted by Greeley from Washington, Feb. 4, *DTri.*, Feb. 6, 1856.
[72] Greeley to Dana, Feb. 1, Jan. 30, 1856, Greeley, *Letters*, 106-110.

CHAPTER 6

FREEDOM WITH FRÉMONT
IN '56

Rise up Fremont! and go before:
The Hour must have its man;
Put on the hunting-shirt once more,
And lead in Freedom's Van!
—An 1856 letterhead.

GREELEY'S political power was at its zenith during the formative years of the Republican party. This prominence gave him great satisfaction, and his optimism soared as he placed his battle plans into operation. He was a warrior clothed with righteousness, and the darts and arrows of his adversaries only pricked him into full cognizance of his immense responsibilities.

The sobering influence of his Washington experiences increased Greeley's confidence in the future of his party. He was sure that if the Republicans adopted a conservative approach to the electorate, they would swell their ranks with Democratic and Know Nothing deserters and march forward to victory. His watchword for 1856 was harmony—disjointed elements must be enticed beneath the Republican standard, and then the whole mass must be leavened and disciplined. With these considerations in mind, he outlined the *Tribune's* procedure to Beman Brockway, an up-state Republican of Free Soil antecedents who had recently been an associate *Tribune* editor. Rashness would be fatal. If a radical were named for the presidency, he would be defeated because the sincere adherents of freedom were in a minority. "What we have to do is to get enough others to go with them to make a majority; and that is a work of extreme difficulty. I shall go for the man who can secure the most strength

151

outside our regular ranks, and let Anti-Slavery men come in when they get ready. I will warrant them all to be in line and hard at work by September."[1]

This was the course of action Greeley adopted after Rust's cane had calmed his temper. He began placing it into effect early in 1856. Around the middle of February, he packed his valise and boarded a westbound train out of Washington for Pittsburgh, where a Republican rally was scheduled for the 22nd. On his arrival, he threw the full weight of his prestige behind a policy of moderation for the young party.

The Pittsburgh gathering was originally designed to promote the presidential aspirations of Governor Salmon P. Chase of Ohio, but such was not its outcome. Chase was too renowned an antislavery enthusiast for Greeley, and the *Tribune* helped alter the purpose of the meeting by assuring its readers that no nomination would be made and that the sole reason for the convention was to perfect machinery for the fall campaign. This step was necessary since the Republicans possessed no national organization.[2]

Greeley wired his paper soon after reaching Pittsburgh that the air was filled with concord and that the general desire was to act firmly, but prudently.[3] The accuracy of this report is doubtful, for the delegates included abolitionists, Free Soilers, antislavery Whigs, Know Somethings, and former Democrats. At any rate bedlam arose from the convention hall on the following day. Owen Lovejoy, a fiery minister of the gospel from Illinois whose abolitionist brother had been murdered by a proslavery mob, delivered the invocation. There was a "suppressed murmur of applause" when he asked God to enlighten the mind of President Pierce and to turn him from "his evil ways," or, if that proved impossible, to replace him with an "honest and God-fearing man."

[1] Greeley to Brockway, June 8 (unless otherwise noted, all dates in this chapter will be understood as 1856), Greeley MSS., LC.
[2] *DTri.*, Dec. 28, 1855; Jan. 17. Crandall, *Republican Party,* 43-53.
[3] From Pittsburgh, Feb. 21, *DTri.*, Feb. 22. Greeley's reports are also published in *Proceedings of the First Three Republican National Conventions of 1856, 1860 and 1864* ... (Minneapolis, 1893), 7-13.

The presence of Greeley ran like an electric current through every conclave he attended, and before the business got under way, he was "vociferously called for." He stood and delivered an important speech. His listeners looked upon him as a staunch radical, and they were unprepared for the conservative words that fell from his lips.[4]

He said his stay in Washington had shown him that the Republicans must conciliate both the southern opponents of the administration and the antislavery Know Nothings. The south, he declared, should be brought to realize that the Republican party desired neither her "injury" nor her "humiliation," but rather "her deliverance from a fearful incubus, and her rapid advancement in all the arts of civilization and peace. If the Southern people fairly understand us, I am sure we should have a strong if not the strongest party in every Slave State. Let us endeavor so to act as at least to offer no impediment to the formation and growth of such a party."

He reaffirmed his dislike of the principle of nativism, but he suggested that "circumstances" had flung "many thousands of good and true Anti-Nebraska men" into the camp of the self-styled American party. "I want these to act with us in the great struggle for which we are now preparing, and I would be careful to do or say nothing which would render such action difficult or embarrassing."

In order to spread the Republican doctrine into the south and to gain the full support of the antislavery Know Nothings, he believed that the platform of the party should rest on a single plank, that of "making every Territory free." Other issues should be forgotten until that had been accomplished. In conclusion he confessed that he was not ordinarily a "cautious" man, but he assured everyone that he was sincere, that what he wished to do was to bind together a

4 George W. Julian, "The First Republican National Convention," *American Historical Review,* IV (Jan., 1899), 313-322. See also Julian, *Giddings,* 326. Russell Errett, "Formation of the Republican Party in 1856," *Magazine of Western History,* VII (Dec., 1887), 180-189.

victorious national party and not just a sectional antislavery clique.

The rank and file was startled by Greeley's remarks, but it is hard to believe that the radical leaders were unprepared. A din shook the rafters for a reply from Joshua Giddings, abolitionist faithful from Ohio. Giddings was ready. Everybody knew, he was sure, that he had served in congress for many years and was well acquainted with the ins-and-outs of the capital. He could truthfully advise his audience not to trust Greeley's or any other advice that emerged from that environment. He favored looking to the northern people for inspiration and leadership. Greeley's timidity reminded him of an old frontier story. Joe and John carved out a settlement. Both were religious, and Joe prayed to God telling him how to bring prosperity to the joint undertaking. John was rather upset by this irreverence, and countered by asking God to "carry it on as you think best, and don't mind what Joe says."[5]

Giddings' prayer went unanswered, for the time being at least. Greeley and his moderate associates carried the day. They seated their favorite, an elderly and well-known former Democrat, Francis Preston Blair of Maryland, as permanent chairman; and they controlled the resolutions committee, which urged resistance to slavery extension by all "constitutional means" and demanded the overthrow of the Democratic regime. Much to Greeley's disgust, Raymond received the honor of embodying these principles in the official address for the convention. Affairs were wound up by selecting a national executive council and by arranging for a nominating convention in Philadelphia on June 17.[6]

[5] Dispatches, ltrs., and editorials, *DTri.*, Feb. 22, 23, 25, 26. See also Julian, *Political Recollections* . . . (Chicago, 1884), 148-149; *Giddings*, 326-327. Wilson, *Slave Power*, ii, 509-510.

[6] Dispatches, ltrs., and editorials, *DTri.*, Feb. 25, 26, Mar. 1. Convention address in *WTri.*, Mar. 8. Greeley to Dana, Mar. 2, Greeley, *Letters*, 123-126. Maverick, *Raymond*, 149, 365-383. William E. Smith, *The Francis Preston Blair Family in Politics* (New York, 1933), i, 319-331.

From Pittsburgh, Greeley returned to the capital, where he stayed until mid-April. Thereafter he remained in and around New York City, except for brief visits to Philadelphia and Washington late in June and early in July. This routine kept his nose to a conservative grindstone. He saw first-hand how difficult it was to gain an advantageous position for his party in the congressional treatment of Kansas, and he became more and more convinced in the face of rapid political developments that his plans for 1856 were correct.

Chief among these developments were the nominations made by the other parties, for the Republicans were the last to place their ticket in the running. Both the Americans and the Democrats selected strong men for the presidency. Both were out to dwarf Republican growth in the north. Greeley realized he had best watch his step.

The regular Know Nothings were first to the post. Meeting in Philadelphia late in February, they chose ex-President Millard Fillmore of New York as their favorite. His running-mate was Andrew Jackson Donelson of Tennessee. The Hindoos recognized a previous error and renounced the pro-Nebraska stand they had taken in June, 1855. This time they adopted compromise resolutions. Their antislavery brothers, however, caused trouble again. A total of 71 delegates, it was claimed, clamored their way into a separate hall. Under the leadership of Lieutenant Governor Thomas A. Ford of Ohio and ex-Governor William F. Johnston of Pennsylvania, they issued a call for a "North American" convention in New York City early in June. They were ready to unite with the Republicans.

The *Tribune* described the Know Nothing convention as having been characterized by "Confusion, Anarchy and Rupture," and cast its spotlight on the secession group.[7] In a report from Washington, Greeley testified that Fillmore's

---

[7] Dispatches, ltrs., and editorals, *DTri.*, Feb. 18-23, 25, 27. Bowles again covered the nativist deliberations. Merriam, *Bowles*, I, 149. Scisco, "Nativism," 172-175.

nomination fell like a wet blanket on the Americans in congress and proceeded to establish the *Tribune's* campaign technique for dealing with the Hindoos. Greeley never gave his adversaries free publicity. He preferred to saturate hostile candidates and platforms with a counter propaganda of insinuation and subtle abuse. The strait-laced Know Nothings as well as the Democrats were laboring to enslave Kansas, he argued. He was glad that the proslavery forces were divided. The anti-Nebraskans ought to be able to triumph on a direct vote of the people. His duty was to flood the country with Republicanism and let the other parties flounder about after the ballots of the slaveholders.[8]

Of course Greeley did not believe this far-fetched interpretation. He knew that the Know Nothings appealed to northern conservatives, and he feared that the anti-administration strength in the free states would be divided, allowing the Democrats to win by a landslide. He underlined his anxiety as he urged Dana to respect the American party and to seize every opportunity to further the Know Something movement. He warned Dana to stop slurring the good name of George Law, for this New York City public utilities tycoon had become a "patriot" when he stalked out of the Philadelphia conclave rather than support his arch-foe Fillmore. "He will never, never give the Hindoo another red cent—nary one," Greeley promised. "On the contrary, he will help us, if that seems the best means of hitting Fillmore. . . . Oh, my friend the wisdom which teaches what should *not* be said, that is the hardest to acquire of all! I confess my own deficiencies therein, but you must gain more of it."[9]

The desideratum that brought forth this rare confession was more keenly appreciated after the Democrats had nominated. They met in Cincinnati early in June and put up James Buchanan and John C. Breckinridge of Kentucky on

[8] From Washington, Feb. 25, 26, *DTri.*, Feb. 27, 28. Greeley to Dana, Mar. 14, Greeley, *Letters*, 131.
[9] Greeley to Dana, Mar. 2, Greeley, *Letters*, 123-126. Greeley's italics.

a platform upholding popular sovereignty and the administration's treatment of the Kansas problem. They showed discernment in picking Buchanan. He had been mellowed by
years of congressional and cabinet experience, and he came
from the critical state of Pennsylvania. Most important, he
had just returned from the post of minister to England, and
was unscathed by the acrimonious controversy raging over
the Kansas-Nebraska act. It would have been difficult to
find a stronger candidate. Greeley feared him more than any
other Democratic contender.[10]

The *Tribune* was waiting for the Democratic nominee with
both barrels loaded. About a week before the convention, it
announced that "Old Public Functionary" Buchanan would
be chosen, "by virtue not of his own strength, but of the
weakness and odiousness of his rivals." The *Tribune* was
confident that the people would not be duped. They looked
upon the Pennsylvanian as an ex-Federalist and as a slave to
the south.[11] There was a slight delay in Cincinnati while the
Douglas and Pierce supporters were being sidetracked, and
during this pause an editorial explained that the delegates were having trouble finding "some northern Benedict
Arnold."[12]

Immediately after the selection of Buchanan, Greeley
requested that the campaign be a clean one. Mud-slinging
was not conducive to harmony, and he knew it would damage
the Republican cause. He assured his readers that he wanted
to be fair to the Democratic hopeful, who was, after all, a
respectable man of unblemished character and reputation;
but the facts were, Greeley added, reverting to his more usual
vein, that Buchanan had no love for the common man and
had sold himself out to the slaveowners who controlled his
party. If he were to win, Greeley predicted, the government
in Washington would protect bondage in all the territories

[10] Greeley to Colfax, May 8, NYPL.   [11] *DTri.*, May 24.
[12] *DTri.*, June 2.

by means of slave codes and this would be disastrous to "Justice, Humanity and Freedom."[13]

The Democrats were incredulous, and one can hardly blame them for refusing to believe that Greeley had reformed. Shortly after this editorial was published, Jeremiah S. Black of Pennsylvania, later Buchanan's attorney-general, passed his opinion of Greeley along to a friend. "No greater service could be rendered to the cause of truth," he raged, "than by putting Greeley where he ought to be. He is a liar and the truth is not in him. He is a mush toad spotted traitor to the Constitution. And he is a knave beyond the lowest reach of any comparison I can make. Shall this political turkey buzzard be permitted to vomit the filthy contents of his stomach on every decent man in the country without having his neck twisted?"[14]

Greeley's intentions were good, whether or not he managed to practice them. The Republican candidate, John Charles Frémont, would have come nearer victory if the 1856 election had been less vituperative.

It is difficult to say exactly when Greeley joined the drive for Frémont, but he was identified as one of its leaders by early spring. After moments of searching doubt, he backed Frémont publicly for two weeks before the choice was made on June 18.

The movement for Frémont seems to have stemmed from the "Jacksonians," and while in Washington Greeley was influenced by these recusants from the Democratic camp. The group was weak in numbers but rich in traditional lore of "Old Hickory." Its members maintained that the regular Democrats had strayed from the beaten path and had for the past few years been following the trail surveyed by the late John C. Calhoun of South Carolina. They believed that their erstwhile party was sacrificing the Union and its liberties in

---

[13] *DTri.*, June 7.
[14] Black to J. Reynolds, June 9. Quoted in Carl B. Swisher, *Roger B. Taney* (New York, 1936), 491.

an effort to extend slavery; they favored congressional jurisdiction over the territories and a repeal of the Kansas-Nebraska act. Gideon Welles of Connecticut, Abijah Mann of New York, and Francis P. Blair of Maryland, along with his two indefatigable sons, Frank, Jr. and Montgomery, were among their leaders, and they hoped that Senator Sam Houston of Texas and Thomas H. Benton of Missouri would join them as they entered the Republican fold.[15]

The opposition to the Democrats evidenced by these men caused Greeley to feel that there was a market for Republicanism in the south. Already it was being exported into Missouri, and the *Tribune* was solicitous in covering the St. Louis political activities of young Frank Blair, whose successes were given as proof of the fact that industrialization was all the majority of the southern whites needed to turn them against plantation culture. Greeley knew that the Jacksonians were out to wean the non-slaveowners from the Democratic party, and it could hardly have been accidental that the elder Blair's journalistic protégé, George Weston of Maine, ran featured articles on southern economic conditions in the *Tribune*.[16]

When addressing the Pittsburgh convention, Greeley took great care to appease the Jacksonians. His letters to Dana from Washington reiterated his hopes. He instructed Dana not to publish any more editorials abusing the slave states. He wanted the *Tribune* to make friends in the south by proving that it sponsored the quarantine of slavery as a means of "regenerating and upbuilding" that section.[17] He expected this course to lead eventually to nation-wide freedom, and he believed that he could show the mass of the southern whites that such a development was to their better interests.

[15] Lewis Clephane, "The Birth of the Republican Party" (pamphlet) (Washington, 1889). Nichols, *Democratic Machine*, 79-91. Smith, *Blair*, I, 285-379.
[16] *DTri.*, Feb. 5, Nov. 5.
[17] Greeley to Dana, Feb. 6, Apr. 2, Greeley, *Letters*, 111-117, 138-142. To Dana, Apr. 11, Greeley MSS., LC.

The clearest example of Greeley's anxiety to win the good graces of the Blair group may be seen in an open letter to Benton published in the *Tribune*. This pronouncement is of importance in showing how far Greeley would go to build a national and not a sectional party. He well knew that Benton's adherence to the Jacksonians would be a feather in the Republican cap.

Greeley was profuse in his apologies when accused of having misrepresented Benton's views on slavery. He vowed no recollection of having said at Pittsburgh that Benton desired emancipation in Missouri. He had only asserted that Benton wanted to see Kansas free. He offered the Missourian full use of the *Tribune* for any statement he wished to make: "He is so greatly my senior in years, in experience, in honors, that I would cheerfully submit to having my mistakes corrected by him through any channel."[18]

This uncharacteristic condescension was insufficient. Benton disliked the sectional hue of the Republican party, and would not enter its ranks, much as he was urged and much as he despised Atchison, Douglas, and the Pierce administration. This persistent refusal to join the Jacksonians was one of the reasons for the Frémont movement. Benton's lovely and accomplished daughter, Jessie, had eloped with Frémont when he was a dashing young army officer. Surely Benton would uphold his own son-in-law.

Greeley's program of harmony called for a candidate who was available to men other than the disgruntled Democrats. He felt that the old-line antislavery partisans, with whom he had long been identified, could not avoid voting the Republican ticket; but such was not the case with the anti-Nebraska Know Nothings, and particularly since the nomination of Fillmore.

[18] From Washington, Mar. 3, *DTri.*, Mar. 6. Benton's reply was carried in *DTri.*, Mar. 28.
Benton did not affiliate with the Republicans even after Frémont's nomination.

Frémont seemed also to fit this bill. Mildly nativist in sentiment, he is said to have first received an offer of presidential support from certain southern Democrats who were anxious to unite with the Americans. He went to Nathaniel P. Banks for advice, and the two agreed that to make the required endorsements of the Kansas-Nebraska act and the fugitive slave law would be morally wrong and politically unwise. Banks had been the titular head of the Know Something detachment since his election as speaker of the house, and he favored Frémont for the Republican nomination.

There were other strings to the Frémont bow. He was well known, having as an army officer engaged in a series of daring explorations in the west which won him a popular epithet, "Pathfinder." More recently, he had participated in the glamorous conquest of California; but after the Mexicans had been routed he became involved in a political quarrel, taking sides against a ranking officer. This indiscretion led to Frémont's recall to Washington and to a court-martial in 1848; but public sentiment was behind him, and he accepted President James K. Polk's remission of penalty only to resign his commission in disgust. Such a gesture went far in clearing his name before the American people, whose non-military minds experienced difficulty in understanding army discipline. Frémont furthered his vindication by returning to California and busying himself as a Democrat in bringing that state into the Union under a free constitution, and he served in congress for a few weeks thereafter as one of her senators. By and large, he seemed to be a clean-cut young man without political scars, a rare specimen in a period of intense slavery agitation.

Frémont looked like a winner all across the board. Greeley, it is true, was not one of his first sponsors before the public, and this delay may be explained by his cautious political attitude and by the fact that there were certain flaws in Frémont's armor not apparent to the inexperienced eye.

161

Greeley did not support Frémont editorially until early in June.

The drive which ended in Frémont's nomination was launched by his wealthy banker friend, Joseph Palmer of California. Palmer visited the east late in 1855 and urged Banks, Henry Wilson, and others to back Frémont as the strongest man the anti-Nebraskans could locate. A boom for the Pathfinder began around Christmas of that year, with Banks and the elder Blair as its most active agents.[19]

Greeley must have felt early whiffs from the Frémont tornado; for, as he complained to Dana, his hotel room in Washington was "the common resort of cigar-smoking, gossiping, political loafers."[20]

His first contribution to the Pathfinder's cause was an unsigned letter published in the *Tribune*. It was dated at Washington on March 16. The style is not Greeley's, but the logic resembles his later editorials on Frémont and his participation in this pronouncement is apparent. Mentioning that Banks had declined the nomination for the presidency and that Seward was expected to do likewise, the writer maintained that a new man with a strong will against the aggressions of slavery was needed. Frémont was his choice.[21] Four days later, Greeley told Dana: "A candidate must have a slim record in these times. I think Fremont or Banks must be put up—perhaps both."[22]

Another indication of Greeley's part in the drive for the Californian may be drawn from Hamilton Fish's correspondence with Weed, although this evidence better evaluates Greeley's prestige in political circles at the capital. Early in January, Fish decided that Frémont would make a strong bid if run on a conservative platform. His view was altered

19 Allan Nevins, *Frémont, Pathmarker of the West* (New York, 1939), esp. 423-427; *The Evening Post: a Century of Journalism* (New York, 1922), 251-252. Smith, *Blair*, I, 323-345.
20 Greeley to Dana, Apr. 2, Greeley, *Letters*, 138-142.
21 From Washington, Mar. 16, *DTri.*, Mar. 18.
22 Greeley to Dana, Mar. 20, Greeley, *Letters*, 131-134.

somewhat by late March, just as the Republican national committee was convening in Washington: "I confess . . . that I cannot be inspired with confidence in any movement that Greeley controls—with all his ability he has a crack across his brain that amounts to little short of derangement & will destroy anything which he may be allowed to head—"[23]

Notwithstanding the verdict of Senator Fish, Greeley steered a steady course. On April 10, the *Tribune* printed a letter from Frémont to Charles Robinson, who had been chosen governor of Kansas by the free state men. The Pathfinder praised Robinson's valor and integrity, and recalled the days when both had worked together against slavery in California, under circumstances said to be similar to those then existing in Kansas. Greeley commented to Dana that the communication would "do good to Kansas if not to Fremont." Colfax was simultaneously writing to South Bend that, confidentially, Greeley was behind Frémont.[24]

After eighteen weeks in Washington, Greeley returned to New York City in mid-April. He reviewed the political situation in an editorial leader appearing on the 29th of that month. He mentioned no names, but his tenor favored Frémont. The nomination, he emphasized, must be made with an eye to the doubtful states, which he listed as Delaware, Missouri, New Jersey, Pennsylvania, Indiana, Illinois, and California. He was confident of all the free states other than the five included above, but he pointed out that thirty-five uncertain electoral votes were needed to win. He concluded that a candidate with a radical reputation would lose everything. Such a selection would throw "the residue of decaying, dissolving Mexico into the folds of the slaveholding anaconda, to be absorbed and digested at leisure. It is to commit

23 Fish to Weed, Mar. 22, Jan. 12, Weed MSS., RRL.
24 Colfax to Alfred Wheeler, Apr. 11, Colfax MSS., LC. Greeley to Dana, Apr. 9, Greeley, *Letters,* 146-148. Frémont's ltr. dated at Washington, Mar. 17, included in Greeley's Washington ltr. Apr. 4, *DTri.,* Apr. 10.
Bowles wrote H. L. Dawes on Apr. 19 that Greeley alone of the *Tribune* staff was warm for Frémont. Merriam, *Bowles,* I, 172.

treason to our cause through a blind, irrational, idolatrous devotion to its leading champions. To such treason we refuse to be a party."[25]

Greeley began to have misgivings about his favorite as the smoke-filled atmosphere of his Washington hotel room cleared from his nostrils. "All would be well if F[rémont] were not the merest baby in politics," he scrawled to Colfax on May 16. "He don't know the ABC[']s . . ." Two days later Greeley reported that he grew "more and more afraid about Fremont. I am afraid he lacks stamina for President, or even for a canvass. . . . I am afraid we shall all be sorry if we get him elected. And I am afr[a]id we can't elect him." Frémont's probable "shabbiness in pecuniary dealing" caused distress. Greeley had recently learned second-hand of a shady transaction involving the Pathfinder's 45,000 acre Mariposa estate in California. He outlined the charge for Colfax. Part of the land had been sold through Benton, who had been given full power of attorney. The first installment had been paid, but Frémont had refused to sanction the contract, although "*he couldn't refund the money*,—and didn't till sometime afterward." Greeley was apprehensive of a public statement exposing this bit of chicanery, which "would kill F[rémont] —and shouldn't it? We mustn't go into this fight mounted on a spavined horse."

Greeley also worried about the North Americans, who were scheduled to convene in New York City on June 12. They were expected to cooperate with the Republicans, who would meet in Philadelphia five days later, but he wondered if their bargaining price for taking Frémont might not prove excessive. For this reason, Greeley toyed with the idea of supporting Banks, who was more acceptable to these anti-Nebraska Know Nothings. "Now you know Banks never liked me," he said to Colfax, "nor I him very much, so there is no love lost between us. I don't know that [he] would even give me that cup of tea I am intent on. But, after all, Banks

25 *DTri.*, Apr. 29.

is a politician—he won't break down under us, nor run away with us." Greeley wanted more information before making a final choice in the *Tribune*. Colfax was still in Washington, and after placing these items before him, Greeley concluded: "Think, inquire and write me."

How Colfax replied to this questioning is not known, but Greeley must have been satisfied. "Yours of yesterday received," he wrote Colfax on May 21. He was still partial to Banks, and suggested Cassius M. Clay, a radical antislavery kinsman of Henry Clay, for the vice presidency. "That ticket would be truly National—Massachusetts and Kentucky, the East and the West; the Free and the Slave, the Old and the New. But if Fremont is not assailable on any personal tack, and don't have to do too much for the North Americans, he suits me very well. He will be overhauled on his Army difficulties, being suspended, &c. and we must not go it blind, but be sure before we start that he will 'run and not faint.' "

Whether or not Greeley would buttress Frémont's preconvention chances with the full power of the *Tribune* hinged upon the demands of the North Americans. He remained in doubt on this point as late as June 1, when he advised Colfax that the convention of North Americans in New York City should pass a resolution favoring fusion and send a conference committee to Philadelphia. "This is what *ought* to be done"; he told Colfax, "it rests with you and other Bogus K[now] N[othing]s to determine what *will* be. I can't undertake to row *that* boat, and shall be out of the way when it runs by." Once again Colfax's response is missing, but it must have met with Greeley's approval, for he replied on June 4 that the *Tribune* would come out for the Pathfinder on the next day.[26]

---

[26] Greeley to Colfax, June 4, 1, May 21, 18, 16, NYPL. Greeley's italics. See also Greeley to Colfax, May 6, 8, 25, NYPL.

The story on Frémont's financial troubles came from John Jay, who got it from Deaning Duer of the firm of James G. King & Sons. Greeley went to see Duer personally on May 19, and told Colfax that the accusation was "not quite so bad as Jay made it, but I still wish F[rémont] had sold Mariposa, or had ratified Benton's sale of it." On the previous day,

Above all else, Greeley wanted the North Americans to delay their nominations until after the gathering in Philadelphia, and then he hoped to hear them echo the Republican ticket. The nativists refused to be sold short, but they were ready to make a deal. Edwin D. Morgan, cool-headed executive chairman of the Republican party, and George Law, prominent North American, agreed that the Manhattan conclave should select candidates informally and then dispatch a delegation to Philadelphia for the purpose of fusion. Banks and William F. Johnston were to be named, the former withdrawing in favor of Frémont and the Republicans accepting Johnston for the vice presidency. Law kept his end of the bargain.[27] The North Americans met on June 12 and exhibited every willingness to take Frémont in the place of Banks when the proper moment arrived. One of their more polished orators praised the Pathfinder as "the man who had grit to climb the Rocky Mountains, half-starved, half-naked, and on his hands and knees." (Loud applause.)[28]

Greeley's editorial leader sponsoring Frémont appeared on June 6, only twelve days before the Californian was named at Philadelphia. Greeley placed this important question before the convention: *"Can the opponents of Slavery Exten-*

Greeley had asked Colfax to find out why George W. Riggs, Washington banker, was hostile to Frémont. Greeley to Colfax, May 18, 19, NYPL. See also Ruhl J. Bartlett, *John C. Frémont and the Republican Party* (Columbus, O., 1930), 39.

The "cup of tea" Greeley was after was probably a cabinet post, possibly the postmaster-generalship. Dana to Pike, Oct. 5, Pike, *First Blows,* 349.

[27] The proposal for this bargain was made by Isaac Sherman to Banks on May 24. There is no direct evidence that Greeley knew of the negotiations before he came out for Frémont in the *Tribune,* but a valid assumption seems to be that he did. An editorial in *DTri.,* June 11, in which he told the North Americans that all the Republicans wanted was to march abreast of them and of any party favoring free Kansas, and specifically mentioning Banks as a possible candidate, indicates that he knew of the deal at that late date. He had washed his hands of the matter, however, and June 11, being the day before the antislavery Know Nothings assembled, was an opportune time for such a statement—giving no clue as to when Greeley got the information.

The details of this bargain may be found in Fred H. Harrington, "Frémont and the North Americans," *American Historical Review,* XLIV (July, 1939), 842-848.

[28] Convention reports and editorials, *DTri.,* June 14, 16, 17. Quotation from Mr. Sperry of Conn. as given in June 16 issue.

sion elect whomsoever they may choose to nominate?" If the delegates answered affirmatively, he favored Seward, although either Chase or Senator Charles Sumner of Massachusetts would be acceptable. In his opinion the reply would be no, and the contest between Banks, Frémont, Governor William H. Bissell of Illinois, and Justice John McLean of Ohio. Banks was out of the picture because he had declared for Frémont, and Bissell was too ill to be considered. As for McLean, his supporters were "all the shaky men," and Greeley would rather he did not resign from the Supreme Court because President Pierce would appoint some "unworthy" in his place and because that tribunal had already "sunk low enough in public estimation."

Greeley picked Frémont because he had desirable connections with former Democrats, and this would preclude the charge that the anti-Nebraskan movement was a "Whig trick." Greeley was pleased by the prospect of having Frémont oppose Buchanan. He asked that "the rival candidates be both Democrats—one for Free Kansas, and the other for the Border Ruffians—and the case will be pretty clear."

Frémont, it was said, had done nothing to offend either the nativists or the foreign born. He was praised as a person of romantic appeal because of his extensive explorations. He had been born poor, but by braving all obstacles he had surmounted his hardships and gained an enviable prestige. No other contender could draw forth such a response from the masses. Here was a young man to lead a young party into a victorious crusade against a senile and Sham Democracy. Greeley did not suggest that the Californian merited the honor, and his pen executed a none too brilliant gyration in disposing of the expected accusations of incompetence and inexperience: "Candidates thus assailed have rarely failed of an election."[29]

This endorsement was all Frémont needed to put him over the top. Greeley quickly forgot his earlier skepticism, and,

29 *DTri.,* June 6. See also *DTri.,* June 11, 12, 14, 16.

chief among a tribe of *Tribune* correspondents, went to Philadelphia for the opening day of the conclave. There was little for these scribes to report, other than harmony and good will, which they dwelt upon long and loud. This gathering, they said, was not a Republican monopoly, but[30]

THE PEOPLE'S CONVENTION

Frémont met with no serious opposition in Philadelphia. Weed thought it unwise to press Seward, and asked him to go on "cheerfully" until the opportune time came. Weed wished to avoid all possible controversy, and was "for yielding to them who desire it, the privilege and responsibility of finding Candidates."[31] Seward coveted the nomination, and he disliked the manner in which Weed and Greeley posed as his friends and yet refused to sustain him. He recalled having implored Weed "to let me publicly decline and save the merit of magnanimity, to let me resign and retire from public life at once and forever, in short to save me or let me save myself from the disgrace of a rejection by my own party in our convention." On the eve of the meeting, he complained of the impression too widely current that "Greeley has struck hands with enemies of mine, and sacrificed me for the good of the cause, to be obtained by a nomination of a more available candidate, and that Weed has concurred in demanding my acquiescence."[32]

Only a few persons were as yet aware of the dissolution of the partnership, and Greeley in his editorial treatment of Seward avoided exposing that fact. Indeed, it seems that Greeley wished to cling to the prestige he had gained as one of Seward's innermost friends, and Weed and Seward had no desire to write him off their book. This course was to have unfortunate consequences for each of the interested parties.

[30] *WTri.*, June 21. See also convention reports and editorials in all mid-June *Tribune* issues.

[31] Weed to Seward, Mar. 15, Seward MSS., Auburn.

[32] Seward to his home, June 14, F. Seward, *Seward*, 277-278. Seward to Weed, Mar. 18, 1858, Weed MSS., RRL.

One obstacle faced Frémont at Philadelphia. This was Supreme Court Justice John McLean, a perennial aspirant for some nomination, but he was blasted aside without difficulty by the Pathfinder's supporters. McLean was backed in 1856 by a group of conservative northern congressmen and Washington journalists. Greeley promised the McLean men that he would back whomever the convention chose,[33] but he hated the "old fogy" and refused to give him a good press.[34]

McLean's followers, consisting mainly of delegates from Pennsylvania, New Jersey, Indiana, and Illinois, were confused by the premature withdrawal and hasty reinstatement of their favorite's name. An informal vote showed Frémont to be in a 5-3 lead, and his selection was made unanimous on the first formal ballot. McLean was furious. He later branded the inept treatment of his candidacy as "a base betrayal of confidence."[35] He distrusted the men behind Frémont, charging that his rival was under the thumb of Blair, Greeley, Wilson, and Weed, "all of whom [are] corrupt."[36]

The need for reconciling the McLean adherents complicated the vice presidential choice. Greeley was not a party to the bargain with the North Americans, and he felt no personal compulsion for upholding it. The nativists were already committed to Frémont. They could not gracefully recede. Both Weed and Seward pinned on Greeley some of the blame for thwarting the deal and for the resulting accusations of bad faith.

Greeley was in search of a ticket which would bring about the greatest possible degree of concord. It was a difficult task. He could not shift his weight to satisfy all factions, and he decided to help tip the scales against Johnston, the North

33 Greeley to I. Washburn, June 13, Washburn MSS., I, LC. See also *DTri.*, June 14.
34 Dana to Pike, May 21, Pike, *First Blows*, 338. See also William Pennington to McLean, June 7, 12; J. A. Bingham to McLean, June 9, McLean MSS., XVIII, LC. *DTri.*, June 12.
35 McLean to Thaddeus Stevens, May 12, 1860, McLean MSS., XIX, LC. *Proceedings . . . Republican National Conventions*, 53-59.
36 Orville Hickman Browning, *The Diary of . . .* , ed. Theodore C. Pease and James G. Randall, I (Springfield, Ill., 1925), July 14, 245.

American choice. The desire of appeasing McLean's supporters seems to have been paramount in Greeley's mind, but
other factors were at work. Some Republicans at Philadelphia were anxious to appeal to the Irish and German immigrants, and the more antislavery delegates objected to the
presence and purpose of the North American conference committee. Finally, the political situation in the critical state of
Pennsylvania was complex. The anti-administration voters
were already fighting among themselves. Greeley felt that to
take a candidate such as Johnston from the Keystone State
would throw them into confusion.[37] Johnston was unaccept-
able for these reasons, and Greeley joined the McLean supporters in giving the vice-presidential bid to William L.
Dayton of New Jersey.[38]

Beyond his part in the nominations, Greeley's hand is
evident in the platform. This document could hardly have
alienated any anti-Nebraskan, for it was couched in phrases
which sparkled harmoniously. It reaffirmed the Declaration
of Independence and the constitution, pledged support to
the glorious Union, asked for river and harbor improvements
and the construction of a railroad to the Pacific, stated that
congress had jurisdiction to prohibit slavery in the territories, condemned the Pierce administration for its aggressive and warlike foreign policy and its treatment of Kansas,
and demanded her admission into the common government
under the Topeka constitution.[39]

Greeley's chest swelled with pride as he returned to New
York City. Seward saw him en route, and related that he was

[37] Greeley to Colfax, May (?), NYPL. Giddings in a ltr. to the
Tribune dated at Washington, June 21, *DTri.*, July 3.
[38] Weed to Simon Cameron, Nov. 12, Cameron MSS., vi, LC. Seward to
his home, July 6, 7, F. Seward, *Seward*, 282-283.
Frémont and Johnston were formally named by the North Americans,
but Johnston was prevailed upon in August to step aside. Nichols, "Some
Problems of the First Republican Presidential Compaign," *American
Historical Review*, xxviii (Apr., 1923), 492-496. Nevins, *Frémont*, 429-433.
Bartlett, *Frémont*, 22-23.
[39] Reprinted in *DTri.*, June 19. See also Charles B. Going, *David
Wilmot* . . . (New York, 1924), 486.

"exultant that he has done the very best thing in the rightest way." Greeley purred with satisfaction as he penned a note to Colfax: " . . . something in my bones . . . tells me Fremont is to be our next President."[40]

He worked like a deacon at a revival to make this prophecy come true. The *Tribune* office became the center for Republican propaganda. As was customary, the *Semi-Weekly* was converted into a campaign edition, with special reduced rates to clubs of readers. Its subscription list jumped to 66,000. Aggregate *Tribune* issues totaled 280,000 by election day. This circulation was a barometer of Republican strength: the four free states east of the Rockies lost to Frémont—Illinois, New Jersey, Indiana, and Pennsylvania —had fewer *Tribune* readers per capita than did the remaining northern commonwealths.[41]

Other Greeley publications supplemented the *Tribune*. He printed a cheap life of Frémont, written in pamphlet form by William F. Bartlett. The short biography came off the press during the first week of August, and the energetic editor was ready to supply 150,000 copies weekly until November.[42] Over and above the continuous stream of campaign speeches and letters which found its way into the *Tribune*, a vast quantity of tracts was published—in German as well as in English, and some, for the Pennsylvania coal fields, in Welsh. In addition to their arduous duties, Greeley and several members of his staff found time to address a number of political rallies in and around metropolitan New York.[43]

The argument Greeley used on the stump and in the *Tribune* may best be analyzed by studying a handbook he compiled for Republican workers and speakers. Selling at one dollar a copy, this little volume had a long title, *A*

---

[40] Greeley to Colfax, June 20, NYPL. Seward to his home, June 27, F. Seward, *Seward*, 279.
[41] See appendices A and B. Among the free states, Frémont also lost California.
[42] Greeley to Colfax, July 30, NYPL.
[43] Editorial references and advs., *DTri.*, June 21 through Oct.

*History of the Struggle for Slavery Extension or Restriction
in the United States . . .*

He opened with a chapter on European and early American slavery. He noted that abroad bondage had gradually died out "in the advancing light of Christianity," but that it still smirched the glory of the United States because of the spirit of the "Virginia Cavaliers." The Revolutionary impulse for freedom had failed to penetrate into the south, he said, and for this reason the nation's history must be written in terms of a struggle for freedom by the north.[44]

The author presented a convincing story by carefully selecting documents to support his concise comments. He viewed the territories as the battlefield over which this war for freedom was being fought. He contended that even the southern Revolutionary leaders, such men as Patrick Henry, James Madison, Thomas Jefferson, and George Washington, had insisted that unsettled land remain free from the scourge of bondage. For this reason they had sponsored the Ordinance of 1787, which had proscribed slavery in the old northwest.

Kentucky had inherited slavery from Virginia, and backward North Carolina and Georgia had decreed that their ceded property remain open to chattel labor; but Greeley emphasized that the constitution contained no direct reference to either slave or slavery.

Migration tested the restrictive principle of the Founding Fathers, he continued. The slaveowners tried, but had failed, to override the Ordinance. Ohio, Indiana, and Illinois entered the Union as free states. The purchase of Louisiana had complicated the struggle, but it had been resolved again with the Missouri Compromise. According to Greeley, the north had been reluctant in accepting that settlement, and the

[44] This chapter shows the influence of Hildreth, and of Adam de Gurowski, a pan-Slav Polish émigré who was writing for the *Tribune*. Hildreth, *Despotism in America* and *Theory of Politics*. Gurowski, *America and Europe* (New York, 1857); *Slavery in History* (New York, 1860).

doughfaces who voted for it had thereby committed political suicide.

Greeley believed that the 1820 period marked the crisis of the battle. The north should have stood firm and outlawed slavery in all the newly acquired territory. Failure to do so had emboldened the slavery protagonists. They had annexed Florida and had entrenched their institution in the old southwest by conquering Texas. The doughfaces had betrayed their constituents by refusing to pass the Wilmot proviso, which would have kept slavery out of all the lands taken after the Mexican War. This defeat had again encouraged the slaveholders; but they had failed to beat down the north in the Compromise of 1850, which had in no particular weakened the Missouri Compromise. In fact, Greeley declared, the north had gained in 1850 by refusing to extend the 36° 30′ line to the Pacific Ocean, which by implication would have allowed the extension of slavery south of that parallel.

The author now reached his climax. The blackest days for freedom came in 1854. He accused a corrupt administration of forcing the passage of Douglas' compact-breaking Kansas-Nebraska bill. This betrayal of confidence had thrown the Kansas question upon the electorate as the major issue of the 1856 campaign. "The struggle respecting Slavery in Kansas," he concluded, "is yet too recent to justify an attempt to write its history."[45]

Stepping from his role as a historian into the more familiar character of a propagandist, Greeley set about playing his part in the drama that was to make Kansas free. In the act that was the year 1856, that territory held the center of the stage. The Republicans couched their lines in the phraseology of forthright congressional restriction, while the Democrats sought the plaudits of the crowd with popular sovereignty.

[45] Greeley, *A History of the Struggle for Slavery Extension* . . . (New York, 1856).

This spectacle was the outgrowth of increased friction in Kansas between the Yankees and the so-called ruffians. Both sides were playing to the voting audience across the Mississippi, and the treaty between Robinson and Governor Shannon was short-lived. The free state forces continued their policy of disobedience to the "bogus" laws and persisted in upholding their independent territorial government. Proslavery Sheriff Jones was too warm-blooded to be so rebuffed. Decked in the full regalia of his office, he strutted into Lawrence, and, as he must have anticipated, a disturbance arose in which he was injured. In reprisal, the United States district court, located at Lecompton, indicted the entire free state administration for treason and issued federal writs to suppress the Lawrence newspapers and dismantle its fortress-hotel. Again the ruffians formed a posse which, under the guidance of a federal marshal, descended upon Lawrence.

This was no comedy. The position of the antislavery cause hinged upon non-resistance to the legal representatives of the government in Washington. Now the so-called territorial ruffianism and federal authority were one and the same. Robinson had no choice but to send his Sharps riflemen from the village, and the posse stalked into the theater unopposed. The hotheads enjoyed themselves. Liquor flowed, type and presses were smashed and thrown into the muddy streets, and the hotel and some private homes were touched off into crackling bonfires. Frightened women and children ran about in dismay, while two free state men were killed, and the same number arrested. In the midst of their own scuffle, it seems, two of the southerners met their death.

Robinson was a first-rate director, but he failed to control all the members of his cast. Non-resistance was a word without meaning to that patriarch of the abolitionists, John Brown, who had migrated to Kansas with the flaming sword of revenge grasped firmly in both hands. Shortly after the Lawrence episode, on the night of May 24-25, he and his stern offspring butchered five southern sympathizers, an

174

infamous deed which brought on a general mêlée. Marauders raided peaceful settlers, stole horses, and laid waste the land. Governor Shannon, never renowned for competence, was unable to stem the chaos. The Pierce administration was obliged to enter the show, or the election would be in jeopardy. Late in July an able executive, John W. Geary, was named governor and dispatched in haste. Under his orders federal troops put an end to the terror and protected the inhabitants,[46] but the *Tribune's* readers never heard of his efficient work.

Under the bright footlights of a national campaign, these disturbances were propitious to hysteria and misunderstanding. Bleeding Kansas became the all important backdrop for the presidential contest. The Democratic press lauded the work of Geary and blared forth in praise of his Kansas policy, while the Frémont journals gave prominence to the sack of Lawrence and depicted the ruffians as running roughshod over peaceful Christians. Only the Republicans, *Tribune* headlines claimed, could bring tranquillity and justice to Kansas.

Greeley was awaiting his cue at the time of the raid on Lawrence. He had warned his readers of[47]

THE THREATENED CIVIL WAR IN KANSAS

The outrage was being plotted in Washington, he wrote. President Pierce had ordered the federal authorities to ally with the Missourians and destroy the homes of the energetic settlers and murder the northern inhabitants. To prevent a frustration of its scheme, the federal government had allowed the ruffians to blockade the Missouri river, thus excluding all free state emigrants. The mails had been

[46] Walter L. Fleming, "The Buford Expedition to Kansas," *American Historical Review*, vi (Oct., 1900), 38-48. Villard, *Brown*, 148-266. Beveridge, *Lincoln*, ii, 306-307, 319-329, 330-336, 403-405, 422-423. A late revisionist study of John Brown is James C. Malin, *John Brown and the Legend of Fifty-six* (Philadelphia, 1942).
[47] Headline to a news article in *DTri.*, May 20.

stopped, and Sharps rifles were being confiscated by what were termed acts of highway robbery.[48] Be prepared, the *Tribune* admonished, "for the fearful collision of steel with steel which it is the manifest determination of the Border Ruffians and their servitors to render inevitable. When that result shall have been achieved, we ask them [the people] to be fully conversant with the facts, and ready to take God to witness that in every step from first to last the Free-State party has been guided and impelled to preserve Peace to the utmost limit consistent with a sacred regard for Justice and Freedom."[49]

Then followed the event which electrified the free states. Lawrence was "devastated and burned to ashes . . . but most of its inhabitants still live. . . . A few bare and tottering chimneys, a charred and blackened waste, now mark the site hallowed to all eyes as that where the free sons of the North have for two years confronted the myrmidons of Border-Ruffianism, intent on the transformation of Kansas into a breeding-ground and fortress of Human Slavery." The *Tribune* wanted it remembered that all this "devastation and butchery" had been consummated "in the name and by the authority of the Federal Union." The president had been "sprinkled from head to foot with the blood of the Free-State men of Kansas, and his whole person illuminated and lighted up with the blaze of their burning houses."[50]

The Democratic press, in extenuation, contended that the northerners had resisted the constituted authorities of the federal government. "That's a lie!" the *Tribune* retorted. "We have the testimony of three men who were in Lawrence . . . and they agree in saying that not a single shot was fired by the Free-State men even at Jones and his ruffians, who so richly deserve death . . ."[51] As for Brown's mass atrocity,

[48] *DTri.*, Mar. 26. See also correspondence and editorials, *DTri.*, Feb. 1, 12, Apr. 15, 22.
[49] *DTri.*, May 20.   [50] *DTri.*, May 26.
[51] Credit for this testimony is given to the Chicago *Tribune*, *DTri.*, May 30.

that was simply a matter of self-defense against overwhelming odds.[52] Such was the *Tribune* version.

Greeley was being swept by the passion of the hour into the chasm of civil war. He had prayed that there would be no occasion to use the Sharps rifles, but he had shown no lack of zeal in shipping them west, and now he helped rush out a military expert in order to uphold John Brown.[53]

The *Tribune* played up the Kansas tumult for all it was worth. Letters, articles, poems, and dispatches, in addition to the editorial page, told a lurid tale. Greeley's Kansas correspondents wrote frequently and much. His regular reporter, W. A. Phillips, kept a constant stream of reports flowing into the paper's columns, although he was "proscribed and hunted like a wild beast" by armed ruffians who had sworn to take his life.[54] The *Tribune* office sponsored a Kansas fund for the relief of the blighted territory, and collected over $20,000, which included many contributions of one dollar. The journal promoted mass meetings and entreated each northern community to form its special Kansas committee in order to foster emigration and to send out material aid. Even *Tribune* advertisements bristled with announcements of books, plays, pamphlets, speeches, and sermons on conditions prevailing in the territory.[55]

Reading Greeley's journal at this late date gives the impression that his staff had no concern for accuracy with regard to the Kansas of 1856. Everything was published which might possibly further the Republican cause. Several times, hardened southerners confessed their Kansas sins on the pages of the *Tribune*.[56] One crusted advocate of negro bondage wrote that he wanted to make Kansas a slave state,

---

[52] Letters and dispatches from Kansas, and editorials, *DTri.*, June 3, 5, 6, 9, 14, 17. Greeley from Lawrence, K. T., May 20, *DTri.*, June 1, 1859.

[53] Greeley from Washington, Apr. 5, *DTri.*, Apr. 8. Card from Greeley to Col. Hugh Forbes, *DTri.*, Oct. 28, 1859.

[54] From Lawrence, K. T., June 3, *DTri.*, June 13.

[55] All pre-election *Tribune* issues.

[56] Examples, *DTri.*, May 15, July 22, and a reprint from the Hartford (Conn.) *Press*, Sept. 3.

but that he detested the fiends sent up from the south for that purpose: "*Talk* of the paupers of the Northen cities as you pleas, they cannt compair with that croud . . . from Charleston, S. C. . . . half starved, raged and louzey. . . . steeling Horses, consealing goods, taking provisions from poor unefending men. . . . sooting people's stock, skinning piggs. . . . *drunk drink, all drunk*—kicking up Jack, insulting the Femail part of comunity. . . . *we want thm no longer. Plenty, thank you.*" If they are not controlled by law, stated the correspondent, suddenly becoming more literate, "we, the citizens will be compelled to rise in mass and drive them from our soil." An introductory note commented that this letter came from Atchison, Kansas, "where no Free-State man could live a day," and that there could be "no doubt of its genuineness."[57]

The *Tribune* overlooked no opportunities. Even the acknowledged fiction turned to the subject of Kansas. The serial changed from Charles Dickens' *Little Dorrit* to a story about the troubled frontier. The author could hardly have claimed to be an authority on the territory, but her yarn was interesting and it dripped pathos. She was Lydia Maria Child, a sweet New England lady overflowing with religious romanticism. Her novel told of some God-fearing northerners who left their beautiful churches and schools to spread the balm of liberty over Kansas. There they met "ruffians, half-tipsy, with hair unkempt and beards like cotton-cards, squirting tobacco-juice in every direction, and interlarding their conversation with oaths and curses. Every one that entered was hailed with the interrogatory,

" 'Stranger, whar are you from?' " And if the response indicated one of the free states,

" 'Damn you, holler-hearted Yankees! What business have you in these diggens? You'd better clar out, I tell yer.' "

The defenseless New Englanders were at the mercy of these brutes, who overran Lawrence, murdered the men, and

[57] From "Pro-Slavery" dated Sept. 17, *DTri.,* Oct. 1. Copied as printed.

frightened the women almost to death. The strain was too great for the heroine, gentle little Alice, who had dreamed blissfully of a "neat little wedded home, cozy and comfortable, with a few simple adornments of pictures and vases." She broke down and sobbed,

" 'I want to go home to my *mother*.' " For three long days pretty Alice lay in a stupor. Then opening her lovely eyes she asked where she was.

" 'You are in Kansas, dear,' " came the sorrowful reply. Sadly, Alice remembered; she told, however, of the vision from which she had just awakened: assistance swept down from the west and made of Kansas a free state, "just like dear New-England"—with peaceful people, farm houses, and barns. The prophecy threw her harassed companions into an ecstasy, and then, "the thin lips of Alice quivered tremulously. It was her last smile on earth."[58] The rescuer, of course, was none other than John Charles Frémont, the Pathfinder of the West.

Tribune readers learned that right-thinking people, not only in New England but all over the world, wanted the Republicans to win in 1856. That outcome alone would save Kansas. The London correspondent described the new party as the hope of European democrats.[59] From the columns of the London *Examiner*, the *Tribune* plucked an appropriate poem by Walter Savage Landor.[60]

> Henceforth, Americans, let none
> Pronounce the name of Washington;
> Whoever shall, that wretch restrain
> From mischief with a ball and chain;
> Let such felonious monster be
> Held doubled under lock and key;

---

[58] "The Kansas Emigrants," *DTri.*, Oct. 23, 24, 25, 28, Nov. 4. *Tribune's* italics. Mrs. Child was the sister of the famed Harvard professor of theology, Convers Francis. Her novel, according to a *Tribune* announcement, was to have been published by C. S. Francis & Co., Boston, but a copy has not been located.
[59] "A. P. C." from London, June 24, *DTri.*, July 7.
[60] Dated Sept. 5 and reprinted in *WTri.*, Oct. 4.

Let our brave Kansas soldiers turn
Their backs on Freedom; let them burn
House, barge, men, women, children till
Not one be left to burn or kill;
And for our toasts we then may sing
President Pierce and Bomba King.

Thomas H. Gladstone visited Kansas, and one of his letters to the London *Times* was prominently reprinted. Greeley pointed to this correspondence as conclusive proof of southern beastliness;[61] but it should be remembered that almost without exception European observers were appalled by American frontiersmen. This kinsman of the famous English statesman falls into that category. Indeed, Greeley himself was to expatiate at length on the low caliber of the Kansas inhabitants when he passed through that territory on his way to California in 1859. Nor did he trouble to lay the blame for this condition on southerners.[62]

In 1856, however, Greeley would have wrecked the *Tribune* building rather than lose Kansas as a campaign issue. It was the most important implement in his tool chest for pounding disjointed political factions into a strong party.

He expected the Democrats to exert every effort in their power to clean up the Kansas situation. The new governor, Geary, showed marked ability as an executive, and the Democratic press left no stone unturned in telling its readers that all was law and order in Kansas. Greeley had anticipated this development. To counter, he had worked hard to get a Republican sounding-board in Washington. In Banks and the house of representatives, he had been successful.

---

[61] Gladstone concluded: "Among all the scenes of violence I witnessed the offending parties were invariably on the Pro-Slavery side." His ltr. is reprinted with editorial comment in *DTri.*, Oct. 27. It is dated at Stockwell Lodge, Surrey, Oct. 9 and appeared in the London *Times* on Oct. 11. See also Gladstone, *The Englishman in Kansas; or, Squatter Life and Border Warfare* (New York, 1857).

[62] From Leavenworth, May 23, and from Manhattan, K. T., May 26, *DTri.*, June 2, 9, 1859.

180

The *Tribune's* audience learned that an earnest group of Republicans at the capital was seeking justice for Kansas, but because of certain doughfaces they were outnumbered. The Democrats controlled the government, and they would enslave the west irrespective of the cost in human lives. One editorial asserted that Douglas had recently "vomited his rage upon the Senate in his declaration, 'We intend to subdue you.' " In thus revealing his intentions towards the free state men in the new territory he was said to have "re-echoed the war-whoop which, from the beginning of things, the principle of Evil in the world has forever shouted in its warfare upon the Good. Darkness has striven against the Light, the Demoniac against the Divine . . . "[63]

Efforts to settle the differences in Kansas were made by congress, but each time they bogged down between an anti-administration house and a Democratic senate. The upper chamber approved a bill backed by Robert Toombs of Georgia. It instructed Pierce to appoint a non-partisan panel of judges, who were to go out to the territory and supervise the compilation of a census and the choice of constitutional delegates. To preclude the charge of ruffianism, the election day was set for November 4, when the Missourians might be expected to be voting at home. Greeley damned this measure, refusing to believe that a dishonest scoundrel like Pierce could name an impartial commission.[64]

The house meanwhile was maneuvering to produce Republican propaganda. The Kansas delegate's post in Washington was claimed by both Reeder and Whitfield, and the lower chamber seized upon this dispute as an excuse for sending a special fact-finding committee out to the territory in order to investigate the respective merits of the two contestants. Three representatives made the trip, two of antislavery and one of southern convictions. Of course the conclusions of the

---

[63] *DTri.*, Mar. 24.
[64] From Washington, Apr. 5, *DTri.*, Apr. 8. The Toombs bill passed the senate on July 8. *Congressional Globe*, 34th Congress, 1st sess., pt. 2 (Washington, 1856), 1574.

181

single proslavery member of the board differed radically from those in the majority report. Greeley was partly responsible for this outcome. He indicated that he was influential in the selections made by Speaker Banks, and that he helped prevent the choice of a moderate as the third man.[65]

Greeley was not in New York City when this report reached the *Tribune* office, which was early in July. Dana launched it with the prediction that it would produce a "profound sensation" throughout the nation. He read the findings with the "strongest emotions," and found them to contain "not a single word of declamation, seldom diverging into argument, but made up almost entirely of a simple resume of the multiplicity of facts established in evidence. . . . Among these facts are a conspiracy and organizations, both secret and open—contemporaneous with the passing of the Kansas-Nebraska bill—to establish Slavery in the Territory by any means and at all hazards."[66]

As Dana wrote this editorial, Greeley was in Washington on an important mission. He hoped to report "that the People's Representatives give the right hand to Free Kansas as a sister State"—which meant to accept the Topeka constitution.[67] He had previously observed that there were only some eighty men of his frame of mind in the house,[68] and he expected the impetus of the Kansas committee report to supply the additional votes needed. When the free state document carried, the Republicans could go to the voters with a clean-cut issue. They could deny the Democratic charge that they were secretly applauding the disturbances in the territory and ask why the senate declined the Topeka remedy.

Greeley remained at the capital for almost two weeks. His task was more difficult than he had supposed. Youthful Galusha Grow, a towering Pennsylvanian, was the chief

---

[65] Greeley to Dana, Mar. 20, Greeley, *Letters,* 131-134. Greeley from Washington, Mar. 25, *DTri.,* Mar. 27.
[66] *DTri.,* July 2.
[67] From Washington, June 29, *DTri.,* June 30.
[68] Greeley to Mrs. R. M. Whipple, Apr. 2, Greeley Transcripts, LC.

sponsor on the floor of the house for the admission of Kansas under the Topeka constitution. He brought his bill to a vote just as the Kansas committee's manifesto was released, but it failed, 107-106. *Tribune* readers were informed that the Fillmore Know Nothings had joined the Democrats and blocked freedom.[69] Greeley would not give up. He resorted to lobbying. The "Demoine Navigation and Rail-Road Company" was seeking an extensive grant of western land. Greeley described it to Colfax as "a New-York concern, in which many good fellows are stockholders." Its backers had agreed to promote Topeka in exchange for assistance in their speculative enterprise. It would be hard to imagine more telling evidence of Greeley's anxiety to tie congress into a knot on the Kansas question than is supplied by this logrolling. He used his influence with at least one representative and served as paymaster for $1000 in lobby funds.[70] Topeka passed on July 3, by a tally of 99-97.[71]

With the controversy thus drawn between the senate and the house, Greeley sought only one thing of Washington. He wanted the congressmen to go home. He feared that an adjustment would prevail, allowing the Democrats to shout that the Kansas differences on Capitol Hill had been resolved. Four days after the success of the free state instrument in the house he urged Colfax to "get adjourned as soon as possible, and avoid all compromises if possible." On July 10, he wrote: "Well, Schuyler, adjourn at the earliest moment,

[69] From Washington, June 30, *DTri.*, July 1.
[70] Greeley to Colfax, July 10, Dec. 28, NYPL. *DTri.*, Jan. 8, Feb. 20, 23, 24, Mar. 16, 31, 1857. *Reports of the Committees of the House of Representatives,* 34th Congress, 3rd sess., III (Washington, 1857), no. 243.
The conflict between Greeley's desire for internal improvements and his anxiety for homesteads will be discussed in chapter VII. A few days previous to the failure of Grow's bill discussed above, Greeley had written from Washington in opposition to the application to the territories of the congressional policy of making land grants through the states to railway companies; he had asked that the settlers have first choice, dated June 27, *DTri.*, June 30.
Some of the details of the Demoine Company may be found in the Weed MSS., RRL, esp. Alvah Hunt to Weed, July 23, Sept. 10, Oct. 13, 1855; Feb. 14, 1857.
[71] *Congressional Globe,* 34th Congress, 1st sess., pt. 2, 1516, 1540-1541.

that's all I have to say. You cannot make it a day too soon."
Six weeks later the legislators were still laboring in Washington's steaming heat, and Greeley inquired of his Indiana friend: "Do you want some nasty fix-up or compromise on Kansas—one that will be hailed by the whole Fillmore and Buchanan press and parties as *a settlement of the Kansas question?* It is to this that you are drifting, and here you will land if you don't contrive to . . . adjourn. What *do* you mean?"[72]

The dispute over Kansas was the foremost among those headlined by the *Tribune* in the 1856 election. Closely affiliated with it was the argument that the institution of slavery made beasts of its advocates. They had no souls, but were servitors of the devil. Such was the *Tribune's* psychological explanation for the so-called ruffians who burned, robbed, raped, and murdered in Kansas.

Events other than the Kansas turmoil assisted in underlining this thesis. Southern hotheads in Washington were unable to resist flourishing their canes and bashing in the skulls of Yankees who crossed their paths, and these brawls were exploited in manufacturing Republican votes. Among a series of threatened and actual outbreaks, two were important.

---

[72] Greeley to Colfax, Aug. 27, July 10, 7, NYPL. Greeley's italics. Hollister, who used the Greeley-Colfax Correspondence extensively and was familiar with Greeley's handwriting, transcribes the first word quoted in the July 10 ltr. as "Hell!" *Colfax,* 100n.

Greeley pleaded with Colfax that the appropriations, which were holding up adjournment, be passed forthwith. He was particularly worried over the proposal of George G. Dunn, Indiana Know Nothing, who was seeking to solve the Kansas problem by a compromise which would, among other things, restore the 36° 30′ division line, make Kansas and Nebraska one territory, and reaffirm the fugitive law. The house, despite its acceptance of Topeka, passed the Dunn bill, 88-74, on July 29. *Congressional Globe,* 34th Congress, 1st sess., pt. 2, 1815-1817.

To his restricted *Daily* audience on Aug. 5, Greeley acquiesced in the support house Republicans had given Dunn, and demonstrated, by analysis of the votes cast, the reluctance of the Buchanan and Fillmore supporters to accord even a minimum of assistance to the cause of freedom in Kansas and Nebraska. His true feelings on the matter may be found in his ltrs. and dispatches from Washington, *DTri.,* June 26, 28, 30, July 1, 2, 3, 4.

The first was the slaying of an Irish waiter at Willard's Hotel. The perpetrator of this crime was impetuous Philip T. Herbert, a Democratic representative from California. He claimed self-defense, but such was not the *Tribune* version. His trial, his ultimate release, the refusal of the house to take any action on his case, and his admission into the Democratic convention at Cincinnati were underscored as examples of the low esteem in which the aristocratic Democrats held all foreign-born.[73] The Irish and Germans should refuse to vote for the candidate of the men who considered, "in the language of the late Gov. McDuffie of South Carolina, 'the laboring classes as dangerous, whether bleached or black' . . ." Buchanan's supporters, the *Tribune* declared, agreed with the Richmond *Enquirer*, which was accused of saying "that Slavery is to be defended and practiced on its own merits, and is as applicable to the white man as to the negro."[74]

The Charles Sumner incident was more significant. Toward the end of May, this Massachusetts senator delivered a harangue on "The Crimes of Kansas." He damned all Democrats, and gave special chastisement to Andrew P. Butler of South Carolina, a senator who was absent at the time.

Preston Brooks, a representative from that state and a kinsman of Butler's, resented the insults heaped upon his family and his commonwealth. He thought that Sumner deserved physical punishment and that it was his duty to deliver it. On the afternoon of May 22, he entered the senate chamber and walked to the front of Sumner's desk. Before Sumner could rise, Brooks rained blows about his head with a gutta-percha cane. Thirty seconds later, Sumner lay stunned on the floor, and Brooks stopped his cudgeling. Greeley reported from Washington that the Massachusetts senator would never fully recover and that he was in danger of softening of

[73] Editorials and Washington and Cincinnati correspondence, all pre-election *Tribune* issues, esp. *DTri.,* May 9, 12, 14, 16, June 4, 9, 11, 13, July 3, 9, 26, 29, Oct. 27.
[74] *DTri.,* June 4.

the brain. Pike observed that "Mr. Sumner lies prostrate and suffering, his head a mass of beaten flesh and suppurating sores."[75]

The Petersburg (Va.) *Intelligencer* regretted that Brooks had dirtied his cane, because such a howl would be raised in the north: "Master Horace Greeley in particular will jump out of his boots and breeches, have about four thousand fits, and thus put up the price of asafoetida and burnt feathers throughout the country."[76]

The Sumner incident was custom-built for Greeley's use. It allowed him to elaborate upon slavery as a vital threat to the country's republican institutions. His paper had outgrown "Facts of Slavery"—a journalistic expedient for warning the northern people of distant dangers. The evil consequences of human bondage were no longer peculiar to the south. The *Tribune* now brought the monstrous specter of slavery into the Yankee living room and seated it before the fireplace.

Sumner's caning took place just as the "Sack of Lawrence" was in prominence, and shared emphasis with that event. The *Weekly Tribune* carried an ink sketch of Sumner,[77] a rare occurrence for the time, and all editions printed the full text of his provocative speech. With constant encouragement from the *Tribune*, indignation meetings took place all over the north. Greeley issued an election pamphlet which included Sumner's oration, the congressional investigations into the attack, and southern editorials praising Brooks.[78]

The *Tribune* asserted that slavery saturated such men as Brooks, Herbert, and Atchison of Missouri with vulgar cowardice. In turn, these southern villains and their deluded political allies, the masses of the slave states and the doughfaces of the north, comprised the Democratic party, which

[75] Pike from Washington, May 31; Greeley from Washington, July 1, *DTri.*, June 3, July 2.
Beveridge, *Lincoln*, II, 340-350.
[76] Quoted in *DTri.*, May 27. [77] *WTri.*, June 7.
[78] All pre-election *Tribune* issues, esp. late May and June.

would continue to rule the country if not ousted in November. "It is high time," the *Tribune* decided, "that this People should take a stand not only against the immediate perpetrators of ruffian assaults but against their confederates and apologists in public life and in the Press. As long as words sincerely spoken can be pleaded as an apology for blows, we shall be regarded by impartial observers as barbarians—and justly so regarded. So long as our truly civilized and refined communities succumb to the rule of the barbarian elements in our political system, we must be judged by the character and conduct of our accepted masters. The youth trained to knock down his human chattels for 'insolence'—that is, for any sort of resistance to his good pleasure—will thereafter knock down and beat other human beings who thwart his wishes—no matter whether they be Irish waiters or New-England Senators."[79]

The so-called southern oligarchs were not only cane-wavers, they were also subtle. They took a step at a time. While their Cincinnati platform promised justice to Kansas under the guise of popular sovereignty, they embraced the principles of Calhoun, which specified protection of slavery by federal bayonets in all the territories. These scoundrels controlled the Democratic party, a pseudo-aristocracy of 60,000 slaveholders ruling a nation of 30,000,000.[80]

Greeley felt the hold of the slaveowners over the south was already shaky, and he hoped to break down the northern fear that a Republican victory would be a prelude to secession. For this reason he repeated arguments used in combating the Nebraska bill. The *Tribune* reassured its audience that there was no danger of disunion and war in the event of a Frémont triumph. These threats were only being used to browbeat the north. Human bondage had impoverished the south. The slaveowners could not fight, they could not even

[79] *DTri.*, May 24.
[80] *DTri.*, esp. Mar. 12, May 6, June 11, 21, 23, July 1, 4, Aug. 2, 11, 12, Sept. 3, Oct. 25.

take the slave states out of the Union. Were they to try, according to the *Tribune*, the southern non-slaveholders would stay their hand. Southern society was depicted as poised on a precipice. The non-slaveholding masses in the south already threatened plantation economy, and they would surely rise in revolt rather than fight for the south's peculiar institution.[81]

Eastern conservatives refused to be weaned from their convictions by Greeley's logic. He could not even entice them from Know Nothing ranks, much less Democratic. He avoided discussing the American party whenever possible, for he believed such a course would increase its prestige. When obliged to mention Fillmore, he did not regard him "as a real candidate for the Presidency, but only as a make-weight thrown in to obscure and conceal the main issue." The Know Nothings, he claimed, were a bunch of hucksters in the pay of the Democrats. Their mission was to frighten the north with cries of disunion.[82]

Realizing that this supposed bugbear of secession could not be uprooted from conservative minds, Greeley relied the more on the working class: "When the great capitalists of the country thus make common cause with those who employ murder, robbery and arson as the means of subduing the free people of the Territories and forcing Slavery upon them, it becomes more than ever necessary for the honest masses who live by their own labor, to rise against this combined power of money and barbarous brutality. . . . Farmers, workingmen, men who wish to leave your children free and independent! It is for you to save the country from the combination which threatens to exclude white laborers from the Territories and hand them over to the sole occupancy of slaves and [s]lave-breeders."[83]

---

[81] *DTri.*, esp. June 23, July 1, 18, 29, Aug. 1, 7, 9, Sept. 12, Oct. 1, 14, 15, 16, Nov. 4, 5.

[82] *DTri.*, Sept. 30.   [83] *DTri.*, Sept. 26.

The *Tribune* vouched that workers who joined the Republican ranks were bettering their lot. Their brothers in the south needed their votes. In that section, whites were being ground into dust by the slaveowners' economic, political, and social pretensions. Northern workers should rush to their assistance by voting for Frémont. Then the non-slaveholders would rise up, take over their local governments, the threats of secession would fade away, and slavery would eventually be outmoded. All these underprivileged fellow workers needed was an opportunity, which would come when the oligarchs were booted from Washington.[84]

Republicanism, after all, sprang from a universal and not a sectional feeling, averred the *Tribune*. It was the answer to man's inner urge for freedom. Public schools were its advance agents, and the educated knew its aim to be the full development of the nation's resources, the diversification of labor, and general prosperity and peace.[85] At this point Greeley called a halt to his usual plea for such controversial legislation as protection for infant industries. This editorial restraint was in accord with his policy of harmony and conciliation.

The *Tribune's* description of Frémont grooved into this pattern of conciliation and appeal for the working class vote. The Republican candidate was described as a rare find who satisfied all comers. A poor man of humble southern origins, his youthful hardships caused him to hate slavery. Honest and uncompromising, he stood for a free Kansas, yet he recognized the constitutional right of each state to control its domestic affairs.[86]

Integrity and hard work, according to the *Tribune*, had dwarfed all obstacles and allowed Frémont to march to success. The dash and courage of his conquests, his physical endurance, and his background in California qualified him to undertake the "most glorious enterprise" of all, that of

[84] See note 80, this chapter.   [85] *DTri.*, Sept. 26, Nov. 26.
[86] All pre-election *Tribune* issues.

removing the federal government from the hands of un-principled politicians.[87] He had proved his executive ability by the "Extraordinary amount of Work which he accomplished in the Senate in Twenty-rne [sic] Days."[88] He was "the scholar, the man of science, the thinker, who has been true to the dreams of his youth and the culture of his early manhood . . ."[89] He would use these talents and this learning to promote the happiness of all. The Pathfinder acknowledged "no American or Anti-American party, Whig, Democrat, Abolitionist, native or foreign, in this canvass; but simply a union of the people, of all parties, on terms of perfect equality, to secure freedom and justice for Kansas, to overthrow the party and policy of the Administration, and by arresting the spirit of Slavery extension and national domination, to put a stop to the sectional agitation that jeopards the peace of the country and destroys its dearest and best interests."[90]

The American and Democratic press was hardly so considerate of Frémont's ability and experience. Greeley had hoped for a clean campaign because he knew the amorphous party created by the Kansas-Nebraska act could not stand united under the pressure of diverse attacks. Until the Republican organization could mature and arm for battle, he realized that it must sponsor a candidate with a romantic, unifying appeal.

Hardly any contender would have fitted Republican specifications in 1856. Frémont did not. He was accused of being a drunkard, a coward, and a slaveowner. Stories were spread that his parents had been married after his birth and that he had been born in a foreign country. He was charged with dishonest financial dealings. Most injurious was the contention that he was a Catholic. Actually he was an Episcopalian, but truth was of little avail. His calumniators offered proof.

[87] DTri., June 19.
[88] DTri. (adv. for the Tribune's pamphlet life of Frémont), July 31.
[89] DTri., July 17.   [90] DTri., June 16.

They said that he had carved a cross on the Rock Independent when making his first western expedition, that when eloping with Jessie Benton he had been married by a priest, that he had sent his ward and niece to a Catholic school, and that his father had been a member of the Church of Rome. With Republican roots growing in part from Know Nothing soil, more damaging statements than these were impossible.[91]

Greeley was wary in meeting these many accusations. He denied editorially that Frémont had been engaged in any shady financial deal. The Mariposa estate figured in this charge, and he rebutted the claim that Frémont had divided it among leading journalists and politicians in order to procure the nomination. He commented that he had only casually heard of the California estate, that he did not believe the Pathfinder claimed rent from his squatters, and that he expected the land to be sold off eventually in small parcels.[92]

The *Tribune* effectively scotched the charge that Frémont had been a cowardly and drunken soldier during the Mexican War by republishing Buchanan's 1852 praise for that part of his rival's career and by running a serial on Frémont's California activities, in the form of personal recollections by one of his men.[93]

Greeley saw that it would be unwise to contradict either the slaveowning or Catholic stories. "Do you not see," ran an open admonition, "that when you indignantly deny that Col. F[rémont] is a slaveholder, an adversary will argue that you tacitly affirm that all slaveholders ought to be proscribed and excluded from office?" The same was true of Catholics.[94] Frémont refused to make a public statement on his religion, and Greeley seconded this decision. But the

91 Nevins, *Frémont*, 444-447.
92 *DTri.*, July 28, Aug. 11, 12, 23, 29, Sept. 3, 5, 6, Oct. 7. See also reply to a letter from E. de Celis, *DTri.*, Sept. 9.
93 *DTri.*, Sept. 20, 22, 23, 24, 25, 26, Oct. 1, 2.
94 *DTri.*, July 9. See also *DTri.*, June 21, 23, 24, 25, July 14, 18, 21, 25, Aug. 6, 29, Sept. 6, 8, 9, 26, Oct. 1, 7.

rumors of popery became a serious menace, particularly in the Know Nothing strongholds in the middle west.[95]

Unfortunately for Frémont, this pressure changed Greeley's mind. He believed that his editorial denials of the accusations, accompanied with the declaration that Catholics had every right to public office, would not suffice. Toward the middle of October, he undertook the publication of a pamphlet in refutation. "As we do not believe that a Protestant is necessarily any better than a Roman Catholic, we have been inclined to make light of the matter," he wrote for the benefit of the Irish and German Catholics; but for the past several months, he added, letters "by the thousands" had begged for conclusive proof of Frémont's protestantism. In this pamphlet he promised to dispose "completely" of the falsehood.[96]

Greeley overreached himself. Beyond normal affidavits, he went to great lengths to show that "there are two Fremonts, both of whom have belonged to the army; both resided in Washington; that they resemble each other, and that the Fremont who is the candidate for President is not that Fremont who was in the habit of attending the Catholic Church."[97] The Know Nothing papers began to laugh at Greeley's "Fishy" Frémont.[98] Matters really reached a climax when the second Frémont swore he had never been inside a Catholic church in Washington. Greeley tried to drop the heated subject by saying that "each has been honestly supposed a Catholic by upright, truthful persons; but the evidence of the contrary is conclusive. Hereafter, let there be no controversy about it."[99]

Circumstances had compelled Greeley to seek a clean campaign, and to sponsor a man of little experience and, he had hoped, immune to hostile attack. Such a course was practical, and Greeley tried to follow it without deviation; but he was not altogether successful. His volatile temper

[95] Nevins, *Frémont*, 444-445. Greeley to Cameron, Sept. 15, Cameron MSS., VI, LC.
[96] *DTri.*, Oct. 11.
[97] *DTri.*, Oct. 16.
[98] *DTri.*, Oct. 17, 23, 31.
[99] *DTri.*, Oct. 21.

made him part and parcel of the tumultuous 1850's. On a number of occasions, the Kansas controversy made him forget his policy of conciliation and lash forth in name-calling diatribes. Even when he tried, he sometimes found it impossible to prevent his vitriolic pen from damning men who disagreed with him.[100]

He made a good effort, and the strength shown by his party at the polls testifies to the high caliber of his work. He became more convincing as he moderated his language. He saw more clearly the need for changing opinions rather than merely blasting forth convictions. He became more logical and less impulsive. He was fast becoming a propagandist unique in American history, an editor with a huge and ever increasing following who willingly accepted his counsel because it was thought to be both reasonable and unselfish.

He was always optimistic when speaking editorially, because he wished to spur his audience to greater deeds and harder work. He urged his readers to solicit more newspaper subscribers, to form more Frémont clubs, and to exert more effort for victory.[101] Even in the *Tribune*, however, he admitted the race would be a close one. He began predicting the result late in July. Buchanan was given every slave state but five. Maryland, Kentucky, and Louisiana would go to Fillmore. He listed Missouri and Delaware as "very doubtful" and noted that the People's Candidate was gaining in both states. All the free states but three were placed in Frémont's column. He feared that defection to Fillmore might throw Illinois to Buchanan, but none the less gave her electoral votes to Frémont. Pennsylvania, New Jersey, and Indiana were uncertain; but Greeley believed Frémont sure to win if he carried any one of the three.[102]

Local elections in August encouraged Greeley, but October brought evil tidings. Pennsylvania went Democratic. The

100 This became more noticeable toward the end of the campaign. *DTri.,* esp. late Sept. and Oct.
101 *DTri.,* esp. Sept. 10, 17, 19, 27, Oct. 2, 6, 9, 20, 25, 29, 31, Nov. 3, 4.
102 *DTri.,* July 22, 23, 24, 25, 31, Aug. 4, 5, 13, 16.

situation in that state reminded him that money as well as words were needed to win elections. He began an onslaught against Democratic graft and corruption, accusing the commercial capitalists of underwriting Buchanan's election.[103] There is evidence that Greeley went out looking for a little money on his own hook. Weed did the Republican party yeoman service in this respect, and he later claimed that he found a willing helpmate in Greeley.[104]

Frémont was beaten on November 4. He carried all the free states but California, Illinois, Indiana, New Jersey, and Pennsylvania. These five, as well as the solid south, less Maryland, went to Buchanan, whose majority in the electoral college was some 50 votes. Greeley's fear proved true. Fillmore split the anti-administration strength in the north, making possible Buchanan's triumph. The Know Nothing nominee won only Maryland, but his popular support cut athwart the nation along the border belt, north and south; and he ran Buchanan a close second in Louisiana and Florida.[105]

Greeley conceded the contest to the Democrats on the night of balloting. He was not discouraged. There was another campaign in 1860—he urged his family of readers to prepare for future battles. They must never give up the struggle for liberty.[106] Colfax visited the *Tribune* building a few days later. "The Republicans here are full of grit," he wrote back to South Bend, "no give up—fuller of elasticity & zeal than any defeated party I ever saw. They are keeping up their Clubs—still working—organizing for 1860 . . . "[107]

[103] Editorials and correspondence from Pennsylvania and Washington, *DTri.*, Aug. 6, 9, Sept. 26, Oct. 1, 2, 6, 7, 10, 11, 14, 16, 18, 20, 21, 22, 25, 27.
[104] (Charles Wright), *The Prospect* . . . (Buffalo, 1862), 20-22. Bartlett, *Frémont*, 56-69.
It would seem that the 1856 Republican "virgin purity" of which Rhodes, *History*, II (New York, 1904), 235, speaks is subject to considerable revision. Weed was the financial wizard of the party, as is shown by his correspondence at RRL.
[105] *Tribune Almanac* . . . *1857* (New York, 1856), 64.
[106] *DTri.*, Nov. 5, 6, 7, 8, 10, 11, 12.
[107] Colfax to Alfred Wheeler, Nov. 13, Colfax MSS., LC.

Greeley added a postscript to another of Colfax's letters. "We have made a great beginning," he judged, "and I trust we have helped Kansas by putting all States west of yours under the government of our friends. I am tired and sore, and a little inclined to rest and quiet, but Kansas will be free."[108]

[108] Colfax to his wife, Nov. 11, Hollister, *Colfax*, 105.

CHAPTER 7

BROADENING THE BASIS
OF REPUBLICANISM

Greeley is not fit for a leader. He is capricious, crochety, full of whims, and as wrong headed as a pig. How he talks on political economy, which he knows so little about!—Theodore Parker to William H. Herndon, August 28, 1858.

GREELEY believed Frémont's splendid showing insured freedom to Kansas, but he was unsatisfied with the scope of the Republican doctrine. It was too narrow. The campaign of 1856 convinced him more firmly than ever that a majority, even in the north, was not antislavery in sentiment.[1] Amidst the relative quiet of a post-campaign year, he returned to his first love: economic development as a means of uprooting slavery and advancing democracy.

He feared that Republicanism would prove to be a flash in the pan. Slavery restriction, after all, was negative in character. It was a destructive and not a constructive principle. He knew it must be buttressed with more tangible aims which appealed to the material welfare of the electorate.

In these years, he never relied upon civil war as a means of eradicating slavery. He wished to avoid a conflict between sections. He was fully aware of the danger inherent in slavery restriction alone. He knew that slave economy was wasteful, that it destroyed the fertility of the land, and that its extension to virgin soil was necessary to its existence. Restriction, therefore, would destroy slavery. It would also create an economic and social vacuum in the south which

[1] Greeley to Pike, Oct. 6, 1856, Pike, *First Blows*, 349-350.

might have frightful consequences for the Union. Some positive economic doctrine was needed.

Greeley wished to kill two birds with one stone. He brought forward his ideas of political economy in the belief that, if adopted by his party, they would provide the margin of northern votes necessary to intrench the Republicans in power and that the application of these ideas would alter the basis of southern life in such a manner as to insure gradual, and peaceful, emancipation.

His doctrine may best be described as economic nationalism. The scope and tremendous natural resources of the country caused him to dream of self-sufficiency. His philosophical background led him to picture America as a harmonious whole, made up of perfectly tuned individual economic units, and flourishing through internal trade independent of markets abroad. Railroads, navigable rivers, and canals would join the thriving communities sprinkled across the nation, and in peace, plenty, and freedom, each man would find work suitable to him, on farm or in factory. To achieve this idealistic interpretation of the future, Greeley considered as immediate and necessary: the availability of free land as homesteads, a protective tariff, internal improvements, and increased immigration.

Homesteads would culminate in a practical restriction of slavery by surrounding the south with a wall of non-slaveholding farmers. The physical fact of a free majority already established in the territories would make slavery extension impossible. Settlement in the west in the advance of industry would entice manufacturers to that portion of the country, a movement which would be facilitated by internal improvements. The production of truck and dairy products would then be rewarded by adjacent markets. The economic advantages of this system would assure its penetration into the south. With a local demand for fruit, vegetables, and milk at his door, the plantation owner would be drawn away from staple crops which both ruined his land and left him at the mercy of periodical fluctuations in world trade. He would grow only enough cotton, sugar, and tobacco to satisfy domestic needs. Under the impulse of a strong protective tariff, the nation-wide expansion of industry would offer jobs to worker and farmer alike, at wages improved by a release from foreign competition. Many agrarian and industrial laborers would be necessary to make this plan feasible, a void which Greeley hoped to fill with immigrant labor.

Such, to his mind, was the most promising economic plan for the nation to follow. His task was to translate this policy into law, which involved political indoctrination. Success depended upon his ability to convince the capitalist and worker alike that the *Tribune* was solely concerned with their best interests.

Greeley always held the needs of the farmer and worker close to his heart. He sincerely called himself a mechanic, nor was he able to distinguish clearly between the entrepreneur and the wage earner. His educational program falls into the same pattern. He sponsored a non-classical, practical and scientific training for the nation's children, with emphasis on part-time employment which would cover much of the expense.[2]

He relied too much on his fond hope that workers would fast become capitalists and own their tools of production. His basic faith in class harmony, in a closely meshed, self-sufficient nation composed of decentralized economic communities, led to his failure to see distinctly the conflicting interests between capital and labor in the 1850's. For this reason, he was willing to accent the conservative side of his economic policy in order to gain political support for the Republican party. While this desire did not cause him knowingly to deviate from his fundamental social idea, he not only refrained from attacking the capitalist, but also applauded

[2] Greeley, *Recollections,* 144-158. See also *DTri.,* Sept. 21, 1853; Apr. 14, May 8, 1854; Nov. 24, 1856; Apr. 4, July 10, Oct. 6, 1857; June 22, 1858; Mar. 17, and speeches reprinted from Calif. papers, Sept. 13, 1859.

those economic developments which, in the latter half of the nineteenth century, allowed the industrialist and financier to emerge economically and politically predominant over the worker and farmer.

In this era, the nation was webbed with railways, and protection and homesteads became the law of the land, but the resultant wealth was not distributed as Greeley expected. Internal improvements centralized industrial growth. The railways carried raw materials to large urban centers. Corporate wealth multiplied, and on a relative basis, the working-men suffered.

Greeley should be accused of shortsightedness rather than bad faith. He worked for labor organization, but that means little within itself. Labor's only weapons were collective bargaining and the strike, and these he opposed. His fundamental attitude made him unsympathetic to class strife, and he sought another answer for the workers.

An illustration of his attitude toward the working class movement may be drawn from the Lynn, Massachusetts shoemakers' strike early in 1860. At a sympathy meeting of New York City workers in Cooper Institute, Alonzo Draper, leader of the Lynn cordwainers, spoke first. Greeley followed.

Draper explained the procedure of a militant union on strike. The owners had received large profits the previous year by cutting down wages. To increase the worker's return, a wage-schedule was proposed; but the operators were refusing to sanction the right of collective bargaining by signing. A strike had been called and was to continue until such recognition was gained.

He assured his audience that the journeymen were enjoying themselves. Union leaders had conducted parades, barbecues, and a carnival. "Their missionaries were all over the State converting the shoemakers to the true faith." (Laughter and applause.) An apprentice system was planned to prevent an oversupply of cordwainers, and scab committees had been established in each ward. Draper closed with an appeal to the New York City workers for material assistance.

Greeley, noted as the workingmen's champion, had been ushered into the hall with loud applause and cheers. He was similarly greeted as he rose to refute Draper at every point. With a finesse which does credit to his understanding of men and his ability as a public speaker, he agreed that the strikers should have sympathy, and that a scale of wages should be adopted; but he urged that the settlement be made not by strike and collective bargaining, but by conference: " . . . whenever either journeymen or employers deem a revision of the Scale just and necessary, they should call a mutual council of delegates from both employers and journeymen, set before them the grounds on which such revision is demanded, and ask their concurrence in the change proposed, or in such change as may be deemed just." If this were done there would be no strikes, he continued. After all, were not the interests of the workers and their masters identical? If shoes could be made cheaper somewhere else would not New England lose all her shoe industries? Strikes would only increase the cost of production and tend to force the shoe trade out of Lynn. If by such means the price of labor were raised too high, thousands would rush into the occupation of making shoes; and wages would drop immediately. He felt that the word of the employers, who said that they could not afford the proposed scale, was as valid as that of the strikers. "If there are too many shoemakers, some must be drawn off into other and less crowded vocations; only thus can the wages of those who remain shoemakers be really permanently enhanced."[3]

The tone of Greeley's address reflected what he openly declared in an editorial, that apprenticing and picketing were wrong, that "while the sellers of Labor have a right to agree on what they consider a fair price for it and refuse to sell for less, they have *no* right to enforce their views on any who do

[3] Reported in *DTri.*, Mar. 28, 1860. *Tribune's* parentheses.

not choose to unite with the[m]."[4] He favored labor unions, but pictured them as loose organizations in which each member controlled his individual action. If workers in eastern industrial centers wished to maintain a high standard of living, he believed that "they must impel a constant stream of emigration from their midst to Illinois, Kansas, Nebraska, Minnesota, and other sections where their labor is in eager demand at good wages and where living is much cheaper than in the crowded cities. In the absence of such emigration, wages will be depressed here by the constant influx of journeymen from the country and from Europe, and no rigor of combination among our resident journeymen can prevent it."[5]

For the workers, Greeley clung to the iron law of wages, although he recognized that unity among operators and investors was general and almost always compact.[6] An employer who paid the "market price" for labor, he once wrote, "is a public benefactor—and none the less so that his business affords him a profit."[7] As for the laborer, "The truth is that the basis of mankind's dealings with each other is not abstract Justice, (as we think it should and ultimately must be,) but Necessity. Buy as cheap as possible and sell for the most you can get. That is the actual law—we did not make it and don't like it, but we are not able forthwith to change it—for we have tried and know."[8]

Thus while Greeley approved of and worked for labor organization, he believed that unions were merely a preparatory step for the ultimate cooperative enterprise which was expected to spring from man's innate goodness. Unions were not and should not be a means of protecting the worker's immediate interests. The laborer could either migrate westward, or follow the Golden Rule and appeal to the Christian instincts of his employer.

[4] *DTri.*, Apr. 6, 1859. Greeley's italics.   [5] *DTri.*, Mar. 23, 1857.
[6] *DTri.*, Apr. 20, 1854.   [7] *DTri.*, Jan. 17, 1855.
[8] *DTri.*, Jan. 24, 1855. Greeley's parentheses.

There was a third alternative. Although certain leaders of the Fourier school in America had alienated Greeley by advocating free thought and free love, he still held faith in a modification of its fundamental plan for labor reform, the workers' cooperative. He closed his address in the Cooper Institute by advising the strikers to establish their own marketing facilities and to produce shoes with their own capital. Then, in place of striking and begging for material aid from fellow workers, they could sell at a profit shoes manufactured by themselves: " . . . does any one seriously doubt that, for every dollar given them outright to sustain their strike, a hundred would cheerfully be paid them for good boots and shoes?" By making and selling their product the strikers could undersell the manufacturers and middlemen and eventually force both from business.[9]

Greeley's reasoning led him to the root of the working class problem, the real wage of the laborer. Although he denied trade unionism the right of collective bargaining and the strike, he thought high wages could be maintained by other means. He placed utmost reliance upon the migration of surplus workers to the frontier. This movement, he was sure, would create labor scarcities in factory centers and keep the worker's income high until the era of "abstract Justice" arrived.

Indeed, Greeley was impelled by social and political considerations to overwork his migration theory. In addition to the normal burden of leveling off urban and farm workers, he expected the nation's economic growth to absorb thousands of immigrants from abroad. Rather than Europe's wares, he wanted her artisans.[10] He believed their man power necessary to the development of America's varied resources. Their contribution was essential to the fulfillment of his social and political doctrine. Before the abolition of slavery, he

[9] *DTri.*, Mar. 17. See also Greeley's address as reported in *DTri.*, Mar. 28, 1860.
[10] Reply to "An Old English Factory Clerk," *DTri.*, Nov. 3, 1853.

BROADENING THE BASIS OF REPUBLICANISM

expected imported labor to further the cause of emancipation by filling the territories with free men and restricting slavery. Once this end had been gained, he wanted to divert the immigrants southward in order that they might resurrect a socially degenerate section by voting the death of African bondage. After abolition, white labor would be needed (and was considered indispensable) for the rehabilitation of the south through industrialization and farm diversification.[11]

Greeley had no qualms about such an influx of labor. His dreams were grandiose. Over and above the immigrants needed to free the south from slavery and to establish factories throughout the Union, he once exaggerated that "We have five thousand million acres and need at least one thousand million inhabitants to cultivate them."[12] His was not a selfish ideal. He felt that his doctrine of economic nationalism would benefit the entire world. If the United States could be so developed by men previously oppressed in despotic Europe, he believed that the example would attract all the Western Hemisphere into its orbit of freedom, and ultimately spread democratic institutions to all corners of the earth.[13]

Greeley's working class program was idealistic in so far as it relied upon the frontier as a direct safety valve for surplus labor. There can be no doubt that western lands drew off a considerable proportion of potential factory labor, but the fact remains that collective bargaining, not vague promises of western farms and far-fetched ideas of Fourierism, was what the urban worker needed in the mid-nineteenth century. At the sympathy meeting in Cooper Institute, Draper and not Greeley showed himself to be a practical friend of labor.

The steady immigration which Greeley encouraged flooded the labor market, and the frontier never functioned as he had

11 Undated addresses in Greeley MSS. and Greeley Misc. MSS., LC. Greeley to Seward, Apr. 29, May 7, 1857, Seward MSS., Auburn. *DTri.*, Mar. 25, Apr. 16, 18, 1857. Greeley, "Mr. Greeley's Letters from Texas and the Lower Mississippi . . . " (pamphlet) (New York, 1871).
12 *DTri.*, Sept. 29, 1853.
13 *DTri.*, esp. Dec. 21, 1853; Apr. 21, 1855; Feb. 6, 1858; Mar. 31, 1859; May 5, 1860.

anticipated. The costs of migrating to the west and of out-fitting a farm were greater than the average worker could afford, even if he possessed knowledge of farming methods and wished to leave the manufacturing center which gave him companionship. Grants to railroads and even more speculative enterprises continued to withdraw the better lands from occupation by the poorer classes, forcing the homesteader to pioneer under the most difficult conditions. The plains presented problems which went unsolved for more than two decades, until marauding Indians were met with Colt revolvers, arid soil was cultivated by dry farming, and timberless land was enclosed with barbed wire fences.[14]

Greeley recognized the tremendous hardships facing the laborer who turned toward western lands. His great desire was to aid him. The oft-quoted phrase "Go West!" is the essence of his advice to the eastern worker, but this counsel was generally accompanied with qualifications which go far to moderate his estimate of the safety valve feature of the federal domain.

Few men in his era traveled more widely or observed frontier conditions more closely than Greeley, and his letters to the *Tribune* offer abundant evidence that the west failed

[14] Walter P. Webb, *The Great Plains* (Boston, 1931). Paul W. Gates, "The Homestead Law in an Incongruous Land System," *American Historical Review*, XLI (July, 1936), 652-681. Carter Goodrich and Sol Davison, "The Wage Earner in the Western Movement," and "The Frontier as Safety Valve: a Rejoinder," *Political Science Quarterly*, L, LI, LIII (June, 1935; Mar., 1936; June, 1938), 161-185, 61-116, 268-271. Murray Kane, "Some Considerations on the Safety Valve Doctrine," and "Some Considerations on the Frontier Concept of Frederick Jackson Turner," *Mississippi Valley Historical Review*, XXIII, XXVII (Sept., 1936; Dec., 1940), 169-188, 379-400. Helene S. Zahler, *Eastern Workingmen and National Land Policy, 1829-1862* (New York, 1941).

See also note 47, chapter I. Robbins' conclusion, *Our Landed Heritage*, 73, that "cheap land acted as a safety-valve for the discontented but only during good times. In general, cheap land can be considered as an aid in balancing the economic order only if viewed over a long-time perspective," is less emphatic than that of Goodrich and Davison. For additional literature on this subject see Everett E. Edwards, "References on the Significance of the Frontier in American History," *Bibliographical Contributions no. 25*, U.S. Department of Agriculture Library (Washington, 1935).

Prof. Paul. W. Gates read this chapter at a formative stage, and made a number of valuable suggestions.

to serve as a refuge for the eastern worker. This is not to say that he thereupon modified his outlook on trade unionism. He did not. He only sought the harder to remove those barriers which he saw obstructing labor migration.

Greeley asserted: "It is idle, it is mockery, to hold up voluntary, unaided immigration to the West, or the Interior, as a cure for the evils of City Pauperism."[15] He pointed out that those workers who had friends or relatives to welcome them into new states or territories were lucky, but that there was a real need for organized migration. He envisaged employment centers in urban communities for the purpose of facilitating contact between the western employer and the employee, and he urged farmers within geographic sections to dispatch one of their number to the city as an employing agent for the group.[16]

Although he depicted the city as the worst possible home for the poor urban worker with a family, he admitted that it was difficult to establish such a man in the west. Single men and women with as little as $10 might set out fearlessly;[17] but as he once wrote to the *Tribune*: "I could not advise a poor man to come West in quest of employment by which to earn his living and that of his family as a hireling; for I believe he can do quite as well and find quite as steady work at the East."[18]

As for knowledge of farming, Greeley insisted that it was essential. Frequently he lectured on scientific methods at state and local fairs,[19] and columns of the *Tribune* were filled with market quotations, crop reports, and technical articles contributed by the agricultural editor, Solon Robinson, and by such proponents of advanced methods as James J. Mapes. Unemployed mechanics and artisans who knew nothing of

15 *DTri.*, Feb. 3, 1855.
16 *DTri.*, esp. Aug. 1, 1854; Jan. 29, 1855; Sept. 18, 1857; June 22, 1858.
17 *DTri.*, Feb. 3, 1855. Greeley from Chicago, Jan. 4, *DTri.*, Jan. 9, 1858.
18 From Prairie-du-Chien, Wisc., Jan. 22, *WTri.*, Feb. 4, 1860.
19 Reprints of speeches, *DTri.*, Oct. 14, 1853; Dec. 6, 1854; Feb. 22, Oct. 19, 1858; Sept. 28, 1859. Greeley, *What I Know of Farming* . . . (New York, 1871).

farming were counseled to learn while working for a good farmer as a hired hand. Their pay, Greeley estimated, would be around $100 a year plus board and room.[20]

Farm equipment was seen to be as essential as the land, and transportation costs were acknowledged a problem. Outlays from $500 to $5000 were recommended, amounts far beyond the means of the average industrial worker.[21] Greeley was apt to assert after such advice that "for the hard-handed plow-jogger, who is poor in coin but rich in children, there is no country to-day so inviting as the broad, free West."[22] Obviously he was thinking, not of urban workers, but of eastern farmers who should resettle themselves, investing in the west the little they had. These were the men who, along with their numerous progeny and immigrants newly arrived from Europe, carried the frontier ever westward, founding for themselves new communities rather than seeking factory jobs in already crowded cities.

Greeley was generous to a fault, and he must have given away considerable sums of money to transport poor men to the frontier, particularly during the period of the Kansas difficulties. Yet, his paper insisted that the northern aid companies were not sending out paupers.[23] The *Tribune* declared that "every energetic, two-handed mechanic or laborer will find work enough in Kansas, if he only carries thither means sufficient to subsist him for the first six months . . . "[24] Another editorial asserted that men of modest circumstances were the desirable settlers for Kansas.[25]

Somehow, paupers got to Kansas, and the results appalled Greeley when he passed through that territory in 1859. His description of these individuals is indeed a sad parody on the

[20] *DTri.*, Feb. 7, 1855.
[21] The best source for Greeley's estimates as to the capital outlay necessary is his letters to the *Tribune* from Kansas and California in the summer and early fall of 1859. These may be conveniently examined in his *An Overland Journey* . . . (New York, 1860).
[22] From Chicago, Jan. 4, *DTri.*, Jan. 9, 1858.
[23] *DTri.*, Sept. 9, Oct. 25, 1854.   [24] *DTri.*, Nov. 12, 1856.
[25] *DTri.*, Dec. 16, 1856.

noble free state men whose praises he had sung with such telling political effect. He wrote the *Tribune* that there were "too many idle, shiftless people in Kansas. . . . those who call themselves settlers, and who would be farmers if they were anything. To see a man squatted on a quarter-section in a cabin which would make a fair hog-pen, but is unfit for a human habitation, and there living from hand to mouth by a little of this and a little of that, with hardly an acre of prairie broken (sometimes without a fence up), with no garden, no fruit-trees, 'no nothing'—waiting for some one to come along and buy out his 'claim' and let him move on to repeat the operation somewhere else—this is enough to give a cheerful man the horrors." He refused to accept illness or the lack of equipment as excuses for this plight, for such a man could hire out "in haying and harvest, and get nearly or quite two acres broken next month for every faithful week's work he chooses to give at that busy season."

Greeley saw other types of settlers in Kansas. The professional speculators were doing well, as were the farmers who had arrived with ample funds in their pockets. He noted but one urban worker whose agrarian future was promising. This was an old New York City friend, formerly an "industrious mechanic."[26]

This trip took Greeley over the broad central section of the federal domain, and confirmed his belief that this land was worthless. Arid, timberless, and desert-like, it was unfit for cultivation. From Salt Lake City he wrote a lady friend: "It is a great way from this to any place where a Christian ought to live voluntarily . . . "[27]

He found the soil and climate improved when he reached California. The greatest need, he declared in the *Tribune*, was the importation of one hundred thousand "virtuous,

<hr>

[26] From Manhattan, K. T., May 26, *DTri.*, June 9, 1859. Greeley's parentheses. Greeley, *Overland*, 64-68. Goodrich and Davison, *Political Science Quarterly*, L, 184.

[27] Greeley to Mrs. Margaret Allen, July 14, 1859, Greeley MSS., LC. See also Greeley's ltrs. in *DTri.*, June 11, 14, 18, 20, July 9, 14, 26, 27, Aug. 13, 16, 30, 1859. Greeley, *Overland*, 71-257.

educated, energetic Women." He also felt that many good farmers from the east could obtain fertile soil if the large and irregular Spanish allocations of land were broken apart. These restrictions looked so formidable that he added: "I believe a young, energetic, intelligent farmer, with a good wife and $2,000 or over, can do as well in California as elsewhere, in spite of the horrible confusion of land-titles."[28]

Large estates such as those held by Spanish grant provoked Greeley. He condemned speculation as "that scourge of the West."[29] He saw that land warrants brought undue hardships to the settlers, forcing the less wealthy into the frontier zone while the speculator clung to the more convenient acres hoping for an increase in value. He concluded: "The granting of large tracts of land to private companies, in order that they may raise the price to settlers, is an outrage which should no longer be tolerated."[30]

Yet in this instance his hands were tied by economic and political considerations. He was anxious to see the nation interlaced with canals and railroads, and realized that such improvements were necessary to western development. He was certainly no socialist in the Marxian sense of the word. He knew full well that land grants offered capitalists the inducements necessary to a risk of their money in this work. He was never able to resolve this problem.

[28] From San Francisco, Sept. 4-5, *DTri.*, Oct. 22, 1859. See also his ltr. from Marysville, Calif., Sept. 2, *DTri.*, Oct. 14, 1859. Greeley, *Overland,* 344-360.

Greeley visited Frémont's Mariposa estate, which was held under Spanish title, but found it inexpedient to do other than praise his 1856 standard-bearer. From Sacramento, Aug. 7, and from the steamboat *Cornelia,* Aug. 15, *DTri.*, Sept. 9, 26, 1859. Greeley, *Overland,* 316-321.

Bayard Taylor was sending California reports to the *Tribune* at this time, and the general survey the two journalists gave frightened one Californian: "Several of us were talking of the wrong impression Horace Greeley's and Bayard Taylor's letters would convey to the people in the eastern states, and might cause them to leave their business and pleasant homes, only to meet disappointment and failure. . . . I advise every one to keep the money it would cost him to come here, and stay in the states." "C. H. P." in the Cleveland *Leader,* Apr. 12, 1860, *Annals of Cleveland,* XLIII, pt. 1 (Cleveland, 1937), abs. no. 3249, pp. 530-531.

[29] From Cleveland, O., Jan. 1, *DTri.*, Jan. 6, 1854.

[30] *DTri.*, Feb. 4, 1854.

There was a tendency on his part to censure Democratic and excuse Republican speculators. Although he disliked political parties and thought they should be broken up every twelve years or so in order to prevent corruption, he saw that a party was needed to implement his political and economic philosophy.[31] When organizing to attain victory, all men, speculators and otherwise, looked like good Republicans to him. He did not believe in "flinging stones at one's own crockery . . . "[32]

In the summer of 1856, he even went so far as to lobby for a grant of about a quarter-million acres to the "Demoine Navigation and Rail-Road Company." Apprehensive of the publicity this endeavor was certain to receive, he promised Colfax an editorial opposing all further railway land grants "at present"; but instead he suggested innocuous alterations in the method and insisted that the policy continue since it had aided internal improvement in several states already.[33] His plan for a Pacific railroad, which was similar to the legislation ultimately approved, was fraught with opportunities for graft in lands, as Pike pointed out.[34]

There was another problem pertaining to farming in particular and western settlement in general which faced Greeley and for which he never found an answer. His was an era of vast expansion in farm machinery. He applauded these inventions, but feared that the small farmer could never equip himself with the advanced tools of his trade. The capital outlay would be too great.

At the same time, his social and economic program called for small holdings in land. Otherwise, he feared, individual initiative would be lost and large estates with tenant labor

[31] *DTri.*, Apr. 11, July 18, Dec. 8, 1854. Pike, "Horace Greeley in 1872 . . . " (pamphlet) (New York, 1873).

[32] Greeley to Dana, Mar. 2, 1856, Greeley, *Letters*, 123-126.

[33] Greeley to Colfax, Dec. 28, 1856, NYPL. *DTri.*, Dec. 29, 1856. See also note 70, chapter vi.

[34] Greeley's editorials, speeches, and an article, *DTri.*, Jan. 13, Feb. 4, 1857; Sept. 13, 14, Dec. 3, 24, 1859. Pike from Washington, *DTri.*, June 3, 1856; Jan. 5, 13, Feb. 4, 1857.

would be the outcome. He favored 160 acres or less in his propagandizing for homesteads and in his agrarian lectures. No man, he argued, should attempt to own more land than he could himself cultivate.[35] Yet, he admired larger holdings on which the latest machines and scientific advancements were utilized.[36] It is possible that he saw a way out in Fourierism. At any rate, he gave Albert Brisbane the use of the *Tribune* as late as 1858 for the promotion of a 100,000 acre "association" with one thousand shares valued at $1000 each. Brisbane planned to have his plantation laid out and inaugurated by hired labor to prevent early disagreements. Thereafter, an initial investment of $2000 would have entitled a family to membership.[37]

Brisbane's scheme was, of course, far beyond the reach of the average worker's pocketbook. Yet, there is no evidence that Greeley offered anything more tangible to the urban laborer. It is well to repeat that the withdrawal of potential factory hands reduced the labor pool in the east. This movement was stimulated by Greeley's propaganda, but it is safe to assume that it would have occurred if he had chosen a profession other than journalism. Historians have been unable to find more than a few isolated instances in which an eastern factory worker successfully established himself on a western farm. During his extensive travels in the 1850's, as has been seen, Greeley noted but one urban laborer who had, with some promise of permanency, so transplanted himself.

Another phase of Greeley's labor program, akin to his constant description of the west as the working man's heritage, defies final evaluation. He was sincere in constantly expounding upon the nobility of labor. He believed that the farmer and the craftsman were the Lord's annointed, and that they would inherit the earth. One can only speculate upon the extent to which this journalistic sympathy con-

---

[35] Greeley's speeches and an editorial, *DTri.*, Oct. 14, 1853; Dec. 6, 1854; Feb. 22, Oct. 19, 1858; Aug. 10, 1857.
[36] From Leroy, Genesee Co., N.Y., Sept. 4, *WTri.*, Sept. 18, 1858.
[37] Brisbane's ltrs., *DTri.*, July 12, 14, 23, Aug. 18, 20, 27, 1858.

tributed to shaping public opinion for the subsequent success of collective bargaining.

In connection with the honor due the laboring man, he believed that the "history of Human Progress" was being written in notices of scientific and mechanical advancements. The machine age engulfing him was looked upon as most promising for the workers. He was confused and over-optimistic. On no apparent grounds other than hope, he anticipated a more equitable distribution of wealth in the wake of new inventions. For this reason he instituted a special department in the *Tribune* for publicizing inventions. He felt that the "path of Empire—journalistic and all other" stretched in that direction.[38] He was personally involved in several such innovations, one of which was a steam plow.[39]

With this attitude, it depressed him to observe that the sentiment of the country was less concerned with improvements along mechanical lines than with speculation and warfare. He might have suspected that machinery could become symbolic of exploitation and death more easily than of prosperity and peace, but he refused to admit it.

On the contrary, he asked why American youth crowded into the cities and strove to get rich quickly through speculation, neglecting inventive and creative enterprise on the farm and in the factory. One explanation might be in the general laudation of conquest and military exploits in the public print: "How can we hope to see peaceful industry duly followed and delighted in while the Press impels the worship of such Juggernauts of imposture and homicide . . . ?"[40]

He was determined that his paper should not cater to this cancerous growth, but results were discouraging. On one occasion he upbraided his readers for their complacent re-

[38] Greeley to Dana, Apr. 7, 9, 1856, Greeley, *Letters*, 142-148.
[39] Greeley to Sanders, Jan. 7, 185(4), HCL. To O. A. Bowe, May 9, 1854, Greeley MSS., NYPL. Greeley wrote Thaddeus Stevens, Jan. 21, 1860, NYHSL, that he had seen Cyrus McCormick about a steam plow while on a lecture trip. He found McCormick "a little closer than the bark on a white oak in winter . . . "
[40] *DTri.*, May 29, 1857.

ception of a *Tribune* account of the excellence of American farm machinery. Had it been a bulletin on the supremacy of the nation's arms in a murderous battle, "no matter on what pretext of quarrel," he wrote in anger, "we should have been required to issue one edition after another till midnight, and then close our office with the demand for extra copies of the electrifying narration still unsatiated." He sorrowed that "we are still essentially barbarians—that is, we judge by brutal standards, and deck with our laurels the brow of overmastering Force rather than that of creative Genius."[41]

In addition to this idealism, the *Tribune* took care to advocate immediate, practical reforms which benefited the working class. The foulness aboard immigrant ships and the frightful slum districts in New York City were exposed, and remedial legislation demanded.[42] Speculation in consumer commodities, particularly foodstuffs, was bitterly attacked. A valiant fight was waged for clean streets, sanitation and health precautions, inspected milk, an orderly city government, and Central Park as a recreational center for the common man.[43] In addition to temperance, Greeley was a leader in the struggle for child labor regulations, the destruction of sweat shops, shorter working hours, and the curtailment of prostitution by offering women a variety of constructive jobs with ample pay.[44]

The point is, however, that nothing in Greeley's working class program prevented his making a strong political appeal to conservatives. True, capitalists were slow to understand his ideas on labor, probably because trade unionism for so little

[41] *DTri.*, Sept. 3, 1855. Greeley was referring to a ltr. from a special Paris correspondent who was covering the "Palace of Industry" exposition, dated Aug. 16 and appearing in *DTri.*, Sept. 1, 1855.

[42] *DTri.*, esp. Nov. 2, 17, 19, 22, 26, 1853; Apr. 26, Nov. 17, 1854; Feb. 19, 1855; Apr. 1, 1856; July 20, 1857; Dec. 20, 1858; Feb. 3, Apr. 3, 1860.

[43] *DTri.*, esp. Oct. 14, 28, Nov. 4, 1853; Feb. 4, Mar. 6, June 1, July 17, Sept. 7, 20, 1854; Feb. 9, May 22, 1856; June 1, 12, 1857; May 4, June 8, Nov. 20, Dec. 4, 1858; Dec. 7, 1859; Mar. 23, 1860.

[44] *DTri.*, esp. Apr. 18, 1854; Jan. 5, Feb. 7, 1855; Nov. 27, 1856; Apr. 9, 1857; July 10, 1858; Apr. 7, 1859; Mar. 19, 1860. Greeley to Mrs. Pauline W. Davis, Sept. 1, 1852, Greeley Transcripts, LC.

as limited, benevolent purposes was considered somewhat radical, and because producers' cooperatives were not quickly recognized as impracticable under current economic and social conditions. By the time of the Civil War, Greeley was being accepted by industrialists and financiers as one of their supporters. While retaining his popularity with labor, he was advancing in every way the economic nationalism which engulfed America in the last half of the nineteenth century. He was an advocate of capitalist expansion in an era when men dreamed in terms of the dollar. Whatever may have been said and thought of his "isms" ten years previously, in 1857 he was attuned to the popular concept of his country's development. He was no harebrained reformer.

Anti-Nebraskan fusion temporarily delayed the promotion of Greeley's ideas on domestic development. His strategy was unaltered, but he could ill afford to jeopardize slavery restriction by tactics which might be acceptable to old Whigs but not to former Democrats. His support of the tariff of 1857, carrying unusually low levies, serves as an example.

This measure originated in Lewis D. Campbell's committee on ways and means, and was sanctioned by the outgoing Republican-Know Nothing house elected in 1854. During the period of the Banks election, the *Tribune* had dealt harshly with Campbell, a moderate Ohio Know Nothing who was slowly becoming a Republican. Greeley was anxious to make amends. "It only remains to say," he editorialized, "that Mr. Lewis D. Campbell—with whom it has not of late been our fortune to agree so generally nor so heartily as we could wish—seems to us to have fairly earned credit by the ability, energy and intelligence which he has evinced in his efforts to reduce the Revenue with as little injury and as much benefit as possible to our imperiled Industrial interests."[45]

This was so much hot air. Just two months previously, Greeley had pleaded for a Christmas present to the poor in

[45] *DTri.*, Mar. 4, 1857.

the form of a protective tariff. "Philanthropists! legislators! Christians!" he had entreated, "help us devise and establish some system whereby there shall always . . . be work at some rate for all who need and will accept it. Help us to replace Charity, to a great extent, by Wages, and thus diminish the moral degradation as well as the pecuniary burdens of Pauperism."[46]

Since the enactment of the Walker tariff of 1846, he had been warning that its low rates would result in a financial disaster. After the slavery question became politically predominant, in non-campaign years, his arguments for protection were distinctive. He believed that excessive importation and speculation were leading to a depression similar to that which struck the country in 1837.[47]

When ridiculed for this consistent pessimism, he replied that California gold was supplying the nation with a period of false prosperity, during which metal was being exchanged for foreign goods. He predicted that the reckoning would be all the harsher when it did come. Already the fruits of impoverishment could be seen growing from the policy of importing fabrics and hardware, of transferring bonds to English capitalists in order to get railway construction materials. Home production was suffering from unnecessary competition, he said, and living costs were rising unduly while opportunities for employment were becoming meager.[48]

Toward the close of 1856, the *Tribune* increased the tempo of its arguments against free trade. A series of editorials was begun, at first dealing specifically with financial conditions in Europe but later blending neatly into a discussion of domestic economics.

[46] *DTri.*, Dec. 24, 1856. See also *DTri.*, Nov. 22, Dec. 4, 26, 1856.
[47] *DTri.*, esp. Sept. 6, 12, 26, Oct. 4, 12, 14, 15, 18, 22, 25, 27, Dec. 2, 7, 1853; Apr. 19, May 3, 25, Oct. 23, Nov. 20, 24, Dec. 12, 15, 1854; Jan. 9, 15, Feb. 5, July 4, 7, 10, 14, Sept. 5, Oct. 3, 23, 30, 1855; Apr. 21, 1856; Sept. 28, Oct. 12, 1857. Reavis, *Greeley*, 329-341, 348-349.
[48] *DTri.*, June 3, July 4, 10, 1854.

These editorials were anti-British and anti-French, predicting a collapse of continental finances and blaming that impending disaster on the English doctrine of free trade and the speculation rife under Napoleon III. English factories were accused of overproduction and of flooding world markets, which was giving rise to an orgy of speculation. The outcome was thought to be inevitable. Economic hardships would unleash political disturbances, and the oligarchical governments of central and western Europe would be overthrown.

While viewing the advent of more democratic governments abroad with pleasure,[49] the *Tribune* was really concerned with the effect of the coming European monetary crisis on the United States. The truth of the matter was, it declared, that the Democrats were in league with the English manufacturers. For that reason, the nation had adopted free trade and was shipping its staple crops to England for fabrication. The *Tribune* maintained that this policy had made the United States economically dependent upon England and Europe. When the approaching downfall took place, the prophecy was that "we shall go with it. We boast of our prosperity, but it is hollow. We are mere colonists and dependents of Europe."[50]

This editorial treatment of the world's fiscal structure was timed perfectly. The next act was Greeley's. He took an extended lecture tour in the late winter and early spring of 1857. What he saw on this trip was most discouraging. The population of the northwest was growing fast, and he felt it would be almost impossible to settle the region too thickly. He observed that homestead legislation would greatly benefit the entire section. On the other hand, he hated to see risky investments in paper towns, and noted that many of the new

49 *DTri.*, Jan. 5, 12, Mar. 12, June 24, 1858.
50 *DTri.*, Dec. 6, 1856. See also *DTri.*, Oct. 9, 27, Nov. 1, 22, Dec. 29, 1856; May 30, June 1, Sept. 27, 1857. Dana and Carey seem to have collaborated in these editorials.

railways were overcapitalized and some were poorly constructed. Spring freshets were washing away tracks laid on the black prairie muck. Why, he asked, were the enormous dividends paid on watered stock not used in maintenance?[51] He feared that speculation was rife and that disaster was inevitable. In Iowa City he observed that "almost every one here who isn't getting drunk is getting rich, or thinks he is."[52]

Returned from the boisterous west to the comparative quiet of his editorial office, Greeley reflected upon the state of the country and scrawled out a series of crisp warnings. Prophets of evil were hardly apt to win popularity, he admitted; but he hoped that his advice would be heeded. "Believing that our current prosperity is bloated, unsound and factitious—that the commercial world is now on the eve of a great revulsion—that a radically new direction should be given to public policy and private enterprise if we would avert this universal peril, we proceed briefly to indicate our reasons for this conviction." California and Australia had thrown too much gold onto the world market. Inflation had resulted. In addition, free trade was causing a superficial prosperity. "Europe, staggering under an Atlas of Public Debt . . . contrives, in spite of her obstructive governments, prodigal courts, standing armies, costly wars, squandering aristocracies, squalid and inefficient peasantries, to run us yearly deeper and deeper into her debt." It was a dismal picture: "Our vigorous youth thus borrows of her senile decrepitude to make the year's ends meet; and the young heir trades off his expectancies at ruinous rates across the counter of the palsied usurer. And now comes our new Tariff to aggravate this tendency by crumbling down the barriers to importation, and thus increase the annual balances against us. We shall naturally buy more wines, more liquors, more iron, more steel, more wool, more sugar, and hardly less of

[51] From Madison, Wis., Jan. 25; Chicago, Jan. 28; Davenport, Io., Jan. 30; Galesburg, Ill., Feb. 7; Princeton, Ill., Feb. 13; Geneva, Ill., Feb. 16; Goshen, Ind., Feb. 17, *DTri.*, Feb. 3, 11, 14, 18, 24, 23, Mar. 2, 1857.
[52] From Iowa City, Feb. 3, *DTri.*, Feb. 20, 1857.

fabrics, because of this alteration: and what beside Bonds have we to sell in excess of last year wherewith to meet the obligations thus incurred?" Nothing, he answered: "Our wealth consists of promises to pay; we grow rapidly rich by converting lands just bought at ten York shillings per acre into city lots which we sell to each other (on credit) at $100 to $5,000 each, and are drinking $5 wine and riding in $1,000 coaches on the strength of the money we shall have when these lots are paid for. The wine is paid for in railroad bonds sold at fifteen or twenty per cent. discount; and we pay the interest on these by selling more bonds. All goes merrily so long as this lasts, but it cannot last forever. We shall wake up some morning and find it brought to a dead halt: every one sees this, feels it, knows it; but each says, 'We shall get *our* Railroad completed meantime, and that makes *my* fortune'; or, 'I shall sell off *my* lots at high prices, and then let the crash come as soon as it will!' We do not say that it must come this year or next; we presume its immediate impulse will be some comparatively trivial probably unlooked-for incident; but its real, ultimate cause will be too much extravagance and high living, too much building and adorning, and too little attention to cultivating the earth; too much buying abroad, and on time, of things which we should make at home and pay for as fast as we use them—all stimulated by a mistaken National policy and a fortuitous increase in the volume of the Precious Metals. That the crash will come too soon for most of us . . . we do most earnestly believe."[53]

Irrespective of the merits of Greeley's prognostications, a financial panic did break in the fall of 1857. He seized this opportunity to inject economic nationalism into the veins of the Republican party. Despite temporary rebuffs, especially from the Free Soil Democratic press, he emerged from the

[53] *DTri.,* Mar. 13. Greeley's italics and parentheses. See also *DTri.,* Mar. 17, 19, 25, 1857.

economic disturbance convinced that his party's 1860 platform would embody his principles of political economy.

The panic broke, not in Europe, but with the collapse of the Ohio Life Insurance and Trust Company late in August, 1857. Before normality returned, it is estimated that 5123 bankruptcies occurred in the United States and Canada, with an aggregate liability of $291,801,000.[54]

Greeley immediately announced his cure for the panic: "We believe a Protective Tariff to be the true National remedy for our present commercial ills. Let it be decreed to-morrow that no Foreign Product that competes with a home-made one shall henceforth enter our ports without paying from 40 to 80 per cent. duty, and our Banks would be all right within thirty days. Confidence would revive; hope would replace despondency; mills, foundries and factories would call for additional hands; and at least Half a Million persons, who have now a miserable prospect for work and food this Winter, would be fully employed in making the Iron, Cloths, Wares, &c., which we shall partly import and partly do without under our present system."[55]

The depression would bring hardships to many, he acknowledged. "But the tendency even of its disasters will in the average be wholesome—toward greater frugality, closer circumspection, more general productive industry, and a contraction or liquidation of debts, instead of prodigal or ostentatious living, reckless adventure, useless or pernicious avocations, and universal expansion. If the medicine is repulsive, it only proves that the patient is very sick. Let him take it with fortitude, fully resolved never to need it again."[56]

This was not the time to set class against class, he counseled: "Realize and inculcate the Harmony of Interests

[54] D. M. Evans, *The History of the Commercial Crisis, 1857-1858* . . . (London, 1859), 34.
The most recent study of this financial crisis follows the *Tribune's* interpretation of its causes. George W. Van Vleck, *The Panic of 1857* . . . (New York, 1943).
[55] *DTri.*, Oct. 2, 1857.   [56] *DTri.*, Sept. 30, 1857.

between Employer and Employed, Farmer and Artisan or Manufacturer, Capitalist and Laborer. All these, in the large, general view, prosper or suffer together, though they may cherish petty or seeming antagonisms. Each for All should be the motto."[57]

Many papers other than the *Tribune* accused the banks of having precipitated the crisis. They, it was claimed, had unnecessarily contracted credits and thereby thrown many sound concerns into bankruptcy.[58] Greeley regretted this course because he favored a national banking system with liberal regulations controlling the issuance of paper currency. Also, he feared an aggravation of the disturbance by a run on the banks. He quickly moved to their defense. In them was the salvation for all. The farmers were in debt, and must pay if the merchants were to remain solvent. As he figured it, the west owed the east and the east owed Europe. The only solution was to ship western grain and livestock immediately to eastern ports and thence to Europe. Money was needed in order to stimulate this movement, and as far as he was concerned the banks alone could produce it. If followed, this procedure would revive business, he claimed. Canals and railroads would be afforded much needed freight; ships would be supplied with cargoes. He called this a "wholesome process of general liquidation."[59]

Greeley denounced as nonsense the theory that a contraction of currency by the banks had caused the collapse. He pointed out that notes were but a small part of negotiable paper. Stocks and bonds formed the greater portion. Depreciation of these holdings was so great that currency reductions were a mere "bagatelle" in comparison.[60]

He maintained that the New York system of free banking, the broad outlines of which were followed by congress in drawing up the national banking act of 1863, was perfect.

[57] *DTri.*, Oct. 16, 1857. [58] Evans, *Commercial Crisis*, 34.
[59] *DTri.*, Sept. 22, 1857. See also *DTri.*, Sept. 10, 16, 1857.
[60] *DTri.*, Sept. 26, 1857.

Under the state law of 1838 and its several amendments, banks were permitted to circulate notes secured by national or New York state public securities and by bonds and mortgages on improved and productive land.[61] This policy had been criticized because the banks were thereby allowed to draw interest from both the bonds and negotiable paper and the bank notes issued. Greeley could see nothing unjust in this scheme. He was perfectly willing that his neighbor should make two or even three profits on the same capital, provided each was based on actual service to the community. According to him, such a system should be established by congress. The sub-treasury method then in use, instituted during the Polk administration and by which the federal government served as its own banker, he termed barbaric. Financial flexibility was needed during panics, he observed, and the Democratic scheme contracted issues of currency at the time when their expansion was desperately needed.[62]

For the moment, Greeley's arguments were not so favorably received as he would have liked. His theories of economic nationalism did not suit the exigencies of party politics; in fact, they did not even convince his editorial family. Dana asserted that the crisis was the result of Wall street speculation and governmental corruption. "The present panic," he asserted in the *Tribune*, "had its origin solely and exclusively with that nest of gamblers, the Brokers' Board." He believed that the secrecy of their operations had undermined confidence within the business world and concluded that an explicit law invalidating dealing in futures was needed.[63]

Pike did not blame free trade, but a reckless system of credits. He went so far in his *Tribune* column as to damn Greeley's pet New York banking system as a failure. "The

[61] *The Banking Laws of the State of New York . . . 1838 to . . . 1854* (Albany, 1854), esp. 3-5, 16, 30, 36-37, 48-49. *DTri.*, Sept. 26, 28, 29, 30, Oct. 1, 5, 7, 14, 1857.
[62] *DTri.*, Aug. 31, Sept. 3, 10, 30, Oct. 5, 6, 20, Nov. 11, Dec. 4, 1857.
[63] *DTri.*, Oct. 1, 1857. See also *DTri.*, Sept. 23, 1859.

much-abused Sub-Treasury," he noted, "is the only remaining memento of pecuniary stability the country holds."[64]

Greeley had to face the truth. The Republican party was not yet strong enough to stand internal dissensions. He began to apologize for his blunt statements on protection and banking.

"We have been falsely charged," he announced, "with abandoning the platform of the Republican party in favor of the establishment of a Protective Tariff. Nothing could be further from the fact. We propose no alteration of the Tariff—recommend none—any more than we propose or recommend a National Bank. The People, whether wisely or unwisely, have chosen a Democratic Congress, which could not be induced to enact a Protective Tariff if it were certain that thus only could thousands of laborers be preserved from starvation and the country from absolute ruin. . . . Believing that a cycle of Hard Money and Free Trade is therefore inevitable, we exhort every one to shape his business accordingly, and not look to the Government for relief that will certainly not be afforded. . . . We do not know that we would even reëstablish the Protective Policy if we could tomorrow, with a full knowledge that it would be warred upon in the future as it has been in the past. Better lie still when we are down than get up merely to be knocked down again."[65]

William Cullen Bryant's *Evening Post*, a New York City journal formerly Democratic in convictions, proposed a debate with Greeley on the tariff issue. He regretted that he could not accept, "as we are deeply interested in the success of the Republican ticket in our State—an interest with which the heart, if not the columns of *The Post* doubtless sympathizes—we defer for some days the discussion invoked by *The Post*."[66] Greeley wanted everyone to understand: "We

---

[64] To the editor of the *Tribune*, undated, *DTri.*, Oct. 21, 1857. Greeley commented that Pike's article included some errors of fact, but that since the advice to get out of debt was sound, the *Tribune* would "gladly" publish it.
[65] *DTri.*, Oct. 26, 1857.   [66] *DTri.*, Oct. 29, 1857.

do not mean to be diverted from the great issue of Freedom against Slavery by any quarrel about Banks or Tariffs."[67]

It was too late for Greeley to try to make amends. The Republicans lost the off-year election of 1857 in New York State. They were attacked for corruption, excessive expenditures on internal improvements, and for fostering a banking system which was detrimental to the economic interests of the masses. Greeley tried in vain to divert attention from the panic to the Dred Scott decision and troubles in Kansas, but the Hards and the Softs united, centered the canvass on local economic issues, and carried the day.[68]

Once the smoke from these local elections had cleared, Greeley estimated the situation anew. He was confident that the Republican cause would ultimately benefit from the panic by adopting his ideas of political economy, but he realized that he must continue to use guarded language when promoting those principles during campaign months.

Early in 1858, he took his annual western lecture tour. Prosperity was returning to the country, he reported. The people had learned the good lesson that they should not go in debt. Some of them had suffered considerably during the depression, and the eviction of settlers from their preempted government land by the Democratic administration in Washington was most unjustifiable. Homesteads, he was sure, were becoming a major political question. More important, the farmers were demanding protection. They were realizing that the middlemen were reaping excessive profits, and they wanted factories moved close to them by means of a tariff. They now saw the value of home markets.[69] Greeley smiled as he announced that the tariff question would "influence powerfully" the 1858 and 1860 campaigns.[70]

[67] In reply to "F. H. K.," *DTri.*, Nov. 6, 1857. See also *DTri.*, Nov. 5, 12, 27, 28, Dec. 9, 1857.

[68] *DTri.*, all Oct. and early Nov. issues. See also *DTri.*, July 19, 1858. Alexander, *New York*, ii, 245-246.

[69] From Chicago, Jan. 4, 11, *DTri.*, Jan. 9, 15, 1858. See also *DTri.*, Jan. 22, June 1, 1858.

[70] *DTri.*, June 2, 1858.

CHAPTER 8

THE DEMOCRATIC PARTY
IS SPLIT

...I advise you privately that: (1) Mr. Douglas would be the strongest candidate that the Democratic party could present for President; but (2) they will *not* present him. The old leaders won't endure it. (3) As he is doomed to be slaughtered at Charleston it is good policy to fatten him meantime. He will cut the better at killing time.—Greeley to William H. Herndon, November 14, 1858.

GREELEY had every reason to soft-pedal his ideas on political economy. The Buchanan administration acted so unwisely as to toss into his lap other issues ready-made for broadening and consolidating Republican support. Conceding Greeley's ability as a protagonist, he was greatly assisted by the mistakes of his political adversaries.

The Democrats misread the 1856 mandate of the American people. Greeley looked upon Frémont's excellent showing as assuring freedom to Kansas, but Buchanan saw in his victory a public desire to get rid of the Kansas problem as quickly as possible, and decided that the best way to do so was to act aggressively and without consideration for the principles of the Republican party. In this he erred. He not only strengthened the Republicans in the north but also split the Democrats. Nothing could have pleased Greeley more. He took full advantage of every opportunity afforded him to increase the Republican following and to drive deep the wedge between the northern and southern Democrats.

The first windfall Greeley received following Buchanan's election was the Dred Scott decision. Shortly after the inaugural in March, 1857, the Supreme Court held the Missouri Compromise unconstitutional. This verdict struck at the basis of the Republican party, which had sprung to life when that adjustment was repealed by the Kansas-Nebraska act. Had the American people been willing to accept the judgment of the court, they would have concurred unanimously that Republicanism was founded on an illegal constitutional doctrine and that the growth of the party had been fostered by an unwarrantable sectional disturbance. Such was not the reaction in the north.

A brief survey of the case shows that it was fraught with political dynamite. Dred Scott and his family had been held as bondsmen by his master, Dr. John Emerson, an army surgeon, at military posts in areas where slavery had been forbidden by free state law and by the 1820 compromise. In 1838, the Scotts returned with their master to his home in Missouri, where they remained in bondage. After Emerson's death, Scott brought suit in a lower Missouri court for his and his family's release, on the grounds that all were so entitled because of previous residence on free soil. A verdict favorable to Scott was awarded in 1850. This decision caused no surprise, for it was backed by precedent.

Two years later Mrs. Emerson, now Scott's legal owner, secured a reversal on appeal to the highest Missouri tribunal. Her counsel successfully argued that whatever Scott's status may have been outside the state, he had returned voluntarily into slavery, and must so remain.

In the meantime, Mrs. Emerson had remarried. Her new husband was Dr. Calvin C. Chaffee, a Massachusetts gentleman of antislavery convictions interested in making of the Scott case a test for the federal courts. To conceal this friendly backing, title to Scott was transferred to John F. A. Sanford, and the suit was carried into the United States district court in St. Louis.

The jurisdictional facilities of the federal government were available under these circumstances only when the defendant and the plaintiff were citizens of different states. So the negro's counsel averred that his client was a citizen of Missouri while Sanford was a resident of New York. Sanford's lawyer, acting nominally to protect his client's property but really to open up the case, entered a plea in abatement contending that the constitution did not recognize the citizenship of either slaves or negroes. The St. Louis district court suspended action on this plea and allowed the case to be argued on its merits. The decision ultimately reached was similar to that rendered by the highest bench in the Missouri jurisdictional system, that a slave who had returned voluntarily into bondage could not be adjudged free. In coming to this conclusion, the federal district court followed a Supreme Court precedent established in 1851.

The above details represent but the first two acts in this important drama. The dénouement could come only in the Supreme Court. Scott's writ of error for appeal was filed during the term which began in December, 1854, but the docket was so crowded that it was not reached until February, 1856.[1]

Considerable speculation arose as to what the decision might be. It was generally known that the court was pro-southern, and it was believed that the negro would be denied his freedom. There were a number of methods by which this might be done. Resort could be had to the plea in abatement and jurisdiction denied; the opinion of the St. Louis district court could be upheld; or judicial review could pass on the constitutionality of the Missouri Compromise. Any one of these grounds would have sufficed, but Chief Justice Roger B. Taney's majority opinion surprised many persons by covering them all.

As the trial proceeded, the court became more and more an arena for controversy. In May, a reargument was ordered, which meant that the judgment would not be thrown into

[1] Swisher, *Taney*, 484-487. The 1851 precedent was Strader vs. Graham, 10 Howard 82.

the midst of the Buchanan-Frémont-Fillmore presidential campaign. This is a probable explanation for the court's hesitancy.

All free soil publicity given the case in the spring of 1856 would have benefited Justice John McLean, who was a contender for the nomination of the People's Convention at Philadelphia and whom Greeley opposed. Hence there is a noticeable lack of editorial comment in the *Tribune*, which may be attributed to political considerations.[2]

The delay likewise pleased Buchanan. It provided what he considered to be the proper moment for the decision. He surmised that the verdict would be agreeable to him. As president-elect, he wished to end slavery agitation, which to his mind could be done by merely suppressing abolitionism. In his inaugural he planned to deal firmly with the question of territorial jurisdiction, showing that it was not within the constitutional power of congress to proscribe slavery. His argument would have more force if the court had previously seized upon the Scott case in order to overrule the Missouri Compromise.

Reconsideration of the Scott suit began in December, 1856. Early in February of the next year, Buchanan wrote a friend on the court to ask when the verdict would be rendered and what its scope would be. He learned in reply that it would come late that month, but that it would not assist him in his

[2] The *Tribune* quotations used by Charles Warren, *The Supreme Court in United States History* (Boston, 1922), III, 5-7, by no means reflect editorial policy, nor are they from Pike's Washington dispatches and letters, as Warren says. They are from "Our Own Correspondent," who signed himself "Index." This was James E. Harvey, who favored McLean's nomination by the Republicans at this time.

Swisher follows Warren in this error, *Taney*, 488-494. Pike was not even in Washington until mid-April, when he took Greeley's place at that post. For the important Harvey items on the Scott case, see the *DTri.*, Feb. 18, 19, 20, 26, 29, Apr. 9, 10, 11, 12, 24, May 7, 14, 15, 1856. See also his ltrs. to McLean, Mar. 30, May 30, June 1, 2, 1856, McLean MSS., XVIII, LC. Greeley to Dana, Dec. 1, 1855, Greeley MSS., LC. To Dana, Apr. 2, 1856, Greeley, *Letters*, 138-40. To Colfax, June 1, 1856, NYPL.

Greeley was in Washington during the heat of this first argument, and the single mention he made of the case may be found in *DTri.*, Feb. 15, 1856.

inaugural address since the right of congress to legislate on slavery in the territories would not be reviewed.

This information was incorrect. Conferences among the judges soon revealed that certainly McLean and perhaps Justice Benjamin R. Curtis of Massachusetts would uphold the 1820 settlement, irrespective of the action of the majority. McLean's reasoning was plausible. To establish Scott's right to liberty, he planned to follow the precedent established by southern courts ten years earlier: if a bondsman became free outside the slave states, he retained that status on his return to one of those commonwealths. To show that this circumstance applied to Scott, McLean found it necessary to prove the legality of the Missouri Compromise.

McLean's determination aroused resolution among the proslavery justices to meet the issue squarely. No other course was open if they expected to counter the free soil pronouncement their colleague was writing, and there is reason to believe that they agreed with Buchanan in thinking the court's prestige would assist in bringing political peace to the country.

So it developed that Buchanan received another letter from his friend on the court. He was advised to state in the body of his inaugural address that the "high and independent character" of the Supreme Court could best be relied upon to settle "a controversy which has so long and seriously agitated the country." Further communications between Buchanan and the pro-southern majority disclosed the full nature of the verdict and that, because of Taney's weak health, it would not be rendered until after the inauguration.

Taney was present at these ceremonies early in March; and, as an example of the absurd suspicions current at the time, he was accused of having whispered something into Buchanan's ear. Republicans claimed that he had thereupon confided judicial secrets, and the address which followed strengthened this story in that Buchanan asked the people to accept peacefully whatever the Supreme Court might say as to the legality of the 1820 adjustment.[3]

The *Tribune* also possessed a confidential channel of information. It had, in general terms, long been ridiculing the court, but in the fall and winter of 1856, this attack was intensified.[4] Two days before Buchanan's inaugural, it imparted editorially: "We learn from trustworthy sources that the Supreme Court . . . will, by a large majority, sustain the extreme Southern ground, denying the constitutionality of the Missouri Compromise. Probably Judges Curtis and McLean will alone dissent. . . . The decree of the Court will, it is supposed, be given in a few days. . . . The majority of this august Court are possibly weak enough to suppose that this decree will tranquilize the country."[5]

Greeley's comments were not published until the next day, for he had just returned from a western lecture tour. He informed the president that the inaugural promise to enforce popular sovereignty in Kansas amounted to naught. At that very moment, Greeley asserted, the highest court in the land was ready to decree "that a slaveholder had the same right to take his slaves into any Territory and hold them there as slaves, and demand the protection of the law in so doing, as a freeman has to take his horse or ox there." Greeley's anger rose as he parroted Buchanan's speech: "You may 'cheerful[l]y submit'—of course you will—to whatever the five slaveholders and two or three doughfaces on the bench of the Supreme Court may be ready to utter on this subject; but not one man who really desires the triumph of Freedom over Slavery in the Territories will do so. We may be constrained to obey as law whatever that tribunal shall put forth; but, happily, this is a country in which the People make both laws and judges, and they will try their strength

---

[3] Swisher, *Taney,* 494-501.

[4] *DTri.,* esp. Feb. 13, Apr. 20, Aug. 28, 1855; June 6, 20, July 30, Aug. 2, Nov. 10, 19, Dec. 16, 1856; Feb. 16, 1857.

[5] *DTri.,* Mar. 2 (unless otherwise noted, the remaining dates cited in this chapter will be understood as 1857).

on the issue here presented." He wished to "whisper" into Buchanan's ear that "true Peace follows Justice."[6]

Chief Justice Taney read his opinion the following day. He remanded the case to its court of origin and instructed that it be dismissed for want of jurisdiction. He reasoned that Scott, a negro and consequently an inferior person, was not a citizen and had no right to sue in a federal court. Scott, the decision continued, had always been a slave because the Missouri Compromise was unconstitutional, and, whatever the temporary effect of his residence on free soil may have been, he had voluntarily returned to Missouri and bondage.[7]

The *Tribune's* fury was directed chiefly against that portion of the decision which declared the 1820 reconciliation illegal. This argument was, to summarize the *Tribune's* stand, mere *obiter dictum*, that is, it was not binding since it was beyond the problem at hand. In order to understand such criticism, it is necessary to examine Taney's treatment in greater detail.

It is generally recognized that American constitutional law is established by the Supreme Court, and it follows that the charge of *obiter dictum* is illogical. Taney had right and precedent for denying Scott the privilege of the court and at the same time reviewing the power of congress to proscribe slavery from the territories. If the verdict relative to the Compromise of 1820 is to be stigmatized, it must be by an examination of its principles.

The majority held the Missouri Compromise invalid, but did not follow identical reasoning in arriving at this judgment. Justice John Catron of Tennessee concurred by arguing that the treaty with France purchasing the Louisiana territory was organic law and that legislation which countered it by restricting slavery was illegal since it had been permitted in that region by France. Justice John A. Campbell of Alabama proved himself a follower of Calhoun.

[6] *DTri.*, Mar. 5.
[7] Swisher, *Taney,* 502-509. 19 Howard 393.

His opinion tended toward the nationalization of slavery by maintaining that Scott was an article of property and therefore could not be taken from his master.

The method of the other five of the majority, and especially Taney's, diverged from Campbell in following federalistic lines. All citizens, Taney maintained, had equal rights in the territories, which were held by the federal government in trust for the states, free and slave alike. At this juncture Taney approached Campbell's reasoning by buttressing his conclusion with a point which was not then accepted. He attempted to read into the constitution the principle of vested property interests. Lawmakers, he ruled, had no authority to debar slavery from a territory because of the fifth amendment. Slaves were property. An act of congress depriving an innocent citizen of liberty or property, he said, "could hardly be dignified with the name of due process of law." Before 1857, the sacred part of the constitution, particularly in Taney's decisions, had been the sovereignty of the people and not the fundamental rights of wealth; the due process clause had been used only to assure trial by jury.[8] Taney's argument applied only to the federal government. It did not deny the right of a state to declare its preference for a free or a slave constitution.

This background is important to an understanding of the *Tribune's* onslaught against the Scott decision. Must the staff in attacking the decree at the same time alienate northern conservatives who sought constitutional protection for their worldly goods? Such a course might prove disastrous to Greeley's policy of harmonizing management and labor, which was essential to Republican growth. Here the resemblance of Taney's logic to that followed by Campbell came in handily, for in the final analysis both treated slaves as property. The *Tribune* need not mention the broad pro-

---

[8] Edward S. Corwin, "The Dred Scott Decision, in the Light of Contemporary Legal Doctrines," *American Historical Review*, xvii (Oct., 1911), 52-69.

tection afforded all capital by Taney's argument. It would with utmost ease lump both opinions together and denounce them as rank Calhounism, a doctrine which treated human beings as property just because of the color of their skin. It would pluck the humanitarian cords of its readers' hearts, mingling into its score the melodious voice of Scott as a fellow man denied his freedom. There was no reason to touch the dissonant note of class conflict.

Thus unencumbered, the *Tribune* beat out a throbbing tune. Greeley was a skillful director. Calhounism, he asserted, had been firmly intrenched in the federal government and could be driven out only by Republican success. He recalled that Buchanan had promised during the 1856 campaign to enforce popular sovereignty in Kansas, and regretted that free soil efforts to convince the northern people of the true aims of the Democratic party had been in vain. Buchanan's inaugural and the Dred Scott decision were ample proof of what the Democrats wanted: "Any slaveholder . . . may plant Slavery in Minnesota or Nebraska to-morrow, in ostentatious defiance of their whole People."[9] The new administration could be expected to maintain human bondage in all the territories with black codes if necessary. Greeley assured his audience that northerners would have nothing to do with the verdict, which was "a *dictum* prescribed by the stump to the bench—the Bowie-knife sticking in the stump for instant use if needed." He declared that the judgment annihilated "all Compromises and brings us face to face with the great issue in the right shape."[10]

The efforts of the conservative press to defend the court were ineffectual, but they did cause Greeley to justify his attack. He swore that he would not go down on his knees before Roger Taney. The "iniquity" of the verdict, violating as it did "the truth of history and the logic even of the law," would be made obvious to all his countrymen "who can read."

[9] *DTri.*, Mar. 9. [10] *DTri.*, Mar. 7. Greeley's italics.

Particularly would he parade its "fundamental denial to the feeble and downtrodden of any right of appeal to the Federal tribunals"; for they above all needed the protection of justice.

He promised that the majority opinion would be reversed: "We mean to create and arouse an enlightened Public Sentiment which shall ultimately place the Federal Government, in all its departments, in the hands of men who love the Constitution and the Union much, but Liberty, Eternal Justice and the inalienable Rights of Man, still more—men who will regard Freedom as the universal and everlasting rule and Slavery as the local and transitory exception . . . " He admitted that the perils of sectionalism were great, but he was more frightened by "the danger that our liberties may be subverted, our rights trampled upon, the spirit of our institutions utterly disregarded, and our great republican experiment turn out a disastrous failure."[11]

Greeley's assistants were more indignant than he. "It is a war upon free labor," one editorial proclaimed, "it is a war upon non-slaveholders, whom the Court seeks to deprive of the power to protect themselves against the competition of slave labor, and to deliver over, bound hand and foot, to the absolute control of a slaveholding Oligarchy."[12] The decision of the Chief Justice was summarized in long discourses which sought to bring out his legal mistakes. The opinions of McLean and Curtis were displayed in full as exemplary of the highest in American legal scholarship.[13] The findings of all the justices were issued in a cheap pamphlet, which went through three editions before the year closed, and remained in print through the campaign of 1860.[14]

[11] *DTri.*, Mar. 12, 16. For comments of the conservative press, see Warren, *Supreme Court*, III, 31-37.
[12] *DTri.*, Apr. 1.
[13] *DTri.*, Mar. 10, 13, 14, 16, 20, 21, 31, Apr. 1, May 20, 28, June 5, 10, July 29.
[14] *DTri.* (advs.), July 6, Dec. 16. "The Case of Dred Scott" (pamphlet) (New York, 1860).

Pervading all this journalistic agitation was a tone of ridicule for the court which seriously injured its prestige for a score of years. Its ignorance and willful misrepresentation were branded as unequaled since the "time that Scroggs sat upon the Bench." Taney in his old age was charged with forgetting the function of a judge and relapsing into the "character of an eager, artful, sophistical, jesuitical, lying advocate—for the suppression of the truth is lying to all intents and purposes."[15] The majority of the judges were said to be in league with the Calhounites, whose next step would be reopening the slave trade with Africa.[16] Then the north would be inundated with bondsmen: "This is all involved in the present decision; but let a single case draw from the Court an official judgment that slaves can be held and protected under National law, and we shall see men buying slaves for the New-York market. There will be no legal power to prevent it."[17]

The identification of the Scott decision with Calhounism furnished Greeley with the weapon for one of his greatest polemical triumphs. The Supreme Court brought Senator Douglas face to face with a grave problem. How could he maintain his doctrine of popular sovereignty after the Scott decision had denied the constitutionality of outlawing slavery in the territories? In Springfield, Illinois, early in the summer of 1857, Douglas attempted to resolve this problem, upholding both the Scott verdict and the Kansas-Nebraska act. The two principles did not conflict, he contended, because local territorial governments—not congress—had the last word. They could, if they wished, withhold police protection from property in bondsmen, which would automatically outlaw enforced negro labor within their limits.

15 *DTri.*, May 20.
16 *DTri.*, esp. Mar. 25, Oct. 30; Jan. 7, Mar. 5, Sept. 1, 2, 1858.
17 *DTri.*, Mar. 11. The Lemmon slave case, then before New York courts, was represented as the trial which would soon allow the Supreme Court to judge that bondsmen could be held and protected in the free states under national law. See *DTri.*, Oct. 1, 2, 3, 5, 6, Dec. 8. Chester L. Barrows, *William M. Evarts* (Chapel Hill, 1941), 83-87.

Greeley scotched this argument in a brilliant editorial. He confessed that it would be strange if Douglas' "readiness of assertion and fluency of speech . . . had not satisfied the great body of his followers that the two apparently incompatible doctrines were easily reconcilable." But he, for one, remained unconvinced. "—Can anybody be duped by this juggle," he queried, "who does not seek to be deceived? . . . Does any American statesman believe the Federal Constitution so inane, so feeble, that it cannot secure the right of a citizen which it expressly guarantees in a district under its undoubted sway, where no State Sovereignty exists to contest and limit its jurisdiction? Are constitutional rights so completely subject to the caprice, and even to the inaction or negligence, of local majorities, often comprising but a handfull of persons? Who *can* believe it?"

Under a conscientious Democratic governor, federal troops would be used to uphold federal law. Greeley asked his readers to compare with Douglas' interpretation of the Scott decision the "more consistent, logical and straight-out pronouncement" of the late Democratic state convention of Texas:

" '*Resolved*, That the citizens of the Southern States have the indefeasible right to carry their slaves into any territory belonging to the United States, and there to exercise and enjoy all the rights of ownership and property, as freely and as fully as in the State from which they emigrate; and that any interference with or obstruction to the enjoyment and exercise of their rights, as Southern citizens, by the Government of the United States, *or by the inhabitants of any Territory*, would be a violation of the rights of the Southern States, which they possess as sovereign States and coequal members of the American confederacy.'

"Of course," Greeley continued, "this statement is abhorrent to us; but if the doctrines of Judge Taney are sound, they lead inevitably to this, and not to Mr. Douglas's equivocating, faith-breaking, duty-evading 'Popular Sovereignty.'"

Greeley concluded that Douglas was a master at the game of "cant, prejudice, sophistry and slang." He observed that the Little Giant had tried to obscure his renunciation of popular sovereignty by venting his rage upon the negro. Such was said to be the technique of all his tribe of demagogues. "Sham Democracy . . . seems incapable of letting the Black Race alone, whence result infinite confusions, hypocrisies, solecisms, and mulattoes."[18]

This thrust at Douglas was more than a denunciation. It was an effort to commit the Illinois senator by virtue of popular sovereignty to the right of the Kansans to choose a slave or a free constitution.

Ironically enough, the implications of the Scott decision were drawing both Greeley and Douglas into the same political kettle, beneath which Calhounism was heating up the fire. Greeley was forced, after the defeat of Frémont in 1856 and the Scott decision in 1857, to accept outright the practical operations of popular sovereignty in Kansas. Such a course offered him the one feasible method of bringing that territory into the Union as a free state. After the 1856 canvass, he was careful not to slacken his activities in dispatching northern emigrants to the new territory.[19] He wanted to obtain an undoubted antislavery majority; for, as he warned his readers, the "good, easy people who dream of moderation or decency in the settlement of the Kansas question have not yet awakened to the character of their Southern rulers."[20]

Theoretically, Greeley still thought that slavery could be excluded from all federal territory by congress; but when

[18] *DTri.*, June 24. Greeley's italics. Douglas' argument was more formally presented in "The Dividing Line Between Federal and Local Authority. Popular Sovereignty in the Territories," *Harper's New Monthly Magazine*, XIX (Sept., 1859), 519-537. Greeley replied to this essay in *DTri.*, Oct. 15, 1859.
[19] *DTri.*, esp. Nov. 12, 15, 25, Dec. 16, 17, 22, 1856; Jan. 5, 7, Mar. 25, 26, Apr. 13, 16, 18, May 16, 23.
[20] *DTri.*, Nov. 10, 1856.

that institution had already gained a foothold in an area, he announced that he would "right heartily" support a doctrine which would allow its inhabitants to override the Dred Scott decision by abolishing slavery.[21]

Emphasizing Douglas' obligations to popular sovereignty showed discernment. Events in Kansas simultaneous with the Dred Scott agitation caused the Little Giant to split the Democratic party—a development for which Greeley had been praying and laboring since 1853.

Kansas had changed since the summer of 1856. The free state men still refused to obey the so-called bogus laws which stemmed from the ruffian legislature, but this condition worried the proslavery forces but little, if at all. Backed by the legal territorial government, they held an election early in the summer of 1857 and chose delegates to a constitutional convention at Lecompton.[22] The northerners refused to participate in this contest, and Greeley stood firmly behind their decision. He contended that the canvass had been so arranged as to prevent a full antislavery vote, and added that in any case criminals from across the Missouri river were sure to flood the polls on the day of balloting and control everything.[23]

What Greeley feared may be gathered from his editorials on the subject. Geary had been replaced as governor by Robert Walker of Mississippi, whom the *Tribune* described as a scheming slaveholder from the heart of the black belt.[24] Greeley knew this picture to be a gross exaggeration. He judged Walker as a moderate and as a keen politician who was eager to bring peace to Kansas. He was frightened lest the new governor be successful in his attempt to organize a party in the territory which, while not aggressively proslavery, would be Democratic. Walker might be able to influence the southern faction at Lecompton and send to

21 *DTri.*, Dec. 15.   22 Beveridge, *Lincoln*, ii, 525-530.
23 *DTri.*, esp. Nov. 7, 12, 26, 29, Dec. 5, 15, 1856; Feb. 27, Mar. 31.
24 *DTri.*, Mar. 17, 18, 21, 23, 25, Apr. 4, 23, 24.

Washington a constitution which, although nominally free, would allow those few slaves already in Kansas to remain enthralled until their death.

This course, Greeley realized, would appeal to a large segment of the northern settlers. It would place the Republicans underfoot in Kansas and jeopardize their position throughout the free states, for the Democrats could with conviction argue that it conformed with both popular sovereignty and the Dred Scott decision. Kansas as a commonwealth would be Democratic, and this outcome would unduly delay Greeley's optimistic timetable for emancipation in Missouri and the other border states.[25]

No man was more relieved than Greeley when the Lecompton document was finished. Walker had been unsuccessful. The instrument embodied the Calhoun concept of slaves as property, and its schedule failed to provide for full submission to the inhabitants of the territory. Instead, they could vote only on the clause which allowed or prohibited further slave infiltrations. Walker, insisting that popular sovereignty was betrayed, broke with the southerners and returned east.

It was a great card for the Republicans when Buchanan decided to push the Lecompton constitution through congress. He was eager to quiet antagonism and thought such a procedure would settle the Kansas question at once.[26]

The worst of the *Tribune's* accusations had come true. Now it could flay the administration for complete servitude to the so-called slavery oligarchs. Greeley did not wait for Buchanan to act. He opened his offensive as soon as he learned of the president's intention. He denounced Sham Democracy for intensifying sectional discord, demanding that a fair vote be taken in Kansas to ascertain if the im-

[25] *DTri.*, June 9, 11, 13, 16, 26, July 8, 9, 10, 11, 14, 20, 21, Aug. 8, 14. See also Robert J. Walker, "An Appeal for the Union," *De Bow's Review*, xxi (Dec., 1856), 589-602.
[26] Beveridge, *Lincoln*, ii, 527-539. All Nov. and early Dec. *Tribune* issues.

migrants wanted the Lecompton, the free state Topeka, or an entirely new constitution.[27]

Buchanan submitted the Lecompton document to congress early in February, 1858. The legislative body at Washington was, by virtue of the 1856 election, strongly Democratic. Had the president's party remained united, it could have prevailed over the Republicans; and Greeley's cries might have been less effective. But Douglas, in the prime of his power and popularity, broke with the regular Democracy. He was up for reelection in the fall; and concerned with his position in the northwest, he saw that if he followed Buchanan his enemies in Illinois could brand him a traitor to popular sovereignty.

This thunderbolt of good news revitalized Greeley's hope that the slaveocracy would soon be overthrown. Temporarily doubtful, he was overjoyed by the assurance that the Little Giant would battle Lecompton. This insurgency represented the first major turn in mid-western politics since the advent of the Republican party.

Greeley found it wise to support Douglas. To allow him to be crucified at the November election in Illinois would set a bad example for other northern politicians who might dream of resisting southern demands. Everything could be lost if this recusancy were not nourished into open rebellion which would shatter the Calhounites. Such was the first goal of Republicanism, and to achieve it Greeley was willing to co-operate with any former adversary.[28] The new party needed additional members, for it was still in a minority. "As to Douglas," he later confided in friendly ears, "I consider him a low and dangerous demagogue—not good enough to be suffered to have the credit of losing his seat through devotion to a great principle. . . . To have such a man ostracized be-

[27] *DTri.*, Dec. 12.

[28] Greeley to Colfax, Dec. 11, 20, 25, NYPL. *DTri.*, Dec. 2. Reinhard H. Luthin, "The Democratic Split During Buchanan's Administration," *Pennsylvania History*, xi (Jan., 1944), 13-35.

cause of his first good deed would have been perilous—disastrous."[29]

Greeley interviewed Douglas twice in Washington. According to one account, he looked like "a Methodist exhorter from the interior of Vermont" as he hurried down Pennsylvania avenue to offer the Little Giant his congratulations and journalistic allegiance.[30] Others claimed that he sold out to Douglas, lock, stock, and barrel. Greeley later vowed that he made no commitments relating to Douglas' 1858 senatorial race in Illinois or to his presidential efforts two years later. It may be that his promise for the 1858 campaign did not pertain to Douglas alone, and it is hardly likely that conclusions as to 1860 were reached,[31] but indications are that the two men at this critical juncture agreed to insist upon popular sovereignty in Kansas in order to defeat the Lecompton constitution in congress and that Greeley pledged *Tribune* backing to the anti-Lecompton Democrats in the fall congressional elections.

Greeley's first major editorial on his return to New York City from Washington early in March resembled those of late 1854: the doors of Republicanism were open to all, and the one requirement for admission was resistance to the Lecompton "fraud." The enemies of this most recent swindle to Kansas, he asserted, were, "so far as they are willing to be so," his political "brethren." He would "urge the re-election of every Democratic or American Member of Congress" who voted against the administration.[32]

Colfax, who had accompanied Greeley on his visits to Douglas, was pleased by this editorial. He wrote from Washington that "Douglas is going to see each one of his men this week personally, & those who express fears that after being cut off by the Adm[inistratio]n, they will be run out by

29 Greeley to F. Newhall, Jan. 8, 1859, Greeley Transcripts, LC.
30 Quoted in Beveridge, *Lincoln*, II, 538.
31 *DTri.*, Jan. 29, Dec. 8, 10, 1859.   32 *DTri.*, Mar. 3, 1858.

Republicans, he is going to read your yesterday's leader to them. He says it is just right."[33]

Greeley had considered a more radical opposition to Buchanan's Kansas policy than to support Douglas, but his new found alliance suited him better. To have declined to join forces would have weakened the opposition to the measure. While he believed that Lecompton's passage would, to Republican advantage, renew bloodshed in Kansas, the sectional risks of such agitation were too great, and he put this temptation behind him. "We have no shadow of doubt," he editorialized, "that the triumph of Lecompton would strengthen and aid the Republican party; but it would do this at a cost which we are unwilling to incur. A year or more of revolutionary strife and general ravage in Kansas, with agitation and turmoil throughout the land, is a price that we do not need or wish to pay for an accession of strength . . ." He preferred to achieve victory "more cheaply, if more slowly, through the gradual diffusion of intelligence and ripening of now immature convictions."[34]

Lecompton passed the senate without difficulty, only David Broderick of California, George E. Pugh of Ohio, and Charles E. Stuart of Michigan among the Democrats bolting with Douglas to oppose it.[35] Slow deliberations in the upper chamber, however, allowed the *Tribune* to perfect its attack and center its pressure on the administration's northern representatives.

The staff excoriated Buchanan. His special message was described as "an elaboration of imposture and iniquity such as no false prophet ever concocted,"[36] and as marked by the same "general complaint of turbulence, faction, lawlessness,

[33] Colfax to Greeley, Mar. 4, 1858, NYPL. See also Greeley to Colfax, Dec. 9, 12, 1859, NYPL.
[34] *DTri.*, Mar. 11, 1858. See also Greeley to Colfax, Feb. 15, 1858, NYPL.
[35] The details of the Lecompton battle in Washington may be found in Hodder, "Some Aspects of the English Bill for the Admission of Kansas," *Annual Report* of the American Historical Association, *1906* (Washington, 1908), I, 199-210.
[36] *DTri.*, Feb. 3, 1858.

rebellion, revolutionary violence, &c." which George III had used in his assaults against the Revolutionary patriots.[37]

Greeley reminded everyone of his pre-election warnings, and pointed with scorn to the president's statement that *"Kansas is at this moment as much a Slave State as Georgia or South Carolina."*[38]

The president's greatest argument in favor of the Lecompton document had been that it would bring peace and quiet to troubled Kansas. Greeley labeled this contention childish. It was to him a naked fact that Buchanan's success would bring civil war to that territory. He declared that the Lecompton constitution could not stand a day unsupported by federal bayonets. He told his readers that the administration recognized this truth and for that reason sought an increase in the standing army so that freedom in Kansas could be subdued by force.[39]

"You say, gentlemen from the South!" Greeley pleaded, "that you don't expect to make Kansas a Slave State—you are only struggling for the abstract principle that a new Slave State may come into the Union, provided there shall be one wanting to come in."[40] Was not this desire, he asked, granted in the proposition that the territory's inhabitants vote on the whole of their constitution? Such was the anti-Lecompton position which both the Douglasites and the Republicans had taken. Nor had it been forced on the Republicans by the exigency of the moment. They had never denied the right of a slave state to enter the Union. They were "too sensible, too practical," he affirmed, "to undertake locking the stable door after the horse has been stolen. They seek to bend the twig, not to break the tree. They would keep Slavery out of (or under in) the Territories, so as not to be troubled with it in the admission of States. And Kansas,

37 *DTri.*, Feb. 4, 1858. See also *DTri.*, Feb. 5, 6, 1858.
38 *DTri.*, Feb. 4, 1858. Greeley's italics. James D. Richardson, ed., *Messages and Papers of the Presidents*, v (Washington, 1897), 479.
39 All *Tribune* issues, Feb., Mar., and early Apr., 1858.
40 *DTri.*, Apr. 5, 1858.

which has taught them how to deal practically with the Slave Power so as to check its advances and transform its triumphs into discomfitures, may teach us [sic] also how to sacrifice our own pride of opinion to the requirements of a practical opportunity for closing an embittered controversy and securing an immense good."[41]

Such reasoning acted as a cohesive agent on the opposition in the house. The parliamentary tactics used to rout the administration were simple. The Republicans, anti-Lecompton Democrats, and northern Know Nothings were to unite and pass the Crittenden-Montgomery substitute, which would require full submission of the controversial document to the people of Kansas. The greatest difficulty in employing this technique came from the radical Republicans, for it meant that they must accede, by implication at least, to the principle of admitting new states even though their constitutions permitted slavery. It was difficult to bring some into line, and the *Tribune*, branding them "impracticables," was energetic in this work.[42]

On April 1, the Crittenden-Montgomery measure passed the house by a 120-112 vote, twenty-two Democrats following Douglas' leadership. The issue was now drawn between the senate and the lower chamber. Though really sceptical of the final outcome, Greeley appeared in high spirits on his editorial page. He announced that a national salute would be fired from the Battery at sunset on the 2nd, and fire-works displayed in Central Park that evening. This noise and exhibition, he said, would celebrate "a triumph of genuine Popular Sovereignty. . . . a victory of Good Faith over Executive Treachery . . ."[43]

Consultation between senate and house leaders followed, and Greeley feared that an adjustment allowing the admin-

---

[41] *DTri.,* Apr. 9, 1858. Greeley's parentheses.
[42] Julian, *Giddings,* 340-351. All *Tribune* issues, Mar., 1858. See also *Congressional Globe,* 35th Congress, 1st sess., pt. 2 (Washington, 1858), 1435 ff.
[43] *DTri.,* Apr. 2, 1858.

istration to emerge with a partial victory would be made. His greatest apprehension, that Douglas might falter,[44] proved groundless, but a compromise was gained and the Crittenden-Montgomery bill defeated.

The accommodation agreed upon was submitted by William H. English, Democratic representative from Indiana who had opposed Lecompton. He suggested that the entire proslavery constitution be placed before the people of Kansas; if accepted, the territory would be admitted as a state and the usual land grants for internal improvements would be made simultaneously; if rejected, admission would be delayed until the population of Kansas had nearly doubled. The Democratic regulars used party pressure and pushed the English measure through the house on the last day of April. Almost half the anti-Lecompton representatives deserted Douglas.[45]

Greeley had no regrets. "Don't be frightened at the looks of English's bill," he wrote Colfax. "It is a vicious blunderbuss, and will kick over those who stand at the breech."[46] Immediately the *Tribune* began supplying the "kick."

The compromise measure did not submit the Lecompton constitution to the people of Kansas, Greeley editorialized. Instead, it was intended as a bribe involving millions of acres of public land should they agree to enter the Union as a slave state. Should they refuse, he continued, they would be penalized by being compelled to remain inhabitants of a territory for several additional years.[47] Branding the proposal hypocritical, he entitled it "Lecompton Junior—the English brat."[48] It only increased sectional agitation. The Republicans, as all reasonable men would admit, had tried to hold the Democrats to their 1856 campaign platform; now it was evident to the world that the Calhounites were in full command at Washington. "Kansas has been fairly won by Free

[44] Greeley to Colfax (Apr., 1858), NYPL.
[45] Milton, *The Eve of Conflict*, 292-293.
[46] Greeley to Colfax, Apr. 21, 1858, NYPL.
[47] *DTri.*, Apr., 22, 24, 26, 1858.   [48] *DTri.*, Apr. 29, 1858.

Labor, in open, arduous, protracted contest," he affirmed. "The judgment of the People is entered up: and it is unworthy of statesmen to resort to pettifogging quibbles and dodges to stave off the execution."[49] He vowed that the free state party would spurn the congressional bribe. "So, Messrs. Lecomptonites," he concluded with confidence, "move on!"[50]

The next move involved the 1858 congressional and state campaigns. Fortuitous circumstances and shrewd political journalism had placed Greeley in an advantageous position for this test. He was able to continue his policy of harmony which had already proved so beneficial to the Republican party.

He met unexpected opposition, however, from certain Republican leaders. Greeley's estimate of the political situation was from a national point of view. He looked upon the interest of certain state politicians in the success of their favorite straight-line Republicans as mere selfishness. He felt that many anti-Lecompton Democrats had been kicked out of their party permanently and that the northern Know Nothing leaders were fast losing their already dwindled political support. The majority within these groups, he thought, would make good Republicans. For his party to refuse them concessions might, on the other hand, force them to join the regular Democracy out of desperation, or at best culminate in another northern political schism such as Fillmore had led in 1856. He was anxious to build up a national organization which would crush the regular Democratic machine in 1860, and for this reason was eager to welcome with open arms all newcomers to the Republican party.

Greeley's plan did not receive universal indorsement among his fellow party members. The Republicans of Illinois were the most vigorous dissenters. Having for years withstood Douglas' taunts and battled to overthrow him, they found it impossible either to trust his motives or to cooperate in his

[49] *DTri.*, Apr. 26, 1858.
[50] *DTri.*, May 1, 1858. See also *DTri.*, late Apr. and early May, 1858.

reelection. Anxious to test their political organization and confident of victory, they had groomed Abraham Lincoln to oppose the Little Giant in 1858.[51]

This mid-western obstinacy placed Greeley in a predicament. He had promised to work for the return of all congressmen who fought against Lecompton, and Douglas was the leader of the important anti-Lecompton Democrats. At first, he sustained Douglas fully, despite increasing pressure from Illinois;[52] but when it became evident that the Lincoln supporters would remain firm, the *Tribune's* stand on the Illinois campaign rapidly became untenable. Accomplished though it was, even Greeley's pen could not blot out Douglas' bitter denunciations of the Republican party.

Doubtless Greeley never expected Douglas to become a full fledged Republican, but the New York journalist was highly wroth with his fellow party members in Illinois. He complained that they had repelled the Little Giant from their midst. Douglas "might have been conciliated and attached to our own side," he said to Lincoln's friend Joseph Medill of the "Chicago, (very) Ill." *Tribune*, but, "instead of helping us in other states, you have thrown a load upon us that may probably break us down. You knew what was the almost unanimous desire of the Republicans of other states; and you spurned and insulted them."[53]

What Greeley wanted above all else was to prevent Douglas' return to the regular Democratic fold. Whether or not the Republicans gained, the Democrats must lose. There was much the *Tribune* would do to contribute to this end.

Greeley was pleased beyond measure when Buchanan showed every intention of opposing Douglas' reelection. He knew this continued animosity would widen the breach

[51] Beveridge, *Lincoln*, II, 544-570.
[52] *DTri.*, May 4, 1858. Joseph F. Newton, *Lincoln and Herndon* (Cedar Rapids, Io., 1910), 140-176. William H. Herndon and Jesse W. Weik, *Herndon's Lincoln* (Springfield, Ill., 1921), II, 390-394.
[53] Greeley to Medill, July 24, 1858 (clipping), Greeley MSS., LC. Greeley's parentheses.

between Douglas and the administration Democrats. To intensify this development, he publicized the charge that certain Lincoln Republicans were conniving with Buchanan's wheel horses in Illinois in order to defeat Douglas.[54]

This journalistic accusation allowed Greeley to kill two birds with one stone. On the one hand, he was painting in black and white the wide divergence between Douglas and the administration, and on the other he was fulfilling his pledge to assist in reelecting all anti-Lecompton Democrats.

He explained his intentions to Colfax. He said he had reliable evidence of the Lincoln-Buchanan "coalition" in Illinois, but had no fear that the schemers could defeat the Little Giant however much they tried. Douglas' anti-Lecompton leadership had popularized the doctrine of popular sovereignty too widely for him to be "beaten before the People." Furthermore, Greeley was glad to be of assistance by publishing the merger story. "Almost all the natural Independents and off oxen in the State take The Tribune," he observed, and his exposé would benefit Douglas "in every bar-room north of Springfield at least."[55]

The pity of the whole business was, he continued to Colfax, that Douglas would try to return to his party since the Republicans had scorned him. "He has got to take a far back seat in the wigwam if he does," Greeley decided. "But no matter what *he* does. Let us have the satisfaction of knowing that *we* have treated him and his friends justly, fairly, honorably. There will be more years after 1858."[56]

It is credible that the moral suasion of a promise so influenced Greeley, but that is only one side of the picture. Throughout his letters to Colfax in this period runs one central theme: he expected his editorial praise of Douglas to be the kiss of political death.

In the early spring of 1858 he complained that Colfax "did wrong to tell Douglas the worst. He can beat Lecompton

[54] *DTri.*, May 11.   [55] Greeley to Colfax, May 17, 1858, NYPL.
[56] Greeley to Colfax, May 25, 1858, NYPL.   Greeley's italics.

and will; and [the administration] must then choose between letting him stay in the party and turning the party out of power. You and I know how Mason, Jeff. Davis & Co. will choose, but we are not required to tell him. He has eyes." He expected Colfax to be more astute in the future. ". . . I wish you would keep Dana advised in my absence at the West," he said in the same letter. "He is shrewd, but green in politics, and don't keep his eye close enough to the field. I know how to favor the Douglas rebellion without weakening his Democratic standing, and shall continue to write during my absence, but there will be occurrences that need to be seized on the instant, and Dana may be at Appleton's or the Opera when he should be studying dispatches. Keep him posted by telegraph and otherwise."

Colfax, however, either disagreed or was prone to forgetfulness. Somewhat later, Greeley summarized his policy toward Douglas again: ". . . it strikes me you ought to see that my evident undertaking to help Douglas will intensify the Lecompton opposition to him. Don't you smell that they all believe already that he and I are in *cahoot*, as they say— secretly leagued to humble and ruin 'the South?' Every thing I have done to favor him since '57 inclusive is treasured up and used to diffuse and deepen the impression that he is a disguised Abolitionist, and virtually of the Black Republicans."[57]

Once the Lincoln-Douglas campaign got under way, however, Greeley's editorial praise of Douglas went into an eclipse. Pressure from *Tribune* friends in Illinois and the Little Giant's attacks on the Republican party necessitated this course. Correspondence from the scenes of the famous debates, generally favorable to Lincoln, made interesting reading for his subscribers,[58] but editorially Greeley was

[57] Greeley to Colfax, Feb. 28, 1860; (Apr., 1858), NYPL. Appleton's was a New York City publishing house which at the time was getting out *The New American Cyclopaedia* . . . , ed. George Ripley and Dana.
[58] *DTri.*, esp. June 17, 26, July 12, 13, 15, 16, Aug. 9, 18, 26, Sept. 4, 7, 14, Oct. 23, Nov. 5, 1858.

almost altogether mum. He washed his hands of the controversial election in mid-May: ". . . we have no counsel to give
to any party in Illinois, nor, since it is morally certain that
either Abraham Lincoln or Stephen A. Douglas is to be the
next Senator, do we wish to interfere in the contest. We *know*
that Mr. Lincoln will prove an excellent Senator if elected;
we *believe* Mr. Douglas cannot henceforth be otherwise."[59]

Greeley's policy during the anti-Lecompton crisis worked
coming and going. Certainly he never expected, did not wish,
Douglas to affiliate with the Republican party; but by praising the Little Giant he hoped to render inevitable an 1860
split in the ranks of the Democrats.

Regardless of what Douglas might do, dissension among
the Democrats would surely increase Republican following.
It was in anticipation of this end that Greeley made his
promise to support the anti-Lecompton Democrats in the
1858 elections. He viewed their insurgency in its broadest
light, as another northern manifestation of disgust against
the so-called Sham Democracy. Some constituents of the re-
bellious representatives would, he was convinced, end up in
the Republican party. He was determined that the *Tribune*
should cash in on this good fortune.

His policy of harmony went beyond the anti-Buchanan
Democrats. It included the northern Know Nothings, whose
leaders likewise had found no haven save with Republican
representatives during the Lecompton struggle in congress.
It was in this phase of his fusion program that Greeley met
with his second reversal in the 1858 elections. In trying to
usher the remaining Americans of New York state into the
Republican ranks, he collided with Thurlow Weed.

Greeley had watched the decline of Know Nothingism with
interest and had made careful preparations for enticing its
political supporters into his party. In order to appease them,

[59] *DTri.*, May 17, 1858. Greeley's italics. See also *DTri.*, July 16, 1858.
Greeley to Herndon, May 29, 1858, Newton, *Lincoln*, 164.

he had demanded a rigid registry law and an interval of one year between naturalization and the right to vote.[60]

He realized that these concessions were not enough, that the basic strength of the Know Nothings had been a conservative attitude toward the slavery controversy. This had given them considerable appeal to the wealthy and, more important, to that section of the country which stood to lose most in the event of warfare between the north and south— the border states. Greeley was laying plans for the 1860 campaign. He wished to gain conservative support in general, and he was particularly anxious to inherit Know Nothing voters in such states as Missouri, Kentucky, Maryland, and Delaware. In order to accomplish this end it was necessary to prevent a repetition of the 1856 oppositional split between Frémont and Fillmore, and this could be done only by purging from the minds of the doubtful the idea that the Republican party was sectional.

Greeley saw that the principle of the Crittenden-Montgomery bill suited his needs. By voting for this measure, the Republicans had committed themselves to the admission of a slave commonwealth should the inhabitants of a territory so elect. What more could the Know Nothings ask? In hopes of driving this point home, Greeley promoted a mass meeting in New York City soon after the passage of the English bill. The rally was later cancelled, but the featured speakers were to have been John J. Crittenden and John Bell, old-line Whig senators from Kentucky and Tennessee respectively, who met with favor in the eyes of the Hindoos.[61]

The crucial test in this scheme for the affiliation of the Americans came in the 1858 New York state election. The Hards and Softs were again at one another's throats, and

60 *DTri.*, Feb. 27, Mar. 24, Apr. 3, 8, May 9, 29, June 17, 25, July 31, Aug. 18; Apr. 9, 12, 15, 1858. Scisco, "Nativism," 232-233.
61 Greeley to Colfax, June 2, 1858, NYPL. *DTri.*, June 18, 1858. Neither of these gentlemen accepted Greeley's invitation "in consequence of previous private engagements." Special correspondence dated at Washington, June 16, *DTri.*, June 17, 1858.

there was no doubt that the Republicans could win alone, but Greeley sought the national prestige which would accompany the Know Nothings into his camp. Such action would go far to prevent a third ticket in 1860. He began cooperating with the American leaders in the late spring of 1858, occupying their platforms as a speaker and writing editorials insisting on fair treatment for them at the Republican state conclave at Syracuse. To ease the anticipated merger, it was arranged that the delegates from the two parties should convene at the same time and place.[62]

Shortly before the two conventions met, Greeley delivered a widely heralded speech at Ulster, New York. Once again he affirmed his devotion to the practice of popular sovereignty and the principle of admitting a slave state should the circumstances warrant such a step. He had indeed come a long way on the road toward conciliation. At times he regretted his course, though convinced that it was the one way to victory. "I think the *Tribune* is getting to be an old Hunker concern," he joked with Pike. "I shall stop taking it soon, if it don't evince a little more reformatory spirit."[63]

Greeley's hopes for fusion were not altogether altruistic. He still wanted a political office. Weed's friends were partly right in viewing the whole affair as a maneuver for the gubernatorial nomination.[64] The Albany boss had both reason and excuse for blocking it. Success would seriously threaten his machine and would, he said, lower the Republican standard. Assistants acquainted him with Know Nothing intrigue in

[62] Notices and editorials, *DTri.*, Mar. 3, May 11, 20, 24, 28, 31, June 10, 17, 18, July 15, Aug. 16, 25, 28, Sept. 6, 1858.
[63] Greeley to Pike, July 7, 1858, Pike, *First Blows*, 422. Ulster speech, *DTri.*, Aug. 20, 1858.
[64] Spaulding to Weed, Aug. 19; William H. Burleigh to Weed, Sept. 3, Weed MSS., RRL. Greeley to J. B. Swain, Aug. 23, 1858, Greeley MSS., NYPL. *DTri.*, Sept. 21, 1858.
Dana told Pike on Sept. 6, 1858: "Horace has gone to Indiana to deliver his agriculture address, and also to be away when he is nominated for Governor, or isn't. . . . The Horatian movement is strong, though both he and I have carefully kept aloof from it." Pike, *First Blows*, 425.

county conventions.[65] Undeniably, the Americans were after his scalp. In Seneca Falls they were chanting[66]

> . . . And those who seek to lead,
> Such as Seward and Thurlow Weed,
> Who ask too much, we do not need;
> As for quiet modest Greeley,
> Satisfied of his abstraction,
> We'll take him in—and trust freely,
> In his good faith to this our faction.

The Associated Press dispatch from Syracuse on the opening day of the two conventions included an interesting sentence: "Horace Greeley's name has been mentioned in connection with the Governorship, and he would be acceptable to the Americans." But Weed was on the scene, for the first time in his life as an accredited delegate. The Know Nothings were spurned without ceremony.[67]

The two conventions met in separate halls, and each appointed a conference committee. The joint group in consultation agreed upon a platform, and the Americans were awarded the short end of the ticket. The Know Nothing convention accepted these conditions with alacrity, and sent its committee with this good news to the Republican assembly hall. But fusion had failed. The Republicans had already adopted their platform, including a resolution of protest against the Dred Scott decision which the Know Nothings were said to oppose. Without further ado, the stronger party named candidates for every office. A more insulting rebuff could not have been concocted. Amid angry speeches, the Hindoos did likewise.[68]

65 All to Weed: H. D. Rich, May 17; Spaulding, June 1, July 15, Aug. 3, 19, Sept. 4; E. D. Morgan, June 1; N. Lapham, June 19; S. P. Allen, July 9; A. H. Schultz, July 21; E. H. Miller, July 21; B. F. Hall, July 29; E. E. Esty, Aug. 7; Jeremiah Petty, Aug. 8; Geo. W. Curtis, Aug. 15; E. B. Morgan, Aug. 25; Charles Cook, Aug. 25, 1858, Weed MSS., RRL. Weed to I. Washburn, Jr., Jan. 17, 1859, Washburn MSS., II, LC.
66 Benson Owen to Weed, Sept. 4, 1858, Weed MSS., RRL.
67 Dispatches, ltrs., and editorials, *DTri.*, Sept. 8, 9, 10, 11, 1858.
68 Scisco, "Nativism," 232-235.

Greeley's public answer flamed with wrath: "The pretended differences respecting a platform are manifestly not the real cause of disagreement. Personal interests, objects, aspirations—'the lust to shine or rule' were the real causes ..."[69] He wanted the people to understand the recent farce at Syracuse: "The Americans were generally ready to fuse on one condition—this, namely, that Mr. Thurlow Weed should take a back seat in the new car." But it was no time for factional strife, Greeley reflected in conclusion. In the congressional districts at least, he was sure that all anti-Lecompton forces could and would unite. Republicans must work hard, he urged, forgetting old dissensions and quarrels.[70]

Such was the setup as Greeley entered the final phase of the 1858 campaign. One aspect of his fusion plan had met with partial success: in general, anti-Lecompton Democratic and American representatives were returned to Washington with Republican support. Hampered on all sides by men who told him to mind his own business, men whom he considered as selfish politicians, Greeley concentrated his editorial talent on defeating the regular Democratic candidates for the house.[71]

As it had been in the 1856 campaign, harmony was again the *Tribune* watchword. Never since 1853 had it been so free from abuse of the south, and one if not all of those few blasts which found their way into its columns drew censure from the editor.[72] There was no change, however, in the method of treating Sham Democracy. Buchanan's followers were bullying aristocrats, made squalid with federal corruption. They continued to use the ruse of disunion in order to frighten the timid in the north and employed repressive tactics to keep the non-slaveholders of the south, who were potential Republicans, under heel.[73]

[69] *DTri.*, Sept. 13, 1858.   [70] *DTri.*, Sept. 14, 1858.
[71] *DTri.*, esp. June 19, 24, 25, July 5, 8, 15, 21, Aug. 4, 5, 23, 26, Oct. 6, 8, 13, 14, 18, 1858.
[72] Congdon, *Reminiscences*, 266-267. *DTri.*, Sept. 18, 1858.
[73] *DTri.*, esp. July 9, 20, Aug. 2, 5, 9, 16, 24, Oct. 21, 1858.

The *Tribune* was incensed that these slaveholders should heap abuse on Republicanism by calling it "Black." Truly, the reply was shouted, it was the one "White" party in the nation. To prove this statement, the *Tribune* pointed to Kansas, where it claimed that federal troops, apparently called to the west in order to quell a rebellion in Utah, were subduing freedom and making way for negro slaves. The Republican party, on the other hand, upheld the traditional liberties of the American people and was therefore gaining in strength as education and culture spread over the land.[74]

No issue which might disrupt the ranks of those crusading against the extension of slavery was featured by the *Tribune*. Temperance was not mentioned, except to promote a better excise bill so as to remove the question entirely from national politics.[75] Articles appeared favoring a mild protective tariff, but declared this to be a problem local to each congressional district.[76]

This editorial policy contributed to success throughout the north. The Republicans carried every free state but California. Lincoln, it is true, won only a moral victory in Illinois by gaining a popular majority. Douglas controlled the state legislature and was sure of his return to Washington. This triumph was the brightest news of all to Greeley, and he seized upon the occasion to defend his attitude toward the Illinois campaign. "Mr. Douglas," he announced to his readers, "has beaten the Republicans and the Administration— we had nearly said combined, but, since that is denied, we will say alike." He was glad that the Democratic party was split. Illinois was a pivotal state for 1860, and the anti-Lecompton Democrats held the balance of power. "He must either be nominated," Greeley asserted of Douglas, "or the Democratic

[74] *DTri.*, esp. July 21, 24, Aug. 6, 7, 10, 14, Sept. 18, Oct. 9, 12, 1858.
[75] *DTri.*, June 9, 22, 1858. See also Greeley to Brockway, Nov. 14, 1858, Greeley MSS., LC.
[76] *DTri.*, June 22, July 9, Aug. 9, 17, 23, 24, Oct. 4, 1858. Greeley would repeat this technique when running for the presidency on the Liberal Republican and Democratic tickets in 1872.

party practically retires from the contest, surrendering the Government to the Republicans."

Greeley could find no reason for complaining about Douglas' recent reorientation toward the regular Democrats. For, as he observed to his *Tribune* audience, "it was obvious that [Douglas] would feel constrained to take a position so near the South Pole as should be necessary to prevent the formation of any considerable Buchanan Democratic party, so as to inclose him between two fires."[77]

Beyond any doubt to Greeley's mind, his anti-Lecompton policy had proved its worth. Faced with imminent collapse of their organization, the northern Know Nothings had little choice but to enter the Republican party; and he was confident that most of the Democratic insurgents would make "sound coin" for the future. "Your course may prove wiser in the long run"; he wrote condescendingly to an ardent Lincoln follower in Illinois, "but ours vindicates itself at the outset." An increase of twenty-five anti-administration representatives from Pennsylvania, New Jersey, and New York was underscored in this letter as an "answer to all gainsayers."[78]

In reviewing the political developments of the past two years, Greeley was convinced that his political plans were feasible. Results, he was sure, would have been even more favorable had his program been generally followed; but his policy of conciliation left no room for recriminations. He determined to stick to his course without flinching. Ostensibly a conservative, he would take his place on the floor of the Chicago Republican convention in 1860.

[77] *DTri.*, Nov. 5. See also *DTri.*, Nov. 12, 17, 19, 23, 30, Dec. 6, 9, 1858.
[78] Greeley to Herndon, Nov. 14, 1858, Newton, *Lincoln*, 240. See also *DTri.*, Nov. 4, 5, 6, 8, 1858.

CHAPTER 9

GREELEY'S CONTENDER
FAILS AT CHICAGO

F. P. Blair, jr. is here, urging us to pour our people into Missouri, where everything looks promising. He is confident of giving her vote to the Republican Candidates in 1860.—Greeley to Seward, April 29, 1857.

THE *TRIBUNE'S* favorite at Chicago was neither Lincoln nor Seward, but Edward Bates, an elderly Whig gentleman from Missouri who had recently manumitted his slaves. The charge of sectionalism against the Republican party brought Greeley to this choice. He recognized that the accusation, as long as it could be plausibly maintained, constituted an ever present danger of disunion; and he feared that, if unchallenged, it would split the potential Republican vote in the north, as Fillmore's candidacy had done in 1856. The nucleus of Know Nothing strength was in the border states, and to prevent a Republican defeat in 1860, Greeley was eager to make concessions to that area.

His method of divesting his party of sectionalism was unusual, but logical. It was to introduce antislavery sentiment below the Ohio river. Economic nationalism, he thought, would turn the trick. He wished to delay his drive for complete freedom until bondage had been proscribed in all the territories and slave culture in the northern tier of southern states had given way to diversified industries and small farms. The inhabitants of Kansas had overwhelmingly rejected the English bill, and he looked upon this result as a victory for the policy of quarantining enforced negro labor. He turned his attention to the next step, emancipation in such common-wealths as Missouri, Kentucky, Maryland, and Delaware. Then and only then could the cotton and sugar plantation owners be rendered impotent in the government at Washington. Peace and prosperity would descend upon the country.

Greeley's hopes ran high as he realized that economic changes were already crumbling the foundations of slavery in certain of the southern urban centers. The emancipationists carried St. Louis in the spring of 1857 and again in 1859. They were ably led by Frank Blair and B. Gratz Brown, congressman and editor of the *Missouri Democrat* respectively, and Greeley regarded their municipal triumphs as democratic uprisings such as no southern state had before witnessed. He was sure that Louisville and Baltimore were next in line, announcing to his readers that he saw "the commencement of a process by which Slavery is speedily to be driven from all the most enterprising and vigorous of the Slaveholding States."[1]

The *Tribune* reprinted a campaign slogan of the St. Louis mechanics,[2]

WHITE MEN FOR OUR CITY,

and

OUR CITY FOR WHITE MEN!

But Greeley failed to comment editorially upon the animosity toward the blacks which was accompanying this political evolution. Blair's program took it into account by calling for colonization. Greeley thought the plan of returning the ex-bondsmen to Africa or of shipping them into Central America impracticable, for he deemed their labor essential to southern welfare;[3] but he publicized colonization in the

[1] *DTri.*, Apr. 15, 1857. See also *DTri.*, Feb. 23, July 3, Nov. 8, 1858; Apr. 5, 6, 8, 9, 1859.

[2] *DTri.*, Apr. 10, 1857. Articles on political and economic developments in the border slave states appear frequently in all *Tribune* editions from 1857 through 1860.

[3] *DTri.*, Dec. 6, 1854. Smith, *Blair*, II, 429-430.

Tribune.[4] He could perceive no profit in facing the racial issue at this time. He knew that emancipation would not stamp out the hatred involved, but it would be a move in the right direction. Sufficient unto the day is the evil thereof.

Another worry was paramount. Human bondage was deeply embedded in southern social life, but Greeley's understanding of political economy gave him confidence that it was doomed. As well as a moral wrong, he viewed it as an inefficient system of production. Already, he reasoned, soil depletion had driven most planters from the eastern seaboard, forcing those who remained to turn their once fertile lands into a breeding ground which yielded field hands for the newer markets along the Mississippi. Now, erosion was threading its way westward. Slavery was consuming the vitals of its existence.

He was convinced that proper husbandry could revive these acres and cause them to bear fruit. The system of settling Kansas with free laborers had been successful. Why not, he asked, employ the same method in the south? As early as 1851 he had asserted that such tactics would "silently and practically dispel the wide-spread delusion which affirms that the Southern States must be cultivated and their great staple crops produced by Slave Labor or not at all."[5] The prospect was now even more promising. His urban emancipation friends would be reinforced by agrarian allies, and the coalition could erase compulsory negro servitude from the statute books of state after state.

The possibility was so attractive that Greeley interested himself in a project for its fulfillment. The workers needed were to come from abroad, and at one time he planned a special trip to Europe in order to arrange for an adequate supply. Northern capital was to back the newcomers, settling them on small farms throughout the border slave zone. Eli

[4] *DTri.*, Jan. 21, Feb. 25, 1858.
[5] From London to the *Tribune*, dated May 23 (1851), Greeley, *Glances*, 83-86.

Thayer, recently of Kansas fame, was also sponsoring the scheme; and he dreamed of prominence in its organization. Greeley was irritated by this idea—he wanted no supposed abolitionist to figure in the public eye. Southern landowners should sell their holdings without suspecting the political motives behind the transfer.[6]

Whether practical or not, the emigration enterprise never materialized. The Civil War provided no opportunity for trial. To Greeley's way of thinking, it was not essential. He based his estimate of future Republicanism in the south on the white agrarian workers and the non-slaveowning small farmers. These men, he felt, could be educated to welcome the light of freedom and to vote the Republican ticket. As it was, they were kept in brutal ignorance by the slavery aristocrats who utilized the psychology of race hatred in order to retain political domination.

This interpretation dictated *Tribune* policy toward the frequent southern commercial conventions held in the pre-Civil War years. Editorials contended that the basic economic problem of the section was never discussed at these gatherings. Agenda took no cognizance of the industrialization of the south. Rather, the slaveholders plotted new and devious ways of bettering their trade relationships with foreign countries, thereby strengthening the market abroad for their staple crops of tobacco and cotton and forcing the poorer whites and slaves into the same social position, that of serfs on vast plantations.[7]

Greeley based his appeal to the non-slaveholders on this indictment of their so-called overlords. He believed that he could attract the small farmers and agrarian workers into the Republican party by offering them factory jobs as well

[6] Greeley to Seward, Apr. 29, May 7, 1857, Seward MSS., Auburn. John C. Underwood to Greeley, Mar. 25, 1857; Seward to Greeley, May 16, 1857, Greeley MSS., NYPL. See also *DTri.*, Mar. 18, 23, 25, Apr. 16, 18, 21, 27, Aug. 3, 1857; Mar. 5, May 27, July 8, Nov. 8, 1858; July 9, Sept. 29, 1859.
[7] *DTri.*, esp. July 23, 1857; Apr. 8, May 15, 21, 27, July 3, 1858; Mar. 11, 15, July 9, 11, 1859.

as food markets in adjacent urban centers. He knew of no political inducement as great as that of material interest.

For this reason he praised the activities of Colonel William Gregg, a southerner who advocated textile manufacturing. The employees at his factory in Graniteville, South Carolina, Greeley told his readers, were "nearly all of the class known at the South as 'poor Whites,' 'Sand-Hillers,' &c., and are summed up by the ebony chattels under the contemptuous designation of 'White Trash'—people who live by a little hunting, a little fishing, some petty thieving around the edges of the plantation, and an infinitesimal quantity of work. They live in the wretchedest log cabins, with hardly a week's food between them and starvation, and in intelligence, in education, in clothing and every other comfort, are below the level of the peasantry of Italy or Ireland." And in the face of these people, the southern commercial conventions announced that "Protection injures the South!" Greeley could dream of nothing more ridiculous. "It diminishes the importance of the cotton-planting, negro-trading handful of White aristocrats who *call* themselves 'the South'; but it elevates and benefits the Poor Whites wherever its influence is felt." He was convinced that eighty per cent of the fair complexioned inhabitants of the region would profit from the tariff, and he therefore regretted that the remaining twenty per cent happened to "own the presses and invent the politicians of that section, leaving the great majority voiceless and without influence."[8]

The effect of this propaganda on northern laborers must not be overlooked. Greeley was out to convince them that they must come to the aid of their southern brothers by becoming Republicans. Hence the *Tribune* devoted increasing space to southern economic conditions. It would be unjust to impugn Greeley's motives. He was striving to decrease, not augment, sectionalism. He thought his chances for introducing the Republican party into the south excellent. He bid

8 *DTri.*, Aug. 13, 1858. Greeley's italics.

actively for the attention of the non-slaveholders. Late in 1858 his paper carried an announcement that several prominent Republicans, including Cassius M. Clay of Kentucky and Frank Blair, had joined in an appeal to the public for funds with which to spread copies of Hinton R. Helper's *The Impending Crisis* through the south. This book, written by a North Carolinian and following closely the *Tribune's* line of argument, had appeared eighteen months before at the list price of $1. The plan was to print 100,000 digests to sell at 16c each. Subscriptions to the general fund and volunteer distributors were requested.[9]

In March of the following year, Greeley joined with a group of journalists and congressmen, including John Sherman of Ohio, in a second urgent appeal for funds. Greeley contributed $100 himself.[10] Until the opening of the 36th Congress some eight months later, however, he was unable to arouse any particular interest in the Helper abridgment. Less than one-third the sum needed had been raised. He chastized his readers in a long leader: ". . . were One Million copies of Mr. Helper's work properly circulated, we do not believe another Slavery Propagandist would ever be chosen President of the United States."[11]

Then, unexpectedly, Helper's book became famous through the length and breadth of the land. Greeley was jubilant. Not only did he view the acclaim it received as highly beneficial to his party but the circumstances which made this publicity possible convinced him that his estimate of political conditions in the south was sound.

The house of representatives was responsible for this stroke of luck. The 36th Congress convened early in December, 1859, with a majority in the house opposed to the Buchanan administration. When the Republicans backed

[9] *DTri.*, Dec. 4, 1858.
[10] *DTri.*, Mar. 16, 1859. The "Compendium" was reviewed in *DTri.*, July 17, 1859.
[11] *DTri.*, Nov. 19 (unless otherwise noted, dates for the remainder of this chapter will be understood as 1859).

Sherman for the speakership, John B. Clark, Democrat of Missouri, introduced a resolution declaring that no one who had endorsed Helper's work was "fit to be Speaker of this House." Debate over this resolution and the antagonism it engendered lasted for almost two months, when the Republicans dropped Sherman and elected the more moderate William Pennington of New Jersey.[12]

Greeley jumped into the fray with utmost vigor. Helper, he vowed, proved that slavery was pauperizing the greater portion of the southern people, and did this good deed by using census statistics which were "as impregnable as the Multiplication Table." Since the slaves could not read, Greeley scoffed at the southern claim that it was incendiary literature. "It is an appeal," he countered, "to Free Whites—to Legal Voters—urging them to use their rightful power to free themselves from the blight of Slavery." Let congress spread news of this scholarly work far and wide. "Meantime —though we have not hitherto done so—we shall procure copies of 'The Impending Crisis' this morning, and have them for sale at our counter, henceforth, at the publisher's lowest prices. We trust the 'Compend' will soon be in circulation at the cost of printing, under the arrangement which was proposed some months ago."[13] Congressional bickering bought speedy results. Soon it was released at 25c a copy, a price which later fell to 20c, $18 a hundred, and $160 a thousand.[14]

The furore raised by the southerners and their sympathizers over this book fortified in Greeley's mind a conviction

[12] *Congressional Globe,* 36th Congress, 1st sess., pt. 1 (Washington, 1860), 3-655. Ollinger Crenshaw, "The Speakership Contest of 1859-1860," *Mississippi Valley Historical Review,* xxix (Dec., 1942), 323-338.

Greeley was first upset that Sherman failed of election on the opening day, then pleased with the assistance being rendered the Helper fund, then angry with the long delay in organizing and with Sherman's failure. He wrote E. Washburne that "the contractors should have been told that they must get half a dozen Dems and Satans out of the House, or they would fare badly as to their Appropriations." To E. Washburne, Jan. 1, 6, 1860, Washburne MSS., vi, LC. Greeley from Washington, Dec. 5, *DTri.,* Dec. 6. See also *DTri.,* Jan. 6, 11, 18, 20, 1860.

[13] *DTri.,* Dec. 7.

[14] *DTri.,* Dec. 20, 26, 27, 28; Mar. 30, 1860.

which only the outbreak of the Civil War would shake. He was positive that representative government had ceased to exist in the south and that the slavedrivers would tremble for the safety of their cherished institution if free discussion and free balloting were allowed. An overt act of secession, he thought, would precipitate such a resurgence of democracy and would smite the southern demagogues from their places of power. As he expressed it, "the Oligarchy are far more afraid of the enlightenment of the Poor Whites than of the Blacks—and with reason."[15] Thereafter he emphasized all news pertaining to southern infringements on the freedom of the press, thought, and speech. Incidents of arrests, book burnings, and mail censorship were ample proof of his interpretation, and they served his purpose far better than editorial logic had ever been able to do. The real disunionists were not the southern people, he reiterated with conviction, but the men who misrepresented them in Washington. Those politicians must be ousted from the federal government so that the true southerners could speak for themselves. He was determined to give the non-slaveowners this opportunity.

Greeley was seeking to broaden the scope of Republicanism, to develop it into a political power which would exercise every constitutional and propagandist means to eliminate African bondage altogether. His methods for the election of 1860 were conservative, but his aim was revolutionary. He was marching to the aid of those whom he considered oppressed in the south. He lived for the day when that section would send to congress "men holding the views and animated by the spirit of Eli Thayer . . ."[16]

This interpretation of southern social and economic conditions formed the foundation for Greeley's political estimate for the coming presidential campaign, as may be seen from an examination of his important editorials and speeches in 1859.

15 *DTri.*, Dec. 15. See also *DTri.*, Dec. 13, 17.
16 *DTri.*, Feb. 6, 1858.

Once the Kansans had spurned the Lecompton constitution, there was no longer anything Greeley could immediately gain by a forthright support of popular sovereignty. He was relieved, but with the idea of a conservative Republican platform for 1860 in mind, he carefully avoided making the demand that congress flatly restrict slavery from all territories.[17] The pressing need of Republicanism, as he saw it, was to launch an administration which *"shall do all in its power to confine Slavery within the limits of the existing Slave States."*[18] Such was the position taken by Washington and Jefferson; slavery was local and freedom national. The constitution prevented the citizens of one state from interfering with the domestic institutions of another, but the territories were the property of the federal government, and must be preserved for free labor. "If I lived in a Slave State," he declared, "I should be there an Abolitionist; living in a Free State, I am a Slavery Restrictionist—that is, a Republican."[19]

The mission of his party was not sectional in scope, he asserted. Already thousands in the slave states prayed for Republican success, and the bulk of the southern people could and must be enlightened: ". . . if the non-slaveholding whites of Delaware, Maryland, Virginia, North Carolina, Missouri, Kentucky, Tennessee and Texas, understood their true interests, and the precise objects of the Republican party, they would rise en masse, wrest the control of those States out of the hands of the Negro Aristocracy, and give their electoral votes to our candidate. That they will ultimately spurn the yoke that crushes them, aspire to the dignity of true manhood, and expel from the soil the blighting curse of Compulsory Labor, is as certain as the decrees of Providence." On the other hand, he saw no reason why the slaveowners should fear a rebellion. The poor and oppressed

17 *DTri.,* July 9, Aug. 6, 14, Sept. 20, Oct. 6, 15, Nov. 29, 1858.
18 *DTri.,* Dec. 9, 1858. Greeley's italics.
19 Speech at Osawatomie, K. T., May 18, *DTri.,* May 31.

263

only sought their democratic rights, and would not harm their former overlords: "They will neither cut their throats, not sack their plantations; but they will marry their proud and portionless daughters, and resuscitate their worn and worthless lands, making their households to be glad with increase, and their hills and valleys to smile with abundance. The hope of the country rests in the non-slaveholding whites of the South."[20]

The time to come to the assistance of these people, he affirmed, was during the 1860 election. He considered it likely that Sham Democracy would be divided in that contest. He could distinguish three different groups within that party, and none of them protected the west from enforced labor or offered aid to the white workers of the south. All three sought to perpetuate slavery by extending it.

The Douglasites seemed to carry the least weight in Democratic councils, Greeley continued. They maintained that the inhabitants of a territory, as though citizens of a state, might have recourse to local unfriendly legislation in order to exclude bondage. Buchanan's followers, on the other hand, contended that slaveholders could settle with their human property on all federal soil, and there receive the protection afforded by the unsleeping guardianship of the Supreme Court. Finally, the Calhounites looked toward congress for "an explicit and formal Slave Code for the Territories." To Greeley it appeared that the Calhounites were gaining domination of the Democratic party, preparing to reopen the slave trade with Africa, and planning expensive conquests below the Rio Grande.[21]

Greeley wanted to win in 1860 in order to frustrate the aims of Calhoun's disciples. This end was possible, as long as the opponents of slavery extension remained united. By a mere tabulation of the 1856 votes, he could prove that the majority had opposed all three Democratic doctrines; but disunity had permitted Buchanan to win. To prevent the

[20] *DTri.*, Aug. 24.　　　　[21] *DTri.*, May 17.

repetition of that disaster, "we propose to fight the next Presidential battle on the platform of essential and genuine Conservatism—anti-Fillibuster, anti-Cuba-stealing, and anti-Slavery-Extension." This policy, he was convinced, would result in success. It would appeal to the sources, as yet undeveloped, of antislavery strength both in the south and in the north, because it offered the one means for national peace.

He was tired of battling against northern conservatives. These "wealthy, timid, and mercantile classes" wanted above all else security for their business ventures, yet they had in the past associated with a party which was intriguing daily to involve the Union in costly domestic and foreign strife. "The Astors, Griswolds, Lennoxes, Crosbys, of our city, and their brethren in other cities," he judged, "ought to be with us, not against us, in the contest of 1860." He did not regard "the Republican as essentially a sectional party," nor was he willing that it should continue "even to *seem* such." He intended to show conservatives that the only way to stop antagonism over slavery was by restricting it.[22]

The Democrats were headed for defeat, he said, if a single ticket were named in opposition to them. Its title was of little importance. Let various localities call it the American, the Republican, or the People's party, as they wished. He did not care. He had but one demand to make for the Republican bloc, that the new administration "exert all its constitutional power, be the same more or less, to confine Slavery within the limits of the present Slave States."[23]

[22] *DTri.*, Jan. 1. Greeley's italics. See also *DTri.*, May 3, 4, 14, 16.
[23] *DTri.*, Jan. 24. See also *DTri.*, Feb. 12, 15, Mar. 14, Apr. 8, 9, 11, 26, May 14, 16, 17, Sept. 14; Greeley's speech at Auburn, Calif., Aug. 6, "Phonographically Reported for the Sacramento Union," and his ltr. from San Francisco, Aug. 20, to the editor of the San Francisco *Times*, reprinted in *DTri.*, Sept. 14, 19.
This series of essays and speeches attracted wide attention. Editorials, dispatches, ltrs., speeches, and reprints showing substantial agreement with Greeley may be found from the following men in *DTri.* cited: Dana, July 2, 19, 22, 25, Aug. 6, 8, 17, 23, 24, Sept. 1, 3, 8; Harvey, May 3; Lincoln, May 24, Sept. 24, 28; Bowles, June 13; Colfax, June 25, July 18; Hildreth,

Greeley's public pronouncements fail to include two essential aspects of his political thinking. For these one must turn to his private correspondence. The first is his intense desire to put into effect his ideas on political economy; the second is his great conceit.

". . . I want to succeed this time," he wrote a friend, "yet I know the country is not Anti-Slavery. It will only swallow a little Anti-Slavery in a great deal of sweetening. An Anti-Slavery man *per se* cannot be elected; but a Tariff, River-and-Harbor, Pacific Railroad, Free-Homestead man, *may* succeed *although* he is Anti-Slavery. . . . I mean to have as good a candidate as the majority will elect. And, if the People are to rule, I think that is the way."[24]

He deemed it his duty before God to defeat the so-called slave-drivers.[25] This mission could be accomplished, he thought, only if the people followed the dictates of his wisdom. He described himself as being in the "position of the rich old fellow, who, having built a church entirely out of his own means, addressed his townsmen thus:[26]

> " 'I've built you a meeting-house,
> And bought you a bell;
> Now go to meeting
> Or go to h---!' "

Greeley believed that John Brown's raid on the federal arsenal at Harper's Ferry in October, 1859, would drive thousands into his church. The *Tribune* featured Brown as a saint sprung from the Book of Revelation to herald the coming of universal freedom. His exploits would drive home, in the north and south alike, the fact that slaveholders, by degrading their fellow men, were endangering their com-

July 20; Broderick, Aug. 22; Bates, Sept. 3; B. Gratz Brown, Sept. 5; H. Winter Davis, Sept. 8.
[24] Greeley to Mrs. R. M. Whipple (Apr., 1860), Greeley MSS., LC. Greeley's italics.
[25] Greeley to Mrs. Margaret Allen, Jan. 6, 1860, Greeley MSS., LC.
[26] Greeley to Pike, Feb. 26, 1860, Pike, *First Blows*, 499-500. Presumably Pike's deletion.

munities.[27] "Believing that the way to Universal Emancipation lies not through insurrection, civil war and bloodshed, but through peace, discussion, and the quiet diffusion of sentiments of humanity and justice," Greeley said, "we deeply regret this outbreak . . ." But Brown and his companions would pay for their deed with their lives, and Greeley would heap no more execration on these brave men's names: "Let their epitaphs remain unwritten until the not distant day when no slave shall clank his chains in the shades of Monticello or by the graves of Mount Vernon."[28]

This theme was continued in a letter to Colfax. Greeley thought the episode at Harper's Ferry brought the peaceful "end of Slavery in Virginia and the Union . . . ten years nearer than it seemed a few weeks ago. I know you are not a Universalist; but wait and see." Then Greeley added a political consideration. He was glad that Brown's exploit came in the midst of the 1859 off-year canvass. He knew that the electorate would be shocked and that many would turn to the less radical candidates. This trend was evident in an effort to link prominent antislavery leaders along with the abolitionists as the instigators of the disturbance.[29] He expected the ballot box outcome to strengthen the conservatives within the Republicans' councils—and Greeley listed himself among such company.

He was pleased to note such a development in the Empire State. In her 1859 campaign, much to the *Tribune's* disgust, Weed had again spurned an alliance with the Americans, who in desperation named part of the Democratic and part of the Republican ticket. Brown's raid was manna from heaven for the Hindoos. It drove the doubtful who were contemplating support of the Republicans into the Know Nothing camp. Weed was frightened. He sent a hasty note to Anson Burlingame, a Republican orator from Massachusetts who had

[27] *DTri.*, esp. Oct. 18, 20, 21, 24, 26, 27, 29, 31, Nov. 2, 7, 11.
[28] *DTri.*, Oct. 19.
[29] Such a charge was leveled against Greeley. *Harper's Weekly*, III (Nov. 12), 722.

won undying popularity by his publicized offers to fight a
duel with Preston Brooks: "Old Insane Brown's madness will
require more work than we supposed necessary. Come to
Albany."[30] It was too late. The Americans proved theirs to be
the balance of power party by electing, with one exception,
those men whom they had picked from the major slates. The
Tribune hastened to point up this result as indicative of
Seward's weakness in his home state. Greeley saw what was
coming, but he had no regrets. He told Colfax that the vote
in New York would "probably help us to nominate a moderate man for Pres[iden]t on our side."[31]

The "moderate man" was Edward Bates, who measured up
to all Greeley's specifications. Bates was fairly well known,
despite the fact that he had been retired from national
politics since 1836; and this was a point in his favor, for
he had not become embroiled in the slavery controversy. He
would attract conservatives, for he was known to be one
himself, having in 1856 presided over the old-line Whig
convention at Baltimore, which supported Fillmore against
Frémont. Yet he could, Greeley thought, be made acceptable
to the strait-laced Republicans; for he had freed his slaves,
opposed the Kansas-Nebraska act, condemned the Dred
Scott decision, and denounced the Lecompton constitution;
and he was identified with the Blair emancipationists in
his local bailiwick in St. Louis. Most important, Greeley knew
Bates as a man who agreed, substantially, with his ideas on
political economy.[32]

The *Tribune* started Bates off on the right foot during the
winter 1858-1859. Through its columns he was made to atone
for his 1856 recusancy by ridiculing the old-line Whig, whom
he was said to have defined as "a respectable gentleman . . .

[30] Weed to Burlingame, Oct. 20, William Whiting Nolan Collection,
HCL.
[31] Greeley to Colfax, Oct. 29, NYPL. *DTri.*, Sept. 21-24, Oct. 8, 27, Nov. 7.
Scisco, "Nativism," 235-238. *Tribune Almanac . . . 1860* (New York, 1859), 48.
[32] Edward Bates, "The Diary of . . . , " ed. Howard K. Beale, *Annual
Report* of the American Historical Association, *1930*, iv (Washington,
1933), v-xvi.

who takes his liquor regularly and votes the Democratic ticket occasionally."[33]

Greeley enlarged upon this remark until he emerged with a full fledged contender for the 1860 presidential nomination. By February, 1859, he was considering Bates seriously. At the time, he was discussing the political situation with Colfax, who as a Bates admirer was cooperating with the Blairs, Samuel Bowles, and others in promoting their favorite.[34] Early in April, Greeley drew the attention of the north to the Missourian. He learned, from some source other than Colfax, that a committee of Whigs in New York City had received but was refusing to make public a letter from Bates. He began writing editorials insisting that this correspondence be published and insinuated that it requested the formal disbandment of the Whig party.[35]

This pressure produced the desired result, the letter appearing within the fortnight. Bates had advocated internal improvements, a protective tariff, and a non-aggressive foreign policy. He termed the "Negro question" one of needless agitation, but he declared himself unaffiliated politically because the Whigs had "ceased to exist as an organized and militant body."

Greeley liked this pronouncement, though he confessed to Colfax that it was rather "Old Fogyish" on the slavery issue and asked that Bates broaden his position so as to include restriction. Meanwhile, he conjectured an explanation of Bates' slavery stand in order to satisfy his readers. He was sure the Missourian had intended to say that slavery was a moral wrong and should be fought with the force of public opinion, but that it was a state issue and, except as it per-

[33] *DTri.*, Nov. 2, 1858. See also *DTri.*, Mar. 1, Apr. 12. An interesting and early notice of Bates is in *Semi-Weekly Tribune* (hereafter referred to as *SWTri.*), May 7, 1852.
[34] Greeley to Colfax, Feb. 18 (15?), 21, NYPL. Hollister, *Colfax*, 142-147. Smith, *Blair*, II, 457-483. Luthin, "Organizing the Republican Party in the 'Border-Slave' Regions: Edward Bates's Presidential Candidacy in 1860," *Missouri Historical Review*, XXXVIII (Jan., 1944), 138-161.
[35] *DTri.*, Apr. 6, 9, 12, 14. Greeley to Colfax, Apr. 3, NYPL.

tained to territories, could not be properly discussed on a national plane.[36]

Soon after this episode, Greeley left New York City on a long overland trip to California. As he traveled through Kansas, he showed his preference for Bates in at least one political address;[37] and while he was absent in the summer and fall of 1859, the Missourian was given excellent press by Dana, who agreed on the expediency of such a nomination.[38]

In October, shortly after his return from California to New York City, Greeley made a partial promise of support, provided Bates should prove "heartily and openly favorable to the policy of confining Slavery to the existing Slave States . . ." The next month, the *Tribune* reprinted with praise what was claimed to be an authoritative interview with Bates. The Missourian sustained congressional jurisdiction in the territories and inferred that he wanted slavery restriction.[39] This stand satisfied Greeley, who informed Colfax that Bates should say nothing more "till the Repub[lican] Convention shall have nominated him. . . . I don't want any thing better."[40]

Soon thereafter, Greeley began his annual winter lecture tour. More extended than usual, it covered all the northwest but Minnesota. His observations while traveling increased his determination to back Bates. Greeley was impressed with two currents in northern political thinking, Douglas' popu-

---

[36] The editorial appeared simultaneously with the ltr., which was dated Feb. 24, *DTri.*, Apr. 16. Greeley to Colfax, Apr. 15, 25, NYPL. For Bates' reaction to this publicity, "Diary," Apr. 20, 1-9.

[37] " . . . I shall be willing and ready to support such a man as John Bell, or John M. Botts, or (better still) Edward Bates, for next President . . . " Speech at Osawatomie, K. T., May 18, *DTri.*, May 31. Greeley's parentheses.

[38] Bates, "Diary," July 27, 36-38. Dana to Pike, Sept. 1, Pike, *First Blows*, 443-444. *DTri.*, May 16, 24, June 6, 11, July 2, 18, 25, 29, Aug. 15, 25, Sept. 3, 5, 8.
Pike seems to have favored Chase. Pike to Fessenden, Sept. 6, Pike MSS., LC. Pike to Chase, May 13; Mrs. Pike to Chase, July 7; May 9, 10, 1860, Chase MSS., xxxiv, xxxv, xxxvii, LC.

[39] The interview was reprinted from the St. Louis *Evening News*, *DTri.*, Nov. 14. For comments upon it see that issue. Bates' reaction may be found in his "Diary," Nov. 8, Dec. 1, 55-56, 71-72. *DTri.*, Oct. 12.

[40] Greeley to Colfax (Nov.) (13?), NYPL.

larity among the Democrats and Seward's in Republican circles. He was pleased by the first of these, but disliked the second.

He was confident that he could use his anti-Lecompton alliance with Douglas in order to embarrass the Little Giant with his own party. Since 1857, he had utilized every journalistic device at his command to widen the breach between Douglas and the administration Democrats.[41] The Little Giant's enormous following in the northwest gave Greeley an opportunity to expand this split, and he hastened to take advantage of it.

In two letters to the *Tribune*, the first from Davenport, Iowa and the second from Mansfield, Ohio, Greeley asserted that Douglas was sure to be selected by the Democrats at their Charleston convention. As he saw it, the purpose of a nomination was to win the election, and the Little Giant, in the eyes of the masses in the free states, was the "champion and embodiment of the principle of Popular Sovereignty by which they were reconciled to the repudiation of the Missouri Compromise." Should he be rejected, Greeley continued, "the very blindest mole will understand that *the principle* wherewith his name is identified is ignored and cashiered . . ." At the same time, it was possible to regard the choice of Douglas with complacency as evidence—which Greeley was not slow to pass on to his readers—that the southerners had lost control of the Democratic party and that "a Democrat may, for once, disobey the mandates of the Slave Power without thereby ruining himself . . ."[42]

Tribune readers failed to follow the ingenious working of Greeley's mind. Criticism of his prophecy concerning Douglas became so general that Greeley prepared a leader in reply. No one, he noted, denied the truth of his prediction; but all

[41] *DTri.*, esp. Jan. 1, 3, 29, Feb. 12, Mar. 1, 28, Apr. 6, 22, 30, May 3, 4, 6, 24, 31, June 24, 28, 30, July 11, 12, 13, 20, 21, 26, 30, Aug. 3, 25, 31, Sept. 2, 15, Oct. 3, 17, Nov. 22, Dec. 8, 17, 20, 22, 28; Jan. 14, 23, Feb. 29, 1860. See notes 28-59, 71-78, chapter VIII.
[42] From Davenport, Io., Jan. 29, *DTri.*, Feb. 7, 1860. Greeley's italics. See also his ltr. from Mansfield, O., Feb. 8, *DTri.*, Feb. 15, 1860.

insisted that it should not have been published. He wished to take a position from which he could attack the Democrats if they passed over Douglas at Charleston. And finally, he boasted, he was looking for a real canvass in 1860, and wanted to beat the best man the enemy could offer.[43]

Greeley's explanation to Colfax was nearer the truth. "Doug[las] is a poor devil," he had decided, "but the influences which are making him the Democratic candidate are not to be despised" and must therefore be treated as a condemnation of "extreme Doughfacism." Greeley did not really expect him to be selected at Charleston, and had written the editorial letters from the west in order to weaken Douglas with the southerners. When the Little Giant had been thrown out of his party, Greeley told Colfax, it would become evident that the good words bestowed upon him had not been wasted. Even more important to Greeley was his feeling that propaganda for Douglas would "help *us* nominate our strongest man."[44]

Greeley believed that an exposition of the Little Giant's strength in the northwest would dampen the sentiment for a radical Republican such as Seward. Conversely, it would improve the chances for a conservative like Bates. If Douglas were selected by a united Democratic party, the Republicans would be hard pressed. Only a person of moderate antislavery repute could defeat him in the doubtful free states, and then only if the anti-administration vote were concentrated. In Greeley's mind Bates was the best contender, since he would make a determined bid for the bulk of Fillmore's 1856 followers in the central layer of states, north and south of the Ohio and Potomac rivers.

So it developed that in the wake of this publicity for Douglas, the *Tribune* gave all out support to Bates. It was too good an opportunity for Greeley to miss. He told his audience that both Seward and Salmon P. Chase of Ohio were

[43] *DTri.*, Feb. 27, 1860.
[44] Greeley to Colfax, Feb. 20, 28, 1860, NYPL. Greeley's italics.

too radical and that he feared neither could carry the crucial states of Pennsylvania, New Jersey, and Illinois. "If, then, our Convention shall decide that it cannot safely nominate Seward or Chase, we hold, with due submission, that the man for the hour is EDWARD BATES of Missouri. Mr. Bates is commended to our judgment because, while essentially a Republican, he has not hitherto been identified with our party, and is not exposed to the unjust prejudices which incessant misrepresentation has excited against our veteran leaders. Born, reared, and always residing in a Slave State, it will be morally impossible to make anybody believe that he meditates disunion as a means of getting rid of Slavery, or that his election would result in disunion. A practical Emancipationist, it would be hard work to make him odious to sane Abolitioni[s]ts, while we might safely count, in his behalf, on the noisy, malignant, untiring denunciations of the little handful of Disunion Abolitionists who refuse to vote even for Seward or Chase, yet insist on damaging these statesmen by speaking well of them. This little coterie of common scolds, who never emancipated a slave and probably never will, will be certain to aid by their opposition the first practical emancipationist ever nominated for the President. . . . 'The Old-Line Whigs' and other supporters of Fillmore and Donelson in '56 would be compelled either to support Bates, if a candidate, or to virtually confess that they oppose him simply because he is averse to the Extension of Slavery. The Tariff men cannot object to him, for he is fully with them. The River and Harbor men will be glad to hail as a candidate the President of the Chicago River and Harbor Convention. As to the Pacific Railroad, the word St. Louis tells all that need be said on *that* subject.

"The gallant Emancipationists of Missouri," Greeley continued, "who have borne the Free-Soil flag aloft in the darkest days, are unanimous and earnest in urging Mr. Bates's nomination. They say that he can carry their State, which we greatly doubt; but he would at least thoroughly contest it, and thereby hasten the day of the consecration of the soil of that noble State to Free Labor alone. So throughout the border line of Slave States: we do not say that Bates would carry one of them, though we believe he would stand a good chance for Maryland and Delaware; but he would have an Electoral Ticket in every one of those States, and a respectable support in each . . ." Finally, such a choice would be "smoke to the eyes o[f] the little junto of workers in darkness who have sold out the remains of the American party to the Sham Democracy, and would find themselves unable to deliver the goods in case Bates were our candidate."[45]

This editorial appeared on February 20, 1860. From that day on, the *Tribune* was a Bates sponsor, although Greeley published letters favoring all candidates and insisted that he would back whomever the convention named.[46] Bates released his views on the slavery question again in March. The federal government, he said, had no control over domestic policy within the states, but exercised full supervision over the territories. In a leader the next day, Greeley praised this declaration. It explicitly avowed opposition to slavery itself, he told his readers, and denied that the constitution "carries that blight into the Territories or anywhere else . . ."[47]

The ensuing spring brought evil tidings to Bates and his admirers. Early in May, the old-line Whigs met with the remnants of the Know Nothings and named John Bell of Tennessee and Edward Everett of Massachusetts. This was water on the Bates fire, and a downpour was pending. The Democrats split wide open at Charleston. Meeting late in April, the delegates failed to agree on either a platform or a candidate and divided into Douglasites and Regulars, the first adjourning to Baltimore and the second to Richmond.

[45] *DTri.*, Feb. 20, 1860. Greeley's italics and upper case. See also *DTri.*, Feb. 28, 1860.
[46] All *Tribune* issues, Mar., Apr., and early May, 1860.
[47] *DTri.*, Mar. 26, 1860. It is not known if Greeley asked for this second pronouncement, but Bates, as has been cited, did not consider the first fully authentic. Ltr. from Bates, Mar. 17, *DTri.*, Mar. 24, 1860.

Each nominated separately after the Republicans had made their selections in Chicago on May 18. The Douglas forces picked their favorite, with Herschel V. Johnson of Georgia as his running-mate; while the Regulars chose Buchanan's vice-president, John C. Breckinridge of Kentucky, with Joseph Lane of Oregon in next place.[48]

This development on the Democratic front was an acid test for Greeley's 1860 program. It virtually assured victory for the Republican candidate. Greeley's action thereafter would disclose the sincerity of his pre-convention stand. Had he been preparing for the worse by attracting conservatives to his party? If so, he could now swap horses before going to Chicago.

Greeley stuck to Bates because he was convinced that such was the proper choice. This selection, he felt, was essential to the promotion of southern emancipation and the orderly exploitation of the nation's resources. He preferred not to interpret the Democratic schism as assuring Republican success. In the interval between the Charleston and Chicago conclaves, the *Tribune* warned its readers that the Democratic factions might rejoin.[49]

Reconciliation was remote, but the possibility thereof upheld Bates. If it occurred, Greeley would find himself in an advantageous position; for the reunited platform could be expected to show concessions to the south, and the *Tribune* could denounce this as a submission of the northern wing of the Democracy to the so-called slave power. On the other hand, he admonished his audience not to be complacent because Douglas had apparently lost his southern backing. The Little Giant could be expected to run regardless, and he would swing a huge vote in the northwest. To Greeley's mind, the Democratic split and the combined Whig-Hindoo nomination made it all the more important that as much of the opposition as possible unite on a conservative Republican who

[48] Dumond, *The Secession Movement* . . . (New York, 1931), 1-59.
[49] All *Tribune* late Apr. and May issues.

could take the wind from the sails of both Douglas and Bell. He wanted the candidate named at Chicago to emerge with a popular as well as an electoral majority, for otherwise secession and even civil conflict might ensue.[50]

There is a final, and equally important, explanation for the course Greeley pursued during this critical period. He did not, in any event, want Seward to win the Republican honors. This, despite Greeley's denial, is perhaps one of the reasons that the *Tribune* tried to move the date of the Chicago gathering to a time earlier in the spring.[51] Greeley knew that a division in the Democratic camp would improve Seward's prospects; for Weed could then claim that anti-administration fusion was unnecessary, that his champion could win by straight Republican ballots.

Seward was the nation's outstanding exponent of the anti-slavery principle in 1860. Greeley judged all prominent radicals as unavailable, but he also hated his erstwhile political partner and feared that his success would strengthen Weed's Albany machine and injure the party by giving free rein to corruption in Washington.

Greeley had formed an aversion to the famous New York statesman. "I was many years intimate with Gov. Seward and devoted to his political advancement," he wrote Colfax early in 1858. "I believe my support never cost him a cent nor in any way involved him. That he never said 'I thank you,' is very well . . . but I cannot remember that Gov. S[eward] ever in his life said to me 'What do you think of the present aspect of affairs? What is our true course in this emergency?' Do *you* happen to know of his ever consulting and counseling with *any body* on terms of equality?"[52]

It is true that since the partnership had been dissolved, Greeley had corresponded intermittently with both Seward and Weed. The old association might have been reestablished if Seward had been willing to accept Greeley's advice, and an

[50] *DTri.*, May 22, 1860.　　　[51] *DTri.*, Jan. 31, Feb. 20, 1860.
[52] Greeley to Colfax, Feb. 5, 1858, NYPL. Greeley's italics.

276

episode late in 1857 showed that this was impossible. It will be recalled that after Seward's reelection to the senate in 1855, the strongest public condemnation Greeley had made of his former comrade had been the charge of refusing to battle against corruption in Washington. Some two and one-half years later, Greeley urged him privately to insist on a curtailment of federal expenditure. Specific suggestions were made. He could reduce government spending "by abolishing the Army—which is an absurd nuisance, unworthy of the XIXth Century—reducing the Navy to six frigates and a few sloops, and cutting down all salaries to what the work is worth. And he who leads Congress in this work," Greeley promised, "may lead the People in any other."[53]

Shortly after receiving this letter, Seward went so far as to bolt Republican ranks in order to vote for a bill which enlarged the army. His fellow party members charged that the additional strength would be used to suppress freedom in Kansas, but Seward followed the creditable reasoning that the president as commander-in-chief had full knowledge of the troops necessary for defense and should be supported.[54]

As for Weed, there was never much chance that he would seek to renew his personal friendship with Greeley. Rather, in a calm and detached manner he blocked Greeley's political pretensions and his efforts to fuse the remaining Americans in New York state with the Republicans.

Weed's lobbying in both Washington and Albany was another important item in preventing reconciliation. Greeley had become convinced that, if nominated, Seward's campaign would suffer from charges of corruption and that, if elected, the federal treasury would be raided.

The *Tribune* began implying that Weed's political methods were dishonest late in 1857,[55] and by the fall of 1860 was

[53] Greeley to Seward, Nov. 19, 1857, Seward MSS., Auburn.
[54] *Congressional Globe*, 35th Congress, 1st sess. (Washington, 1858), 412-413, 430, 518-519, 757, 763-765, 876. Blatchford to Greeley, Feb. 22, 1858, Greeley MSS., NYPL.
[55] *DTri.*, Oct. 6, 1857. See also *DTri.*, July 19, 21, 24, 1858.

openly condemning them as foul. This attitude pervaded the entire staff, and Seward was blamed as much as Weed. Pike wrote Senator Fessenden that Seward's congressional activities were a "part of the hateful plundering policy that marks and degrades New York politics & which is poisoning those of the federal gov[ernmen]t. We have got to make war on that policy & slay it or it will be the death of the [R]epublican party and perhaps the government itself. I never knew the time when Seward did not vote on the stealing side."[56]

This sentiment gathered momentum in the *Tribune* as 1860 approached. When a new Republican governor, Edwin D. Morgan, was inaugurated at Albany early in 1859, Greeley privately advocated that constant pressure be exerted upon him to prevent peculation.[57] Throughout that year and the early part of the next, the *Tribune* fought to force the railroads of the state to pay tolls on their freight, the returns to be used in canal maintenance and improvements. The canals were state owned and were suffering from competition. It was pointed out that Albany lobbying obstructed this legislation, as well as enactments which would adjust freight rates and prevent the excess charges of short over long hauls. Informed readers could see that Greeley was hitting at Weed's machine.[58]

The *Tribune* gave editorial publicity in the spring of 1860 to a charge that Weed was a lobbyist,[59] and contended that the corrupt influences which were passing a monopolistic New York street railway bill at Albany were injuring the Republican party. Additional lines were greatly needed for Manhattan's transportation system, and Greeley favored a plan which would benefit the municipal government by turning all profits above a reasonable sum into the city treasury. Weed,

---

[56] Pike to Fessenden, Apr. 9, 1858, Pike MSS., LC.
[57] Greeley to Brockway, Nov. 14, 1858, Greeley MSS., LC.
[58] *DTri.*, July 19, 21, 24, Sept. 13, 1858; Sept. 26, Nov. 9, 10, 19; Jan. 4, Feb. 20, Mar. 19, 21, Apr. 2, 11, 1860. See also E. Corning to Weed, Mar. 13, 20, 24, 27, 1858, Weed MSS., RRL.
[59] *DTri.*, May 1, 1860. See also "Turk" from Albany, *DTri.*, Feb. 15, Mar. 3, 1860.

however, had become interested in the matter some years previously, and was working to satisfy all private economic interests of any weight by pooling most of the franchises into the gridiron railway measure.[60] The bills as drawn up granted interlocking directorates construction rights in perpetuity on all the city's main thoroughfares as well as on all those which seemed destined to bear heavy traffic in the future. The *Tribune* opposed these bills in several strong editorials, but they passed toward the middle of April.[61]

At this point, Greeley's opposition to Albany corruption ceased until after the Chicago convention. The Seward movement was too strong, and he did not wish to jeopardize the chances of its champion, if nominated, in the November election.

Greeley had praised Governor Morgan's inaugural promise to root out extravagance and fraud,[62] but now he requested that the gridiron bills be signed: ". . . there is a very general desire," Greeley volunteered, "to get rid of protracted wrangle—to have more railway accommodation and less jaw about it. . . . And besides, men of all parties are deeply interested in the proposed roads, including some of Gov. Morgan's political and personal friends, whom he must hate sorely to disoblige, in a matter which they regard as of vital consequence." Morgan did not take Greeley's advice. He returned the bills, five out of the six unsigned, protesting that since they granted monopolies in perpetuity they were

[60] Examples, all following to Weed: S. Draper, Apr. 9, 1854; A. J. Steward, Apr. 13, 1858; Richard Schell, Nov. 27, 1858; D. P. Barhydt, Jan. 9, Mar. 29, 1860; H. R. Runsen, Feb. 10, 1860; John A. Cook, Mar. 29, 1860; J. A. Haddock, Apr. 19, 1860, Weed MSS., RRL.
Wright, *The Prospect*, 17-24.
Dana wrote Pike on Mar. 8, 1860, Pike, *First Blows*, 501, that George Law was outmaneuvering Weed in this deal; but apparently the two men got together. J. F. Cummings to Weed, Mar. 17, 1860; and (?) McLean to Weed, Mar. 21, 1860, Weed MSS., RRL. A year earlier, D. R. Martin had written A. H. Schultz, Mar. 29, Weed MSS., RRL, that "we Republicans want all the money we can raise & what a lift here is. There is from one to two millions of clean dollars in this scheme . . . "
[61] *DTri.*, Nov. 10, 11, 19, Dec. 1; Mar. 7, 9, 12, 16, 23, 1860.
[62] *DTri.*, Jan. 4, 1860.

harmful to the welfare of the people.[63] The vetoes were overridden without serious difficulty, and Greeley hastened to
blame as much of the scandal as he could on the Democrats.[64]

He was immensely relieved, however, when the legislature
adjourned a few days later. "... let us be reverently thankful
for all mercies," he said in a leader, "we do not believe it
possible that another body so reckless not merely of right but
decency—not merely corrupt but shameless—will be assembled in our halls of legislation within the next ten
years."[65] He realized that the condition of New York politics
would handicap the Republican party throughout the Union
if it were known. Although he opposed Seward's nomination
at Chicago, he perhaps spoke the truth when he later said
that he "carried none of New-York's dirty linen to the
Chicago laundry . . ."[66]

It may be seen that Greeley was playing his anti-Seward
cards close to his body. Though opposing Seward's nomination, he was preparing himself for such an eventuality. He
would not challenge the Albany machine until after the
Chicago convention.

A question as to Greeley's personal integrity is involved
at this point. Although many Republican leaders knew of
the rift, and references to it had appeared in northern journals,[67] the general public was ignorant of the dissolution of
the Weed-Seward-Greeley partnership until after the Republicans passed over Seward late in May, 1860. It can be
said that both Weed and Seward were anxious to regain
Tribune support, and made several direct efforts to that
end;[68] but, unsuccessful because of Greeley's adamant atti-

[63] Lincoln, *Messages*, v, 238-242. *DTri.*, Apr. 16, 1860.
[64] *DTri.*, Apr. 17, 18, 1860. *Laws of the State of New York*, 83rd sess. (Albany, 1860), 1033-1052.
[65] *DTri.*, Apr. 18, 1860. Seward was also relieved. H. Heniore (?) to Seward, Mar. 20, 1860, endorsed by Seward with a note to Weed; and Seward to Weed, Apr. 21, 1860, Weed MSS., RRL.
[66] *DTri.*, May 26, 1860.
[67] *DTri.*, May 7, 26, 28, 1860.
[68] Weed to Seward, July 13 (1858), Seward Collection, RRL (this citation furnished by Prof. Van Deusen of the University of Rochester). Weed to Greeley, Dec. 18 (1857?); Blatchford to Greeley, Feb. 22, 1858, Greeley

tude, they were in no position to publicize their discord with him. They expected and would need his journalistic assistance in case Seward were named. Greeley, likewise, maneuvered himself into a position from which he could back Seward if the senator were chosen at Chicago. The problem is, did Greeley utilize his supposed friendship with Seward to help defeat the latter's nomination?

The answer is, yes. In his private political conversations at the time, Greeley was seldom if ever straightforward. He gave the impression that he would rather see Seward president than any other contender.[69] His editorials favoring Bates rang with a tone of comradeship for Seward. He repeated that since four free states—Illinois, Indiana, Pennsylvania and New Jersey—were doubtful, 1860 was not the year for such a radical choice as the New York contender, but added that he hoped the time would soon come.[70] Seward and his supporters were not caught flat-footed. In their correspondence they admitted that Greeley had left their camp, and at one time Seward believed that the public was aware of the rupture,[71] but they hoped to have the support of his paper, and were glad of the increased prestige which their presumably close connections with the editor gave them. However they did everything possible to diminish his influence. Gree-

MSS., NYPL. An undated ltr. from Blatchford to Weed, Weed MSS., RRL, is of interest: "Dear Weed I have just seen Greeley—he says he will meet you at my office at 12 O. C. Wed." See also Seward to Dana, Jan. 27, Dana Misc. MSS., LC.

[69] Among a number of references on this point, the three following are most interesting: J. B. Taylor to Seward, July 14, 1858, Seward MSS., Auburn, "I saw Greeley yesterday afternoon & had two hours talk with him. [H]e is all right as a Book on Every thing[,] as Strong for Seward or More So if Possible, than Ever[.]" Charles Leib to Cameron, Jan. 2, 1860, Cameron MSS., IX, LC. "Horace Greel[e]y was here [Chicago] yesterday. I had a short interv[i]ew with him in which he said that he feared and the friends of Mr. Seward feared that he could not be elected, if nominated." J. B. Hall to Blatchford, Oct. 14, Weed MSS., RRL, endorsed with these words in Blatchford's hand, " . . . Greeley came to breakfast with me this morning—he is deluded."

See also, all to Weed: Dana, Oct. 7; R. S. Oakley, Dec. 24; James Parker, Jan. 12, 1860; Charles G. Halpin, Feb. 10, 1860; D. F. Miller to Greeley (copy? to Weed), Mar. 19, 1860, Weed MSS., RRL.

[70] All *Tribune* pre-convention issues, esp. *DTri.*, Mar. 24, 26, Apr. 2, 1860.

[71] Seward to Weed, Mar. 18, 1858, Weed MSS., RRL.

ley was anxious to be a delegate to Chicago, but Weed dominated the New York delegation, and Greeley was left out. In desperation, he seized an opportunity to attend as a substitute from Oregon, a situation made possible by transportation difficulties.

Greeley arrived in Chicago three days before the deliberations began and attempted to win the support of the doubtful states for Bates. The elderly candidate himself, in accordance with the ritual for presidential aspirants, stayed home in St. Louis. Seward likewise waited in Auburn to receive with graceful surprise the news of his nomination. Weed, surrounded by New York followers and the band hired to play the triumphal march, roared in on a special train to fix up matters. His lieutenants headed like homing pigeons to the nearest bars, to influence voters. Lincoln remained in Springfield, but was ably represented by Judge David Davis, Norman B. Judd, and other managers.

On May 16, the assemblage moved into the Wigwam, a large frame building erected for the occasion. Seward entered the convention as the strongest contender, and his defeat resulted in part from the influence which Greeley wielded against him. The less informed delegates were surprised that the popular editor was not sponsoring New York's choice, and his words seemed stronger because it was supposed that his old connections with Seward had but recently, if at all, broken. Efforts were made by James Watson Webb of the New York City *Courier and Enquirer*, Henry J. Raymond, and others, to counter Greeley's prestige by representing him as a disappointed New York office-seeker. The letter which Greeley had written Seward late in 1854 was referred to, but not produced, in proof. Neither Greeley nor the Sewardites yet openly attacked each other. Both were thinking of the canvass in November, and were anxious not to injure party morale.

Greeley's favorite, however, had been weakened by Bell's nomination and particularly by the Democratic split at

Charleston. Other causes for Bates' failure were the antipathy of foreigners, especially the Germans, toward a man who had canvassed for the American party nominee in 1856, and Bates' long delay in occupying Republican ground. Colfax was of the opinion that many of the more extreme anti-slavery delegates believed him an old-line Whig until after the nomination.[72]

Working in conjunction with the Blairs, B. Gratz Brown, and others, Greeley never slackened his efforts for Bates until the doubtful states, with Pennsylvania leading, broke for Abraham Lincoln. At about midnight on May 17-18, Greeley was discouraged and wired his paper that the opposition to Seward was unable to unite and that New York's favorite would be selected.[73] Normally an early retirer, Greeley was too aroused to do much sleeping. It was during the small hours of the morning following that Lincoln's agents clinched the doubtful state delegations. Balloting began on May 18, and Greeley was active in holding the Bates group together until the swing to Lincoln became irresistible. Hannibal Hamlin of Maine became the vice-presidential candidate.[74]

The convention councils had been influenced by Greeley's energy and persistence, and the Sewardites were quick to lay full blame upon him for the defeat of their hero. "Yesterday was a sad day to many in Chicago," one wrote on May 19. "When it became evident that Seward was to be sacrificed tears flowed like water among the vast throng. I never saw a scene so truly affecting. . . . The white livered old cuss was jubilant. To his venom the result was attributable, but of this you may be certain, that no man ever heard a greater

72 Hollister, *Colfax*, 147.
73 Greeley's Chicago dispatches may be found in *DTri.*, May 14 through May 19, 1860.
74 *DTri.* editorials are filled with explanations of Greeley's Chicago activities, late May and early June issues. The best study of the convention itself is William Baringer, *Lincoln's Rise to Power* (Boston, 1937), 188-295. Henry M. Field, *The Life of David Dudley Field* (New York, 1898), 131-140, gives an account of Greeley on the night May 17-18.

amount of honest talk in regard to himself in the same space of time than Hoss Greel[e]y." Weed was smarting for revenge when he wrote Seward: "Greeley was malignant. He misled many fair minded men. He was not scrupulous. He said to some that you could not carry New York and that 20 of our delegates were against you."[75]

There were other factors in the Seward failure. Lincoln's availability proved attractive to a convention of heterogeneous elements. He was the choice of those free states which went to Buchanan in 1856 and this was the controlling consideration with the majority of the delegates. The outstanding Republican politicians of Indiana and Pennsylvania, Henry Lane and Andrew Curtin, led the doubtful states to the Lincoln banner because Seward was too renowned as a radical. Lincoln's nomination, furthermore, was a move to promote Republicanism in the west, and marked an alliance of the Pennsylvania and New Jersey protectionists with the homesteaders. Finally, Weed's cohorts in Chicago were rowdy and conceited—drinking much and boasting of their well-filled campaign chest—and the charges of corruption against the Albany machine injured the cause it was promoting.[76]

Although they were fully aware of other reasons for Seward's collapse, Weed and his assistants exaggerated Greeley's influence at Chicago. They found this the most feasible tactics to retain their control of New York state and to assure themselves a lion's share of patronage from the Lincoln administration. *Harper's Weekly,* mildly Democratic in tone, noted that the *Tribune* "has been the creator of the Republican party," claimed Greeley was to a large degree responsible for Seward's failure, and concluded: "Hitherto Mr. Greeley has been generally considered by his friends an

[75] Weed to Seward, May 20 (1860), Seward Collection, RRL (this quotation furnished by Prof. Van Deusen of the University of Rochester). C. C. Washburne to E. Washburne, May 19, 1860, Washburne MSS., IX, LC.
[76] James A. Hamilton, *Reminiscences of* . . . (New York, 1869), 453-454. *DTri.,* May 22, 1860. Luthin, *The First Lincoln Campaign* (Cambridge, 1944), 136-167; "Abraham Lincoln and the Tariff," *American Historical Review,* XLIX (July, 1944), 609-629.

ardent and conscientious man, who rose above petty considerations of personal spite and personal aggrandizement; the
true story of his desertion of Seward will, doubtless, confirm
this impression, and will show that in his action at Chicago he
rather played the part of Brutus than that of Judas."[77]

There is, indeed, little to sustain the Weed-Seward charge
that Greeley was motivated solely by spite. His position was
similar to that taken four years previously, for in neither
campaign could he foresee a popular majority with a radical
Republican. There was reason to complain of his refusal to
combat Seward forthright and unequivocally. Yet, Greeley
had to keep the *Tribune* free for all eventualities. He was not
a man who crossed his bridges before reaching them.

Nor did Lincoln's stalwarts have anything for which to
thank Greeley. They remembered him as the journalist who
had been kind to Douglas in 1858. As one of them remarked,
Greeley's "semi-dictation" at the convention had availed him
nothing, for he had not elevated Bates: "Horace's legs are
not long enough, Caesar like[,] to 'bestride this narrow
world' or even the [R]epublican portion of it, no living man
is tall enough to make automatons of our party, Douglass
[*sic*] may make his *servants* step to the music of his whistle
but Mr. Greeley . . . will do well to read [A]Esop on the
crow's imitation of the eagle."[78]

Greeley was personally pleased that he had met and worst-
ed Weed, as he believed single-handed. "Do you see how the
heathen rage?" he berated Pike, enjoying himself immensely.
"How the whole weight of their wrath is poured out on my
head?" Colfax also received his share of reproach for not
walking into Weed's jaws. "As to Chicago," Greeley wrote,
"I don't see why more of you did not come on to help, when
the matter was so vital. My share of the load was unreason-
ably heavy, considering where I live, and the power of the

[77] *Harper's Weekly*, IV (June 2, 1860), 338.
[78] Nathaniel Vose to E. Washburne, May 20, 1860, Washburne MSS., IX,
LC. Vose's italics.

soreheads to damage me. . . . I don't think *you* wanted to come face to face with Weed in a case wherein his heart was so set on a triumph. . . . I ought not to have been obliged to expose myself to the deadliest resentment of all the Seward crowd as I did. But what I must do, I will, regardless of consequences."[79]

Although Greeley had been outmaneuvered by the Lincoln faction and knew it, Chicago was not without compensations. His personal acclaim was great. He was stared at, pointed out—and booed or greeted as the party's savior. Complete strangers sought his gems of political wisdom. As he told his readers, his mind "had been long before deliberately made up that the nomination of Gov. Seward for President was unadvisable and unsafe . . ." He had favored Bates because such a campaign would have restricted slavery, given an impetus to the cause of emancipation in Missouri, and calmed the slave states, as he said, into accepting "Republican ascendancy." Even now, he concluded, when all his friends were "raining bouquets" on Lincoln, he wished to repeat that he thought Bates would have been the wiser choice.[80]

[79] Greeley to Colfax, May 26, 1860, NYPL. Greeley's italics. To Pike, May 25, 1860, Pike, *First Blows*, 520.
[80] *DTri.*, May 22, 1860. See also Hollister, *Colfax*, 147-148. Baringer, *Lincoln*, 217.

CHAPTER 10

NOT COMPROMISE, BUT WAR

A civil war, forsooth, in behalf of slavery! The absurdity is immense.—Dana in the *Weekly Tribune*, February 2, 1856.

THE tumultuous imbibing of John Barleycorn, the smoke-filled back rooms, the horse-trading maneuvers of Judge David Davis and other floor managers for Lincoln proved too much for the reforming editor from New York City. Greeley was without peer in partisan journalism, and he could hold his own in debates and parliamentary tussles; but the double-dealing and the roaring, raucous crowd confused him. What control he had once exercised over the Republican party had slipped from his hands. The day of the professional politician had dawned anew, and Greeley's efforts to dominate the convention went for naught. His power, as it had been in the years before the Kansas-Nebraska bill, was again one of influence, not of direction.

A cycle of Greeley's life had elapsed. He had picked up the scattered parts of the antislavery movement, and he had ingeniously bolted them into an engine of great political strength. He saw the danger inherent in a misuse of this machinery. He wanted to employ it gingerly, to restrict slavery and nothing more. He wished to return anew to his doctrine of economic nationalism as a means of altering social conditions in the south. He realized that any merciless attempt to rip negro bondage from southern culture would result in war and discord and misery, and would destroy, in his time at least, the chances for the democratic improve-

287

ments on which he had set his heart. It was with this knowledge, and with this fear, that Greeley bestirred himself to procure the Republican nomination for a man whom he deemed acceptable to the south—or at least to the border and central layer of slave states, which in the final analysis would control the decision of the gulf region.

Although he had considered Bates a wiser choice, Greeley accepted the verdict of his fellow delegates at Chicago with alacrity. The ticket was cut to his pattern of expediency for the doubtful free states. Lincoln was known to be a conservative as well as a Republican, and his strength at Chicago came from those northern commonwealths which went for Buchanan in 1856: Indiana, Illinois, Pennsylvania, and New Jersey. Greeley knew that Lincoln would be victorious. The refusal to nominate Seward or another renowned radical seemed to him wise. It denied southern hotheads a bludgeon by which they might beat their masses into secession. While Lincoln's candidacy would not directly assist the emancipation drive so ably led by Baltimore's most notable firebrand, nativist Henry Winter Davis, and by young Frank Blair in St. Louis, the platform called for economic measures which would in the long run peacefully eliminate slavery. Southern non-slaveowners, Greeley felt, were imbued with a Jacksonian love for the Union, and they would fight for a separate government only if their aristocratic overlords could convince them that their rights were being trampled. No one could justly claim that Lincoln contemplated an invasion of the south, and Greeley rested assured that threats of disunion were the mouthings of political charlatans.

Greeley's anxiety to halt the antislavery tornado may be seen in the conservative platform drawn up at Chicago. He served on the resolutions committee, and the document which emerged shows his strong influence. He later affirmed that he labored "long and earnestly" to divest this party pronouncement of all features "needlessly offensive or irritating" to the south. Specifically, he claimed credit for having blocked "the requirement that Congress shall positively prohibit Slavery in every Territory whether there be or be not a possibility of its going thither."[1]

This interesting statement was made in February, 1861, when the Republicans in Washington, concerned over possible border slave state secession, were following their platform of 1860 to the letter in organizing the territories of Nevada, Colorado, and Dakota without clauses proscribing slavery therein. At this time Douglas taunted his opponents with the charge that they had accepted his principle of popular sovereignty.[2] He was, in marked degree, correct. Greeley supervised that partial acceptance at Chicago when working on the Republican platform. This document berated the Democrats for refusing to admit Kansas to the Union as a free state, maintaining that such was the popular mandate of the inhabitants of that territory.

Greeley's chief aim in 1860, both in backing Bates for the Republican nomination and in formulating a conservative declaration of party policy, was to draw as much free state strength away from Douglas as was possible. This end Greeley could best accomplish, he felt, by removing the charge of sectionalism from his party. He knew that to insist upon a congressional edict against slavery within territories where that institution was economically infeasible was a senseless provocation. Troubles in Kansas had taught him that were the administration in Washington against the extension of slavery, there would be in the future no difficulty in ushering territories with climate and soil similar to that of Kansas into the Union as free states. This position Greeley had taken when sponsoring the Crittenden-Montgomery substitute, when supporting Douglas' reelection to the senate, when delivering a widely publicized speech at Ulster, New York, and when sponsoring the absorption of the remaining New York

[1] *DTri.*, Feb. 20, 1861. See also *DTri.*, Feb. 22, 1861.
[2] *Congressional Globe*, 36th Congress, 2nd sess., pt. 2 (Washington, 1861), 1391. *U. S. Statutes at Large*, xii (Boston, 1863), 172-177, 209-214, 239-244. James G. Randall, *Lincoln the President* (New York, 1945), i, 126, 229-231.

state Know Nothings into the Republican party in 1858, and he upheld this position as he promoted the nomination of Bates in 1859-1860. On the other hand, Greeley consistently maintained that congress had the power to outlaw slavery in any territory, "whenever," to quote the Chicago platform, "such legislation is necessary . . ."

Other parts of the platform bid for the foreign vote by denouncing the rabid nativists, and made due obeisance to the constitution, the Union, and the Declaration of Independence. Here Greeley again ran afoul of that messiah of the abolitionists, Joshua Giddings, who, venerable with age, rose haughtily from his chair and stalked toward the Wigwam door. Greeley had only mentioned Jefferson's great document, and Giddings insisted that the equality clauses be quoted. Catcalls and cheers gave way to orations on the point in dispute, and finally the old man, backed by the Sewardites, was satisfied. Thus was the one radical plank nailed to the Republican bandwagon. Of far greater importance were the resolutions pertaining to economic policy: homesteads, tariff, and internal improvements.[3]

After twenty years of agitation, Greeley stood at the threshold of his greatest public achievement, the homestead law. Such legislation had been gaining favor, particularly in the west, since the panic of 1857, and Greeley believed it would not be denied the frontiersman even if the Republicans lost in 1860. This consideration was partly responsible for the *Tribune* letters during the previous winter which had prophesied success for the Little Giant at the Democratic convention. Douglas had long been known as an advocate of free land, and Greeley confided to Colfax that his compliments for the Illinois senator were designed in part "to *pin* him on the Homestead."[4]

[3] Platform printed in Greeley, *American Conflict*, I, 319-321. See also Baringer, *Lincoln*, 259-263. Gustave Koerner, *Memoirs of* . . . , ed. Thomas J. McCormack (Cedar Rapids, Io., 1909), II, 84-87. *DTri.*, May 22 (unless otherwise noted, all dates used in this chapter will be understood as 1860).
[4] Greeley to Colfax, Feb. 20, NYPL. Greeley's italics.

NOT COMPROMISE, BUT WAR

The demand for a quarter-section to be given any man who would till the soil was the keystone in Greeley's theory of labor reform, and the logical culmination of the *Tribune's* antislavery crusade. Speaking in Kansas in 1859, Greeley asserted that "Land for the Landless" was more vital than congressional restriction of chattel labor; for he deemed it "the more effective and enduring barrier to the spread of Slavery." A mere platform announcement sponsoring homesteads was hardly sufficient for him. He insisted that the Republicans on Capitol Hill manufacture ammunition for his editorial guns.[5] He felt that if such a bill could be pushed through congress, Buchanan would veto it, thus clarifying a first-rate campaign issue. All was done to Greeley's satisfaction. Galusha Grow, of Pennsylvania, secured house approval of his homestead bill in March, 1860. Southern opposition to the parceling of the western prairies into small farms was of course stronger in the senate, where Tennessee hillman Andrew Johnson had difficulty in obtaining even a semblance of the house version. A conference committee brought forth a virtual acceptance of the senate proposal. Greeley wrote Colfax that the Republicans acted wisely in sustaining any compromise which would prove agreeable to the upper chamber, "though you knock a plank in the Chicago Platform which I fixed exactly to my own liking." Johnson's measure passed in June, but Buchanan refused to sign.[6] The *Tribune* danced with glee. True Republican policy, it testified, was to be found in Grow's bill, for Johnson's was but "a half-loaf." And yet, tired old aristocratic Buchanan had refused even these crumbs to the masses. The delighted editor reminded his readers of the grave danger involved in elevating a man to the presidency who had never associated with the poor. Lincoln, he promised, favored a

[5] Greeley to Colfax, Feb. 14, 1859, NYPL. Speech at Osawatomie, K. T., May 18, *DTri.*, May 31, 1859.
[6] Greeley to Colfax, June 20, NYPL. George M. Stephenson, *The Political History of the Public Lands, from 1840 to 1862* (Boston, 1917), 195-220.

land policy for the people, but would have accepted even a half-way enactment.[7] Greeley also made this point clear in his campaign addresses to the working classes in and around New York City, and he wrote privately that the "Free Land or Homestead bill is our tower of strength in the North-West."[8]

A harder nut to crack was protection for American industries. The problem lay in the Free Soil crust of the Republican party, for these men were clinging to their Democratic ideas of free trade as beneficial to the consumer. Greeley had to steer a middle course to satisfy these recalcitrants and at the same time attract the tariff enthusiasts of Pennsylvania and New Jersey to the Republican banner. He employed moderation in wording the protection plank at Chicago, and followed a cautious editorial policy. He urged his congressional friends not "to drive the wedge butt-end foremost, nor lose all in attempting to grasp too much." By this advice he meant protective duties on iron, fabrics, and luxuries, but none on coal or any other commodity which might be convincingly paraded in the Democratic press as an unnecessary burden on the laborer.[9] At the same time, he stressed what he termed the "great fraud" of 1844. The Democrats had carried Pennsylvania by claiming that James K. Polk and George M. Dallas favored the high tariff of 1842; but this duplicity could not be repeated in 1860, for the people were now too well informed by such papers as his own.[10]

The Pacific railroad held the spotlight of the third item on his economic agenda, internal improvements. His construction plan was similar to that later adopted. Congress

[7] *DTri.*, June 21. See also *DTri.*, June 25, 26.
[8] Greeley to George W. Wright, Oct. 18, 1859, Schurz MSS., LC. Notices, editorials, and articles, *DTri.*, Jan. 23, 26, 30, Feb. 7, Mar. 6, 19, 20, June 7, 15, Aug. 11, Oct. 11, 22. William E Dodd, "The Fight for the Northwest, 1860," *American Historical Review*, xvi (July, 1911), 774-788.
[9] *DTri.*, Mar. 3. See also *DTri.*, Jan. 31, Feb. 2, 7, 9, 10, 1859; Mar. 9, Apr. 27, June 7, 15, 18. Greeley to Justin S. Morrill, Feb. 22, 25, 1859, Morrill, "Notable Letters from My Political Friends, ii," *Forum*, xxiv (Nov., 1897), 270-271. Greeley to Colfax, Feb. 4, 1859, NYPL.
[10] *DTri.*, Aug. 4, Sept. 10, 26.

should offer a contract demanding the completion of the railway within ten years. All groups of capitalists interested should submit bids on their estimates of the cost over the route they preferred, and the coveted prize should go to the company asking the least governmental assistance, which was to be paid in bonds, land grants, and timber rights. Greeley was partial to a central route through Kansas and the newly discovered gold fields about Pike's Peak, which he had visited amidst much fanfare as he crossed the Rocky Mountains in 1859. Such an undertaking, he observed, would pay dividends, for settlement would soon be sufficiently advanced for its maintenance. He undoubtedly believed that the financiers who backed the enterprise would take a similar view. He was not, however, so undiplomatic as to speculate upon the eastern terminus in the *Tribune*—he had a number of subscribers in and around Chicago—but he was surely thinking of St. Louis, which would thereupon become a city teeming with free laborers anxious to uphold Frank Blair and the cause of emancipation.[11]

Greeley lavished praise on Lincoln as the candidate who would foster the peaceful eradication of slavery through economic developments. In a manual compiled for campaign speakers, Greeley sought to show that the Republican policy was in the best traditions of American democracy. Reprinted were the principal letters and addresses of all the candidates, the platforms of the parties, and "a history of the struggle respecting slavery in the territories, and of the action of congress as to the freedom of the public lands . . ." It was said to be unbiased. By late August, 10,000 copies had been sold, and the work was entering its seventh printing.[12]

Both Greeley and Dana spoke to local Wide-Awake clubs, putting the popular handbook to practical use. They ex-

---

[11] *DTri.*, Feb. 28. See also note 34, chapter VIII.
[12] *WTri.* (adv.), Aug. 25. Greeley and John F. Cleveland, *A Political Text-book for 1860* . . . (New York, 1860). The price was $1 per copy. The joint author was Greeley's brother-in-law, the *Tribune* and *Almanac* statistician.

horted complete organization and the polling of a full vote in November.[13] Greeley was worried lest his teammates fall into the dissolute ways of the so-called Democratic ruffians. Instead of luring voters by demon rum, he advised young Republican workers to study and master the Lincoln-Douglas arguments, and devote their leisure to converting reluctant friends. "So shall you be an effective worker for the cause of Free Labor, without having to put at hazard your social and moral well-being or the bread of honest industry and manly independence."[14]

Greeley made it easy for his cohorts to follow this paternal counsel. He flooded the country with printed material. Fatigue seemed never to touch him, although his letters during these hectic days were infrequent and scrawled with utmost haste, and he complained of being worn with work and anxiety. His efforts were not in vain. The *Semi-Weekly* became the *Campaign Tribune*, but its circulation was only a fraction of that in 1856. The *Weekly* more than compensated for this disappointment. Its mailing list numbered more than 200,000 throughout the year. Greeley claimed 1,500,000 readers, and he took pride that each of his aggregate 300,000 copies passed through five hands: "As subscribers are often exhorted not to lend their papers, we are moved to say that we shall be glad to hear of *our* subscribers lending theirs as widely as possible."[15] In addition to his personal appearances on the campaign platform, his volume summarizing the political issues, and the *Tribune* itself, auxiliary publications streamed from Greeley's presses. Important Republican documents and addresses were circulated in cheap pamphlets. Lincoln's Cooper Institute oration and his debates with Douglas were at the crest of the current, followed by Seward's "Irrepressible Conflict" and his moderate senate pronouncement on the admission of Kansas, delivered on the

---

[13] Notices in *DTri.*, July 19, 20, 30, Aug. 6, 15, 23, 27, Sept. 10, 19, 21, 25, 27, 28.
[14] *DTri.*, May 29.
[15] *DTri.*, Mar. 3. Greeley's italics. See appendices A and B.

eve of the Republican convention to capture supporters who might otherwise judge him too radical.[16]

According to the *Tribune*, Seward had failed because Lincoln was a true conservative. The "House Divided" speech declared only that slavery should not be extended. "This would place it where Washington, Jefferson, and Madison placed it—in the way of ultimate extinction by the operation of natural causes, and in the peaceful legislation of the people of the States where it exists. Such is the orderly and conservative policy of Abraham Lincoln and of the Republican party. It was the policy of the great men in the days when there were giants in the land."[17]

Editorial treatment of Lincoln must have seemed a bit sudden to the *Tribune's* readers, for it had never considered him seriously as a Republican contender. Greeley had first met the Illinoisian in 1848, when both were Whig representatives in Washington. Mutual respect had grown up between them,[18] but so completely did they differ in temperament nothing approaching a friendship had been formed. At one point before the Chicago convention assembled, Greeley had privately judged Lincoln a logical choice for the vice-presidential nomination, but this preference had never received full editorial backing, because of the *Tribune* drive for Bates and its conviction that only one former Whig should be on the Republican ticket.[19] Lincoln's forensic ability had been recognized by Greeley at least as early as the Lincoln-Douglas senatorial race,[20] and the Cooper Institute speech delivered on February 27, 1860, in New York City had won more *Tribune* applause than was normally given to such efforts. With this exception, Lincoln had been accorded only

16 Editorial notices and advs., *DTri.*, Jan. 24, Feb. 11, 20, 28, Mar. 3, Apr. 3, May 10, 23, June 9, 11, 18, 22, July 7, Sept. 17, 18.
17 *DTri.*, May 30. See also *DTri.*, May 21, 23, 24, 28, June 1, 6, 20, July 4, 18, Aug. 11.
18 Lincoln to Charles L. Wilson, June 1, 1858, Lincoln, *Complete Works* ..., ed. John G. Nicolay and John Hay (New York, 1905), i, 238-39. Greeley, *Letters*, 24-26; *Recollections*, 226.
19 Greeley to Colfax, Feb. 3.
20 *DTri.*, June 24, 1858. See also *DTri.*, July 6, 30, 1857.

the pre-convention editorial space and praise handed out to any one of a half-dozen other favorite sons.[21]

Immediately after Lincoln's nomination, the *Tribune* began to laud him as an able statesman who had struggled from the impoverished surroundings of a log hut to command the respect of a nation. He was painted as the true political descendant of the Revolutionary fathers, and as a man of the people who would cherish and sustain the Union as had Andrew Jackson and Zachary Taylor before him. He would draw the nation's stable, peace-loving workers and farmers to the Republican banner, while Sham Democracy consisted of a cabal of mercantile, commercial, and plantation capitalists, plus a motley crew of urban ruffians.[22]

Two of Lincoln's adversaries were denounced as hypocrites. John Bell, claimed by the *Tribune* as a dilapidated Tennessee war horse, had been fighting other people's battles for many a year. This time he was backed by Democratic money for the sole purpose of beclouding the nuclear theme of slavery restriction and frightening the timid of the north with the ruse of disunion.[23] As for Douglas, he was conducting a "vague" campaign.[24] The Dred Scott decision had split his principle of popular sovereignty down the middle, and he was standing on the free soil half in the north, and the slavery-extending remainder in the south. Greeley so feared Douglas' power in the northwest that when he wrote about the Little Giant, his pen dripped venom: "It is a shame to our politics that any public man should in his public capacity so equivocate and deceive, so abandon the truth and so stick to false-

[21] *DTri.*, Dec. 4, 1858; Oct. 12, 1859; Jan. 31 ("Abram [*sic*] Lincoln"), Feb. 20, 25, 27 (on the eve of the Cooper Institute speech, "It is not probable that Mr. Lincoln will be heard again in our City this year if ever."), 28, Mar. 3, 6, 7, 12, 29, Apr. 6. *WTri.*, Mar. 3. Greeley from Davenport, Iowa, Jan. 29, *DTri.*, Feb. 7.

An interesting account of Lincoln's reading the proof of his Cooper Institute speech at the *Tribune* office is carried in Henry B. Rankin, *Intimate Character Sketches of Abraham Lincoln* (Philadelphia, 1924), 189-192.

[22] *DTri.*, May 30, Sept. 10, Oct. 4, 17, 23, 26, 27.

[23] *DTri.*, July 16, Aug. 13, 16, 25.   [24] *DTri.*, July 12.

hood, that, were it done in private life and done openly, he would be left without name and credit enough to buy a pint of rum on trust in a corner grocery."[25]

John C. Breckinridge, on the other hand, was a manly fellow—he was just on the wrong side. He came out openly and admitted that he wanted the negro driven across the free plains of the west; he met the issue of the hour squarely; it was a pleasure to oppose him.[26] The fundamental question before the electorate was the ethics of slavery. If enforced labor benefited the nation, it should be extended; if not, it should be quarantined within the slave states until it died a normal death. A brief conversation with a "Southron" or a doughface would display this essential difference between a pro and an antislavery advocate: ". . . he contemplates the needs of a talking animal, while you regard primarily those of an immortal soul."[27]

The Kentuckian's prestige in the north was being injured, averred the *Tribune*, by that scoundrel Douglas, who was portraying his Democratic adversary as a disunionist. It was true that Breckinridge was being supported by southern hotheads, but he was no secessionist. To prove its point, the *Tribune* placed Breckinridge's acceptance letter and a pro-Union speech before its readers.[28]

The people must decide between Lincoln and Breckinridge. On the one hand marched honesty in government, peace with all foreigners, an orderly development of the country's resources, and the ultimate extinction of chattel labor. On the other slouched corruption, oligarchy, costly wars with foreign powers in an effort to extend slavery, a policy of free trade which compelled all farmers to accept the prices set upon their produce by British imperialism, and the social spread

[25] *DTri.*, Oct. 6.   [26] *DTri.*, July 18, 19, Aug. 13, Oct. 12, 13, 19.
[27] Greeley in the New York *Independent,* July 19.   This was a religious paper of wide circulation in the north.   His more pronounced antislavery declarations in the campaign and secession periods are to be found in its columns.
[28] *DTri.*, Sept. 13, Oct. 19.   For ltr. and speech, *DTri.*, July 10, and *SWTri.*, Sept. 7.

of slavery until it encompassed the working classes, white and black.[29] The choice was obvious, and Greeley expressed his faith in the future: "The signs of the times indicate that the Republican President will be inaugurated, as it were, by universal consent, amid an era of good feeling."[30]

To bring his audience into any anticipation of this era of good feeling, Greeley had to meet an argument reiterated by the Democratic press in both northern and southern states. These journals contended that the measures recommended by the Republican party would bring about the freedom of large numbers of slaves with ruinous effect to the south. Only on a basis of slavery could two races live together in peace. Emancipation had ruined the British West Indies, and brought negro and white man into disastrous social, professional, and economic competition. The *Tribune* replied indirectly but decisively. In treating the question, discretion had to be employed, for the south had no monopoly on race hatred. With an election at hand, Greeley saw no reason for the *Tribune* to solve the problem of the freedman overnight. His own views may be drawn from previous and subsequent pronouncements. He looked with disfavor on racial amalgamation, but wanted the blacks to become citizens. Civil rights should be proffered slowly. First the ex-slaves must be given the privilege of enjoying their own homes, of spending the just return of their own labor. Then they must be educated, taught to save and to improve their economic status. In the early stages there would be no competition between the whites and the blacks. The former would be trained as skilled technicians in factories or scientific tillers of small farms. The latter would remain for a time as plantation hands. It was foolish to speak of colonizing them. "They will all be needed here, and will be a more healthy, cheerful, tractable body of laborers than the planters can find beside. Now they are good for nothing, because they have no rights, no social position,

[29] *DTri.*, June 18, 19, July 4, Aug. 8, Sept. 12, Oct. 20.
[30] *DTri.*, July 10.

298

no hopes, no friends."[31] Eventually Greeley believed that they would gravitate into the gulf zone, where they would live alone and govern themselves within the Union.[32]

No stress was placed on these beliefs in the campaign of 1860. Instead, the *Tribune* carefully refuted the factual argument of the economic starvation of the British West Indies.[33] Rather than by emancipation, Jamaica had been hard hit by soil depletion and the anaconda of British imperialism. The first had driven sugar culture to more fertile regions, and the second had bankrupted the planters by compelling them to pay ruinous prices for British timber and foodstuffs when these items could have been purchased cheaper in the United States. By 1860, economic improvement was said to be noticeable. The freedmen had taken over the former plantations, and were breaking them down into small farms and diversifying the crops. Soon the colony would be self-sufficient, and would be able to compete anew with the other sugar zones.[34] Hildreth made a special voyage to survey the progress of former slaves in British Guiana. In a series of articles, he judged their advancement as nothing less than remarkable, considering the beastly past from which they had so recently emerged.[35] A correspondent in Canada joined the chorus. Negroes in that northern colony, newly arrived from the slavedriver's tyranny, were developing into peace-loving, law-abiding citizens.[36]

[31] *DTri.*, Dec. 6, 1854.
[32] "For the present the great mass of American Blacks must remain commingled with the whiter races.
"Ultimately the Gulf States will be mainly their home.
"Liberia? Let all go thither who will.
"The Civilization and Christianization of Africa is a noble enterprise." Lecture notes (delivered after the Civil War), Greeley MSS., LC.
[33] A moderate but typical proslavery view may be found in *Harper's Weekly*, III (Sept. 3, 1859), 562.
[34] *DTri.*, July 1, 1857; May 17, Aug. 17, 1859; Mar. 3. Ltr. from "Viator Veritatis," *DTri.*, Aug. 6, 1858. See also Hildreth, "The 'Ruin' of Jamaica," American Anti-Slavery Society *Tracts*, no. 6.
[35] *DTri.*, Apr. 21, May 4, 5, 26, June 16. An editorial, *DTri.*, May 4, announced Hildreth as the author of these articles.
[36] *DTri.*, Oct. 24, Nov. 2, 11, 27, 1857.

Thus were the Yankee mechanic, farmer, and merchant
assured by indirection and analogy that manumission would
not wreck the slave states with servile insurrections, but what
of the southern whites? Would they not sever the Union
rather than abide a Republican president? Greeley's method
of allaying such a fear as this was the same he had employed
since the Kansas-Nebraska bill was presented in the senate.
The great bulk of the southerners were humble, hard-working
farmers, who needed the political assistance of their northern
brothers. Only a Republican victory would allow these depressed individuals to speak for themselves and thus prove
the close interrelation of their interests with those of the
northern masses.[37]

Greeley entreated the free state voters not to swallow the
falsehoods of the proslavery press. The fire-eaters were using
belligerent language as a political weapon. Southern economy depended upon the maintenance of the Union.[38] The
oligarchs, he reiterated, "aim to bully the Free States out of
their choice for President; or, that failing, to drag the border
Slave States into a rebellion which, however it may result
directly, will have the effect of chaining those states more
completely to the car of Slavery. The game is a bold one, but
will not win. The Union will stand; the Slave States will not
secede from it; and if a few restless, baffled political plotters
shall implicate themselves so deeply as to render their own
flight into exile inevitable, it will be all the better for the
tranquillity, the harmony, and the prosperity of the American Republic."[39]

The successes of Frank Blair were indicative of the future.
The south was swarming with potential Republicans, who
were prevented from exercising their free judgment by
southern tyranny, but 1864 would see the Republicans
carry several slave states.[40]

[37] DTri., esp. Jan. 10, Mar. 12, 23, Oct. 13.
[38] DTri., Aug. 30, Oct. 13, 17, 20, 24, 26, Nov. 2.
[39] Greeley in the New York Independent, Aug. 16.
[40] DTri., Aug. 15, Sept. 12, Oct. 13, 19, 22, 23.

Already, Greeley claimed: "Thousands there will vote for
Lincoln, as tens of thousands would do if they dared and were
allowed to do so." His faith in southern free soil sentiment
was bolstered by increased demands for his journal. "Thousands" in that section took the *Tribune* already, although
"hundreds" were compelled to see their copies "stolen and
burned, the Post-Office conniving at the robbery." Were
Lincoln once in office and the heavy hand of intimidation
lifted from the minds of the non-slaveowning whites, the
Tribune's circulation would jump, and Republicanism would
spread like wildfire.[41]

For those who might have been sceptical of Greeley's
interpretation, there were additional assurances. The *Tribune's* correspondents in the south were unanimous in their
opinion. There would be no secession, there would be no war.
Republican clubs were being formed in both Portsmouth and
Wheeling, Virginia. Forecast of a large vote for Lincoln
came from Maryland. A Texas farmer sent "three cheers for
Abe" because that candidate was a conservative who would
"allow us Southerners to enjoy our own opinion, and if we
want to keep our niggers he will be the last man to interfere."
A gentleman in Louisville wrote to say there would be no
disruption of the Union, for Kentuckians would acquiesce
peacefully in Lincoln's election. An observer in Richmond
gave the seemingly contradictory but interesting testimony
that the larger and more influential Virginia landowners
favored a free soil triumph as the best way to avoid a sectional disturbance wherein "the North, in order to gain an
easy victory, would need to do little more than furnish arms
to the non-slaveholding whites of the South." From Memphis
came these reassuring words: "Sentiments of disunion are
uttered only by violent political aspirants, and are seriously
entertained by no one possessed of an ordinary amount of

41 *DTri.*, July 23. See also *DTri.*, Aug. 15. Clement Eaton, "Censorship
of the Southern Mails," *American Historical Review*, xlviii (Jan., 1943),
266-280.

common sense. Let not threats, or predictions of disunion, intimidate the friends of honest dealing and righteous government. None but the veriest fire-eaters contemplate disunion; they are but an insignificant clique, utterly powerless against the people. The masses are heart and soul for the Union . . ."[42]

Greeley called particular attention to a "genuine" letter from an overseer of an Alabama plantation as evidence of the coming white rebellion against the slaveocracy. This man feared that "agitators would make the Northern people believe that the South is united to a man. There could not be a greater mistake. The people are divided into two classes— the rich and the poor—who are as distinct and separate as the North Pole is from the South Pole." Only on election days would the aristocrats condescend to speak to their social inferiors, and then just long enough to get their votes. Now, the tables were turning. He demanded that his fellow workers in the north give him and his companions "Truth, Equality, Justice."[43]

To appeals for advice from the slave states, Greeley gave editorial answer. His southern friends were worried as to how they should conduct themselves at the ballot box. Vote for Lincoln, or not at all, counseled Greeley. They should agree "on the hour at which you will together go quietly to the polls and offer your votes . . . if they are refused, or if they are accepted and then destroyed or not returned, *your* duty is performed." He had recently heard that Baltimore was sure to go Republican. He doubted this, but admired the confidence which prompted the prediction. Such faith would soon "render her the Gibraltar of Republicanism in the East of Slavedom, as St. Louis is in the West. The oligarchy under-

[42] "J. R. S." from Memphis, July 12; H. R. Helper from New York City, Nov. 1, enclosing a ltr. from a friend in Richmond; "Danell" from Louisville, Oct. 19; "Farmer" from Bold Spring, McLennan Co., Texas, July 19; "A Maryland Republican" from Russville, Md., Oct. 27; Daniel Collins from Portsmouth, Oct. 26; "C. A. G." from Wheeling, Va., Oct. 16; *DTri.*, in order as listed, July 19, Nov. 5, Oct. 26, Aug. 11, Oct. 30, 30, 20.
[43] "V" from Montgomery Co., Ala., Aug. 4, *DTri.*, Aug. 22.

stand this. They dread the election of Lincoln as insuring a revolt, not of their black slaves, but of their white ones. . . . A few hotheads. . . . may really mean to break up the Union whenever they shall have ceased to rule it; but any move in that direction will only precipitate the disaster they are seeking to avert. There will be no need of sending troops to the South to put down a slave-breeders' insurrection there; the *real* unionists of the South will deal with the hotheads most effectually. They will neither need nor desire external aid."[44]

Reading his reports from the south and incorporating their meaning into his partisan journal gave Greeley courage in his convictions, but he was unable to hide his anxiety altogether. One admonition from the south was timely. A gentleman in Savannah denied that disunion was "apprehended," but went on to urge that "Lincoln should be elected, if at all, *by a majority of the people*. For the South's sake he should be, not only a 'Constitutional President,' but also the 'People's President.' " This correspondent begged the northerners to vote for Lincoln and give him an overwhelming triumph.[45]

When the Democratic party was seen to be irrevocably divided, Greeley commented that Lincoln might receive ever so many electoral votes, but he could not be expected to gain the popular majority. This outcome would give the disunionists propaganda for secession.[46] Surprisingly to the *Tribune*, Douglas' slave state following seemed small.[47] Charges of sectionalism against Lincoln and the Republican party became more telling as the campaign mounted in intensity, and Greeley regretted anew—in the *Daily Tribune* only—that Bates had not been selected at Chicago.[48] The October elections assured Lincoln's success in Indiana and Pennsylvania; he would certainly be the next president.

[44] *DTri.*, Oct. 12. Greeley's italics.
[45] "W" from Savannah, Oct. 18, *DTri.*, Oct. 26. Tribune's italics.
[46] *DTri.*, June 25, 26.   [47] *DTri.*, July 2, 24.
[48] *DTri.*, Aug. 20.

Once more Greeley turned southward and pleaded for peace:
"And, again, it is most desirable that the sensible, patriotic
citizens—who are far more numerous in the Slave States
than they would seem to be if we judged the South by what
appears in her newspapers—should interpose at once to stop
the ridiculous gasconade of disunion which some who know
better, with many who know scarcely any thing, mischie-
vously persist in. It is now clear that this exerts, and can
exert, no influence over the Free States, except to confirm
them in their fixed resolve not to be bullied out of their convictions by menaces which strike at the root of constitutional
government, and that make a mockery of elections. To undertake to browbeat the North out of her convictions by threats
of rebellion and revolution, is to renounce the whole machinery of popular elections, and to convert our country into
another Mexico or New-Granada, where each election is expected to be followed by a civil war between those who carried
it and those who were defeated."[49]

As the canvass closed, the question of disunion was foremost in Greeley's mind. Yet in the *Tribune* he appeared as
confident as ever: "We dare the Fire-eaters to submit the
question of Secession or No Secession because of Lincoln's
election to the popular vote of their own people. They will
be badly beaten in every State but South Carolina, and
probably beaten in her popular vote also. And let them be
assured of this—that they cannot make feints of jumping
out of the Union and expect the North to hold them. Whenever any considerable section of this Union shall really insist
on getting out of it, we shall insist that they be allowed to go.
And we feel sure the North generally cherishes a kindred
determination. So let there be no more babble as to the ability
of the Cotton States to whip the North. If they *will* fight,
they must hunt up some other enemy, for we are not going to
fight them. If they insist on staying in the Union, they must
of course obey its laws; but if the *People* (not the swashy

[49] *DTri.*, Oct. 13.

304

politicians) of the Cotton States shall ever deliberately vote themselves out of the Union, we shall be in favor of letting them go in peace. Then who is to fight? And what for?"[50]

Lincoln's election on November 8 was but a brief interlude of joy amid the bitter concern Greeley felt for the Union. On the next day he repeated that peace would be maintained in any event. He would never compromise the position of the north, nor would he countenance war. The right to secede was a revolutionary one, but it existed none the less. "We hope never to live in a republic whereof one section is pinned to the residue by bayonets." He stressed that the step must be taken by the southern states "with the deliberation and gravity befitting so momentous an issue." The hotheads must not harangue their fellow citizens with rancor, prejudice, and misrepresentation: ". . . let the act of secession be the echo of an unmistakable popular fiat. A judgment thus rendered, a demand for separation so backed, would either be acquiesced in without the effusion of blood, or those who rushed upon carnage to defy and defeat it would place themselves clearly in the wrong."[51]

Greeley's basic condition for peaceable secession was a solemn and deliberate judgment on the part of the people of the slave states. For this reason, to take from their context and use singly such eye-catching quotations as "Wayward sisters, depart in peace" is to distort his intent.[52] Nor was his policy "an editorial flash."[53] Nine years earlier, when discussing South Carolina's perennial threats of withdrawal, he said: "If a State, by a decided, unquestionable majority of

[50] *DTri.*, Nov. 2. Greeley's italics and parentheses.
[51] *DTri.*, Nov. 9. See also *DTri.*, Nov. 16. Greeley's reply to "R. S.," *DTri.*, Dec. 15. Greeley in the New York *Independent*, Nov. 8.
[52] Examples, Avery Craven, *The Coming of the Civil War* (New York, 1942), 428. Samuel E. Morison, *The Oxford History of the United States,* II (Oxford, 1927), 153-154. John B. McMaster, *A History of the People of the United States . . .* , VIII (New York, 1913), 492. Rhodes, *History*, III (New York, 1904), 140-142, 165-166.
Peaceable secession editorials in the *Tribune* and other northern journals may be examined in *Northern Editorials on Secession,* ed. Howard C. Perkins (New York, 1942), I, 332-379.
[53] Suggested by Randall, *Lincoln the President*, I, 207n.

her People, should resolve to quit the Union, we should prefer to let her go rather than retain her by Military force. . . . If any did [go], she would be glad to walk in again before she had been out two years."[54]

Changed in only one particular were his more elaborate ideas on secession as they unfolded anew in the fall, winter, and summer of 1860-1861. He not only felt it impracticable for a single state to leave the Union, but also viewed such a step unconstitutional. "We do not talk of subduing her," he hastened to add, "we only say that her position as a seceding and *quasi* independent State in the heart of a Federal Union will be anomalous and untenable."[55] Agitation over slavery had trained him to think in terms of sections rather than individual commonwealths, and this mental transition allowed him to reduce the idea of small segments making an exit from large economic and strategic entities to an absurdity: ". . . Governor's Island should not be at liberty to secede from the State and Nation and allow herself to be covered with French or British batteries commanding and threatening our City."[56] He concluded that the Union was in its constitutional nature "irrevocable," and that only the earthquake of a sectional revolution could "shiver it."

This revolutionary right Greeley proffered to the "eight Cotton States," and to any other contiguous slave commonwealths desiring to join them.[57] The situation as he saw it might become analogous to the American Revolution, and might again demand the application of Jefferson's "great principle" embodied in the Declaration of Independence: ". . . that governments 'derive their *just* powers from the *consent of the governed*: and that, whenever any form of government becomes distructive [*sic*] of these ends, it is the *right of the people to alter or abolish it* . . .' " If this principle, Greeley continued, "justified the secession from the British Empire of Three Millions of colonists in 1776, we do not see

[54] *DTri.*, Oct. 17, 1851.   [55] *DTri.*, Nov. 30. Greeley's italics.
[56] *DTri.*, Dec. 17.   [57] *DTri.*, Nov. 16.

5. The "Mustang" Team, by Currier & Ives. Astride horse and on wagon: Greeley, Bennett, Raymond, Frémont, unidentified, Webb

The Weekly Tribune.

CHARLES SUMNER.

COL. JOHN CHARLES FREMONT.
[FROM A PHOTOGRAPH BY ROOT.]

THE PEOPLE'S CONVENTION.

A STRAIGHT-OUT PLATFORM.

FREMONT NOMINATED FOR PRESIDENT.

VICE-PRESIDENT NOT YET NOMINATED.

FIRST DAY'S PROCEEDINGS.

From Our Own Reporters.

PHILADELPHIA, Tuesday, June 17, 1856.

At a quarter past 10 o'clock the doors of the Musical Fund Hall on Locust street, assigned for the assemblage of the Convention, were opened and the delegates entered the Hall. The Committee of Arrangements had assigned seats for the different delegations. The arrangements for the accommodation of the Press were of the most creditable character, and the Committee has the thanks of all the Reporters in attendance. In point of intelligence, intellectual and moral worth and personal standing in society, no Convention ever called in this country has shown a superiority in the delegations represented, while an equality in these respects has been very rare. A good proportion of those in attendance have occupied high and responsible stations in the National and State Legislative Councils or in the Judiciary or Executive Departments of the Government; others have held high positions at the bar, in commerce, and in private life, and their very names have always carried with them a moral weight that indicates upon which side in a great contest the truth rests.

As the delegation from Kansas entered the Hall, it was met with six loud and enthusiastic cheers. The whole number of delegates in attendance was between six and seven hundred, all of the delegations being

CHARLES SUMNER, the distinguished Massachusetts Senator, was born in Boston, January 6, 1811, and hence is now in the full maturity of manhood. His father was Charles Pinckney Sumner, a descendant of an ancient Boston family, and for many years the Sheriff of Suffolk County. A man combining integrity of purpose with urbanity of manner to an uncommon degree, he was held in high and deserved honor by the great mass of his fellow-citizens. Mr. Sumner received his early education at the Boston Latin School, was graduated with brilliant reputation at Harvard University in the year 1830, and soon after commenced his professional studies at the Law School in Cambridge. He was a favorite pupil of the late Justice Story, and, at his instance, was appointed editor of *The American Jurist*. Admitted to the Boston bar in 1834, he was at once recognized as a young man of rare legal erudition, of singular devotion to study, and of elegant classical attainments. He became reporter to the United States Circuit Court soon after commencing practice, and three volumes of reports attest his assiduity and legal acumen in that office. During the absence of Professors Greenleaf and Story he lectured, at the request of the Faculty, for three successive Winters, to the classes in the Cambridge Law School. He won golden opinions from the students who enjoyed his instructions, and enlarged the basis of his professional reputation.

Deciding to devote some years to the study of

June 7, 1856   June 21, 1856

6. Sketches from *Weekly Tribune*

why it would not justify the secession of Five Millions of Southrons from the Federal Union in 1861."[58]

Greeley believed the application of Jefferson's principle would either allow the unionist masses of the south to overthrow their leaders, or the cotton states to depart peacefully. The first alternative seemed by far the more probable. He viewed his policy as essential in upholding the unionists in the south, whom he presumed to be in the majority. He considered that every effort was being made to carry secession over the heads of the rank and file. Such chance correspondence as he smuggled out of the slave states strengthened his views. From Charleston, South Carolina, came word that "Lincoln's election will lead to attempts at Secession, but I am convinced that they will not be supported by the majority of the people, even in the State of South Carolina."[59] "Virginia is as true as steel to the Union," witnessed a Richmond scribe. It was felt in Savannah that the unionists of Georgia would eventually triumph, if only the north were firm but pacific, and time for reflection were allowed. One observer noted as he passed through Tennessee to Atlanta that the people were "almost to a man" for the Union. A non-slaveholder from the banks of the lower Mississippi entreated the northerners not to desert his cause: "The Union men of the South only wait for you to show your strength."[60]

The northern display of strength, as far as Greeley was concerned, was not in assuming a war-like attitude, but rather in refusing to compromise the victory won in November. The Republican triumph, he wrote, "was not the cause of the secession movement, but only seized as affording a

[58] *DTri.*, Dec. 17. Greeley's italics and textual errors. *The Complete Jefferson*, ed. Saul K. Padover (New York, 1943), 28.
[59] From Charleston, Nov. 7, *DTri.*, Nov. 10. This correspondent, probably James E. Harvey, changed his outlook without apologizing as the situation demanded. Other ltrs. and dispatches may be found in *DTri.*, Nov. 19, Dec. 3, 13, 14, 21, 28, 29; Jan. 16, 1861.
[60] "E. P. U." from Raymond, Hinds Co., Miss., Feb. 7, 1861; (?) from Atlanta, Dec. 22, and from Macon, Dec. 24; (?) from Savannah, Dec. 10; "Our Own Correspondent" from Richmond, Nov. 29; *DTri.*, in order as listed, Feb. 18, 1861; Dec. 28, 28, 15, 3.

favorable opportunity for bringing it to issue."[61] Sensibly, he wanted to do nothing which might play into the hands of precipitant South Carolina: "What she expects and desires is a clash of arms with the Federal Government, which will at once commend her to the sympathy and cooperation of every Slave State, and to the sympathy (at least) of the Pro-Slavery minority in the Free States. It is not difficult to see that this would speedily work a political revolution, which would restore to Slavery all, and more than all, it has lost by the canvass of 1860."[62]

Greeley's confidence in the feasibility of a peaceful solution to the southern problem was complete. He continued to seek the emasculation of the armed forces of the federal government as late as December, 1860.[63] His horror of warfare urged a bloodless solution. "War is a hideous necessity at best," he warned, "—and a civil conflict—a war of estranged and embittered fellow-countrymen—is the most hideous of all wars."[64] This prospective civil war was particularly repellent because of the uncertainty of a northern victory. Were the gulf region alone united, it could hardly be defeated: "Five Millions of People, more than half of them of the dominant race, of whom at least Half a Million are able and willing to shoulder muskets, can never be subdued while fighting around and over their own hearthstones." Furthermore, victory, if achieved, would at best be a barren one. He doubted that even then the Union could be restored and anticipated the trials of the Reconstruction era. If the seceding states were beaten, he asserted, "they would no longer be equal members of the Union, but conquered dependencies. Suppose they could be overcome and their military forces destroyed: what then? Can you compel them to send members to Congress?"[65]

[61] *DTri.*, Nov. 30.
[63] *DTri.*, Nov. 21, Dec. 1.
[65] *DTri.*, Nov. 30.

[62] *DTri.*, Dec. 17. Greeley's parentheses.
[64] *DTri.*, Nov. 16.

To avoid war, to protect southern unionists, and to safe-guard his moral concept of the right of a section to choose its own government, Greeley continuously expressed certain conditions he considered necessary to secession. These were three in number: a free and open discussion of the problem by the citizens of the section contemplating withdrawal; a deliberate and democratic election which would exhibit beyond any shadow of a doubt that the majority of the southerners involved really wanted to leave the Union, and had not been bribed, intimidated, or forced by the slave-holders to take that stand; and, finally, if the verdict were for splitting the government, peaceful negotiations in Washington between the representatives of the southern and northern people, either in the form of a convention or of a constitutional amendment, legalizing Jefferson's revolutionary right. Until these negotiations were completed, and the common federal property equitably divided, Greeley maintained it the duty of the government at Washington, whether headed by Buchanan or Lincoln, to continue the enforcement of federal laws throughout the land.[66]

In emphasizing these conditions, Greeley exhibited a grave misunderstanding of the south. He counseled delay because he wished to give the sentiment of the supposed unionist majority time to crystallize. As the seven states of the lower south, which formed the first Confederate government, left the Union in the winter of 1860-1861, *Tribune* readers were informed in no uncertain terms that the non-slaveowners were browbeaten or duped, that elections to the secessionist conventions were unduly rushed, and that popular referendums were not contemplated.[67] Certain important facts supported this interpretation. The secessionist leaders found it neither wise nor necessary to secure a solemn and deliberate mandate from their people. Only by the decisions

[66] *DTri.*, Nov. 12, 16, 19, 20, 21, 24, 27, 30, Dec. 4, 6, 8, 10, 12, 17; Jan. 7, 1861. Greeley in the New York *Independent*, Nov. 15, 22, 29, Dec. 6.
[67] All *Tribune* issues, Dec.; Jan., Feb., Mar., 1861. Esp. *DTri.*, Mar. 20, 1861. See also Greeley in the New York *Independent*, Mar. 21, 1861.

of hastily elected conventions were six of the cotton states carried out of the Union. Texas, the seventh and last in the original group to secede, held a referendum and joined the neighboring nucleus in a common government. Considerable opposition to secession came from citizens throughout the gulf zone who saw no reason for such action before positive Republican assaults had been made against the rights of sovereign states. Similar efforts to obtain pro-secessionist conventions in Arkansas, Tennessee, North Carolina, and Virginia were unsuccessful. These four states left the national government only because of the crisis, which seemed to many the proof of northern aggression, at Fort Sumter in Charleston Harbor in the early spring, 1861.[68]

It is not surprising that Greeley should exaggerate unionist feeling in the south and should misjudge the acumen of the secessionist leaders. He knew little about that region. Suspicion and passionate hostility towards him and his paper had blocked his travel thence. It was a foreign nation as effectively sealed as China. He was a man of intelligence, a keen student of social and political trends; yet he never had the opportunity to see for himself what the south was like. In February, 1861, he was scheduled to deliver a literary lecture before a society of fine arts in that "Gibraltar of Republicanism," St. Louis, but it had to be cancelled for fear of mob violence. After the war was over and the smoke was clearing away from the bloody battlefields, Greeley recalled the bitter secession crisis. He remembered the difficulty that his correspondents had experienced in getting their data out of the south to the *Tribune* office, and he suggested, mildly enough, that if the hotheads had permitted the Republican aims to be more understood among their fellow citizens—just as the southerners had spokesmen in the free states—then four frightful years of carnage might have been avoided.[69]

[68] David M. Potter, *Lincoln and His Party in the Secession Crisis* (New Haven, 1942), 188-218, 306-313.
[69] Greeley, "Letters from Texas," 43-44. See also George W. Patterson to Weed, Mar. 18 (1861), Weed MSS., RRL.

310

By the time of the crisis of 1860-1861, the north and the south had passed the point of understanding. They spoke to one another in a foreign tongue. Southern editorials show that the slave state estimate of the north was as askew as was Greeley's of the south. Slaveowning journalists were as confident as was the New York editor that there could be no real opposition to their course. There is no evidence that Greeley exercised more than a modicum of influence over the southern decision to leave the common government. The *Tribune* was neither read nor understood to any degree in the south. Various southern journals were aware of the New York paper, but its words were scarcely passed on without prejudice.[70] Editorial gibes from the Mobile *Daily Advertiser* ring with the tone of the *Tribune*—with Greeley the butt: ". . . the crafty old incendiary who has been preaching aggressive abolition from youth to grayhaired age is getting down on his knees at last to the power he has so often challenged and defied." Later this journal predicted that the *Tribune* office would be torn into shreds by starving men left unemployed because of secession. As for Greeley, the mob would "ornament a lamp post with his lovely person."[71]

[70] The lead in the view that the *Tribune* fostered secession in the south seems to have been taken, for political reasons, by Weed during the 1872 presidential campaign, ". . . Letter . . . to Thomas C. Acton" (pamphlet) (New York, 1872), 4-6.

[71] Mobile *Daily Advertiser*, Dec. 23, Nov. 24. Other references of interest: Norfolk *Southern Argus*, Nov. 19, 21, 27, Dec. 4; Augusta (Ga.) *Daily Constitutionalist*, Nov. 23; Baltimore *Daily Exchange*, Dec. 3; Wilmington (N. C.) *Daily Journal*, Dec. 8; Richmond *Enquirer* (daily), Nov. 19, Dec. 7, 15, 25; Baltimore *Sun*, Dec. 6; Augusta (Ga.) *Daily Chronicle and Sentinel*, Dec. 12; "Pink" from N. Y. C. to Charleston *Daily Courier*, issues Nov. 20, 30, Dec. 1, 11, 24, 25; New Orleans *Daily Delta*, Nov. 22, Dec. 13, 20, 21; New Orleans *Commercial Bulletin* (daily), Nov. 22, Dec. 4, 11, 29; Vicksburg *Weekly Sun*, Nov. 19, 26; Mobile *Daily Advertiser*, Nov. 23, Dec. 6, 7, 21, 29. See also *Southern Editorials on Secession*, ed. Dwight L. Dumond (New York, 1931).

The sources have not been exhausted, and evidence that the *Tribune* did embolden the south to secede may be found in the Memphis *Daily Avalanche*, Nov. 19; Savannah *Daily Republican*, Dec. 7, 8; and the Augusta (Ga.) *Daily Constitutionalist* published a speech made by H. L. Benning on Nov. 19 in the state assembly in which reference is made to Greeley, issues for Dec. 18, 19. See also Troup (pseud.), "To the People of the South. Senator Hammond and the *Tribune*," *Tract No. 3* (pamphlet) (Charleston?, 1860).

In the north, Greeley's doctrine of peaceable secession had the indirect effect of bringing that section more whole-heartedly into the war. The *Tribune* audience, and indeed the great majority of northerners, debating with themselves the rights and wrongs of allowing the south to depart if she earnestly desired to do so, were outraged by the haste of her exit and the farewell gesture of the attack on Fort Sumter. This assault on the flag of the Union occurred when President Lincoln, in conformity with Greeley's wishes, was trying to send provisions to that southern fort. Thus, in the eyes of the *Tribune's* followers, not only had all Greeley's conditions for peaceable secession been skirted, but also one of his basic premises, that federal authority and law be upheld in the south until withdrawal had been sanctioned by a federal convention or a constitutional amendment, had been flouted. This circumstance added to the feeling in the north that secession was the work, not of the supposed mute and unionist majority, but of a powerful and unscrupulous cabal, unable to achieve its end through any means other than battle. From the first, the Civil War was in keeping with the popular conception of all modern armed struggles: each opponent felt itself unitedly at war with an enemy who was under the dictatorial heel of a treacherous oligarchy.

There is no substantial evidence which questions Greeley's integrity and honesty in offering a means of peaceable secession to the cotton states.[72] His activities during the war sustain the interpretation that he misunderstood that section, and because of that misunderstanding had reason to feel that his offer of peaceable secession, if tried, would test the strength of unionist sentiment in the south, and if necessary, provide a tranquil means for the exit of that region from the national government. As the war broke, he looked anxiously through rose-colored spectacles in search of a non-slave-

[72] For another and provocative interpretation, see Potter, *Lincoln*, 51-57; "Horace Greeley and Peaceable Secession," *Journal of Southern History*, VII (May, 1941), 145-159.

owners' rebellion. As the turmoil gained in intensity, he peered into every corner and crevice of the south to find sentiment for the Union, or to establish some basis for a negotiated peace. Frustrated by failure, he demanded southern emancipation not only as a social advance but also as a military expediency. Lincoln's pronouncement of freedom, he hoped, would tear the Confederacy apart by servile disturbances and instill into the Union a partnership which the southern whites had failed to provide.[73]

Although he misunderstood the south, Greeley would have willingly granted disunion rather than barter away the hard-won fruit of the antislavery victory in 1860. He took a firm stand against any compromise on the part of the north for two reasons. He believed the southern leaders unable to carry the secession question before their people, and concluded these politicians were utilizing the threat of withdrawal in order to cause the free states to back down from their position on the slavery issue. To retreat, he feared, would weaken if not destroy the roots of democracy he was nourishing in his home section. The north could no longer afford to be bound down by what he considered the reactionary economic and social doctrine of the south. In 1854 he had written Theodore Parker: ". . . I fail to realize the advantages of disunion, whether outwardly or otherwise, until we shall have truly Free States to break off, as well as undeniably Slave States to separate from."[74] The first part of this statement came to pass with Lincoln's victory which, although a plurality only, included a majority of the votes cast in the north.

In this frame of mind, Greeley countered last minute compromise measures with unvarying antipathy. The senate resolution offered by aging Senator John J. Crittenden of Kentucky came nearest to success. It would have abrogated the features of the fugitive slave law obnoxious to the north,

[73] Ralph R. Fahrney, *Horace Greeley and the "Tribune" in the Civil War* (Cedar Rapids, Io., 1936).
[74] Greeley to Parker, Mar. 23, 1854 (copy), Parker MSS., MHSL.

313

while eliciting a repeal of the free state personal liberty laws. By the passage of a series of fundamental enactments, which "no future amendment of the Constitution shall affect," Crittenden expected to make his settlement permanent. The articles would have denied congress the power to abolish slavery on federal property or within the District of Columbia unless the inhabitants consented and both Virginia and Maryland had already so acted, would have permitted inter-state and inter-territorial traffic in bondsmen, would have authorized the common government to sue the locality refusing to return a negro to his rightful owner, and, most important, would have specified that "in all the territory of the United States now held, or hereafter acquired, situate north of latitude thirty-six degrees and thirty minutes, slavery or involuntary servitude, except as a punishment for crime, is prohibited while such territory shall remain under territorial government. In all the territory south of said line of latitude, slavery of the African race is hereby recognized as existing, and shall not be interfered with by Congress, but shall be protected as property by all the departments of the territorial government during its continuance [as a territory]."[75]

It was unthinkable that Greeley could have accepted Crittenden's adjustment in its entirety. Any man who had opposed finality for the Compromise of 1850 could hardly have been expected to consider seriously not only the perpetuity of slavery in the south but also its extension everywhere within the United States south of 36° 30', and possibly into Mexico, Cuba, and Central and South America. The *Tribune* offered not one olive leaf to the south, which, in view of the subsequent reluctant secession of Virginia, North Carolina, Tennessee, and Arkansas, was a decision of grave consequence. This attitude caused Greeley to be tossed unceremoniously from conservative ranks—he was still known as a Bates man in Chicago—into the far left of the radicals.

[75] Potter, *Lincoln,* 103-110.

His inconsistency was apparent rather than actual. Greeley would compromise on a candidate, but not the gains made against slavery. Throughout his career, he had refused to retreat an inch from what he judged to be the intent of the constitution in regard to slavery; and, as was evidenced by his work on the Republican platform of 1860, he felt that he must at least pay lip service to earlier precedents covering the possible admission of a slave state into the Union. He had always viewed the Missouri Compromise as a blunder on the part of freedom; and, unable to obtain the Wilmot proviso, he had sustained the 1850 settlement only because he interpreted it as doing nothing more than sanctioning the entrance of a slave commonwealth should one such knock at the door of congress. He had opposed the Kansas-Nebraska bill until it had become an accomplished fact, and then maneuvered to make of it the best possible free state success. Within the framework of the constitution and in complete respect for the sovereignty of the states, Greeley sought to foster economic changes which would doom slavery and institute a plausible social system in its place. He had never offered any adjustment to the south other than those already in existence. Nor in 1860 would he burn his fingers as he had done a decade earlier by allowing a dubious rewording of his interpretation of the law of the land.

Before his reading audience, he defied all attempts at negotiation. Lincoln had been chosen on a platform opposing the extension of slavery, and the *Tribune* riveted him to his pledge. Were the president-elect to sacrifice that issue he would not only prove unfaithful to trust but would also incite rather than quell the agitation for secession in the south. "Let it be fully and fairly understood that the benefits of the Union are mutual—that we don't want the South to remain in the Union out of charity to us—and this eternal menace of Nullification and Secession will be hushed forever."[76] Greeley was determined that the Calhounites, who had failed

[76] *DTri.*, Nov. 19.

to frighten the free states before the balloting, would not succeed thereafter. "For the North to proffer any concessions or assurances now would be to proffer a premium on rebellion, a bounty for sedition."[77] Constitutional government was itself a compromise. *"Before making any new contract with the Fire-Eaters, we want it distinctly understood that they will abide by the old one."*[78] No one could deny that Lincoln had been selected as the legal head of the common government. The *Tribune* was proud to "state in the most positive terms, that Mr. Lincoln is utterly opposed to any concession or compromise that shall yield one iota of the position occupied by the Republican party . . . in May last . . ."[79] Greeley denounced his fellow party members in Washington who were toying with compromise. He branded as guilty of timidity the congressional committee of 33 seeking conciliation. He advised the dormant congress to pass the homestead measure, the moderate tariff sponsored by industry-loving Justin S. Morrill of Vermont, a judicious Pacific railway bill, to make the necessary appropriations, to abolish the franking privilege, to admit Kansas as a free state, to stop agitating the "Nigger question" by going in for "the Union, the Constitution, and the enforcement of the laws," and to "go home."[80]

In view of his estimate of the political situation in the south, it is difficult to censure Greeley's outspoken stand. But his armor is not without its dents. His major reason for opposing the Crittenden plan so violently was that he knew, once it reached the stage of being referred to the northern commonwealths for ratification, it would be accepted. He had admitted privately that a majority in the north was not heartily antislavery in sentiment. He realized that although Lincoln had gained a majority of the free state votes cast, factors other than the quarantine of slavery had entered into

[77] *DTri.*, Dec. 24.   [78] *DTri.*, Nov. 20. Greeley's italics.
[79] *DTri.*, Dec. 22.
[80] *DTri.*, Jan. 11, 1861. See also *DTri.*, Dec. 3, 6, 12, 14, 15, 20, 22, 24, 28, 31; Jan. 4, 7, 14, 17, 22, Feb. 4, 25, Mar. 12, 1861.

the picture. Greeley had worked too hard for a homestead, tariff, and internal improvement platform, and he had traveled too widely in the north since the panic of 1857 not to perceive that economic factors had swelled the total for Lincoln. Greeley feared another political tussle with the southern hotheads. They seemed to be playing the game for keeps. He saw that the free states would back down when, faced with a canvass beclouded more than ever with southern threats of disunion and war, a ballot on some such scheme as Crittenden's was held. After the Civil War, he had this to say: "And the danger was imminent that, if a popular vote could have been had (as was proposed) on the Crittenden Compromise, it would have prevailed by an overwhelming majority. Very few Republicans would have voted for it; but very many would have refrained from voting at all; while their adversaries would have brought their every man to the polls in its support, and carried it by hundreds of thousands."[81]

Here Greeley is justly open to the charge of inconsistency. How could he insist that the slave states submit their secession resolutions to popular referendums, and not do likewise with an adjustment plan in the north? There are extenuating circumstances. Greeley convinced himself that whereas the free commonwealths had voted upon the slavery question in November, the slave states had not cast their ballots for or against disunion. Eight years previously in connection with the Maine law, he had explained to a friend that a referendum is an essential part of a true democracy, but is necessary only when a body of men such as a convention or a legislature wishes to take an action not contemplated by the people at the time those representatives were selected.[82] Yet, in connection with the slavery issue and the voters of the free states, even remembering that in Greeley's opinion the

[81] Greeley, *Recollections*, 397. Greeley's parentheses. For a full analysis of the issues in the 1860 election, see Luthin, *The First Lincoln Campaign*, esp. 220-221.
[82] Greeley to H. B. Anthony, Nov. 27, 1852, Greeley Transcripts, LC.

problems of human bondage and homesteads, the tariff, and internal improvements were irrevocably intertwined, it is hard to see how he could have satisfied his conscience that in sustaining Lincoln in November a majority of the northern people had been unalterably opposed to compromise.

One explanation of this inconsistency, and the gravest condemnation which can be leveled at Greeley during these trying days, is the fact that the intransigency he displayed in 1860-1861 coincided with and sustained his political ambitions. In dealing with his career,.the student can never separate clearly the editor's personal pretensions from his public utterances. At which time the one motivated the other is a question that even he would have been hard put to answer. The *Tribune's* onslaught against compromise, at least in part, was a continuation of the feud between Greeley on the one hand and Seward and Weed on the other. Following Lincoln's success in November, Weed began publishing conciliatory editorials in his Albany *Evening Journal*, and the *Tribune* staff was convinced that Seward had inspired if not written these articles.[83] This conclusion was given credence by Seward's stand in the congress which was to expire with Lincoln's inaugural. Overnight the New York senator ceased to be known as a firebrand radical and was recognized a compromising conservative. Both he and Weed appeared anxious to sustain the essential outlines of Crittenden's proposal. It now seems evident that Seward was playing for time in which to bring border state unionism to the surface. The *Tribune*, however, gave him no credit for his diplomatic juggling of the secession problem during the interregnum, when the critically situated commonwealths of Missouri, Kentucky, and Maryland—not to mention the central slave states which later seceded—were tottering on the brink of disunion. Instead, Greeley's paper damned Seward as a time-serving employee of the Albany boss, whose unsavory con-

[83] Seward to Weed, Dec. 3, Weed MSS., RRL.

nections with New York City capitalists were said to have shaped Seward's cowardly course in Washington.[84]

Immediately upon his failure at Chicago, Seward's thoughts turned to the supremacy of Weed's machine in New York state.[85] By what means might the Weed forces crush Greeley's temporary ascendancy in state and national political circles? Late in May, Raymond wrote an insulting open letter in which he gave his rival editor full credit for Seward's rebuff and condemned Greeley as a sneaking little office-seeker.[86]

This pronouncement hoisted the curtain on four weeks of furious journalistic combat. Greeley tore into Raymond with sharpened claws and gnashing teeth. He knew why the "little villain" had bedecked himself in sackcloth. Raymond wanted to go to the senate, and for that reason had hastened to announce that Seward was heart-broken and would retire from public life in March, 1861. Greeley scoffed: "It is like the inscription on the Parisian tombstone—'Here lies Pierre Drouot, the tenderest and best of husbands. His disconsolate widow still keeps the shop, No. 17, rue Lepelletier.' "[87]

As good a newspaperman—and poor a controversialist— as Raymond should never have slugged it out with Greeley in the editorial ring. But the *Times* persevered, assisted by Webb's *Courier and Enquirer*. Soon, both Raymond and Webb were so dazed that they were hitting one another. The *Tribune* editor retired to a corner and beamed as he pointed to their contradictions and to Webb's public admission that the Sewardites in Chicago had attempted to undermine Greeley's influence by insinuations against his character.[88]

[84] *DTri.*, Dec. 6, 15, 19, 20, 31; Jan. 4, 17, 22, 24, 25, 1861. Philip S. Foner, *Business and Slavery; the New York Merchants and the Irrepressible Conflict* (Chapel Hill, 1941). Potter, *Lincoln*, 28-314.
[85] Seward to Weed, May 18, 24, 27, Weed MSS., RRL.
[86] Reprinted from the *Times* in Barnes, *Weed*, II, 273-276. Partly reprinted in *DTri.*, May 25.
[87] *DTri.*, May 28.
[88] All *Tribune* issues, late May and June.

In denouncing Greeley, Seward and his allies for the first time acquainted the public with the letter he had received from the *Tribune* office in 1854. Raymond based his whole argument of Greeley's ingratitude toward faithful and trusting friends on this dubious bit of evidence, without quoting it verbatim in the *Times*. Greeley saw his opportunity. For three long weeks he clamored that the letter be published in vindication of his honor. Seward had asked his wife to forward to Weed the original of this famous epistle as early as June 1, two weeks before it was made public.[89] Why its release was delayed is hardly a mystery. Weed's sanctimonious utterances feigning ignorance of Greeley's political ambitions and the insidious defamations of Greeley's honor being spread by Raymond and Webb would have carried more weight had the letter never seen the light of day. But Greeley roared and raged—daily, semi-weekly, and weekly. Weed had no choice. The letter was released amid anticlimatical overtones in mid-June. Greeley published it in every issue of the *Tribune* and it was copied into every paper of prominence in the north. Greeley was then able to state with telling effect that his withdrawal from the partnership had been unequivocal and that in Chicago he had acted as a free man in the best interests of his party.[90]

By July the fracas between Greeley and the Albany machine had subsided—on the surface. When Lincoln's victory was seen to be assured, Greeley leveled the *Tribune's* main battery against corruption in New York state.[91] These broadsides may have had their legitimate target, but another aim seems to have been to destroy Weed's control over the legislature and open the way for Greeley's triumphant entry into the senate at Washington as successor to none other than

[89] Seward to Weed, June 1, 7, Weed MSS., RRL.
[90] Barnes, *Weed*, II, 271-286. Seitz, *Greeley*, 183-184. Bancroft, *Seward*, I, 540-541. John W. Forney, *Anecdotes of Public Men*, II (New York, 1881), 95-101.
[91] *DTri.*, Aug. 7, 20, 21, 24, 30, Sept. 11, Oct. 1, 8, 23, 26, 29.

William Henry Seward. This was more than Weed could stomach.

The battle broke into the national arena when the new legislature met in Albany early in 1861. The Republicans were in full control, but inroads had been made into Weed's ranks, and his men sized up their radical adversaries with a jealous eye. Greeley was optimistic. He was being mentioned for the postmaster-generalship in Lincoln's cabinet,[92] but he refused to press his claim because he feared his name would further antagonize the south and because he preferred the senatorship. This decision, he thought, would give him bargaining power with the incoming administration. In mid-November, he wrote Brockway, his special emissary at the New York state capital: "I know nothing about Senator— that is, the prospect. I *guess* that Seward means to be elected, and then expects to step out and have everything fixed for [William] Evarts. But (between us) S[eward] will not be invited to take a place in Mr. Lincoln's cabinet, whatever else may betide. He will probably be offered a first-class Mission; but even that is not certain if he insists on being elected to the Senate. However, I only guess this; about the cabinet, I think I *know*."[93]

Before the legislature in Albany were two major questions: how should it instruct Seward to vote on the compromise proposals before congress; and, since it was evident that Seward would either retire from public life or enter the cabinet, whom should it name in replacement? Weed's power was strong enough early in January to secure a conciliatory resolution,[94] but the *Tribune* campaign against peculation and a mounting sentiment for a firm antislavery stand told heavily

[92] S. P. Chase, "Diary and Correspondence of . . . , " *Annual Report* of the American Historical Association, *1902* (Washington, 1903), II, 485-487.
[93] Greeley to Brockway, Nov. 17, Greeley MSS., LC. Greeley's italics and parentheses.
[94] *Laws of the State of New York*, 84th sess. (Albany, 1861), 819-820. Weed to Seward, Jan. 9, 1861; S. C. Davidson (wire) to Seward, Jan. 11, 1861, Seward MSS., Auburn. See also *Journal of the Assembly of the State of New York*, 84th sess. (Albany, 1861), 76-77. *Journal of the Senate of the State of New York*, 84th sess. (Albany, 1861), 57-58.

against the Albany machine as the senatorial election approached. The chief contenders were Greeley and an eloquent New York City lawyer, William Evarts, backed by Weed. Ira Harris of Albany, with support from the western part of the state, was the third man in the race. The Republican caucus on February 2 was deadlocked for eight ballots with Greeley and Evarts polling about the same number of votes. Then Weed acted. On the ninth, he switched his support to Harris, who thereby gained the Washington post.[95] The *Tribune* hastened to represent this as a reversal for Weed, but the Albany boss was confident of Harris' reliability. Weed rejoiced as he sat down to write a friend: "We have, after a desperate struggle, with all the Radicals against us, and with other disadvantages, paid the *first installment* on a large Debt to Mr. Greeley. Fearing that we would not elect Evarts, Harris (who has *always* been with us) was held in Reserve."[96]

Greeley said he regretted the use of his name in connection with the senatorship, for it compelled him to journey to Washington during the inaugural and seek patronage for his supporters. Yet it is hard to believe that he would have been absent from the nation's capital during these critical days. He wanted to continue the bitter warfare he had been conducting for four months against Seward and other Republicans who favored a compromise policy toward the south. He reported to Brockway from Washington on the last day of February that Lincoln was a good man, but no Jackson. He feared the anti-Seward men would fail to control the government because the president was "in the web of very cunning spiders and cannot work out if he would," a situation which gave the "compromisers full swing." But Greeley was encouraged on March 12. He thought the "corruptionists" sure

95 Alexander, *New York*, ii, 361-366.
96 Weed to A. C. Wilder, Feb. 3, 1861, Charles E. Brown Collection, RRL. Weed's italics and parentheses. Greeley, on the other hand, wrote Capt. Sam Strong, Feb. 20, 1861, Greeley Transcripts, LC: "I am to meet Judge Harris next Sunday by appointment, and I shall then know how I stand with him."

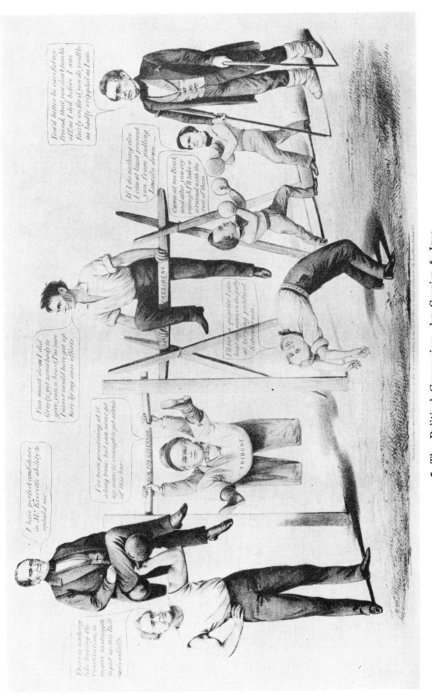

7. The Political Gymnasium, by Currier & Ives

Everett, Bell, Greeley, Webb, Lincoln, Douglas, Breckinridge, Seward

8. "The Impending Crisis"—or Caught in the Act, by Currier & Ives. Webb, Greeley, Raymond, Seward (Arrest of Greeley as Seward, grasping the famous 1854 letter, sinks into political oblivion.)

to get three-quarters of the political plums going to New York because Seward had managed to worm his way into the inner councils as secretary of state, but the anti-Seward group—in Salmon P. Chase, Montgomery Blair, Edward Bates, and Gideon Welles—had gained four out of seven cabinet posts. Greeley was lavish in praise of Chase. That able and uncompromising Ohioan had become secretary of the treasury only "by the determined frank and clear-headed sagacity of Old Abe himself, powerfully backed by Hamlin, who is a jewel. All the Kitchen Cabinet, including the female President were dead against him."[97]

Greeley's political ambition thus takes its place as one of the factors shaping *Tribune* policy during the crisis of 1860-1861. Events, however, pushed their way relentlessly forward. South Carolina left the Union late in December, 1860, and during the ensuing six weeks, was followed in this course by Georgia, Florida, Alabama, Mississippi, Louisiana, and Texas. Having solemnly pronounced their independence, these seven states sent delegates to Montgomery, Alabama in February, 1861. Within a short time, they had adopted a plan of union and were proceeding with the establishment of a new general government.

These developments had no effect whatsoever on Greeley's refusal to compromise. He continued to insist that federal authority in the south be maintained until withdrawal had been negotiated in accordance with his conditions, and refused to face realistically the ever increasing probability of war. His nationalism alone was insufficient to make him choose armed conflict. His religious convictions and his belief in the revolutionary right of a people within a large geographical section to select their own government were against such an outcome—yet neither was an obstacle to a war of self-defense. He should have realized sooner than he did that armed con-

[97] Greeley to Brockway, Mar. 12, Feb. 28, 1861, Greeley MSS., LC. Randall, *Lincoln the President*, I, 313, despite Greeley's earlier reference to Hamlin in his Mar. 12 ltr., transcribes the last sentence: "All the Kitchen Cabinet, including the Senate President, were dead against him."

flict was inevitable because of the existing circumstances, yet, in keeping with his determined character, he had made up his mind that the secessionist leaders were involved in a bold gamble, and almost to the bitter end, expected them to back down.

Dana assured Greeley that the southerners were in no position to fight, and that even if war came the battle would be neither long nor bloody. The managing editor stood in the vanguard of those members of the staff who believed that slavery had weakened the south to the point of exhaustion. For several years past, he had been handling the *Tribune's* military department, and had acquired a considerable faith in his knowledge of the art of war.[98]

His influence may be found in the *Tribune* throughout the secession crisis, but it manifested itself clearly only toward the end of November. He was make-up editor of the *Weekly*, and roughly seventy-five per cent of the *Tribune's* readers were subjected to a smaller dose of peaceable secession than normally would have been the case. Sunday was his day off,[99] and Greeley's gloomiest moods were reflected in the Monday morning dailies. Early in December, the *Tribune* began accusing Buchanan of treason for his failure to dispatch additional troops and supplies into the south.[100] Greeley was becoming belligerent. He stressed peace the less, and threatened the so-called southern oligarchy with war if they persisted in their haste to sever the Union. "A Government is not to be dissolved in a pet nor a pout," he warned. "All great political changes, if peaceful, are to be effected with gravity, deliberation, decorum. But let not the South rush

[98] *DTri.*, June 27, 1859. The best source for Dana's estimate of southern strength and his strategic plan for that section's defeat is *DTri.*, Jan. 31, Mar. 10, 26, 1856. See also Greeley to Dana, Feb. 1, 6, 1856, Greeley, *Letters*, 108-110, 113-115.

[99] Greeley to B. Taylor, Aug. 16, NYHSL. To Pike, July 1, 1857, Pike, *First Blows*, 375.

[100] *DTri.*, Dec. 6 through Feb., 1861. For the changing evaluations of Buchanan's policy, see Frank W. Klingberg, "James Buchanan and the Crisis of the Union," *Journal of Southern History*, IX (Nov., 1943), 455-474.

into civil war under the impression that the sword alone can cut the cord that binds her to the North; for it is not so. Let her make a straightforward appeal to the manly self-respect of the North, saying in substance, 'I am tired of you—let me go!'—and we feel very certain that her request will be complied with. To plunge the country into civil war is much more likely to consolidate the Union than to destroy it."[101] Greeley was still thinking in terms of a non-slaveholders' rebellion. He believed that the seceding states were "all liable to insurrections at any moment . . ."[102]

Greeley left for his annual winter lecture tour in mid-January. This journey strengthened his stand against the south. It was not accidental that the trip took him through Springfield, Illinois, where he called on Lincoln. The New York journalist wanted to buttress the president-elect's attitude against compromise and to promote an anti-Seward cabinet. It is said that Greeley's opinion on appointments was "freely solicited and given" during a conversation lasting for several hours. More important, Greeley found *Tribune* subscriber Lincoln[103] with views on the secession crisis similar in some respects to his own: any pre-inaugural remarks made by the president-elect would be quickly twisted by the secessionist leaders to their own advantage, and the unionist sentiment in the south would profit most from silence on Lincoln's part.[104] Greeley could talk—and did. That evening, his high pitched voice reached "a very large audience." His listeners were invigorated by "his emphatic anti-compromise declarations," and were "in high glee over the gratifying assurance he is claimed to have received of the President elect to adhere firmly to the doctrines embodied in the Chicago platform." The great anxiety was reported to be that "a sufficient number of weak-backed Republican

101 *DTri.*, Dec. 28.   102 *DTri.*, Dec. 29.
103 Herndon, *Lincoln*, II, 363.
104 *DTri.*, Nov. 17, 21, Dec. 22. Potter, *Lincoln*.

Congressmen" would be mustered to adjust the controversy before the new administration entered office.[105]

Greeley was absent from the *Tribune* office for five weeks. If he mailed any peaceable secession editorials back to New York City, they never saw the printed page. His managing editor was busy redefining and clarifying the *Tribune's* policy.

Dana was more than an authority on warfare, he was a diplomat. He did his work unobtrusively, for he wished to spare Greeley's feelings—and keep his job. Nor was it a difficult task, for Greeley had never said that the federal government should not defend itself.

Dana reasoned that secession without war was impossible. In no case would the stars and stripes be dishonored. If the hotheads were successful, a conflict would ensue. All citizens, he argued, had spent blood and money in the acquisition of new territory, and the north would never permit the slave states to walk off with joint belongings. Federal court and postal buildings in the cotton zone belonged to the public as a whole, as did the southern forts. Revenues due the common government must be collected in Charleston and other such ports. Should any group of individuals in that region undertake to nullify the laws of the United States or to attack its property, it would become the duty of the president to maintain his authority, with force, as commander-in-chief of the army and navy, if necessary.[106]

With Greeley away, Dana proceeded to refute the principle of peaceable secession. Disunion was geographically impossible, he announced. The south depended upon federal law to prevent the escape of her slaves into Canada, and the Mississippi was an artery of commerce vital to the mid-west. Those "ingenious speculators" who along with Greeley thought blood would flow only from a "willful determination to

[105] Associated Press dispatches from Springfield, Feb. (5), 6, *DTri.*, Feb. 6, 7, 1861.
[106] *DTri.*, Dec. 3, 11, 12, 15, 21, 22, 25, 28, 29; Jan. 4, 8, 10, 11, 12, 15, 16, 17, 18, 19, 21, 22, 1861.

'coerce sovereign States' unnecessarily" were due for a big surprise.[107] The commonwealths which were seceding would either voluntarily return to the Union, or hostilities would commence when men from the "rebel" states fired on federal forts or marched on Washington. It would be a short struggle. The navy would merely blockade the southern coast, and then the "laws of trade" would strangle the slave states. Cotton and tobacco shipments would be routed through the interior of the free states, and the north would prosper. Already New York City's commerce was said to be expanding. Under these circumstances, there would soon arise in the south a powerful party which would insist on restoring the Union. Should the southern confederacy attack the northerners, they would rise up as one man, draw on their superior resources, and crush the rebellion in a trice. The slave states were bound to the Union "by geographical necessities, and by a wise and beneficent Constitution whose stipulations must be enforced, they cannot escape the destiny imposed upon them as members of a common Government."[108]

When Greeley arrived in New York City late in February, Dana had hoisted to the *Tribune's* mast-head:[109]

NO COMPROMISE!

———◇———

NO CONCESSIONS TO TRAITORS!

———◇———

The Constitution as it is

Assaults on Weed were stronger than ever; and as Seward pleaded with the senate for a considerate approach toward the south, the *Tribune* italicized quotations from earlier speeches in which he had categorically affirmed he would never seek to appease that section. Daily diatribes called Buchanan a scoundrel and a knave and demanded that his administration clean house of all sympathizers with secession and rush rein-

[107] *DTri.*, Jan. 31, 1861.
[108] *DTri.*, Jan. 26, 1861. See also *DTri.*, Jan. 23, 24, 25, 30, Feb. 2, 1861.
[109] *DTri.*, Feb. 18 through Mar. 1, 1861.

forcements to the endangered forts. Greeley's return changed none of this.[110]

On the contrary, his jaw was set as he braved the winter winds and headed for the *Tribune* building. Soon he would descend upon Washington, an uncompromising Yankee searching for political morsels in the midst of a pack of patronage hunters. He would not bow down to the south, but as stubborn as ever, he had not yet reconciled himself to an all out war as the only alternative. His insistence that federal rights in the south be maintained, combined with his continuing faith in a strong southern unionist sentiment and with Dana's optimistic strategical outlook, had slowly changed his attitude regarding a show of force by the north. By February, he felt the national government must display firmness. Otherwise the seven cotton states which had already withdrawn would form a government of their own and overrun federal property in the south with impunity. This exhibition of national weakness would lower the prestige of the Washington government in the eyes of both northern and southern unionists. With this idea of intransigeance in his mind, he wrote an acquaintance in England: "I think we are now likely to avoid the rock of compromise, and to settle our difficulties in or out of the Union in a manly way, and that the present arrogance of our slave holding oligarchy is not much longer either to disgust or amuse the civilized worlds."[111]

By the day of the inaugural, Greeley's uncompromising attitude caused him to be denounced as a leader of the warhawks. James W. Nye, a New York politician, wrote his ally Seward on February 23 in ringing denunciation of Greeley's stand. Nye had just attended a dinner intended to indorse the *Tribune*. He went to spy upon a "set of men not altogether our friends." He found an air of discontent, and was sure the

[110] All *Tribune* issues, late Jan., Feb., and early Mar., 1861.
[111] Greeley to Samuel P. Shaw, Feb. 20, 1861, *Saturday Review of Literature,* xxvi (May 1, 1943), 13.

Tribune would not break the Seward ranks in New York state although Greeley's associates had tried to gain Lincoln's ear as he passed through the city on his way to Washington and "induce him to believe that all of the Republicans were for war[.]" Nye was disgusted. "Imagine Greel[e]y booted & Spurred with Epaulets on his Shoulders and with a whetted blade in his hands marching at the head of a column: Shade of a Scott defend us: The idea of Greely turning warrior, is too ridicul[o]us to be thought of:"[112]

Regardless of such opinions as Nye's, Greeley remained adamant. Lincoln's inaugural contained no direct reference to compromise proposals, and the *Tribune* praised it. The president was said to have correctly and judiciously assured the south that the constitution would be upheld, state sovereignties respected, the Union maintained, the forts strengthened, and the revenue in southern ports collected. Greeley was especially pleased: "The Address can not fail to exercise a happy influence on the country. The tone of almost tenderness with which the South is called upon to return to her allegiance, can not fail to convince even those who differ from Mr. Lincoln that he earnestly and seriously desires to avoid all difficulty and disturbance, while the firmness with which he avows his determination to obey the simple letter of his duty, must command the respect of the whole country, while it carries conviction of his earnestness of purpose, and of his courage to enforce it."[113]

Lincoln's inaugural failed to elicit the pro-Union sentiment from the south Greeley seemed to expect. The New York journalist saw fit again to warn the secessionists against their precipitant haste. His belief in peaceable secession had not been dampened by the president's failure to offer such a course. Overthrow of the legal government, Greeley said, "accompanied by the stealing of forts, mints, and custom-houses,

[112] Nye to Seward, Feb. 23, 1861, Seward MSS., Auburn.
[113] *DTri.*, Mar. 5, 1861. See also dispatches from Washington, *DTri.*, Mar. 5, 1861.

and by piratical acts of war, cannot be tolerated. It must be resisted to the last extremity. Otherwise, law is a mockery, and anarchy and chaos come again. If the Southern States wish to take charge of their own destiny in peace," they must let their people "fairly vote upon the question, and not cheat and force them into Disunion . . ." Four days later, he went so far as to admit that the choice for the north was between compromise and the preparation for war, and he chose the latter. Whether or not secession was a means of intimidation, his section was now faced with a *de facto* Confederate government which demanded seemingly humiliating conditions for remaining in the Union. He finally realized that the north would be driven to a positive stand: "We hope the position assumed will be a proud and manly one; we cannot believe it will be a tame submission. . . . The way, and we fear the only way, of preventing a war, as the alternative of submission, or a treaty, is to be fully prepared for it."[114] He advised against attack, but Lincoln did not thereafter move fast enough in refusing to mediate with the Confederacy and in reinforcing Sumter. It was time for decided, energetic, effective action. The majority of the "loyal subjects of Jeff. Davis"[115] believed that the free states were ready to submit; and delay, Greeley counseled, would only give credence to that absurdity.[116]

Thus, even before the crisis at Sumter, Greeley's peaceable secession argument merged with Dana's belligerency. This outcome followed naturally not only from Greeley's insistence that federal property in the south remain immune to seizure by force, but also from his contention that the southern masses really loved the Union. Only by taking a warlike attitude, and if necessary actually fighting, could the non-slaveowners be brought to rebellion and the fire-eaters routed.

April brought hectic days, but Greeley had the faith of his convictions. To his mind, everything possible had been

[114] *DTri.*, Mar. 16, 12, 1861.   [115] *DTri.*, Mar. 27, 1861.
[116] *DTri.*, Mar. 23, Apr. 3, 4, 1861.

done to prevent war. Now, if the secessionist cabal precipitated an armed conflict, he would battle in self-defense. The *Tribune* stood ready and waiting to carry its readers into a holy struggle against the evils of human bondage which sought to destroy their democracy. "Within a few days at farthest," read an editorial early in April, "the cannon of the insurgents will be battering down the defenses and slaughtering the defenders of the American Union." Without provocation, "Slavery makes open war upon that Union which has so long been its protection and security."[117] Any government which tamely accepted the insults of the south "confesses itself a humbug and a bastard."[118] On April 13, Greeley announced that Sumter had been fired upon: ". . . the great Cotton Rebellion inaugurates in blood its more direct and manly efforts to subvert the Federal Constitution and Government, and build up a Slaveholding Oligarchy on their ruins. Having chosen its ground and its time, it may of course count with reason on a temporary advantage. But the end is not yet. Let none doubt the ultimate triumph of Right."[119]

As the smoke cleared across Charleston harbor, Dana's importance on the *Tribune* staff rose. Greeley could rightfully claim little knowledge of strategy and tactics, and in this field deferred to his managing editor.

In mid-May, while chopping trees on his tiny farm at Chappaqua, Greeley's axe slipped and cut his knee. The injury was painful, and his blood was bad. He remained in his cottage for over a week, and a full month later, wrote his friend Margaret Allen that the wound was just beginning to heal. He seemed to feel he could afford to be absent from the *Tribune* office and take a much needed rest, but he did have an opinion on the conduct of the war. He told Mrs. Allen that he did not want it hurried, but "quietly pressed to a righteous conclusion."[120]

117 *DTri.*, Apr. 5, 1861.   118 *DTri.*, Apr. 9, 1861.
119 *DTri.*, Apr. 13, 1861.   See also *DTri.*, Apr. 15, 17, 25, 1861.
120 Greeley to Mrs. Margaret Allen, June 17, 1861, Greeley MSS., LC.

Greeley must have thought Dana was living up to this desire, else on reading the *Tribune* in his seclusion at Chappaqua, he would have taken steps to moderate its editorial tone. Dana believed that four months was long enough and carried the *Tribune* along with him. On June 26, he blazed forth with this advice to the untrained federal troops:[121]

THE NATION'S WAR-CRY.

Forward to Richmond! Forward to Richmond!
The Rebel Congress must not be allowed to meet there on the 20th of July!

By that date the
place must be held by the National Army!

The outcome of such pressure as this was the first battle of Bull Run. The Union force turned and fled. Such an insight into the staggering cost of the Civil War was hard for Greeley to bear. He suffered nervous prostration. Level-headed Beaman Brockway believed him faced with softening of the brain. With a quivering hand, he apologized to his audience for his paper's military editorials—and in a short while Dana was looking for other employment.[122]

This disastrous defeat was the beginning of Greeley's doubts as to the ability of the north to win the war. For a period of several months, he would urge energetic prosecution of hostilities; then for a time, and with an attitude recalling the days when he had sponsored peaceable secession, he would

---

[121] *DTri.*, June 26 through July 4, 1861. Fahrney, *Greeley*, 83-96.
[122] Dana, *Recollections of the Civil War* (New York, 1898), 1-2. Brockway, *Fifty Years*, 154.
In his apology, Greeley said: " . . . the watchword 'Forward to Richmond' is not mine. . . . Henceforth, I bar all criticism in these columns on Army movements, past or future . . . . the subject is closed and sealed." *DTri.*, July 25, 1861. Dana, in a long personal letter written shortly after his dismissal from the *Tribune*, sets forth some of the circumstances of his departure, but fails to mention specifically his military editorials, attributing the matter entirely to personal jealousies on the part of Greeley and other members of the staff. To Pike, Apr. 9, 1862, Pike MSS., Calais (Me.) Public Library.

counsel meditation.[123] Greely, "booted & Spurred," was not a very imposing figure.

As the struggle ended with General Grant's march on Richmond—just before Lincoln fell to the bullet of an assassin—Greeley poured forth the grief in his soul: "I am becoming still more alienated from the religion which passes among us for Orthodox and Christian. Its teachers and leading professors are loudest in the cry for bloodshed and vengeance against the beaten, prostrate Rebels. They want to erect the gallows all over the South and hang the baffled traitors whom we have not killed in battle. I am sure Jesus of Nazareth is not truly represented in this spirit. As for me, I want as many Rebels as possible to live and see the South rejuvenated and transformed by the influence of Free Labor. I should deem it a calamity to have Jeff Davis die these ten years.

"I have not usually believed that we should win, because I could not believe that we *deserved* to win. We are a Pro Slavery people to-day. In the great city of Philadelphia, which gave Lincoln nearly 10,000 majority in '60, and again in '64, a black Union soldier is not allowed to ride in their street-cars; I tried to pilot through a most respectable colored clergyman, but was obliged to give it up. By all ordinary rules, we ought to have been beaten in this fight and the more consistent and straight-forward worshipers of Satan triumph."[124]

In the seventeen years remaining in his life, Greeley sought to eradicate the scars of the Civil War. His attitude was consistent with a statement, written in 1857, in connection with capital punishment: ". . . recognizing the truth that it is better some should die than all be benighted and enslaved, we could level a deadly weapon at the breasts of an embattled host, if we felt sure that the cause of despotism, of tyranny, or moral and intellectual darkness, must stand or

123 Fahrney, *Greeley*. Linn, *Greeley*, 190-192.
124 Greeley to Mrs. R. M. Whipple, Apr. 13, 1865. Greeley Transcripts, LC.

fall with that host. But, let the battle be fought and won, the enemy crushed or captive, if an order were to reach us from headquarters to shoot or hang the prisoners, we should falter and shrink from its execution . . ."[125] Following this doctrine with a creditable consistency, Greeley went bail for the scarred and broken Jefferson Davis in 1867; and in 1872 ran for presidency on the Democratic and Liberal Republican platform of reconciliation. But at this late date, the northern politicians were the hotheads, and waved the bloody shirt so effectively that they slaughtered his candidacy.[126]

Such was the bitter harvest which Greeley reaped from his antislavery crusade. The party for which he was so largely responsible had become the intrenched party of the north, determined on vengeance. The wages of battle were hatred, and Greeley saw his hopes of a harmonious society within the nation crumble about his feet. Much of his career had been spent in vain.

[125] *DTri.*, July 13, 1857.
[126] Earle D. Ross, *The Liberal Republican Movement* (New York, 1919).

APPENDICES, BIBLIOGRAPHY
AND INDEX

APPENDIX A

STATE	1854	1855	1856	1858	1860
Maine	8.9%	7.6%	11.8%	6.8%	10.4%
New Hampshire	7.3	7.2	10.4	9.1	11.2
Vermont	13.2	11.8	18.7	19.0	21.8
Massachusetts	8.0	8.1	9.0	6.9	6.5
Rhode Island	12.0	14.3	16.7	19.0	11.3
Connecticut	11.6	10.7	10.9	12.3	12.8
New York	12.5	14.0	14.5	12.0	14.4
New Jersey	4.4	4.5	5.4	5.7	5.4
Pennsylvania	2.7	3.5	3.8	4.1	6.0
Ohio	5.9	6.1	7.7	5.7	5.9
Indiana	3.7	4.1	5.1	4.8	5.0
Illinois	7.6	8.1	6.7	5.1	4.2
Michigan	11.2	13.0	11.7	7.9	7.0
Wisconsin	14.5	12.9	11.6	7.0	7.9
Minnesota	* —	12.4	12.7	9.0	11.3
Iowa	9.2	10.0	7.8	6.9	9.1
California	10.0	8.6	8.6	8.0	6.2
Oregon	* —	3.4	7.6	6.7	6.0
Nebraska	0.4	5.8	1.9	* —	7.9
Kansas	1.7	* —	4.6	10.0	13.1

These figures, taken from *Tribunes* and from *Whig* and *Tribune Almanacs*, were obtained by dividing voting totals into *Tribune* circulation by states. They are intended to be indicative only. Percentages for the slave states are too low to warrant inclusion.

* Data not available.

APPENDIX B

TRIBUNE CIRCULATION, 1853-1861

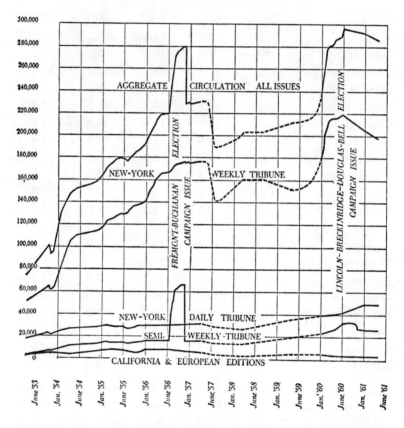

Solid line data from *Tribune* and private correspondence. Broken
line data, during the depression of 1857, from
private correspondence alone.

338

COMMENT ON FOOTNOTES

1. All *Tribune* citations, unless otherwise indicated in the text or footnotes, are taken from the editorial page.

2. Omissions within quotations are the author's.

3. In those chapters in which the events are largely limited to the same year, after a point indicated by a footnote this year is assumed, rather than repeated.

4. To decrease footnotes, a number of citations are combined, wherever logical, in one footnote. In these cases, the last item in the text is the first cited in the footnote.

5. Abbreviations:

DTri.	*Daily Tribune*
HCL	Harvard College Library, Cambridge, Mass.
LC	Library of Congress, Washington, D.C.
MHSL	Massachusetts Historical Society Library, Boston
NYHSL	New York Historical Society Library, New York City
NYPL	New York Public Library, New York City
RRL	Rush Rhees Library, Rochester, N.Y.
SWTri.	*Semi-Weekly Tribune*
WTri.	*Weekly Tribune*

SELECTIVE BIBLIOGRAPHY

PART I

MANUSCRIPTS (USED IN WHOLE OR IN PART)

John Bigelow Papers, New York Public Library.
Blair-Lee Papers, Princeton University Library.
Blair Family Miscellaneous Papers, Library of Congress.
Francis Preston Blair, Jr., Papers, Library of Congress.
Charles E. Brown Collection, Rush Rhees Library, University of Rochester
Simon Cameron Papers, Library of Congress.
Salmon P. Chase Papers, Library of Congress.
Schuyler Colfax Correspondence, Library of Congress.
Thomas Corwin Papers, Library of Congress.
Charles A. Dana Miscellaneous Letters, Library of Congress.
Edward Everett Manuscripts, Massachusetts Historical Society Library, Boston.
Hamilton Fish Papers, Library of Congress.
Margaret Fuller Papers, Harvard College Library.
Gist-Blair Collection, Library of Congress.
Horace Greeley Manuscripts, Library of Congress.
Horace Greeley Miscellaneous Manuscripts, Library of Congress.
Horace Greeley Manuscripts (the Ford Letters), New York Public Library.
Horace Greeley Transcripts, Library of Congress.
Greeley-Colfax Correspondence, New York Public Library.
Adam de Gurowski Papers, Library of Congress.
Mrs. H. C. Ingersoll Manuscripts, Library of Congress.
John McLean Papers, Library of Congress.
Justin S. Morrill Papers, Library of Congress.
Theodore Parker Papers, Massachusetts Historical Society Library.
James S. Pike Manuscripts, Calais (Me.) Public Library.
James S. Pike Papers, Library of Congress.
Carl Schurz Papers, Library of Congress.
William H. Seward Collection, Rush Rhees Library, University of Rochester.
William H. Seward Collection, Seward home in Auburn, N.Y.
William H. Seward Letters to S. B. Ruggles, Library of Congress.
John Sherman Papers, Library of Congress.
Thaddeus Stevens Papers, Library of Congress.
Charles Sumner Papers, Harvard College Library.
Lyman Trumbull Papers, Library of Congress.
Benjamin F. Wade Papers, Library of Congress.
Israel Washburn, Jr., Papers, Library of Congress.
Elihu B. Washburne Papers, Library of Congress.

BIBLIOGRAPHY

Thurlow Weed Manuscripts, New York Historical Society Library, New York City.
Thurlow Weed Papers, Library of Congress.
Thurlow Weed Papers, Rush Rhees Library, University of Rochester.
Henry Wilson Letters, Library of Congress.
John R. Young Manuscripts, Library of Congress.
Miscellaneous letters from Charles A. Dana, Harvard College Library; and in the Gerrit Smith Papers, Library of Syracuse University.
Miscellaneous letters from Horace Greeley, Boston Public Library; the Harvard College Library; the Historical Society of Pennsylvania Library in Philadelphia; in the Lincoln Collection, Library of the University of Chicago; Massachusetts Historical Society Library; the New York Historical Society Library; the New York State Library in Albany; in the Gerrit Smith Papers, Library of Syracuse University; Yale University Library; and a lecture manuscript of Horace Greeley's, Bucks County Historical Society Library in Doylestown, Pa.
Miscellaneous letters from Henry J. Raymond, New York Historical Society Library.
Miscellaneous letters and papers from George Ripley, Massachusetts Historical Society Library.
Miscellaneous letters from Thurlow Weed, Harvard College Library.

PART 2

OFFICIAL AND SEMI-OFFICIAL PUBLICATIONS

The Congressional Globe.
Reports of the Committees of the house and senate.
United States Statutes at Large.
United States Supreme Court Reports.
A Compilation of the Messages and Papers of the Presidents, 1789-1897, ed. James D. Richardson, 10 vols., Washington, 1896-1899.
New York (State) Court of Appeals, *Reports of Cases Decided* . . .
Journal of the Assembly of the State of New York.
Journal of the Senate of the State of New York.
The Banking Laws of the State of New York . . . 1838 to . . . 1854, Albany, 1854.
Laws of the State of New York.
State of New York Messages from the Governors, ed. Charles Z. Lincoln, 11 vols., Albany, 1909.

BIBLIOGRAPHY

PART 3

CONTEMPORARY NEWSPAPERS AND PERIODICALS

(Used for the dates given, or for period covered by this monograph)

The American Laborer. . . , 1842-1843.
Augusta (Ga.) *Daily Chronicle and Sentinel*, 1860-1861.
Augusta (Ga.) *Daily Constitutionalist*, 1860-1861.
Baltimore *Daily Exchange*, 1860-1861.
Baltimore *Sun*, 1860-1861.
Charleston *Daily Courier*, 1860-1861.
Frank Leslie's Illustrated Newspaper, 1857-1860.
Harper's New Monthly Magazine, 1859.
Harper's Weekly, 1859-1861.
Memphis *Daily Avalanche*, 1860-1861.
Mobile *Daily Advertiser*, 1860-1861.
New Orleans *Commercial Bulletin*, 1860-1861.
New Orleans *Daily Delta*, 1860-1861.
New York *Independent*, 1860-1861.
New York *Tribune* (*Weekly, Semi-Weekly*, and *Daily*).
Norfolk *Southern Argus*, 1860-1861.
Putnam's Magazine.
Richmond *Enquirer* (daily), 1860-1861.
Savannah *Daily Republican*, 1860-1861.
Tribune Almanac and Political Register . . . , 1856-1862.
Vicksburg *Weekly Sun*, 1860-1861.
Whig Almanac and Political Register . . . , 1852-1855.
Wilmington (N.C.) *Daily Journal*, 1860-1861.

Annals of Cleveland, 1818-1935, XXXVII-XLIII, Cleveland, 1937.
Northern Editorials on Secession, ed. Howard C. Perkins, 2 vols., New York, 1942.
Southern Editorials on Secession, ed. Dwight L. Dumond, New York, 1931.

PART 4

CONTEMPORARY WORKS AND PAMPHLETS

There is no complete bibliography of Horace Greeley's published writings. The original of Nathan Greeley's compilation is in the Greeley Miscellaneous Manuscripts at the Library of Congress. An abridgment of it appears in *Proceedings at the Unveiling of a Memorial to Horace Greeley*, Albany, 1915.

William Atkinson, *see* listing under Horace Greeley.

343

BIBLIOGRAPHY

Albert Brisbane, *Association; or, A Concise Exposition of the Practical Part of Fourier's Social Science*, New York, 1843.

———, *Social Destiny of Man; or, Association and Reorganization of Industry*, Philadelphia, 1840.

"The Case of Dred Scott" (pamphlet), New York, 1860.

Lydia Maria Child, "The Right Way the Safe Way, Proved by Emancipation in the British West Indies and Elsewhere" (pamphlet), New York, 1860.

Cassius M. Clay, *see* listing under Horace Greeley.

Lewis Clephane, "The Birth of the Republican Party" (pamphlet), Washington, 1889.

John F. Cleveland, *see* listing under Horace Greeley.

Charles T. Congdon, *Tribune Essays . . . 1857-1863*, New York, 1869.

Charles A. Dana, *see* listing under George Ripley.

———, "Proudhon and his Bank of the People," reprinted in *Proudhon's Solution of the Social Problem*, ed. Henry Cohen, New York, 1927.

Stephen A. Douglas, "The Dividing Line Between Federal and Local Authority. Popular Sovereignty in the Territories," *Harper's New Monthly Magazine*, xix (Sept., 1859), 519-537.

Friedrich Engels, *see* listing under Karl Marx.

D. M. Evans, *The History of the Commercial Crisis, 1857-1858...*, London, 1859.

"Fun From Under the Old White Hat" (pamphlet), New York, 1872.

Joshua R. Giddings, *History of the Rebellion: Its Authors and Causes*, New York, 1864.

Thomas H. Gladstone, *The Englishman in Kansas; or, Squatter Life and Border Warfare*, New York, 1857.

Horace Greeley, "An Address on Success in Business . . ." (pamphlet), New York, 1867.

———, *The American Conflict. . .*, 2 vols., Hartford, Conn., 1864, 1866.

———, ed., "Art and Industry as Represented in the Exhibition at the Crystal Palace, New York—1853-4 . . ." (pamphlet), New York, 1853.

——— and Henry J. Raymond, "Association Discussed; or, The Socialism of the Tribune Examined" (pamphlet), New York, 1847.

———, "The Dishonor of Labor," *Autographs for Freedom*, ed. Julia Griffiths, 2nd series, Auburn, N.Y., 1854, 194-197.

——— and Robert Dale Owen, "Divorce: Being a Correspondence Between . . ." (pamphlet), New York, 1860.

———, *Essays . . . [on] Political Economy . . . as a System of National Coöperation for the Elevation of Labor*, Philadelphia, 1869.

BIBLIOGRAPHY

Horace Greeley, *Glances at Europe: In a Series of Letters...*, New York, 1851.

——— *et al.*, *The Great Industries of the United States...*, Hartford, Conn., 1872.

———, *Hints Toward Reforms...*, New York, 1854.

———, *A History of the Struggle for Slavery Extension or Restriction...*, New York, 1856.

———, "Horace Greeley jugé par lui-même" (pamphlet), Washington, 1872.

———, "Mr. Greeley's Letters from Texas and the Lower Mississippi: to Which Are Added his Address to the Farmers of Texas, and his Speech on his Return to New York, June 12, 1871" (pamphlet), New York, 1871.

———, *The Life and Public Services of Henry Clay, Down to 1848*, by Epes Sargent. Edited and completed at Mr. Clay's death by Horace Greeley, Philadelphia, 1852.

———, *An Overland Journey from New York to San Francisco...*, New York, 1860.

——— *et al.*, "People's College: An Address ..." (pamphlet), New York, 1859.

——— and John F. Cleveland, comps., *A Political Text-book for 1860: Comprising a Brief View of Presidential Nominations and Elections...*, New York, 1860.

———, "Principles of Political Economy," by William Atkinson, with an introduction by Horace Greeley (pamphlet), New York, 1843.

"The Greeley Record" (pamphlet), Washington, 1872.

——— *et al.*, *The Religious Aspects of the Age...*, New York, 1858.

———, *What I Know of Farming...*, New York, 1871.

———, "What the Sister Arts Teach as to Farming" (pamphlet), New York(?), 1853(?).

———, ed., *The Writings of Cassius Marcellus Clay...*, with a preface and memoir by Horace Greeley, New York, 1848.

Adam de Gurowski, *America and Europe*, New York, 1857.

———, *Russia as It Is*, New York, 1854.

———, *Slavery in History*, New York, 1860.

A. Oakey Hall, "Horace Greeley Decently Dissected ..." (pamphlet), New York, 1862.

Murat Halstead, *Caucuses of 1860: A History of the National Conventions...*, Columbus, 1860.

James P. Hambleton, *A Biographical Sketch of Henry A. Wise...*, Richmond, 1856.

Hinton R. Helper, *The Impending Crisis of the South: How to Meet It*, New York, 1857.

———, *Compendium of the Impending Crisis...*, New York, 1859.

BIBLIOGRAPHY

Thomas W. Higginson, "A Ride Through Kansas" (pamphlet), New York, 1856(?).

Richard Hildreth, *Archy Moore, the White Slave.* . . , New York, 1857.

————, *Despotism in America.* . . , Boston, 1854.

————, *The History of the United States.* . . , 6 vols., New York, 1849-1852.

————, "The 'Ruin' of Jamaica," American Anti-Slavery *Tracts*, no. 6, New York, 1855.

————, *Theory of Politics.* . . , New York, 1854.

Charles W. Johnson, pub., *Proceedings of the First Three Republican National Conventions of 1856, 1860 and 1864.* . . , Minneapolis, 1893.

Edward McPherson, *The Political History of the United States of America, During the Great Rebellion*, Washington, 1864.

Karl Marx, *The Eastern Question.* . . , ed. Eleanor M. and Edward Aveling, London, 1897.

———— and Friedrich Engels, *The Civil War in the United States*, ed. Richard Enmale, New York, 1937.

"The North and South" (pamphlet), New York, 1854.

Robert Dale Owen, *see* listing under Horace Greeley.

William A. Phillips, *The Conquest of Kansas, by Missouri and Her Allies.* . . , Boston, 1856.

James S. Pike, "Chief Justice Chase" (pamphlet), New York, 1873.

————, *First Blows of the Civil War*, New York, 1879.

————, "Horace Greeley in 1872 . . ." (pamphlet), New York, 1873.

Henry J. Raymond, *see* listing under Horace Greeley.

Logan U. Reavis, *A Representative Life of Horace Greeley*, New York, 1872.

James Redpath, *The Roving Editor: or, Talks with Slaves in the Southern States*, New York, 1859.

George Ripley and Charles A. Dana, eds., *The New American Cyclopaedia.* . . , 16 vols., New York, 1858-1863.

Solon Robinson, *Facts for Farmers.* . . , New York, 1864.

————, *Hot Corn.* . . , New York, 1854.

Bayard Taylor, *At Home and Abroad*, New York, 1860.

Eli Thayer, *A History of the Kansas Crusade.* . . , New York, 1889.

————, *The New England Emigrant Aid Company.* . . , Worcester, 1887.

Troup (pseud.), "To the People of the South. Senator Hammond and the *Tribune*," *Tract No. 3*, Charleston(?), 1860.

Henry Villard, *Lincoln on the Eve of '61: A Journalist's Story*, ed. Harold G. and Oswald G. Villard, New York, 1941.

Thurlow Weed, " 'What I Know About' Horace Greeley's Secession, War and Diplomatic Record. A Letter Written (not

BIBLIOGRAPHY

Published) in 1870 . . . to Thomas C. Acton" (pamphlet), New York, 1872.
Henry Wilson, *History of the Rise and Fall of the Slave Power in America*, 3 vols., Boston, 1875-1877.
(Charles Wright), *The Prospect. . .* , Buffalo, 1862.

PART 5

AUTOBIOGRAPHIES, MEMOIRS, COMPLETE AND SELECTED WORKS, AND PUBLISHED DIARIES AND LETTERS

Mary C. Ames, *Outlines of Men, Women, and Things*, New York, 1873.
————, *see* listing under Alice and Phoebe Cary.
Thurlow W. Barnes, *see* listing under Thurlow Weed.
Edward Bates. "The Diary of. . ," ed. Howard K. Beale, *Annual Report* of the American Historical Association, *1930*, IV, Washington, 1933.
John Bigelow, *Retrospections of an Active Life*, 5 vols., New York, 1909-1913.
James Gillespie Birney, *Letters of. . .* , *1831-1837*, ed. Dwight L. Dumond, 2 vols., New York, 1938.
Anne Charlotte Lynch Botta, *Memoirs of. . .* , ed. Vincenzo Botta, New York, 1894.
Albert Brisbane, A Mental Biography, with a Character Study by his wife Redelia Brisbane, Boston, 1893.
Wiley Britton, *Memoirs of the Rebellion on the Border, 1863*, Chicago, 1882.
Beman Brockway, *Fifty Years in Journalism. . .* , Watertown, N.Y., 1891.
Orville Hickman Browning, *The Diary of. . .* , ed. Theodore C. Pease and James G. Randall, 2 vols., Springfield, Ill., 1925, 1933.
James Buchanan, *The Works of. . .* , ed. John B. Moore, 11 vols., Philadelphia, 1908-1910.
Alice and Phoebe Cary, *A Memorial of. . .* , by Mary C. Ames, New York, 1875.
William Henry Channing, *Memoir of. . .* , by Octavius B. Frothingham, Boston, 1886.
Salmon P. Chase, "Diary and Correspondence of. . ," *Annual Report* of the American Historical Association, *1902*, II, Washington, 1903.
Lydia Maria Child, *Letters of. . .* , with a biographical introduction by John G. Whittier and an appendix by Wendell Phillips, Boston, 1883.
James F. Clarke, *Anti-Slavery Days*, New York, 1883.
————, *Autobiography, Diary and Correspondence*, ed. Edward E. Hale, New York, 1891.

347

BIBLIOGRAPHY

Howell Cobb, "The Correspondence of Robert Toombs, Alexander H. Stephens, and. . . ," ed. Ulrich B. Phillips, *Annual Report* of the American Historical Association, *1911*, II, Washington, 1913.

Charles T. Congdon, *Reminiscences of a Journalist*, Boston, 1880.

Moncure D. Conway, *Autobiography, Memories and Experiences of*. . . , 2 vols., Boston, 1904.

Charles A. Dana, *Recollections of the Civil War*. . . , New York, 1898.

James C. Derby, *Fifty Years Among Authors, Books and Publishers*. . . , New York, 1884.

Ralph Waldo Emerson, *The Letters of*. . . , ed. Ralph L. Rusk, 6 vols., New York, 1939.

Friedrich Engels, *see* listing under Karl Marx.

Maunsell B. Field, *Memories of Many Men and of Some Women*. . . , New York, 1874.

John W. Forney, *Anecdotes of Public Men*, 2 vols., New York, 1873, 1881.

Octavius B. Frothingham, *Recollections and Impressions, 1822-1890*, New York, 1891.

———, *see* listing under William H. Channing.

Edwin Lawrence Godkin, *Life and Letters of*. . . , ed. Rollo Ogden, 2 vols., New York, 1907.

Horace Greeley, . . . *on Lincoln, with Mr. Greeley's Letters to Charles A. Dana and a Lady Friend*, ed. Joel Benton, New York, 1893.

———, *Recollections of a Busy Life*, New York, 1868.

———, "Recollections of. . . ," by Thurlow Weed, *Galaxy*, XV (Mar., 1873), 372-382.

°Rufus W. Griswold, *Passages from the Correspondence and Other Papers of*. . . , ed. W. M. Griswold, Cambridge, 1898.

Adam de Gurowski, *Diary*. . . , 3 vols., Boston, 1862-1866.

James A. Hamilton, *Reminiscenses of*. . . , New York, 1869.

Marie Hansen-Taylor, *On Two Continents; Memories of Half a Century*, New York, 1905.

John Hay, *Lincoln and the Civil War in the Diaries and Letters of*. . . , ed. Tyler Dennett, New York, 1939.

Thomas W. Higginson, *Contemporaries*, Cambridge, 1900.

———, *Letters and Journals of*. . . , *1846-1906*, ed. Mary T. Higginson, Boston, 1921.

Thomas Jefferson, *The Complete Jefferson*, ed. Saul K. Padover, New York, 1943.

George W. Julian, *Political Recollections, 1840 to 1872*, Chicago, 1884.

Gustave Koerner, *Memoirs of*. . . , *1809-1896*, ed. Thomas J. McCormick, 2 vols., Cedar Rapids, Iowa, 1909.

BIBLIOGRAPHY

Abraham Lincoln, *Complete Works of. . .* , ed. John G. Nicolay and
   John Hay, 12 vols., New York, 1905.
————, *Intimate Character Sketches of. . .* , by Henry B. Rankin,
   Philadelphia, 1924.
Alexander K. McClure, *Recollections of Half a Century,* Salem,
   Mass., 1902.
Karl Marx, Friedrich Engels; Historisch-kritische Gesamtausgabe,
   Werke, Schriften, Briefe, pt. 3, II, Berlin, 1930.
Theodore Parker, *Life and Correspondence of. . .* , by John Weiss,
   2 vols., New York, 1864.
Donn Piatt, *Memories of the Men Who Saved the Union,* New
   York, 1887.
Henry B. Rankin, *see* listing under Abraham Lincoln.
Henry J. Raymond, "Extracts from the Journal of. . . ," ed. his
   son, *Scribner's Monthly Magazine,* XIX (Nov., 1879; Jan., Mar.,
   1880), 57-71, 419-424, 703-710.
Solon Robinson, Pioneer and Agriculturist; Selected Writings, ed.
   Herbert A. Kellar, 2 vols., Indianapolis, 1936.
Carl Schurz, *The Reminiscences of. . .* , 3 vols., New York, 1907-
   1908.
William H. Seward, *. . . at Washington as Senator and Secretary*
   of State; a Memoir of his Life, with Selections from his Letters,
   1846-1861, by Frederick W. Seward, New York, 1891.
George W. Smalley, *Anglo-American Memories,* New York, 1911.
Alexander H. Stephens, *see* listing under Howell Cobb.
Bayard Taylor, *The Life and Letters of. . .* , ed. Marie Hansen-
   Taylor and Horace Scudder, 2 vols., Cambridge, 1884.
————, *The Unpublished Letters of . . . in the Huntington Library,*
   ed. John R. Schultz, San Marino, 1937.
Robert Toombs, *see* listing under Howell Cobb.
Henry Villard, *Memoirs of. . .* , 2 vols., Boston, 1904.
Thurlow Weed, *Life of . . . including his Autobiography and a*
   Memoir. . . , ed. Harriet A. Weed, with the memoir by Thurlow
   W. Barnes, 2 vols., Boston, 1884.
————, *see* listing under Horace Greeley.
John R. Young, *Men and Memories,* ed. May D. R. Young, 2 vols.,
   New York, 1901.

(Miscellaneous letters from Greeley published in newspapers
and periodicals before and since his death, are numerous. Those listed
in the footnotes, aside from *Tribune* citations, are: *Collector,* XVI
(Mar., 1903), 53; *Forum,* XXIV (Nov., 1897), 270-271; *Saturday*
Review of Literature, XXVI (May 1, 1943), 13; and New York *Sun*
(Nov. 26, 1893.)

349

BIBLIOGRAPHY

PART 6

BIOGRAPHIES, GENERAL WORKS, MONOGRAPHS, AND ARTICLES

Charles F. Adams, *Richard Henry Dana, a Biography*, 2 vols., Boston, 1890.

DeAlva S. Alexander, *A Political History of the State of New York*, 4 vols., New York, 1906-1923.

Philip G. Auchampaugh, *James Buchanan and his Cabinet on the Eve of Secession*, Lancaster, Pa., 1926.

Frederic Bancroft, *The Life of William H. Seward*, 2 vols., New York, 1900.

William Baringer, *Lincoln's Rise to Power*, Boston, 1937.

Chester L. Barrows, *William M. Evarts*, Chapel Hill, 1941.

Louise Barry, "The Emigrant Aid Company Parties of 1854," and "The New England Emigrant Aid Company Parties of 1855," *Kansas Historical Quarterly*, XII (May, Aug., 1943), 115-155, 227-268.

Ruhl J. Bartlett, *John C. Frémont and the Republican Party*, Columbus, O., 1930.

Albert J. Beveridge, *Abraham Lincoln, 1809-1858*, 2 vols., Boston, 1928.

Ray A. Billington, *The Protestant Crusade, 1800-1860*, New York, 1938.

Frank W. Blackmar, ed., *Kansas, a Cyclopedia of State History*, 2 vols., Chicago, 1912.

Willard G. Bleyer, *Main Currents in the History of American Journalism*, Boston, 1927.

Gamaliel Bradford, *As God Made Them; Portraits of Some Nineteenth-Century Americans*, Boston, 1929.

Paul H. Buck, "The Poor Whites of the Ante-Bellum South," *American Historical Review*, XXXI (Oct., 1926), 41-54.

Harry J. Carman and Reinhard H. Luthin, "The Seward-Fillmore Feud and the Crisis of 1850" and "The Seward-Fillmore Feud and the Disruption of the Whig Party," *New York History*, XXIV (Apr., July, 1943), 163-184, 335-357.

Harry J. Carman and Reinhard H. Luthin, "Some Aspects of the Know-Nothing Movement Reconsidered," *South Atlantic Quarterly*, XXXIX (Apr., 1940), 213-234.

Edward Channing, *A History of the United States*, VI, New York, 1925.

Arthur C. Cole, *The Irrepressible Conflict, 1850-1865*, New York, 1934.

Henry S. Commager, *Theodore Parker*, Boston, 1936.

John R. Commons, "Horace Greeley and the Working Class Origins of the Republican Party," *Political Science Quarterly*, XXIV (Sept., 1909), 468-488.

BIBLIOGRAPHY

William M. Cornell, *The Life and Public Career of Horace Greeley*, Boston, 1882.

Edward S. Corwin, "The Dred Scott Decision, in the Light of Contemporary Legal Doctrines," *American Historical Review*, xvii (Oct., 1911), 52-69.

Andrew W. Crandall, *The Early History of the Republican Party, 1854-1856*, Boston, 1930.

Avery Craven, *The Coming of the Civil War*, New York, 1942.

Ollinger Crenshaw, "The Psychological Background of the Election of 1860 in the South," *North Carolina Historical Review*, xix (July, 1942), 260-279.

———, "The Speakership Contest of 1859-1860," *Mississippi Valley Historical Review*, xxix (Dec., 1942), 323-338.

Francis Curtis, *The Republican Party . . . 1854-1904*, 2 vols., New York, 1904.

Elmer Davis, *History of the New York Times*, New York, 1921.

Sol Davison, *see* listing under Carter Goodrich.

William E. Dodd, "The Fight for the Northwest, 1860," *American Historical Review*, xvi (July, 1911), 774-788.

Dwight L. Dumond, *The Secession Movement. . .*, New York, 1931.

Clement Eaton, "Censorship of the Southern Mails," *American Historical Review*, xlviii (Jan., 1943), 266-280.

Everett E. Edwards, "References on the Significance of the Frontier in American History," *Bibliographical Contributions no. 25*, U.S. Department of Agriculture Library (Washington, 1935).

Charles W. Elliott, *Winfield Scott*, New York, 1937.

Sumner Ellis, *Life of Edwin H. Chapin, D.D.*, Boston, 1882.

Russell Errett, "Formation of the Republican Party in 1856," *Magazine of Western History*, vii (Dec., 1887), 180-189.

Ralph R. Fahrney, *Horace Greeley and the "Tribune" in the Civil War*, Cedar Rapids, Iowa, 1936.

Francis Fessenden, *Life and Public Services of William Pitt Fessenden. . .*, 2 vols., Boston, 1907.

Henry M. Field, *Life of David Dudley Field*, New York, 1898.

Carl R. Fish, *The Rise of the Common Man*, New York, 1927.

Emerson D. Fite, *The Presidential Campaign of 1860*, New York, 1911.

Walter L. Fleming, "The Buford Expedition to Kansas," *American Historical Review*, vi (Oct., 1900), 38-48.

Alexander C. Flick, ed., *History of the State of New York*, 10 vols., New York, 1933-1937.

Philip S. Foner, *Business and Slavery; the New York Merchants and the Irrepressible Conflict*, Chapel Hill, 1941.

Octavius B. Frothingham, *George Ripley*, Boston, 1883.

Claude M. Fuess, *Daniel Webster*, 2 vols., Boston, 1930.

Paul W. Gates, "The Homestead Law in an Incongruous Land

BIBLIOGRAPHY

System," *American Historical Review*, XLI (July, 1936), 652-681.

Charles B. Going, *David Wilmot. . . ,* New York, 1924.

Carter Goodrich and Sol Davison, "The Wage Earner in the Western Movement" and "The Frontier as Safety Valve; a Rejoinder," *Political Science Quarterly*, L, LI, LIII (June, 1935; Mar., 1936; June, 1938), 161-185, 61-116, 268-271.

James P. Hambleton, *see* Part 4.

Bray Hammond, "Free Banks and Corporations: The New York Free Banking Act of 1838," *The Journal of Political Economy*, XLIV (Apr., 1936), 184-209.

Ralph V. Harlow, *Gerrit Smith, Philanthropist and Reformer*, New York, 1939.

——, "The Rise and Fall of the Kansas Aid Movement," *American Historical Review*, XLI (Oct., 1935), 1-25.

Fred H. Harrington, "Frémont and the North Americans," *American Historical Review*, XLIV (July, 1939), 842-848.

George H. Haynes, "The Causes of Know-Nothing Success in Massachusetts," *American Historical Review*, III (Oct., 1897), 67-82.

William H. Herndon and Jesse W. Weik, *Herndon's Lincoln*, 2 vols., Springfield, Ill., 1921.

Mary T. Higginson, *Thomas Wentworth Higginson. . . ,* Boston, 1914.

Frank H. Hodder, "A Famous Chapter in American Politics," *Dial*, XLVII (Sept. 1, 1909), 120-122.

——, "The Genesis of the Kansas-Nebraska Act," *Proceedings* of the State Historical Society of Wisconsin, *1912* (Madison, 1913), 69-86.

——, "The Railroad Background of the Kansas-Nebraska Act," *Mississippi Valley Historical Review*, XII (June, 1925), 3-22.

——, "Some Aspects of the English Bill for the Admission of Kansas," *Annual Report* of the American Historical Association, *1906*, I (Washington, 1908), 199-210.

Richard Hofstadter, "The Tariff Issue on the Eve of the Civil War," *American Historical Review*, XLIV (Oct., 1938), 50-55.

Ovando J. Hollister, *Life of Schuyler Colfax*, New York, 1886.

Richard Hooker, *The Story of an Independent Newspaper*, New York, 1924.

Charles F. Horner, *The Life of James Redpath. . . ,* New York, 1926.

Frederick Hudson, *Journalism in the United States from 1690 to 1872*, New York, 1873.

Lurton D. Ingersoll, *The Life of Horace Greeley. . . ,* Chicago, 1873.

William H. Isely, "The Sharps Rifle Episode in Kansas History," *American Historical Review*, XII (Apr., 1907), 546-566.

BIBLIOGRAPHY

Allen Johnson, *Stephen A. Douglas: A Study in American Politics*, New York, 1908.

———— and Dumas Malone, *Dictionary of American Biography*, 21 vols., New York, 1928-1944.

Samuel A. Johnson, "The Emigrant Aid Company in the Kansas Conflict," *Kansas Historical Quarterly*, vi (Feb., 1937), 21-33.

————, "The Genesis of the New England Emigrant Aid Company," *New England Quarterly*, iii (Jan., 1930), 95-122.

George W. Julian, *The Life of Joshua R. Giddings*, Chicago, 1892.

————, "The First Republican National Convention," *American Historical Review*, iv (Jan., 1899), 313-322.

Murray Kane, "Some Considerations on the Frontier Concept of Frederick Jackson Turner," *Mississippi Valley Historical Review*, xxvii (Dec., 1940), 379-400.

————, "Some Considerations on the Safety Valve Doctrine," *Mississippi Valley Historical Review*, xxiii (Sept., 1936), 169-188.

Abraham D. H. Kaplan, "Henry Charles Carey, a Study in American Economic Thought," *Johns Hopkins University Studies. . .*, series xlix, no. 4, Baltimore, 1931.

Frank W. Klingberg, "James Buchanan and the Crisis of the Union," *Journal of Southern History*, ix (Nov., 1943), 455-474.

John A. Krout, "The Maine Law in New York Politics," *New York History*, xvii (July, 1936), 260-272.

————, *The Origins of Prohibition*, New York, 1925.

Edgar Lanfsdorf, "S. C. Pomeroy and the New England Emigrant Aid Company, 1854-1856," *Kansas Historical Quarterly*, vii (Aug., Nov., 1938), 227-245, 379-398.

William A. Linn, *Horace Greeley*, New York, 1903.

Reinhard H. Luthin, "Abraham Lincoln and the Tariff," *American Historical Review*, xlix (July, 1944), 609-629.

————, "The Democratic Split During Buchanan's Administration," *Pennsylvania History*, xi (Jan., 1944), 13-35.

————, *The First Lincoln Campaign*, Cambridge, 1944.

————, "Organizing the Republican Party in the 'Border-Slave' Regions: Edward Bates's Presidential Candidacy in 1860," *Missouri Historical Review*, xxxiii (Jan., 1944), 138-161.

————, *see* Harry J. Carman.

John B. McMaster, *A History of the People of the United States. . .*, viii, New York, 1913.

Charles A. Madison, "Albert Brisbane: Social Dreamer," *American Scholar*, xii (Summer, 1943), 284-296.

James C. Malin, *John Brown and the Legend of Fifty-six*, Philadelphia, 1942.

Augustus Maverick, *Henry J. Raymond. . .*, Hartford, 1870.

353

BIBLIOGRAPHY

George S. Merriam, *The Life and Times of Samuel Bowles*, 2 vols., New York, 1885.

George F. Milton, *The Eve of Conflict; Stephen A. Douglas and the Needless War*, Boston, 1934.

Stewart Mitchell, *Horatio Seymour of New York*, Cambridge, 1938.

Samuel E. Morison, *The Oxford History of the United States. . .* , 2 vols., Oxford, 1927.

Frank L. Mott, *American Journalism*, New York, 1941.

Gustavus Myers, "History of Public Franchises in New York City (Boroughs of Manhattan and the Bronx)," *Municipal Affairs*, IV (Mar., 1900), 71-206.

Joseph S. Myers, "The Genius of Horace Greeley," Ohio State University *Studies in Journalism*, no. 6, Columbus, 1929.

Elias Nason and Thomas Russell, *The Life and Public Services of Henry Wilson*, Boston, 1876.

Allan Nevins, *The Evening Post: a Century of Journalism*, New York, 1922.

————, *Frémont, Pathmarker of the West*, New York, 1939.

Joseph F. Newton, *Lincoln and Herndon*, Cedar Rapids, Iowa, 1910.

Roy F. Nichols, *The Democratic Machine, 1850-1854*, New York, 1923.

————, *Franklin Pierce*, Philadelphia, 1931.

————, "Some Problems of the First Republican Presidential Campaign," *American Historical Review*, XXVIII (Apr., 1923), 492-496.

James Parton, *The Life of Horace Greeley*, Cambridge, 1896; (first edition, New York, 1855).

Louis Petzer, *Augustus Caesar Dodge. . .* , Iowa City, 1909.

Thomas M. Pitkin, "Western Republicans and the Tariff in 1860," *Mississippi Valley Historical Review*, XXVII (Dec., 1940), 400-420.

George R. Poage, *Henry Clay and the Whig Party*, Chapel Hill, 1936.

David M. Potter, "Horace Greeley and Peaceable Secession," *Journal of Southern History*, VII (May, 1941), 145-159.

————, *Lincoln and His Party in the Secession Crisis*, New Haven, 1942.

Albert Post, *Popular Freethought in America, 1825-1850*, New York, 1943.

James G. Randall, *Lincoln the President*, 2 vols., New York, 1945.

Perley O. Ray, "The Genesis of the Kansas-Nebraska Act," *Annual Report* of the American Historical Association, *1914*, I, Washington, 1916.

————, *The Repeal of the Missouri Compromise. . .* , Cleveland, 1909.

Logan U. Reavis, see Part 4.

BIBLIOGRAPHY

Whitelaw Reid, *Horace Greeley*, New York, 1879.
James F. Rhodes, *History of the United States.* . . , 7 vols., New York, 1893-1906.
————, "Newspapers as Historical Sources," *Atlantic Monthly,* ciii (May, 1909), 650-657.
Lisette Riggs, "George and Sophia Ripley," unpublished doctoral thesis, University of Maryland, College Park.
Roy M. Robbins, "Horace Greeley: Land Reform and Unemployment, 1837-1862," *Agricultural History*, vii (Jan., 1933), 18-41.
————, *Our Landed Heritage, the Public Domain, 1776-1936,* Princeton, 1942.
Earle D. Ross, *The Liberal Republican Movement*, New York, 1919.
Constance M. Rourke, *Trumpets of Jubilee*, New York, 1927.
Robert R. Russel, "The Pacific Railway Issue in Politics Prior to the Civil War," *Mississippi Valley Historical Review*, xii (Sept. 1925), 187-201.
Thomas Russell, *see* listing under Elias Nason.
Lucy M. Salmon, *The Newspaper and the Historian*, New York, 1923.
Carl Sandburg, *Abraham Lincoln; the War Years,* 2 vols., New York, 1939.
Epes Sargent, *see* listing under Horace Greeley, Part 4.
Carl Schurz, *The Life of Henry Clay*, 2 vols., Boston, 1915.
Louis D. Scisco, "Political Nativism in New York State," Columbia University *Studies in History, Economics and Public Law,* xiii (New York, 1900-1901), no. 2, 203-457.
Mary Scrugham, *The Peaceable Americans of 1860-1861.* . . , New York, 1921.
Don C. Seitz, *Horace Greeley*, Indianapolis, 1926.
Frederick W. Seward, *see* listing under William H. Seward, Part 5.
Fred A. Shannon, "The Homestead Act and the Labor Surplus," *American Historical Review*, xli (July, 1936), 637-651.
William E. Smith, *The Francis Preston Blair Family in Politics,* 2 vols., New York, 1933.
Charles Sotheran, *Horace Greeley and Other Pioneers of American Socialism*, New York, 1915.
George M. Stephenson, *The Political History of the Public Lands, from 1840 to 1862*, Boston, 1917.
George A. Stevens, *New York Typographical Union No. 6*, Albany, 1913.
Henry L. Stoddard, *Horace Greeley, Printer, Editor, Crusader,* New York, 1946.
Candace Stone, *Dana and the Sun*, New York, 1938.
Carl B. Swisher, *Roger B. Taney*, New York, 1936.
Eli Thayer, *see* Part 4.
Alice F. Tyler, *Freedom's Ferment*, Minneapolis, 1944.

BIBLIOGRAPHY

Glyndon G. Van Deusen, "Thurlow Weed: A Character Study," *American Historical Review*, XLIX (Apr., 1944), 427-440.

————, *Thurlow Weed, Wizard of the Lobby*, Boston, 1947.

George W. Van Vleck, *The Panic of 1857...*, New York, 1943.

Oswald G. Villard, *John Brown...*, Boston, 1910.

Charles Warren, *The Supreme Court in United States History*, 3 vols., Boston, 1922.

Walter P. Webb, *The Great Plains*, Boston, 1931.

Jesse W. Weik, *see* listing under William H. Herndon.

John Weiss, *see* listing under Theodore Parker, Part 5.

Henry Wilson, *see* Part 4.

James H. Wilson, *The Life of Charles A. Dana*, New York, 1907.

Barton H. Wise, *The Life of Henry A. Wise...*, New York, 1899.

Francis N. Zabriskie, *Horace Greeley...*, New York, 1890.

Helene S. Zahler, *Eastern Workingmen and National Land Policy, 1829-1862*, New York, 1941.

INDEX

abolitionists, 152, 226-27, 267; Greeley's opinion of, 32-33, 36, 41, 129-30, 247, 263, 273
African slave trade, 51, 63, 85, 233, 264
Alabama, 302, 323
Albany *Evening Journal*, 12, 52, 318
Allen, Margaret, 331
American party, *see* Know Nothings
American Revolution, used as argument for peaceable secession, 306-7
American System, 26
American Temperance Union, 93
anti-Lecompton D e m o c r a t s, *see* Douglas
anti-Nebraska fusion, *see* Republican party
antislavery crusade, 3, 71, 98, 276; and Greeley's career, 22, 25, 29-42, 49-52, 73-75, 83-89, 98, 124, 127-33, 189, 213-14, 221-22, 230-32, 253, 313, 334
Arkansas, 310, 314
Arnold, Benedict, Buchanan compared with, 157
Associated Press, 4, 251
Astor family, 265
Atchison, David R., 160, 186; senate race with Benton, 45-47; Kansas activities, 132, 134, 140, 142
Atchison (Kan.), 142, 178

Baker, George E., 118
Baltimore (Md.), 256, 274, 302-3
Banks, Nathaniel P., Jr., elected speaker, 142-49; favored Frémont, 161-62; considered for presidency, 162, 164-67; named Kansas committee, 180-82
Barnum, Phineas T., 19
Bartlett, William F., 171
Bates, Edward, 265n; contender for 1860 Republican presidential nomination, 255, 268-70, 272-76, 282-90, 303, 314; in Lincoln's cabinet, 323
Bell, John, early attitude of Greeley toward, 249, 270n; presidential candidate, 274-76, 282, 296
Bennett, James G., 4, 15-16, 80
Benton, Thomas H., 164, 165n; senate race with Atchison, 45-47; praised, 66; efforts to attract into Republican party, 159-60
Big Springs (Kan.), 135
Birney, James G., 47

Bissell, William H., 167
Black, Jeremiah S., 158
Blair, Francis P., Jr., political activities, 159, 255, 256, 288, 293, 300; endorsement of Helper's *Compendium*, 260; Bates supporter, 268, 269, 283
Blair, Francis P., Sr., permanent chairman Pittsburgh convention, 154; backed Frémont, 159, 162, 169; supported Bates, 269, 283
Blair, Montgomery, 159, 269, 283; in Lincoln's cabinet, 323
Blatchford, Richard M., 64n
border slave states, slave trade regarded as essential to, 51; loyalty predicted in event of secession, 60, 63; desire to introduce Republicanism into, 123, 153-54, 158-60, 196-98, 255-64, 273-74, 286-88, 300-303; in secession crisis, 318
Boston *Atlas*, 8, 116n
Botts, John, 270n
Bowles, Samuel, opposed to Kansas-Nebraska bill, 52-53; contribution to split of Know Nothings, 116-23, 138, 155n; said Greeley backed Frémont, 163n; agreement on 1860 campaign, 265n, 269
Breckinridge, John C., vice presidential nominee, 156-57; presidential nominee, 275, 297-98
Brisbane, Albert, influence on Greeley, 23, 24n; articles in 1858 *Tribune*, 210
British Guiana, 299
British West Indies, 298-99
Brockway, Beman, former associate editor *Tribune*, 151-52, 321-23, 332
Broderick, David, 240, 265n
Bronson, Green C., 100, 105n
Brook Farm, 6, 9, 22, 24
Brooks, Preston, 185-87, 268
Brown, B. Gratz, 256, 265n, 283
Brown, John, 131, 174-77, 266-67
Browning, Orville H., 3
Bryant, William C., 52, 126, 221
Buchanan, James, presidential nominee, 156-57, 167, 191, 193-94; elected, 194, 284, 288; Dred Scott case, 223, 225-29, 231; split with Douglas, 237-48; analysis of administration, 264; veto of homestead legislation, 291-92; in secession crisis, 309, 324

INDEX

Buffalo *Republic*, 52
Bull Run, first battle of, 332
Bunker Hill, 123
Burke, Edmund, influence on Seward, 71
Burlingame, Anson, 267-68
Burns, Tony, 85-86
Butler, Andrew P., 185

Calhoun, John C., influence on Democratic party, 45-46, 158-59, 187, 229-31, 233, 237, 238, 243, 264; and secession sentiment in slave states, 315-16
California, 48, 253; admission to Union, 29, 37-38, 62, 137; election of 1856, 161, 163, 171n, 194; Greeley's visit, 180, 208; gold and 1857 panic, 214, 216
Campbell, John A., 229-30
Campbell, Lewis D., 144-45, 213-14
Canada, 62, 299
capital punishment, 22, 333-34
Carey, Henry C., 59, 215n
Carlyle, Thomas, 72
Cary, Alice, 19
Cary, Phoebe, 19
Cass, Lewis, 36
Catholic Church, attacked by Know Nothings, 81-83, 117-20; Frémont said to be member, 190-92
Catron, John, 229
Central Park, 18, 212, 242
Chaffee, Calvin C., 224
Chapin, Edwin H., 19
Chappaqua (N.Y.), 16, 108, 331-32
Charleston *Mercury*, 60, 119
Charleston (S.C.), 60, 271-72, 274-75
Chase, Salmon P., contender for Republican nominations, 152, 167, 270n, 272-73; in Lincoln's cabinet, 323
Chicago (Ill.), 43, 275, 293
Chicago Republican Convention, *see* Republican party
Chicago River and Harbor Convention, 273
Chicago *Tribune*, 52
Child, Lydia M., 178-79
Cincinnati (O.), 114, 156-57, 185, 187
Civil War, Greeley's responsibility for, 14, 30, 58, 177, 307-9, 312-24, 327-31
Clark, John B., 261
Clark, Myron H., prohibitionist, 81; elected governor New York, 93, 98-101, 103n, 104-7, 114, 122
Clay, Cassius M., 165, 260

Clay, Henry, 48, 165; influence on Greeley, 25-26, 35-37
Cleveland, John F., 293n
Cleveland *Leader*, 52
Colfax, Schuyler, friend of Greeley, 19; editor, 87; elected house of representatives, 87, 139; said Greeley backed Frémont, 163; New York City visit, 194-95; conferences with Douglas, 239-40; views on 1860 campaign, 265n, 269, 283; reproached for absence from Chicago convention, 285-86. For correspondence with Greeley, *see* Greeley, Horace
collective bargaining, opposition by Greeley, 28, 199-201
Colorado Territory, 289
Compromise of 1850, included popular sovereignty and fugitive slave law, 29, 37-38, 43-44, 85; Greeley's attitude toward, 36-42, 173, 314, 315; impact on Whig party in New York state, 80-81
Confederate government, early formation of, 309-10, 323; Greeley's reaction to its demands, 330; Richmond established as capital, 332
Congdon, Charles T., associate editor of *Tribune*, 7-9
congress, pressure to reject Kansas-Nebraska bill, 54-56, 64-68; mileage graft published, 90; difficulties in Kansas, 137-38, 181-84, 237-48; homestead legislation vetoed, 291-92; compromise tendencies condemned, 316
Connecticut, 64, 103-4, 122
conventions, Greeley's dislike of, 88, 91
Cooper Institute, 199-203, 294-95
cooperatives, Greeley's belief in, 202
Corning, Erastus, 64n
Crittenden, John J., early attitude of Greeley toward, 249; compromise proposal on eve of Civil War, 313-14, 316-19
Crittenden-Montgomery substitute, 242-43, 289
Crosby family, 265
Crystal Palace, 18
Cuba, 48, 50, 62, 314
currency, Greeley's views on, 26, 219-21
Curtin, Andrew, 284
Curtis, Benjamin R., 227-28, 232
Cutting, Francis B., 64n, 65

INDEX

Dakota Territory, 289

Dallas, George M., 292

Dana, Charles A., managing editor *Tribune*, 6-7, 13; on Greeley's 1854 political hopes, 98; split in Know Nothings, 111-13, 116-25, 138; over-confidence, 125; urged to moderate editorial tone, 125, 147, 159; and 1855-56 speakership contest, 142-47, 150; asked to assist Know Some-things, 156; Kansas report, 182; on 1857 panic, 215n, 220; Greeley crit-ical of, 247; Greeley's 1858 political aspirations, 250n; agreement with 1860 campaign plans, 265n, 270; absurdity of civil conflict over slavery, 287; in 1860 campaign, 293-94; belligerent attitude toward slave states, 324, 326-28, 330; mili-tary policy of *Tribune*, 331-32; dis-missal, 332

Dana, Richard H., Jr., 16

Davenport (Iowa), 271

Davis, David, 282, 287

Davis, Henry W., 265n, 288

Davis, Jefferson, 43, 247, 333-34

Dayton, William L., 170

Delaware, hope for emancipation in, 51, 256, 263; loyalty predicted in event of secession, 60; and 1856 election, 163, 193; and 1860 cam-paign, 249, 274

Democratic party, ineptitude of lead-ers, 30; Greeley's dislike of and early hopes for split in, 34-35, 41-42, 49; early difficulties over Kan-sas-Nebraska legislation, 64n, 65, 103-4; disintegration, 80-84; Vir-ginia 1855 campaign, 116; Georgia 1855 platform, 121; New York state 1855 election, 126-29; early troubles in Kansas, 134-38, 140-43; and 1855-56 speakership contest, 143-49; and 1856 election, 155-58, 167, 173-88, 193-94; opposed by Jacksonians, 158-59; won New York state election, 222; division over slavery question, 223, 235-54, 264-65, 270-76, 282-83; in 1860 campaign, 292, 294, 303; Greeley nominated for presidency, 334

Demoine Navigation and Rail-Road Company, 183, 209

Dickens, Charles, 178

District of Columbia, 38, 120, 314

Dodge, Augustus C., 43

Donelson, Andrew J., 155, 273

Douglas, Stephen A., sponsors Kan-sas-Nebraska bill, 42-44, 53-55, 65, 68, 143, 144, 173; and 1856 election, 157, 160, 181; reelected to senate, 233-48, 253-54, 285, 289; and 1860 election, 264, 270-72, 275-76, 289-90, 296-97, 303

Douglas County (Kan.), 140-41

Draper, Alonzo, 199-200, 203

Draper, Simeon, 64n

Dred Scott decision, 30, 222, 251, 268; examined, 223-32; implications on popular sovereignty, 228, 231, 233-37, 296

Duer, Deaning, 165n

Dunn, George G., 184n

education, Greeley's views on, 21, 198

emancipation, Greeley desired by peaceful, economic means, 25-33, 45, 153-54, 158-60, 196-99, 255-64, 287-88, 293, 300; a military expe-diency, 313

Emerson, John, 224

Emerson, Mrs. John, 224

English, William H., 243-44, 249, 255

Europe, visited by Greeley, 32, 39, 111-13, 118n; reported outlook on 1856 election, 179-80

Evans, George H., 28

Evarts, William, 321-22

Everett, Edward, 55, 115, 274

Facts of Slavery, 33-35, 186

Fenton, Ruben E., 89n

Fessenden, William P., 55-56, 149, 278

Fillmore, Millard, 144, 155-56, 160, 188, 194, 244, 249, 255, 268, 272, 273, 283

Fish, Hamilton, 95, 145-46, 149, 162-63

Florida, 62, 173, 194, 323

Foot, Solomon, 89n

Ford, Thomas A., 155

Fort Sumter, 310, 312, 330-31

Fourier, Charles, 23-24; influence on Greeley, 25, 202, 210; attacked by Raymond, 76

Francis, Convers, 179n

Franklin, Benjamin, 12

free love, alienated Greeley from Fourierism, 24, 202

Free Soil Democrats, component part Republican party, 3, 86-89, 127-29, 151-52; and 1848 election, 36, 80; Greeley refused affiliation, 36, 41, 74; press opposed Kansas-Nebraska bill, 52; and 1857 panic,

INDEX

217; Republican 1860 platform, 292

Free State party (Kan.), early organization, 135-38; Wakarusa War, 140-43; led by Robinson, 163; and 1856 election, 174-84; Lecompton constitution, 236-44; triumph, 255, 257

free states, democratic treatment of negroes favored, 33; peaceable secession as a factor in unifying, 312

free thought, alienated Greeley from Fourierism, 24, 202

Frémont, Jessie B., 160, 191

Frémont, John C., presidential nominee, 151, 158-71, 175, 179, 187, 189-94, 196, 208n, 223, 249, 268

Fry, William H., associate editor *Tribune*, 7-8

fugitive slave law, 38, 39-41, 85-86, 184n, 313-14

Fuller, Henry M., 144-45

Fuller, Margaret, 17

Gadsden purchase, 29n, 62

Galena (Ill.) *Jeffersonian*, 52

Gardner, Henry J., 120-22, 138, 144

Garrison, William L., 33

Geary, John W., 175, 180, 236

George III, Buchanan compared with, 240-41

Georgia, 121, 172, 307, 323

Giddings, Joshua, 154, 290

Gladstone, Thomas H., 180

Glover, Joshua, 85

Godkin, Edwin L., 6, 15, 18

Graham, Sylvester, 20

Grand National Council, governing body Know Nothing party, 113; Cincinnati meeting, 114; Philadelphia meeting, 116-23, 125, 138-39, 143, 144

Graniteville (S.C.), 259

Grant, Ulysses S., 333

Great Britain, 32, 45, 102, 214-15

Greeley, Horace, founder and editor of *Tribune*, 4-5, 7-8; personal description, 10-11; early life, 11-13; *Tribune* established, 13-14; style, 14; character and family life, 14-18; friends, 19; interest in reform movement, 19-22; social philosophy, 22-28; correspondence with Colfax, 24n, 47, 68, 73, 74, 87, 94-95, 98, 104-5, 138-39, 164-65, 171, 183-84, 194-95, 239-40, 243, 246-48, 267-68, 270, 272, 276, 285-86, 290-91; clash with southerners, 28-30; optimistic

nationalism, 31; solution for slavery, 31-33; antislavery propaganda, 33-35; early opposition to slavery extension, 35-37; interpretation of 1850 compromise, 37-39; and 1852 campaign, 39-42; awareness of threat to Missouri Compromise, 44-48; nature of objections to Kansas-Nebraska bill, 49-52; leadership against popular sovereignty, 53-56; defense of *Tribune's* mature attack against Kansas-Nebraska bill, 58-59, 63-64; belief bill will be defeated, 64-65; final battle before passage, 65-67; attitude after passage, 68

Partnership with Weed and Seward, 68-73; early disaffection, 73-75; resentment of Raymond, 75-80; political ambition and 1854 campaign, 80; prohibition, 81-82; nativism, 83; anti-Nebraska fusion, 83-85; fugitive slave law, 85; abortive sponsorship of Republican party, 86; design to combine anti-Nebraska and anti-rum issues, 87-89; opposition of Weed and Seward, 89-91; views on conventions and editors as candidates, 91-92; conferences with Weed and altered policy, 92-97; outmaneuvered by Weed, 98-99; support of Whigs, 100-103; discouragement over canvass, 103-6; partnership dissolved, 106-11; European visit, 111-12; policy toward Know Nothings, 112-13, 118n; return from Europe, 123-24; other reforms secondary to Republican cause, 124

Overconfidence in 1855 political outlook, 125-27; prohibition issue submerged, 127-28; fusion and the Republican party, 128-29; denial "Black Republicanism," 129-30; early view Kansas, 130-33, 136-37; plans 1856 campaign, 137-38; American party 1855 victory, 138; changed tactics toward Know Nothings, 139-40; arrival in Washington for speakership contest, 140; assisted by events in Kansas, 140-42; evaluation of political activities in Washington, 142-47; caned by Rust, 147-49; criticized by non-Democrats, 149-50; sobering influence of Washington experiences, 150; zenith of political power, 151; strategy for 1856 cam-

360

INDEX

paign, 151-52; Pittsburgh convention, 152-55; reaction to Know Nothing and Democratic nominations, 155-58; hesitation before supporting Frémont, 158; desire to appease Jacksonians, 158-60; anxiety over anti-Nebraska Know Nothings, 160-61; Frémont's candidacy weighed and accepted, 161-67; Philadelphia convention, 167-68; disappointment of Seward and McLean, 168-69; vice presidential candidacy, 169-70; platform, 170; return from convention, 170-71; campaign propaganda, 171-73; Kansas as principal issue, 175-77, 180-82; lobbyist for Topeka constitution, 182-84; indignation at Sumner incident, 185-86; opinion of secession threat, 187-88; appeal to farmer and worker, 188; economic principles in abeyance, 189; wary in meeting charges against Frémont, 190-92; campaign work evaluated, 192-93; predictions of outcome, 193; last minute activities in Pennsylvania, 193-94; undismayed by defeat, 194-95; assured of Kansas freedom, 195-96

Economic nationalism analyzed, 196-99; attitude toward labor organization, 199-202; theory of westward migration, 202-10; faith in nobility of labor and mechanical progress, 210-12; practical demands for working class, 212; strong appeal to economic conservatives, 212-13; political expediency and 1857 tariff, 213-14; prophecies of coming depression, 214-18; demand for protection, frugality, and class harmony, 218-19; defense of banks, 219-20; ideas on political economy temporarily rebuffed, 220-22; New York state 1857 defeat, 222; continued confidence in economic principles, 222

Anxiety to split Democrats, 223; windfall in Dred Scott decision, 223; absence of 1856 editorial comment on case, 226; assault on Buchanan's inaugural address, 228-29; Scott decision attacked, 230-32; polemic triumph over Douglas, 233-35; drawn by decision toward support of popular sovereignty, 235-36; view of Lecompton convention, 236; fear of Walker and re-

lief at his failure, 236-37; Buchanan assailed and Douglas upheld, 237-41; principle of admitting slave state conceded, 241-43; English bill condemned, 243-44; outlook on 1858 campaign, 244; rebuffed by Illinois Republicans, 244-48; Know Nothing fusion and gubernatorial hopes blocked by Weed, 248-52; outcome of 1858 elections, 252-54; ostensibly a conservative at Chicago, 254-55; desire to introduce Republicanism into slave states, 255-58; faith in non-slaveholding whites, 258-60; promotion of Helper's *Compendium*, 260; attitude toward 1859-60 speakership contest, 260-61; mistaken view of slave states fortified, 261-62; estimate of 1860 campaign, 262-65; conceit and concern with economic principles, 266; outlook on Brown's raid, 266-67; pleased by 1859 New York state election, 267-68; Bates groomed as 1860 contender, 268-70; Douglas' nomination predicted, 270-72; all out support for Bates, 272-74; Bates sustained despite adverse circumstances, 274-76; opposition to Seward, 276; suggestions on disarmament ignored, 276-77; distaste for corruption and Weed's lobbying, 277-79; acquiescence in gridiron bills, 279-80; question of personal integrity, 280-81; activities at Chicago, 281-84; other factors in Seward's defeat, 284-85; criticized by Lincoln stalwarts, 285

Satisfaction at results of Chicago convention not wholehearted, 285-88; positive prohibition of slavery extension in platform blocked, 288-90; Declaration of Independence quoted, 290; homesteads, 290-92; protective tariff, 292; Pacific railroad, 292-93; publication of campaign literature, 293-95; Bell, Douglas, and Breckinridge criticized, 296-97; Republican triumph amid era of good feeling predicted, 298; problem of freedmen, 298-99; answer to disunionists, 300-3; misgivings over continued threats to Union, 303-4; peaceable secession, 304-9; misunderstanding of slave states, 309-10; attacked by southern press, 311; honest in offering

361

INDEX

INDEX

364

INDEX

Platte country, *see* Kansas and Nebraska

political parties, Greeley's view of, 25-26, 70, 84, 88, 209

Polk, James K., 161, 292

popular sovereignty, and Compromise of 1850, 29, 38, 40; Kansas-Nebraska bill, 30, 38, 43-44, 48-68, 132-33; Democratic 1856 platform, 173-84, 187, 228, 231; Greeley, Douglas, Dred Scott decision, and Lecompton crisis, 233-44; issue in 1858 campaign, 244-54; and 1860 canvass, 263-65, 270, 288-90

Portsmouth (Va.), 301

prohibition, advocacy dropped to sponsor Republicanism, 3, 124, 127-28, 253; Greeley's interest in and New York state 1854 election, 22, 81-84, 86-89, 91, 93-94, 96-102

protective tariff, favored, 26-29, 31-32, 44-45, 71, 124, 197-98, 213-18, 221-22; and 1858 campaign, 253; and 1860 canvass, 269, 284, 290-92

Proudhon, Pierre Joseph, 7

Pugh, George E., 240

railroads, and western land grants, 183, 208-9; *see also* Pacific railroad

Ray, Charles H., 52

Raymond, Henry J., editor, 4, 53, 75; and Weed-Seward-Greeley partnership, 75-80, 89, 109-11; elected lieutenant governor New York, 99-101, 103n, 105-7, 127; at Pittsburgh convention, 154; and 1860 attack on Greeley, 282, 319-20

Reconstruction, Greeley's attitude toward, 202-3, 333-34; trials of anticipated, 308

Redpath, James, 131

Reeder, Andrew H., 134-38, 181

referendum, Greeley's view on, 317

reform movement, 6, 19-32, 70-73, 81; *see also* antislavery crusade

registry law, 83, 248-49

Republican party, and antislavery crusade, 3, 30; early expression of doctrine, 37; formation demanded by Pike, 67-68; Weed-Seward-Greeley partnership and early demand for fusion, 70, 80-111; name first carried in *Tribune*, 86, 88; Philadelphia Grand National Council, 111-24; and 1855 elections, 125-30, 137-39; importance of early Kansas struggles, 125, 130-38; Greeley's 1856 plans, 126, 137-38;

150-52; and 1855-56 speakership contest, 139-40, 142-50; Pittsburgh convention, 152-55, 160; and 1856 nominations, 158-71; Kansas issue in 1856 campaign, 173-84; introduction of Greeley's economic doctrines, 196-99, 212-13, 217-22; New York 1857 defeat, 222; strengthened by Buchanan, 223, 226; stand in the Lecompton struggle, 237-44; and 1858 elections, 244-54; Greeley's 1860 strategy, 248-49, 254-66; New York 1859 election, 267-68; Bates as contender for 1860 nomination, 268-76; Greeley's opposition to Seward, 276-82; Chicago convention, 282-88; Chicago platform, 288-93, 315-18; and 1860 election, 293-305; secession crisis, 316-17, 325-26, 328-29; and 1872 election, 334

Rhode Island, 64, 103-4, 122

Richardson, William A., 65-66, 144

Richmond, Va., 274, 332, 333

Richmond, Dean, 64n

Richmond *Enquirer*, 185

Riggs, George W., 165n

Ripley, George, literary editor *Tribune*, 9

Robinson, Charles, 135, 140-41, 163, 174

Robinson, Solon, agricultural editor *Tribune*, 9-10, 205

Rochester Ladies' Anti-Slavery Society, 32-33

Rochester *Union*, 52

Rockwell, Julius, 138

Rusk, Thomas J., 64n

Rust, Albert J., 147-50, 152

safety valve theory, 28, 62, 201-10

St. Louis (Mo.), possible terminus transcontinental railway, 43, 45-46, 273, 293; activities of emancipationists in, 159, 256, 288, 293, 302; Greeley's lecture in canceled, 310

St. Louis *Missouri Democrat*, 256

Sanford, John F. A., 224-25

Saratoga (N.Y.) Convention, 88, 92-100

Savannah (Ga.), 60, 303

Schoolcraft, John L., 72-73

Schouler, William, 53

Scott, *see* Dred Scott decision

Scott, Winfield, 39-41, 75, 329

secession, deemed a political threat by Greeley and *Tribune*, 30, 58-64, 67-68, 121, 187-89, 261-64, 288, 296-

366